Nov. 25 - 1981

FROM THE WRONG
SIDE OF THE TRACKS

By Dolores Barnes Wilson

Best Wishes to
Alean & Marlene Swanson

Sincerely
Dolores Barnes Wilson

"From the Wrong Side of the Tracks" is a
true story of the Barnes family whose
trials and tribulations and even happy
times during the 1930's are revealed.
Some names have been changed out of
respect for surviving relatives.

Printed by
ARGUS PRINTERS
Stickney, S. D.
1980

Dedication

This book is dedicated to the memory of my Mother and Father, and to the generation who lived through the Great Depression; the common people who despite their "blood, sweat and tears" still maintained a faith in God and their hopes for a better tomorrow.

Father
Sylvester Raymond Barnes

Mother
Josephine Mary Drees

Foreword

Mitchell, South Dakota, was one of the many "Boom towns" that were springing up on the wide open spaces of the midwest when my father, Sylvester Raymond Barnes, arrived here in the year of 1910. The small town had been incorporated in 1881 and was named in honor of the president of the Milwaukee railroad, Alexander Mitchell. It had once been a tiny village located along the banks of the James River, but because of the ever present flood danger, the railroad decided to build near a more suitable location, so the residents of Firesteel moved three miles west to what is now the city of Mitchell.

My father was born in Vernon Springs, Howard County, which is a small hamlet near Cresco, Iowa. He was brought into life in a stone house located near the scenic Turkey River. His parents were Sylvester and Catherine Barnes, whose ancestors migrated from New York state. Sylvester joined the Union Army and served in Civil War. Dad was one of twelve children who lived close to the land on which they were born. His father was a prominent farmer and local postmaster. Although theirs was a close knit family, there wasn't enough farm ground for all to share, so the youngest brothers decided to leave the state of Iowa and follow the exodus to South Dakota where there were fertile lands and endless prairie.

The young brothers, Mark, Frank and Lee, along with my father, first settled in the small town of Armour, South Dakota, where they engaged in a bakery and cafe business.

After a few years, three of the brothers decided that Mitchell was a far more enterprising little city so again they packed their belongings into a camelback trunk, hitched a team of coal black horses to a rubber-tired buggy and headed for the Corn Palace city. The year was 1910.

Mitchell was a bee hive of activity when they slowly drove through the rutted dirt streets with wooden boardwalks. They observed the construction of many new buildings including houses, hotels, livery stables and restaurants. Within a few short hours all three had "hired on" in an occupation suited for them. Dad worked as a brick layer at the construction site of the Navin Hotel, which was completed in 1911.

So began a new way of life for the three Iowans who were destined to remain for the most part of their lives in their newly adopted home town of Mitchell.

5

From the lush green valleys along the Mississippi River, from a town named Wabasha, my mother answered the call of the Dakota land and left her farm home in 1912.

She and her older sister, Caroline, arrived on the Chicago-Milwaukee train and liked what they saw as they walked the main street in search of a place to stay. They found cheap lodging at Mrs. Kempton's "rooming house." The next day they were employed at the "Beanery" (Interstate Lunch Room) located in the Milwaukee depot. The passengers from the trains, the railroad workers and the townspeople found the home-cooked meals and lunches to be nourishing and delicious. Mama was "chief cook and bottle washer" and her sister was a "Harvey girl," or waitress.

In this newly constructed brick and masonry depot, my parents met and fell in love "at first sight." The handsome blue eyed Irishman and the pretty dark haired farm girl decided they were meant for each other. After a short courtship they were married on November 24th, 1914, at the Catholic parsonage. Father Coleman O'Flaherty officiated at the single ring ceremony.

So began a happy marriage of good times and bad, "for better or worse," in "sickness and in health," till death did part them after thirty-five years of marriage. Their union brought forth nine children.

The wind-swept prairies that beckoned to my parents those many years ago have now reclaimed them and they are entombed in Calvary Cemetery. Mitchell. They left no mark on the history of this community and only a few of the townspeople can recall their names. They are probably only remembered by me and the remaining clan of the Barnes family whose heritage we share.

DOLORES WILSON

Contents

Birthplace and First Home

"I'd give all of my tomorrows for just one yesterday" is a line from a song that illustrates the feelings of many people like myself in the summer of our years. If we had the chance to turn back the hands of time, where in time and place would we want to remain forever? I'm sure most of us would like to return to the "age of innocence" and to the carefree days of our childhood.

For many, the past is forgotten or lost in the cobwebs of an elusive memory. But for me it keeps coming back like a song, and the melody becomes sweeter as the years go by. It seems only yesterday and not almost a half century ago when I can recall my first awareness of who I was and where my roots began.

First I want to inform my readers that I'm not a professional writer, nor do I have any degrees in journalism. This story is a true account of one family's survival during the Great Depression and the events that took place during our "growing up" years in Mitchell, South Dakota.

I am sure it was around the age of three or four when I first became aware of my earthly surroundings. The flashbacks of time come and go like a beacon. A fondness for playing in a pile of dirt and sometimes getting a spanking. Being jealous of my younger sister because she was the baby of the family. Taking an afternoon nap with my mother. The buzzing of a pesky fly waking us up again. Watching the bedroom curtains swaying in the breeze from an open window. The fun of walking through the mud puddles after a summer shower and trying to catch a fluttering butterfly as it caressed the wild flowers in our back yard.

My birthplace was located almost at the end of the block on 721 North Edmunds, adjacent to a lumber yard and the Omaha railroad tracks. An oil station was directly across the street. The house was wood with a small porch extending to the front and back. Four small rooms had to expand to accommodate nine people. There must have been a bed in every room. People often asked my parents in jest, "Do you folks sleep standing up?"

There was no indoor plumbing. An unpainted privy sat near the alley and an ash pile near the fence line. Our water supply was kept in a deep dark well, a large wooden barrel caught the rain water that flowed from the eaves. Mama was forever washing clothes, either on the washboard or in a creak-

9

ing, leaking, wooden washing machine. We may have been poor but "scrub brush clean."

I was the sixth child born on May 11, 1924. We three younger children were like stairsteps with only one year difference in our ages. Sometimes I felt like a twin to my brother Bobby or sister Neeney. But it was a happy childhood at the time and I enjoyed many hours of fun and games with so many brothers and sisters. We didn't know that we were born into the poor society of the town.

Hard times were already pressing during the late twenties, for our family as well as countless others. It took a lot of groceries to feed an ever-hungry brood of seven children, even though the basement bulged with the jars of fall canning.

We children usually wore "hand me downs," or were given rummage from some charitable association like the Salvation Army. To keep bread on the table, my dad worked at many "jack of all trades" jobs. With his limited schooling he had to accept the menial jobs. If he was lucky a few paint jobs came along to bolster his self image. During the winter months he worked part time in the Purity and Equity Dairies where he could buy skim milk for five cents a gallon. The T. P. Navin saloon often hired him as an extra bar tender to sell beer and lunches.

Prohibition and Bootlegging

Many people remember the days of Prohibition with fond memories and can recall many tales about buying illegal whiskey and "bending the law of the land." Saloons were allowed to sell 3.2 beer or "near beer" as it was aptly named. The foaming mugs and bottles sold across the bar satisfied some of the local gentry but not the hard drinkers who wanted a bigger kick than a glass of "suds." Since selling whiskey was against the law and stiff fines and jail sentences were given to offenders, it still didn't halt the "rum runners" or "bootleggers" in and around Mitchell. Business was flourishing and the "white lightning" or "moonshine" was being sold in pints, quarts, jugs and in gallon cans.

We kids knew who the bootleggers were; not just the riff-raff of the town but a few prominent businessmen and even an officer of the law. Neighborhood kids used to look for empty whiskey bottles and sell them back to the "bootleggers" for one cent each. One who lived near the roundhouse pond raised the ante to two cents. He owned a classy looking green and white roadster.

To keep ahead of the law, many bootleggers had to find secret hiding places for their "hootch." It was stashed in caves, haystacks, basements and even buried in the graveyard. Many unsuspecting farmers uncovered large caches of moonshine during the spring plowing season and some of them jumped on the bandwagon and sold it in the surrounding communities. People were hard up and there was no conscience about being an accessory to the "Big Wigs" or "Kingpins" as they toured the towns looking for the poor folks to help them sell their merchandise.

I remember well the night my dad was approached by a man they called Lou Bronko. He stepped out a a luxurious maroon car, was well dressed, puffed on a long black cigar. We kids jumped up on the running boards and looked inside at the fancy leather seats. But Lou told us to "scoot" when my brother kept beeping the horn. When Dad told us to get into the house, I felt that there was something they wanted to discuss in private. The bootlegger convinced my dad that "everybody's doing it" and "it doesn't hurt anybody to make a little on the side."

I'm sure there were others in our neighborhood who also had their home bars but no one wanted to admit it. People were known to "squeal" on their friends and relatives when the federal agents made inquiries. I knew Dad and Mother tried to hide the selling of booze from us kids but there was a noticeable number of new friends and relatives coming to our door, usually at night. It was during a teachers' convention when business was more brisk than usual when Mama almost got "pinched" one day.

She and a neighbor lady were taking a "coffee break" when they took note of two more customers getting out of a taxi cab and coming towards the house. "Two more teachers who want to paint the town red," they laughed as Mama proceeded to open the door.

Mama's suspicions were quickly aroused when she noticed the two "ladies" were overly dressed and their make-up didn't look quite natural. Curls of flaming red hair and heavily rouged lips didn't seem to fit the image of a prim school teacher. When one of them asked for a half pint, the voice sounded too masculine to belong to a woman.

Mama told them to wait and she would bring out the whiskey. Knowing by now that they were two Federal agents (revenuers), posing as women, this called for some quick strategy and to let them know she was too smart to be trapped by amateur sleuths. Quickly she told her friend Margy to fill a bottle from the vinegar barrel that sat on the back porch. Before the agents would pay fifty cents for the prohibited beverage, they wanted to taste the concoction so an arrest could be made. It took one sip for the agent to realize that they had been foiled again and he angrily smashed the bottle against a tree. They swore that they would get even with Mama the next time. Mama smiled as she watched the agents walk back to the waiting taxi, still trying to appear ladylike in their red wigs and three-inch high heeled shoes.

The "Revenuers" finally had the last laugh when a bottle of bootleg whiskey was found in the trunk of Dad's car. He had been stopped for a minor traffic violation. How scared I was when I saw the police car drive into our yard! They told Mama that Dad had been arrested, along with five other townspeople.

Although Mama was more than worried, it wasn't as bad as she thought. The prohibition agents didn't really want the small town bootleggers, they wanted the big suppliers. So after a court appearance, Dad decided to testify in Federal Court in Sioux Falls, South Dakota. "Bootlegger Lou" was headed for the "big house."

For some reason Mama and we three younger children

were allowed to make the trip also, all expenses paid for by the state. Who could ask for anything more?

The neighbors must have thought we were going on a vacation instead of a court appearance as we boarded the passenger train at the Omaha depot. I'm sure our eyes were as big as saucers as we watched all the sights from the window of the train, as we wended our way over hill and dale.

The larger-than-Mitchell city of Sioux Falls was a sight for sore eyes as our taxi driver gave us a "Cooks tour" of the grand avenues and boulevards before we registered at the Cataract Hotel on Phillips Avenue.

For three long glorious days we enjoyed the elegant sleeping and eating accommodations. I felt like a real live princess as I followed Mama and Dad around the confines of our penthouse. I especially liked the bathroom where I played with the water faucets that sprayed hot and cold running water.

But all good things have to end and it was time to say "good-bye" to the high living "high rise" and come back down to earth. Dad and Mama were glad the trial was over and were more than willing to leave the bootlegging to others. Our neighborhood seemed strange for a while but the experience was soon forgotten and we were just plain folks again. AND still poor!

T. P. Navin and Sons' Saloon
in the 1930's

The Wrong Side of the Tracks

It can be said that we children weren't born with "silver spoons" in our mouths but we became accustomed to our way of life. Yet, I often heard the phrase about living on the wrong side of the tracks and I began to notice that there was always a railroad track not too far from our front door. Mama often talked about the people who enjoyed the better things in life on the other side of town, "the upper crust." It made a lot of difference to some people if a family owned their stately mansions or rented a tumble down shack near a railroad track. At an early age I sensed that because we were poor, we would have to take the back seat for the more affluent society, a feeling that remained with me throughout my childhood.

My fears began to multiply during the bitter cold winter of 1930. I knew Mama was worried about my dad being out of work and sometimes her anxiety would erupt into an argument. I hated to see them argue and many times I would hide beneath my bed and hold my hands over my ears so I wouldn't feel the hostility. Dad was usually in misery anyway from aching teeth and didn't have the money for a dentist. Mama told him, "Get up to see Doc Sweeney and have all those teeth pulled out. You can pay him in the spring." Dad angrily replied, "I won't need the teeth if I don't earn any money to buy groceries."

To make matters worse, the landlord was coming to the house to collect the rent that was past due. Dad kept putting him off in hopes an extra job would pay off the mounting bills. I was becoming accustomed to the face of the man who was going to kick us out, "lock, stock and barrel." I began to fear the skinny old man. I thought he was evil. Mama called him "Simon Legree," or the old "skinflint" who was too tight to fix up the many houses that he owned around town. Sometimes we kids were told to be quiet as a mouse when Mama didn't want to answer the door. From behind the curtains we watched him walk briskly to his old automobile that looked as dilapidated as his real estate. When he was out of sight everyone relaxed until his next visit.

Old John soon tired of waiting for the rent money so tried the next best thing to rid his premises of us—a three-day eviction notice was handed to Dad by the local sheriff. Where were we going to live? It was cold outside, 20 below zero.

The next day a house was found on the far west side of Mitchell which needed some repair and was a little too close to the railroad track, but "beggars can't be choosers." It was going to be a hardship for Dad and the older members of the family to walk about fourteen blocks to school and town. To own a car at that time would have been impossible.

With so few home furnishings in the small house, it didn't take long to dismantle the iron beds, box up the kitchen utensils and remove the few pictures and calendars from the wall. (The holes in the walls became visible when the pictures came down.) "Why, in God's Name, does everything happen to us?" "When it rains it pours," Mama fumed. The weather wasn't cooperating on moving day. The ground was covered with a sheet of ice and the wind was howling around the door. Our Uncle Pete was having a hard time trying to maneuver his old truck close enough to the front porch. He was the only relative with a vehicle in running condition.

The rooms were almost cleared except for the linoleum rugs and the pot-belly stove. Dad and Uncle Pete pulled on their gloves to dismantle the stove pipes which were still too hot to handle. We kids stood waiting, wrapped in our warmest clothing, while the stove was hoisted out of the door, followed by a trail of ashes. The worn, faded rugs were quickly rolled together and tied.

The little house was now empty and humble looking. It seemed cold and lonely. I felt sad to leave the only home that I ever knew. It was like losing something very dear to me. "Come on, let's go," Dad called from the truck as I jumped inside, holding my doll under my coat. Mama closed the door of the house for the last time and climbed in beside me, and muttered, "Get the hell out of here—I never liked this place anyway."

MY SECOND HOME — WEST 4TH STREET

Time does change everything and the old neighborhood was soon a thing of the past. There were oodles of kids on the west side of town and most of their families were like us, poor as church mice.

Our house was a ramshackle cement structure with more than enough room for all of us. I did worry somewhat about the railroad track that was only a few yards away. During the railroad track that was only a few yards away. During the night we were often awakened by the rumbles and groans of a slow moving freight winding its way out of town. After the train had passed, I would lie awake and listen to the whistle wailing its lonely departure.

Money was becoming harder to come by and the country was already engulfed in a worsening economy. Our neighbors and our family were all in the same boat. "Why don't you go to the county for help?" a neighborhood lady asked. "You have to forget your pride." Everyone in town knew the people who received relief from the county. Their names were printed in the local newspaper. Dad finally went to the courthouse to beg for his family to keep their heads above water. The coal bin was soon filled with a half ton of coal and a few weeks supply of groceries were bought at John Cramptons store. There was one more request. Mama needed a doctor for her baby who was due in a few weeks. When the time came, she could call Dr. Earl Young, who was the county doctor for the needy. (At the age of 41, Mama was really too old to have another baby, but during that period it wasn't unusual for women to bear children until they reached the change of life.)

Mama was a large enough woman without being pregnant and she tried to conceal her ballooning figure from the neighbors. She used to complain to Dad, "How am I going to hide a watermelon?" Dad only laughed and told her, "I think you're going to have twins." She might as well have, as our baby brother weighed in at 14½ pounds at birth.

At this tender age I couldn't understand the "why and wherefore" about babies coming into the world. Mama and Carrie, conversing about the preparations, belied all the stories about the stork dropping the baby down the chimney or finding an infant on a doorstep tucked into a wicker clothes basket.

The neighbor ladies all helped Mama prepare her layette and brought hand-me-downs from their youngsters. Aunt Carrie donated crocheted booties and a cap and sweater set. The outing flannel for the stacks of diapers was purchased at a general store. I loved to look at the tiny wardrobe, with embroidered flowers that splashed across the kimonos, pink and blue ribbons that entwined around the necklines, the doll-like white stockings and the pretty celluloid rattle, waiting to be held by a tiny hand.

My younger sister, Neeney, wasn't too thrilled about the little stranger who would soon replace her as baby of the family. She liked to sneak the nursing bottles, fill them with water and drink the contents. This was done in the privacy of the closet. I was always ready to reveal her secret and warned her. "I'm going to tell Mama on you and you're going

16

to get a good licking." My threats never had much of any effect on her because she always "had her own way."

I knew Mama's "time" had come when my Aunt Carrie was brought to our house by Uncle Pete. It was almost twilight and we had just finished eating supper. Aunt Carrie had brought along an extra box of bread, rolls and cookies. She set her suitcase in the closet and proceeded to help with the dishes. Mama's sister tried to act cheerful but I could tell by her eyes that she was worried about the impending birth.

"You kids get to bed early tonight," we were told by our already nervous father. Any emergency always made him jumpy. Aunt Carrie asked if there was a neighbor with a phone to call the doctor. Dad had already asked Mr. Crampton, who ran the grocery store next door.

I couldn't sleep as I lay in the crowded bed with my two sisters. I was afraid that Mama might die. What would we do without a mother? I had heard some of the neighbor ladies telling about women who died when their babies came into the world. All of us were born at home except brother Bobby. Mama was ill with pneumonia at St. Joseph's Hospital when he arrived on April fools day.

During the night I could hear the sounds of voices below us and I knew that Mama was in pain as the moans became more audible. Then I heard the slamming of a door and I knew that Dad was going to call the doctor.

It seemed like a very long time before I heard the crunching of the doctor's car wheels in the snow-covered yard. By the light of the moon we could see that the good doctor had arrived in time; it wouldn't be long now. "Please don't let Mama die," I prayed.

After watching the doctor leave again from our upstairs window, we kids waited in the darkness and wondered if everything was all right. My sister said she thought she heard a baby crying. "Were Mama and the baby alive?" I wondered to myself. The suspense was awful.

After what seemed to be an eternity the hallway door was opened and Aunt Carrie shouted, "You can all come down now." I was the last to go down the stairs, wrapped in a blanket to ward off the cold that permeated the house.

The kitchen was warm and cozy and there was a pot of coffee brewing on the cook stove. When Dad was nervous he drank coffee. I shyly approached Dad as he sat on a kitchen chair holding the newest addition to our household. "What

17

do you think of your little brother?" he quietly asked me. My childish heart was filled with emotion as I gazed upon the sleeping infant. I thought he was more beautiful than any baby I had ever seen. "Hello, Jimmy," I whispered. The name James Patrick had been chosen long ago. I wasn't disappointed that the little sister that I was hoping for turned out to be a boy. "Can I hold him for a little while?" I begged.

"I'll let you hold him for just a minute," said Dad, placing the new-born child into my arms. I could feel the warmth of the tiny body nestled in the flannel receiving blanket. "Look at his red face. He sure has a lot of hair. How come he makes those funny faces? Look at his hands; they look so big," were comments made by the family as they took their turns holding baby Jimmy. Sister Neeney was already showing her disapproval of losing her place of honor as the baby of the family. She didn't want to look at this little intruder. "You will get used to him," soothed Aunt Carrie to my pouting sister. "In a few months he will be fun to play with."

The baby was taken back into Mama's bedroom and we kids went back upstairs to bed. I couldn't sleep. I was waiting for the sunrise so I could see our baby brother again.

After weeks of seeing the care and feeding of Mama's new offspring, I felt I was able to bathe, powder, diaper, feed and burp my baby brother. Mama did allow us to cuddle him for a few minutes, her ever watchful eye on his soft spot and warning us never to bump his head or allow it to bob up and down. In a few short months I'm sure he became as tough as shoe leather after being passed from one family member to another.

The daily sponge baths were soon replaced with a submersion in an oversized enameled dishpan. Before this could be done the kitchen had to be as hot as a blast furnace, although the outdoor air was now very warm from the noonday sun. Mama didn't take any chances of Jimmy catching cold or pneumonia.

The makeshift tub filled with warm sudsy water and a floating bar of soap was placed on the kitchen table. After feeling the temperature with her elbow, Mama plunged Jimmy into his bath while we kids circled the table to watch the kicking and splashing. He was then rolled into a warm towel and patted dry, the ever ready can of talcum powder standing by. Sometimes cornstarch was used when there wasn't any extra money for powder, or a dab of lard for diaper rash.

Resting on a nearby chair were the small garments that

Mama stitched together on her sewing machine. The flannel diapers, undershirts and kimonos were the same sizes as my doll clothes. I loved to feel the little knitted booties that were tied with pretty colored ribbon. During that time all babies wore long white stockings which were pinned to the diapers. So when the baby was "soaked to the gills," so were the stockings and everything else.

In a twinkling of an eye, Mama had her baby dressed, careful not to twist a chubby arm or leg. When finished he looked just like a kewpie doll that I once saw in a store window.

By this time Little Jim was hungrily sucking on his fist and beginning to whimper for a warm bottle of milk. (His formula was canned milk and syrup.) While Mama warmed the milk in a pan on the cookstove, we kids jostled the bed to keep him content. The milk was then sprinkled on Mama's wrist to insure the right temperature. The bottle was propped on a rolled-up diaper to keep it in place. In no time at all the contents of the bottle were emptied and Jimmy lay fast asleep while the warm sunlight from the bedroom window cast a halo of gold around his curly head. It was time to tip-toe out of the room and back into the kitchen where Mama was busily sorting clothes for the never-ending laundry. Only now her burden was made a little easier. Dad had purchased a new soft rubber wringer washing machine. Such luxury, no more scrubbing on a washboard.

The month of March was going out like a lion, engulfed in the bitter cold winds and snow squalls of a dying South Dakota winter. Although the old weather-beaten concrete house was winterized with tar paper and cardboard covers for the doors, windows and foundation, it was still cold enough so we could see our breath in the drafty bedrooms on the second floor, where we older children slept.

Our baby brother Jimmy shared Mama's bed, protected from a "roll over" by several large pillows. For awhile Dad had to sleep on an uncomfortable day bed. At that time many infants slept with their mother in a safe and warm environment. Also there was the ever-present danger of the flu and pneumonia which no drugs would then combat. Mama never forgot the sorrow of losing her first born child to pneumonia.

Jimmy's life, too, was threatened by a respiratory ailment complicated by a series of convulsions that wracked his small body till his skin turned blue. It was touch and go for many weeks before Dr. Earl Young, with his black bag of medicine

19

bottles and Mama with a few home remedies, conquered the malady and brought the roses back to Jimmy's cheeks.

How happy I was the day I heard the good doctor tell Mama, "I think he is finally out of the woods." From that moment on, the curly haired blue eyed baby was the object of our affections in a large household of now healthy children.

Christmas Time

My growing up years in Mitchell were both bitter and the sweet but I honestly believe the good times outweighed the sad occasions.

One of the happiest times of the year was the Christmas season. Santa Claus was a man who brought toys and goodies to the children in other neighborhoods but never to ours. At an early age Mama told us that the fairy tales about the jolly old man were only stories affluent parents told to their children, as they could afford the gifts that were asked for. "There is no Santa Claus." I think she told us the bitter truth so we would understand when Christmas arrived and we didn't receive presents like some of the neighbor kids. Yet I

**Christmas tree and decorations
on Mitchell's Main Street**

continued to believe in the miracle of the jolly Santa in the red suit with his prancing reindeer who flew through the air like thistle down. Many times I would awaken my little sister and whisper, "Did you hear that scratching noise on the roof?" "I think it's Santa Claus." "Oh, go to sleep, that's just a mouse. Besides, there ain't no Santa Claus. Mama said so." And she would thump her pillow and roll over and fall back to sleep.

One special Christmas comes to mind. It was the year of 1929 and I was a young lady of four.

Christmas morning wasn't too different from any other morning. We kids opened a few small trinkets that we found in our stocking. There was no tree. Mama was busy in the kitchen baking some pies to take over to Aunt Carrie's where we were going to spend the day. "Can we go out and play in the snow?" we asked her. "Better not, you might get your clothes all wet, then you won't have anything to wear." So we kids just sat by the large bay window and watched the swirling snowflakes.

"Hey, Ma, there's a big truck pulling into our yard," shouted one of the brothers and we all ran to see what the commotion was all about. "I can't imagine who that can be," said Dad as he pulled on his overcoat and walked out on the porch. With noses pressed to the frosty window panes, we watched two men open the doors of the truck and set some cardboard boxes on the ground.

Soon Dad came back into the house, followed by the men carrying the boxes. There was a happy grin on his face. "Merry Christmas, children," the strangers shouted. "We ran into Santa Claus this morning and he asked if we would help him deliver these presents to the Barnes family."

"See, I told you there was a real Santa Claus," I told my sister as we all edged toward the presents that were being distributed to each member of the family.

The boys were wild with excitement, tearing open their packages of games, toys, bags of nuts and candy and even some new jackets and caps with ear flappers.

Neeney and I were anxiously waiting for our gifts that were at the bottom of the box. Two parcels wrapped in scarlet ribbon were given to us by Santa's helper. "Say thank you," Mama reminded us as we scurried into the bedroom. "Thank you," we shouted over our shoulders.

I couldn't believe my eyes when I lifted the lid off the box. Inside was a beautiful doll with golden curls and pink lips that were parted to reveal two pearly white teeth. Her eyes were closed, fringed with long lashes. They flew open when I gently lifted her into my arms, and were blue, just like mine. The soft cuddly body was dressed in a pink organdy and lace pinafore, a matching bonnet adorned with satin ribbons perched on top of her head. Her chubby feet were encased in pink booties. My heart overflowed with joy as I hugged her close to my breast. I felt like a new mother in my childish imagination. Sister Neeney was not as enthralled with her doll. She wanted a fire truck instead. "You can have my old doll," she pouted and threw it on the bed. A cry of "Mama" came from the discarded doll. I picked her up and smoothed her curls. "Now I have two babies to love," I crooned to myself.

The good Samaritans who brought our Christmas cheer were members of a businessmen's club. They called themselves The Goodfellows—and that they were. Over the years we became accustomed to these dedicated men who gave of themselves so others less fortunate might enjoy a happier holiday.

After all the excitement had died down, we had a chance to examine all the presents that the Goodfellows left at our house. The brothers were already engrossed in reading the books about Tarzan of the Apes, Dick Tracy, and Flash Gordon. Their bags of candy and nuts were almost empty. Little brother Bobby was zooming around the house on his hands and knees, pushing his new fire engine. Neeney was trying to take it away from him.

"Won't Aunt Carrie be surprised to see my new doll?" I questioned Mama as she placed the aromatic, still warm pies into a cardboard box.

"I'm sure she will," she answered, "and wait till she sees your new coat."

I had almost forgotten about the tweed coat with the fur collar and cuffs that fit me to a "T." This was no hand-me-down, but my very own.

"Boy, I'm getting hungry," Dad shouted from the front room. "You guys better get ready or I'll leave without you. We're supposed to be over there by noon." "Over the river and through the woods, to Carrie's house we go," he sang as he swung my little sister and me upon his knees and pretended to gallop like a horse over the fields of snow.

Getting dressed around our house was hectic, to say the least. The search for an elusive sock or a suit of underwear left the dresser drawers in a jumbled mess and the brothers often fighting over a belt or neck tie.

"If I hear one more word I'm coming in there with the broomstick," Mama called from the kitchen where she now was in the process of curling up her hair. (This quick curl method was to place a two pronged curling iron into the red hot coals of the cookstove, then twirl the iron around the hair to create a coiled hair-do.)

"The iron was too hot," she fumed. The smell of singed hair filled the kitchen and chased away the fragrance of the apple pies. "Now remember, before anyone leaves this house, I'm holding inspection," Mama informed the family. "I can't get this knot out of my shoestring," Bobby wailed. "Someone help me." "Shut up and get a fork," suggested brother Don.

"I can't find the comb," came another complaint. "I can't get this zipper closed." "You better get those shirt tails tucked in. One day out of a year you're going to look decent."

"I'm sure glad Christmas comes but once a year" an exhausted Mama said as she took one more peek behind the ears and under the chins to check on the high water marks, and then smoothed down the cowlicks on the boys' unruly hair. Looking over to where we girls stood all neatly dressed and ready to go, she sighed, "I wish I would have had all girls."

It was a long walk from our house to Aunt Carrie's place and the weather was cold with a snow covered ground. Yet, our hearts were filled with the Christmas spirit and we knew that we were in for a great feast of turkey and all the trimmings.

"Now mind your manners when we get there or you'll get it when we get back home," Mama warned everyone as we trudged along. "Rememer now, you kids have to wait till the grownups eat first." There wasn't enough room around the table for everyone to be seated at the same time. My mind wasn't on the food. I was content with my new doll that I clutched tightly in my arms.

Uncle Pete already had a path shoveled through the snow from the road to the house when we arrived and everyone stomped the snow from his feet before going in. Aunt Carrie was at the door to take our coats, scarfs and mittens which were taken to the kitchen to dry off near the huge cook stove. "Merry Christmas, Merry Christmas!" We exchanged greetings with our relatives while peeking at the dining room table,

24

laden with a gigantic golden turkey, surrounded by steaming bowls of potatoes, gravy, creamed peas and carrots and an assortment of cole slaw, pickles and other relishes.

While the grown-ups dined on the delectable banquet and exchanged the latest gossip, we kids tried to keep our mouths from watering until it was our turn.

It wasn't hard for me to find something to do because Carrie's home was like a miniature library, with magazines, books, scrapbooks, and a wonderful stereoscope with pictures from all over the world.

"O.K., kids, come and get it," shouted Aunt Carrie after the large round oak table had been cleared of the dishes and then filled again with a generous supply of food. The brothers tried to argue about the seating arrangement until Mama warned them again, "Just wait till I get you home!" It was always our mother who had to discipline us children. Dad never wanted to. I don't ever remember him laying a hand on anyone of us. Aunt Carrie said grace and all the Barnes clan dug in like seven little pigs in the straw with their mother.

After everyone had eaten till their stomachs hurt, Mama, Aunt Carrie and sister Evie cleared the table and prepared to wash the stacks of dishes and pots and pans. I wanted to help, too. Mama always let me wipe the dishes at home. "You can put all the silverware in the cupboard drawers," Carrie said. "And when you're finished it will be time to go into the parlor and see what Santa Claus left under our tree. Everyone pushed and shoved behind our aunt as she led the way through the house.

"Close your eyes now and don't peek till I tell you to open them," said Aunt Carrie, who was ready to open the folding doors. The large oak doors then swung wide to reveal a room full of mysterious beauty.

In the center of the room stood a magnificent Christmas tree glowing with lights of green, red, blue, orange and even lavender, clinging to the lush green branches of an evergreen. Strings of white fluffy popcorn and beads of ruby red cranberries entwined between the glittering strands of tinsel. Perched on the low hanging branches was a red cardinal and two bluebirds made out of blown glass. The gasping sounds of "Ohs" and "Ahs" filled the parlor as we all gazed in awe at this wonderful tree. There was never a Christmas tree at our house.

To add to the decorations was a homemade chain of

colored paper extending from each corner of the room, hanging in the center was a large red ruffled bell.

Neatly piled under the tree was an assortment of packages, each one tied with loving care by our dear Aunt Carrie who was placed on this earth to bring a little happiness to all who knew her.

Even though our gifts were dime store novelties, they were very much appreciated during those hard times. The brothers received a bottle of Rose hair oil to control their unruly hair, or maybe a pair of socks. We girls were tickled pink with our presents of toilet articles and hair ribbons or barrettes. Mama's passion was jewelry so a shiny pin from the store made her smile. It would look elegant on the fur collar of her coat. Dad was happy to receive a maroon tie, a change from the black one that he wore on dress-up occasions.

"Aunt Carrie, I feel bad because we couldn't give you a present," I sadly told her as she adjusted the satin bow in my hair. If Dad gets that job at the dairy after Christmas then maybe we'll have some money."

"Never you mind. Just to make someone happy is all the present I need." She hugged me close to her ample bosom and gave me a big kiss.

A few games of bingo were then played with our cousin Delmar who always received more than his share of gifts. Being an only child meant he would get the better things in life.

"Well, you kids better get your coats on, it's beginning to get dark," Dad announced after we finished a light lunch of fruit nectar and Christmas cookies. "The snow is coming down a little heavier now and it will be pretty deep by the time we get home." We all scrambled into the kitchen, sat on the floor and pulled on our overshoes.

And so ended another happy holiday at Aunt Carrie's house. Our spirits were lifted as we kids sang "Jingle Bells" while trying to step into Dad's footprints in the deepening snowdrifts. Aunt Carrie, Uncle Pete and cousin Delmar stood on the front porch, shouting, "Have a happy New Year." When I looked back I could see the lights from the Christmas tree glowing through the frosted windows—a sight no artist could paint. For my parents, it was a special day, but what about tomorrow? Would the hard times continue to deprive our family of the necessities of life in the coming new year? Only time would tell.

PEACE ON EARTH?

Our family didn't always share the traditional holidays with our relatives. Sometimes there were hard feelings and we were on "the outs," especially with our mother and Uncle Pete who brought out the worst in each other.

I recall one memorable Christmas eve when we were all invited to share in the singing of carols and to have a cup or two of Aunt Carrie's delicious egg nog, something we kids always looked forward to.

Everything started out on a cheery note as we kids tramped through the snow on the heels of our mother while Dad stayed home with baby Jim, and to keep the stoves fired up with coal.

Answering our knock on the door, a voice inside hollered, "Come in if your nose is clean."

"Sounds like Pete has already fallen into the egg nog barrel," Mama laughed as she shoved the door open.

Righ away we all knew that Uncle Pete was "half stewed" by the silly smirk on his face. "I hope he and Mama don't get into it," I prayed. This is Christmas eve and there should be peace on earth, good will to men, including our sometimes obnoxious relative."

Mama tried her best not to get "hot under the collar" when insults entered into every topic that was discussed. Aunt Carrie kept changing the subject when she thought they came close to argument. Uncle Pete had painted the kitchen the day before and invited one and all to inspect his artistic talent. We all praised his work to keep him in a good humor. (He never could paint as well as my dad who was almost a professional.)

Mama chose to hold her tongue while her brother-in-law was beginning to get under her skin. Looking up at my mother who was at least a head taller than he, he again tried to "get her goat."

"It's a hellava lot better paint job than old Bill Barnes could ever do. He's about the sloppiest painter in town."

That insult did it. Mama raised her arm, doubled up her fist and let him have it—a right to the jaw. He fell backwards and landed behind the cookstove with a startled look on his face. "He asked for it," she announced to the shocked on-lookers.

"Come on, kids, let's get out of here," Mama fumed as

she pushed us out the back door. "It will be a cold day in hell before I ever set foot in this house again, Christmas or no Christmas." As for me, I was filled with mixed emotions of not enjoying our eggnogs and decorated cookies, but still glad that Mama finally gave Uncle Pete exactly what he deserved, a good right to the jaw.

The eventful day usually dawned on a crisp cold morning, the house chilly until the two stoves were fired up. The first thing Mama would do was check on her mouse traps scattered throughout the house. Sometimes they were filled with dead mice. The lifeless rodents were tossed out of the back door where a neighbor's hungry cat enjoyed a tasty breakfast.

"Is anyone getting up around here?" asked Mama. She thought everyone should be out of bed by 6 a.m. "Those two old red roosters have to be killed and in the oven by nine o'clock." She continued to rattle the pots and pans until everyone climbed down the stairs.

Dad never wanted to slaughter his prized roosters or hens, so the job was left to Mama who seemed to have a good stomach for almost anything.

After cornering a few of the largest roosters and grabbing them by the feet they were carried, squawking, behind the chicken coop where they were beheaded.

The still warm bodies were placed in a bucket of scalding water to remove the feathers, then singed over an open flame to rid the fine hair and pin feathers. After a thorough cleansing in cold water, then cleaned, the plump roosters were filled with dressing and shoved into a hot oven.

The delicious apple and pumpkin pies were baked the night before, the tin pans of jello were placed on the chilly back porch that served as our makeshift refrigerator. I recall the year when Mama went to the porch to bring in our dessert and found that a rooster had somehow gained entry and had pecked out all of the fruit from the containers of jello. That old red rooster was lucky to escape with his life.

By the time the oil-clothed dining room table was set and loaded down with our annual feast, everyone was as hungry as a bear and there were no holds barred. The older kids always picked out the choicest parts of the chicken, while my plate more often contained a wing and I never got the wish bone. Everyone believed their wish would come true if it was broken in their favor.

"I'm just stuffed," or "I can hardly breathe," moaned a satisfied bunch of kids who had licked the platter clean. "Do you want your pie now or later?" Mama asked, "or why don't you go outside and walk it off?" Mama used to say that I always ate like a bird or nibbled like a mouse. It took me a long time to clean my plate. By the time the table was cleared I'd still be eating.

The Christmas holidays were a great time for all of the neighbor kids to gather around to see what Santa Claus brought. In our neighborhoods there was never anything too expensive to brag about. There were more than enough sleds to go belly flopping down the steep snow packed hill that ran past our house. Located at the bottom was the ice covered Roundhouse pond. (This winter playground became alive during the holidays with the children from the south side of town.) The steep hills surrounding the pond were ideal for sleds or any homemade toboggans of cardboard or snow shovels. What fun it was playing crack the whip, broomstick hockey or fox and goose. Little brother Jimmy enjoyed frolicking in the snow and being pushed around on his sled till his cheeks turned rosy from the winter winds. When our hands and feet became numb from the cold we warmed them near a crackling bonfire built from the scraps of wood that were found on the hillsides.

All too soon the fun and games were over as the late afternoon sun began to hide in a maze of purple clouds and the shadows from the hills were creeping across the ice covered pond. It was time to head for home and a supper time of goulash, the leftovers from the noonday Christmas banquet.

The Circus

Mama never had to ask our dad to entertain us when we were only babes in arms. He had a natural talent for singing, dancing, spinning a yarn or making funny faces when we were in pain from a bruised knee, a tummy ache, or burning up with fever. The discomfort was soon forgotten when our attention was focused on the bedroom wall, watching the shadows of animals and birds that came to life, manipulated by Dad's hands.

My brother Bobby, sister Neeney and I never tired of his riddles and the stories he told us as he tucked us into bed. "Tell us about the little elephant that jumped the fence," we begged him for the umpteenth time.

"O.K. One more time and then the sandman is coming," he would answer. "I asked my mother for fifty cents to see the elephant jump the fence. He jumped so high, he hit the sky, and never came down till the Fourth of July."

"Did you really work in a circus and see all those wild animals and funny clowns?" we asked.

"I sure did," he laughed, "and someday I'm going to take you kids to the circus, and boy, will we have fun."

With that often repeated promise, Dad would quietly close the door and leave us to dream of that wonderful world of make believe in a balloon filled never-never land.

It was around the age of five when I began to take note of the local happenings around town by listening to the grownups talk. One evening I overheard Dad tell Mama, "There are circus posters plastered all over town. The Ringling Brothers and Barnum and Bailey circus will be in Mitchell soon and I don't know if I should tell the kids, but they will hear about it anyway. You know I've always promised to take them but we can't afford it right now. The older boys can get jobs watering the elephants for free passes. So that takes care of them."

"Can't you scrape up a few dollars somewhere?" Mama implored. Maybe 'T. P.' will loan you some."

"I doubt it," Dad replied. "I've already been paid in advance on that last paint job."

"Well, I can do the next best thing. We can get up at the crack of dawn and watch the circus train unload."

When I heard this exciting news, I raced into our bed-

Camel and rider in circus train parade

room to tell my brother and sister. "There's a big circus coming to town and we're going to watch the train unload all of the wild animals and maybe we will see some clowns." We could hardly contain ourselves, waiting for that eventful day to happen.

Mama didn't have to tell us twice to get up and dress on that memorable day. Our coveralls, socks and sandals were neatly placed under the bed the night before.

"They better put on some sweaters, too. It's pretty cool outside," Dad called from the kitchen. "The sun hasn't come up yet to take away the chill." We ignored the breakfast that Mama prepared for us. We were just too excited to eat.

"Wait till I finish this cup of coffee, then we'll go," Dad said, while we sat around the table trying to hurry that last sip of brew to his lips.

It seemed another eternity before Dad cranked up our old car and we were on our way to the Omaha railroad yards where the circus train was due to arrive momentarily. By the time we arrived we could see a good sized crowd of people by the dawn's early light. They, too, were searching for a good spot from which to observe a once-in-a-lifetime sight. Many were seated on the roofs of their trucks and cars. The low buildings surrounding the tracks were filled to capacity with a grandstand audience.

"Is there room for a few more up there?" asked Dad, trying to squeeze us next to a fat man who looked like Humpty Dumpty sitting on a wall. When the jolly stranger moved over there was more than enough room for all of us.

No sooner were we settled among the excited onlookers when we heard someone shout, "Here she comes, here comes the circus train." All eyes were strained and looking into the golden glow of the rising morning sun, when the steam engine came into view, white smoke puffing. A long piercing whistle warned everyone to clear the tracks.

The wooden box cars, brightly painted with the name of the circus emblazoned in large letters, moved slowly into the railroad yards. The steel wheels groaning and squealing from the weight of its precious cargo, ground to a sudden halt.

Unmindful of the gawking townspeople, who kept their distance, the roustabouts and animal handlers began their everyday chore of getting the show set up.

"Look at those elephants," Dad exclaimed as he diverted our attention to the immense animals being led down a gang-plank by a fast moving trainer. "They have to do all the heavy work, see! That long trunk is just like a hand to pick up things."

"It would be fun to feed them some peanuts," sister Neeney told me. "They might step on you with those big feet," I warned her, yet knowing that she wasn't afraid of man nor beast.

I moved a little closer to Dad when the cats inside their steel barred cages roared their disapproval about being jostled about. A shiver went down my spine when they snarled at us and flicked their tongues across sharp fanged teeth. Everyone was hypnotized by the beasts of the jungle.

"That's a man-eating tiger," said one woman, pointing toward a gold colored animal with black stripes. "Just think, there's a wild animal trainer named Clyde Beatty who gets into a center ring cage with these wild animals, protected only by a whip and a chair." Everyone marveled at this fear-less man who was billed as the "World's Greatest."

"What are those funny looking things called?" we asked Dad, observing some long-necked docile appearing animals who seemed too timid to walk down the ramp.

"Those are lamas. They come from a far away land," Dad answered, "and you know the name of those creatures with the strange looking humps."

"Camels," we all answered as if we were having a lesson right there near the circus train. I had learned all about animals with strange sounding names from looking through Aunt Carrie's scrapbooks.

The morning sun was becoming warm by the time the horses and ponies were hustled down the wooden chute amid the clatter of pounding hoofs and the shouts of the dusty unkempt roustabouts. They were being herded across the tracks and down a long dusty road toward the circus grounds on the north edge of town. The Cassem family owned the spacious meadow land where most of the tent shows were held. In just a few short hours the greatest show on earth was going to be seen by thousands.

The crowd began to disperse, pile back into their cars and trucks, satisfied that they had enjoyed a free sneak preview. Because of the hard times, only the more affluent families could afford to take their children through the main gate and buy the cotton candy and toy balloons.

"Where are the clowns, Dad?" we asked, taking a last look at the now silent circus train before climbing into the front seat of our old car. "Are they still sleeping?"

"We won't be able to see the clowns this year," he softly replied. But I promise you the next time a circus comes to town we will all be there and maybe watch an elephant jump the fence. We were pacified with the same old story.

Watching the arrival and the departure of the circus trains became a yearly ritual as I was soon growing up from a tousle-haired moppet into a gangling pre-teenager. Our financial status remained the same. Dad's promise of taking us to a circus began to fall on deaf ears. Yet, I felt a kinship with him as we watched the fascinating scene of the circus world. I often wondered if our lives would be happier if we could leave the humdrum life of the small town and join the vagabonds who were here today and gone tomorrow. Did my dad have a secret yearning to leave all of his troubles behind and hide himself behind the laughing face of a clown? Was he ever sorry that he was saddled with a large family, with not enough money to care for them?

My thoughts about him were more than answered when he grabbed us kids by his strong work-worn hands and wistfully told us, "Well, I guess it's time to go home now." Hurrying across the darkened railroad tracks, we could hear the echoing sounds of the circus train fading away in the dying night. "Farewell, farewell! I'll be back another day."

I was eighteen years old before I finally went to my first circus and it did indeed fulfill all of my expectations. The glitter and razzle dazzle of the big top was worth every nickel that came from my pocket. And the funny lovable clowns looked exactly as I had pictured them in my childhood dreams.

First Grade

I should have been enrolled in the first grade in 1930 but Mama decided since we lived so far away from the school that I should be kept home another year. This was disappointing to me as I was very anxious to begin my reading, writing and arithmetic. Every day I would watch the neighbor kids pass by our house, carrying their school books and sack lunches. When Mama saw the big tears I tried to hide, she assured me I would be better off having my younger sister, Neeney, by my side when I entered the first grade.

During the bitter cold weather that dropped the temperatures down to ten and twenty below zero the following winter, I was glad that Mama did make the right decision about my welfare. I can recall watching the school children braving the blowing snow and freezing winds, their heads wrapped with heavy scarves, and boots and overcoats encrusted with ice from the unrelenting blizzards. The strong winds often forced the children to walk backwards when the snow blinded them. Our kitchen looked like a Chinese laundry from the frozen clothing draped over a make-shift clothesline, or on chairs near the cook stove to dry them so they could be worn again the next day. I began to realize what it was going to be like for me to battle the cold South Dakota winters when I would have to walk those many blocks to school.

It was with great joy the day in the fall of 1931 that my younger sister, Neeney, and I were ready to enter the first grade at Whittier school next to Central and Junior High schools at 410 West Second Street.

Our big sister, Evie, took us to be registered. Mama remained at home with baby brother Jim. Evie was to be the spokesman for us on many occasions.

The weather beaten school building was already showing its age. The two-story structure had been erected in 1881. In the early days it was in the center of the block and served all grades and high school. In 1931 there were six rooms with four grades and two combination classes.

The first grade was on the southwest corner of the school where we shyly followed sister Evie through the door and took note of a pretty young woman sitting at a large wooden desk. She smiled sweetly and introduced herself as Miss Stella Johnson. While Evie supplied all the information that was necessary, I was observing the room where I would spend the next

Left front, blonde first grade teacher, Miss Stella
Johnson; in center, Ruth Wagner, principal; behind her, Miss Marian Cooley (others unidentified).

nine months. I can still recall the somber looking faces of
George Washington and Abraham Lincoln gazing down at
me from the wall. An octagon shaped wooden clock had a
pendulum which swung back and forth inside a glass case.
There were two pretty pictures of a long-haired boy in a
fancy blue suit and a small child holding an orange. I
learned all about the "arts" in a few weeks. The portraits
were "Blue Boy" and "Baby Stewart." The huge blackboard
was located on the east wall with pieces of chalk resting on
the ledge. I was anxious to show off and so picked up some

School children in front of old Whittier school, 410 West Second

chalk to show the teacher that I could write my name. I was already a year older than most of the class. I would be eight years old the following spring.

When Miss Johnson repeated our names, Norma and Dolores, as she filled in the registration cards, I felt grown up and important. At home we were called Neeney and Lorsey and a few other nicknames that we didn't approve of, such as tomboy or tuffy, and skinny or kitty cat.

The thought of going to school didn't impress my little sister, so during the first week she sneaked away and went home during the recess period. Miss Johnson finally decided to seat the two of us together in my desk to change Neeney's attitude toward school. The idea worked and in no time Neeney settled down to the daily routine.

Although we were sisters under the skin, we didn't look too much alike and our personalities were as different as day and night. Neeney was blond, brown eyed, short and bossy. Other classmates soon learned she was to be reckoned with. If she did not like the way some kids mentioned her tomboy antics, she didn't hesitate to wrestle them to the ground.

I was the shrinking violet and would not fight back no matter if a classmate pinched, pulled my hair or marked my dresses with ink. I suffered in silence because I didn't want to be called a tattle tale. Neeney finally realized my torment and vowed she would get even with the "preacher's kid" who sat behind me. I'll never forget the time when we chased Mildred home from school, but by the time I caught up with them, Neeney had already pushed my tormenter into a mud puddle. I picked up Mildred's hat that was lying nearby and threw it in the mire. She never bothered me again, nor did anyone else.

There are many fond memories that pervade my mind of those bygone days in the first grade; learning to read the Dick and Jane books; a hallowe'en party; wanting to be a "flowering buttercup" in a school program but not able to afford the costume; drawing pictures of everything under the sun and proudly taking them home to Mama and Dad; memorizing a poem or a song. One was "My Dog." "My dog is fond of playing but, oh, he is wise. To know what he is saying, just look into his eyes." Or, "Would you like to live in the sky and sit on the clouds as they go sailing by? You could visit the moon and the stars and the sun; now that I would think, would be fun." The first grade was a pleasant experience.

The old school building is gone but not forgotten. It has been moved and made into an apartment building. Still remembered are some of the children who were my classmates in that long ago. They were Dorothy Kirkpatrick, Jackie Russell, Donald Roller, Patsy Staire, Patsy Eastman, Donna Belle Jones, Mary Jane Coulteaux, Earl Hilton, Eileen Ganschow, Norma Towler, Robert Jacobson, Jackie Harkness, Donald Faber, Lois Newlon, Polly (?), and the preacher's girl, Mildred McGovern.

I didn't mind the long walk to school, skipping along with the neighbor kids, always trying to keep my dresses neat and my shoes free from the mud and the dusty roads.

But all too soon the beautiful Indian summer was stripped of its warm sunny days by the cold winds of winter. Our wardrobes were quickly changed from cotton dresses, anklets and sandals to the bulky wool coats, dresses, four buckle overshoes and the fleecy long-legged underwear that kept us from freezing our butts off. Maybe we kept warm from itching induced by our woolly garments.

During the cold months it took a lot of grit to face the elements each day. An extra supply of handkerchiefs was needed to stop the flow of runny noses. It was especially hard on me. Mama spent a lot of time rubbing my frozen feet back into circulation when I came from school.

Most of the school children in our neighborhood found the going easier when they joined forces, so it was a familiar sight to see about a dozen kids banded together walking toward the school house. Some of those brave souls who lived in our neck of the woods were the families of Pluff, Kelly, Norris, Lambert, Downs, Messerli, Obermuller, Durst, Forbes, Ganschow and Westendorf. I hope some of these people are still among us and will enjoy reading my story about the "good old days." (?)

Religion, Moving Again, and Changing Schools

"Now I lay me down to sleep, I pray to the Lord my soul to keep.

"If I should die before I awake, I pray to God my soul to take.

"God bless Mama, Dad, Donnie, Delly, Buddy, Evie, Bobbie, Neeney, Jimmy and me—and make me a good girl. In the name of the Father, Son and Holy Ghost. Amen."

I used to repeat this prayer every night before I went to sleep.

I often wondered why our family didn't attend church like some of the others in our neighborhood. Mrs. Forbes, the fat lady who talked a great deal, went to church about every night and twice on Sunday. Mama said she wasn't as religious as she made herself out to be, and her kids were as mean as the devil. A person doesn't have to go to church to be religious. "Just follow the Golden Rule."

There were some devout Catholics, some "holier than thou" Methodists, a few pious Lutherans and one or two "Holy Rollers" in our midst. We knew that we were baptized Catholic and most of our friends and relatives were of the same denomination. I didn't like it when some of the neighbor kids called us "cat lickers" or "fish eaters."

Mama always admired the Salvation Army people because of their helping hands for the needy. They nourished the body as well as the soul and asked for money from the business people of the town.

The first time I ever heard a preacher-man was when the local captain of the Army came to our house to offer salvation. I thought he was a policeman and hid behind my mother's skirts. On his second visit there were two women along and Mama was asked to join them in prayer. I wondered why Mama cried when she knelt down beside the kitchen chair. Did they make her feel ashamed because she didn't go to church? While she stood by the door, wiping her tears on her apron, she promised to be present at the next citadel service. It happened only one time, in gratitude for all the kindness that the Salvation Army extended to our family. Although she was reluctant to attend her own church, she was instilled with Catholic doctrine, taught to her by a strict, domineering German father.

Children from the practicing Catholic families were enrolled at Notre Dame Academy, a private institution located next to the Holy Family Church. When a child was in the second and third grades, it was time for his (or her) First Communion. It did take more money for books and tuition and a family was expected to donate their share for the support of the church and school. A few coins in the collection basket was about all that my dad could afford. It was up to the bankers, doctors, lawyers and prominent business people to keep the church and school out of debt.

"If those three kids are going to Notre Dame next year, we are going to have to move closer to town," Mama told Dad, after a few of their Catholic friends inquired about our religious upbringing. (We had to make our first communion if nothing else.)

And so the search began anew for some cheap housing. Mama hoped it wouldn't be close to another railroad track. The situation looked brighter this time. We were in luck. A neat but modest frame house was located on West 10th Street, not too far away from my birthplace on north Edmunds.

After living in the barn-like structure on West 4th, we found our new home was somewhat cramped. No wonder the brothers were scrapping more than usual. It was just too close for comfort. I guess you can say we were "thicker than six in a bed." None of us had the luxury of sleeping alone. It wasn't much fun to wake up and have a foot sticking in your face. "Ma, he's kicking me," was a familiar cry from the back bedroom. Many times a broomstick smacked across the quilts by an angry mother, stopped the complaints. That old broomstick was feared by all of us. "If you don't hear, you're going to feel," she would tell us.

We three youngest children were finished with our first year at the Whittier school and looked forward to the "lazy, crazy days of summer."

It was a better section of town and "chuck full" of kids from every walk of life. There were more little boys to play with than girls but boys were becoming more interesting, as I grew older. I took a "shine" to a little blond boy named Cecil Kapperman. I guess you can say he was my first boy friend.

The summer of '32 passed by quickly and it was time to

prepare ourselves for another big change in our young lives. We were definitely going to be enrolled at the Catholic school. The neighbor kids told us that our teachers looked like black and white ghosts and didn't have any hair on their heads. I had never seen a nun or priest before and I had second thoughts about going to the school at 200 North Kimball Street.

Mama and Dad tried to stretch their extra pennies that summer so that we would have better clothes to wear to the more conservative school. Dress pants and shirts for my brothers and neat dresses and shoes for us girls. No pajamas or slacks allowed. One girl did appear in a pajama outfit and was sent home from school. Mama also bought me a tam because women and girls had to have their heads covered while in church.

The playground was already crammed with children, fathers and mothers, when we arrived on that first day of school. I don't think anyone paid any attention to us amid all the excitement. Bobby left our company to join a game of "you're it."

After watching the little strangers, we entered the side door to try and find the second grade room. I was already wondering if I was going to like my school mates after listening to Mama's comments about their families being the high-brows of society. Would these more affluent children think that they were better than we were? Only time would tell.

My fears soon vanished after one of the little girls took me by the hand and showed the way to our classroom. "My name is Dolores," she told me, happily. "What is yours?" I couldn't believe that anyone else had the same name as I did.

After all the commotion of finding our desks, I sat down, hands folded and waited to see what my teacher looked like. I feared for the worst.

Suddenly a black and white clad woman hurried through the door and stood near a large desk at the front of the room. "Hello, boys and girls, how nice to see you again," she addressed the students, who smiled back with genuine affection.

While she welcomed the children, I was studying her attire—the black robe-like dress that rustled as she moved about the room, the black beads that hung from a belt around her waist. I thought she must be uncomfortable wearing the tight fitting cloche around her head.

Holy Family Catholic Church, built in 1886, addition in 1912

The snowy white bib across her bosom made her look like a plump penguin. Then I noticed her face. It was pale without a trace of make-up, but her clear blue eyes reflected her inner beauty. "You and I are going to be good friends by the time you leave the second grade," she said. We newcomers were asked to call her Sister Annunciata, who was one of the many instructors at Notre Dame Academy.

In a few days I felt that I was truly being accepted by the other children. After a period of giving me the once-over, a few whispers and some giggles, I was welcomed into their group. I soon found out that not all of the students were rich kids. There were quite a few from the lower income bracket. "Birds of a feather flock together," so naturally I was more at ease with my own kind. But there was one common bond. We were all Catholics and our minds were going to be indoctrinated on the same wave length about our creation. Learning our prayers began immediately under the tutoring of Sister Annunciata, Sister Winifred, Father O'Connor and last but not least, Father William Brady.

Because we kids weren't familiar with priests, I must say I was afraid and insecure of these religious teachers of the gospel. Were they contented people, I wondered, or sad like the pictures of the saints who looked down in sorrow from the walls of Aunt Carrie's house? I think I expected them to wear long white robes with a halo around their heads instead of the black suits with the tight fitting white collars.

The very first week we children became acquainted with Father Brady, I tried my best to look and act well mannered as we waited for him to speak to us.

Father Brady was a large, robust, broad shouldered man. Silver strands of close cropped hair encircled his head like a wreath. From behind a pair of gold spectacles, his eyes were penetrating but kindly. A serene face widened into a smile as he gazed upon the children of his parish.

We children absorbed every word he said when he finally spoke in a slow articulate voice with a slight Irish lilt. He laid the ground rules for our conduct, on and off the school grounds. Notre Dame students were expected to be as good as gold.

And so along with our ABC's, we were learning the doctrine of the Catholic Church, the mysteries of our beginnings, our relation to the Father, Son and Holy Ghost, and why we must obey the commandments of the church. There were

44

many prayers to memorize and to recite several times a day. Our life style was being changed and we were learning the meaning of discipline and the do's and don'ts for a good Catholic.

I was determined that I would faithfully obey every rule and have clean thoughts at all times.

"Don't eat meat on Friday." We were lucky to afford meat at all.

"Remember to keep one's head covered while in church and don't laugh or talk during the service." And don't swear like some of the rest of the family.

Attend mass every Sunday unless there is a very good excuse. On Monday mornings the sisters checked all students to ask if they attended church the day before.

Could an eight year old child keep from committing a sin while living in a household of eight rambunctious children? At an early age I was developing a very guilty conscience.

While I took my new found religion very seriously, not so with my younger sister, Neeney. She didn't like to toe the mark for anyone, even the nuns and priests. It was during one of our meditation periods after school that she demonstrated outrageous behavior.

We were in the church with some of the other students saying our prayers, when Neeney left our flock, climbed on over the communion railing, picked up the priest's silver bell, then proceeded to ring it vigorously while some of the children stared in shock. I thought for sure that she was going straight to hell and I warned her that I was going to tell Mama. On the way home that afternoon, she promised that she would change her ways if I kept the secret about the episode. I don't think she feared hell and damnation; it was the thought of Mama's hard callused hand warming her rear.

The fall term of school moved into the winter months and it was tough sledding for the family again. The house on West Tenth was just too dinky and the rent too high. Just when we kids adjusted to a new environment it was time to pull up stakes again. Our next move would take us to the south side of town, due south of the Milwaukee railroad tracks. But we would continue our schooling at Notre Dame. It would be unthinkable to change schools as we children were being prepared to make our first Holy Communion in the spring.

There were a few tears of sorrow when we departed from

the home on West Tenth Street and a few who thumbed their noses. Some of the families that we left behind were Dabbler, Dicky, Watson, Pooley, Madison, Dickinson, Kapperman, Andrews and Zimmer. I did feel sad about leaving one person, my boy friend, Cecil Kapperman. He and I were destined never to meet again.

THE HOUSE ON THE HILL

"You're just going to love this place," Dad promised Mama as we all piled out of our truck laden with our "early Salvation Army" furniture. The landlord, a Mr. Jones, offered Dad three months rent free if he would repair the roof and foundation, clean out the basement and paint the interior. It sounded like a real bargain to all of us.

There was a mad dash to inspect the two-story, drafty, nine-room house while Dad, Mama and the older brothers set up the two cast iron stoves (the range in the kitchen and the pot belly in the living room). Everyone "pitched in" to help carry the heavy iron beds, springs, the bulky mattresses and the stacks of quilts and blankets into the four bedrooms upstairs. I soon found out that we had more elbow room but not enough beds to go around. We three girls would still have to share a bed, two on one side and one on the other. There was one consolation, we would be as snug as bugs in a rug.

With all of the excitement going on about getting settled, we overlooked the fact that it was going to be a long, long cold walk to the school on the other side of the tracks. "I don't want you kids crossing the railroad tracks. It is too dangerous," Dad warned. But the danger was worth the chance after we tried to walk the many blocks around Sanborn street and just about froze to death. I was always in tears by the time I reached the school. The good Sister Winifred often rubbed the circulation back into my numbed feet. It was a hardship for all of us, getting to school and trying not to miss church on Sunday. I was beginning to envy the children who lived only a "stone's throw" from town.

The school children on the edge of town and the farm kids brought their lunch in paper bags and metal buckets. Mama placed the minced ham sandwiches, an orange or apple, along with a generous piece of cake, into a large tin syrup pail. A cup of hot cocoa could be purchased for one cent from the school kitchen. For a change of diet, we often traded food with our pals who chose to share our lunch.

Some of our select group were Pat Condron, Demitrius Kaponin and Mary and Earl Allington. We shared many good times and a few bad ones with this foursome.

While walking home from school together we often stopped to watch the construction of the Roxy Theatre, owned by Nelson Logan. Rummaging in the alley, we looked for the unwanted and broken items thrown into garbage boxes behind Newberry's Dime Store. One afternoon we discovered a discarded carton that was unopened, but after a series of kicks, balls of yarn spilled out and we then proceeded to fill our arms with the colorful thread. "Won't Mama love this stuff?" we thought as we headed for home with our treasure.

No sooner were we in the house when there was a loud knocking at the door. When Mama answered she was confronted by an angry, red-faced man who demanded the yarn that we had stolen. Sister Neeney and I were shaking in our boots as Mama tried to explain to the manager that an innocent mistake had been made; besides, she didn't know how to knit anyway. I wondered to myself, "Will this be considered a sin when I go to my first confession?" My religious training was off to a bad start.

The snow packed winter months were soon melting away into the sunny spring season. The lilac bushes were pushing out their tiny buds on their greening branches while robins slowly returned to their northern homes. It was becoming difficult to concentrate on my studies while the noises and smells of spring were calling to me. It was going to be so nice to walk barefoot again in the cool grass.

Meanwhile the nuns and priests were preparing us for the last few weeks of catechism. There were so many things to learn before our first confession. The nuns repeatedly told us to make a good confession and not to leave any sins in our souls. I honestly couldn't think of anything bad, except fighting with my brothers and sisters and that was hard not to do. So I decided that I would have to make up a few sins, like stealing cookies from Mama's cookie jar, sassing her (I knew better than to talk back to Mama). My sister Neeney and I practiced going to confession every night before we went to sleep. "Are you going to be scared?" I asked her. "What's there to be scared about?" she sleepily answered. I was already dreading going into that dark confessional in a few days.

"Bless me, Father, for I have sinned," I barely whispered when I heard the voice of Father Brady telling me to begin.

My knees were shaking and my heart was pounding as I knelt in the tomb of darkness. I was indeed sorry for being such a terrible child and I hoped that the good Lord would wash my sins away. I felt like a ton had been lifted from my shoulders when the priest told me that I could leave. I was so weak I could hardly stand. I hurriedly walked past the other waiting children and went back to our school room where I sank behind my desk, emotionally drained. It was a very depressing experience for a little eight year old girl. Why was it so miserable to be good?

The sisters assured us that the first milestone had been passed and the next step would be a glorious event, when we would be blessed with our first Holy Communion. A gift of rosary beads, medals, a prayer book and other Catholic items were presented to each child. My heart was filled with joy as I gazed upon the beautiful white prayer book, etched in gold. On the cover was a tinted picture of five angels gathered around a gold chalice. (That small prayer book is now worn and yellowed with age and the angels on the cover are fading like my memories of that yesterday.)

Mama was also being pushed for time as she tried desperately to finish our communion dresses before that eventful day. The yards of white organdy were difficult to style into the pleats, tucks, puffs, and ruffles of our miniature wedding dresses. There were more than a few choice words directed at her old sewing machine when the bobbin was clogged and cutting the thread. It was the first time Mama was ever challenged to work with the fancy material like organdy and lace and I knew that it was certainly going to be the last time. "Damn it, anyhow," this repeated phrase sounded sacrilegious while she was stitching on our holy garments.

Sister Neeney and I stayed away from her territory near the bay window, but tried on our dresses to insure the right length. I felt sorry for Mama as I looked into her anxious eyes as the beads of sweat trickled down her face and neck, staining the collar of her dress.

"I've done the best I can," she finally sighed as she held up the completed gowns for our inspection. We all agreed that she had created masterpieces.

I rushed into the bedroom and quickly slipped the dress over my head. A chair was pushed in front of the mirror so I could see what I looked like. While I stood caressing the tiny ruffles and puffed sleeves, Mama came into the room

Our First Communion, May 1933

and tied the wide sash into a large perky bow. "You look just like a little angel," she sighed, trying not to show her emotions, but I could see the tears she tried to hide as she turned and went back to her daily routine. Mama wasn't in the church when we made our first communion and I don't know why she chose to remain at home.

"Remember now, don't you kids eat or drink anything until after communion tomorrow," we were told as we went to bed early. For some reason I felt awfully hungry and my throat was already as dry as cotton. A sip of water would help.

The first thing that I noticed when I awoke was the sound of rain drops spitting against the window panes. Sunday morning, May 7, 1933, dawned on a gray, misty world. "Oh no," I moaned, "we'll all get wet." I shook my little sister awake and reminded her not to drink any water. I could hear Mama and Dad in the kitchen. Brother Bobby appeared in the doorway and we couldn't believe our eyes. It was the first time we had ever seen him dressed up. His outfit was a black suit, white shirt, a stiff bow tie and black shoes. His dark hair was neatly combed and his handsome face was wreathed in a big grin. "How do I look?" he asked as he turned about to show off his finery. "You look very nice," I answered as we scrambled past him. "You better sit down on a chair so you won't get mussed up. Our taxi is coming in about an hour."

Dad was about half dressed with his shirt tail hanging loose. Mama was nervously looking for his one and only tie. He didn't have a good Sunday-go-to-meeting suit; only mismatched coats and trousers. Still I thought he looked as handsome as any of the bankers, doctors or other professional men who walked into the church with an air of superiority.

It didn't take long to slip into my white panties, under skirt and long stockings. Mama made some elastic garters to hold them in place. I could see myself in the shiny black patent leather shoes which were purchased at the Burg shoe store by a friend of the family.

Neeney wasn't as thrilled about getting dressed in the communion gowns and she fussed when Mama combed her hair for the third time. Mama worried that our white stockings would be mud splattered by the time we arrived at the church and maybe the veils would get wet.

At last we were all ready to experience one of the most memorable days of our lives (except Mama). She decided at the last minute that she wasn't going. I sadly waved to her as she stood by the open screen door as our taxi drove out of the muddy yard. I so wanted her to be there to share the joyous day.

When we arrived at the school, I hurried along with my sister and brother to receive our last minute instructions before going to the huge stone church. Such a commotion. There were mothers, fathers, relatives and priests blocking the hallways and students running to the bathrooms for one last chance. There was no turning back once we began that long ceremony. Our wispy veils were securely attached to our heads, tiny satin ribbons falling to the shoulders, the prayer books and rosaries were taken from the boxes and placed between our clasped hands. A few particular mothers (especially concerned with details) stayed to the last, coaxing an unruly cowlick into place, rebuttoning a jacket or smoothing out a wrinkled stocking. I'm sure the sisters were crossing their fingers and breathing a prayer of relief when we proceeded to march in formation toward the church. After taking a few steps I felt my garters slipping down my legs and resting above my knees. With my hands clasped around my prayer book, there was nothing I could do. My stockings would just have to bag.

Leading the young communicants were two older girls dressed in white flowing gowns, trimmed with silver and gold bands of ribbon, matching the halo-like garlands in their hair. They represented angels as they slowly ascended the concrete steps that led into the vestibule, the paper wings attached to their shoulders rose and fell in graceful movements.

I tried to compose myself but was overcome with a feeling of rapture as I walked down the aisle of the candle-lit Cathedral. I could hear the angelic voice of Sister Winifred mingled with the soft, vibrating music of the pipe organ, singing one of the beautiful hymns of the church. Every pew was decorated with white satin bows where the relatives were seated in a reserved section. I peeked at Dad as I passed by. I knew that his heart was overflowing with pride and love for his three children who were being given one of the greatest sacraments of the church.

When Sister Annunciata gave a signal each child knelt to the floor, then took their place in the long pew. Everything progressed smoothly as the solemn procession finally ended. I relaxed momentarily to observe the colors of the stained glass windows, showered in an iridescent beauty from the sunshine that had broken through the clouds. Garlands of spring flowers banked the altar and at the feet of the blessed Virgin Mary, flames flickered from the candle holders, casting shadows across the faces of the other marble statues that we learned to idolize.

The atmosphere seemed strange and like a dream when I felt my sister poke me and say, "It's your turn to go up there."

I could feel my heart throbbing in my throat and the butterflies in my stomach as I passed through a flower covered archway and knelt at the altar railing. I looked up and took note of the crucified Christ, hanging on a golden cross. I had been taught to know and to love Him by the dedicated sisters and priests. My childish sins had vanished. I am sure I touched a piece of heaven as I received my first Holy Communion.

There were many smiles of relief and tears of happiness as we passed the congregation on the way out of the church. By this time I was a dazed and weak-kneed little girl who was also hungry and thirsty for a cool glass of water.

The sisters provided a light breakfast in the school gym before we had our class picture taken by a local photographer, Mr. Hersey. I thought I was a privileged character because I was placed directly behind Father Brady.

Most of the children in this picture are now aging grandparents who have watched their own families grow up and find their place in the world. A few have passed away, some have gained recognition for their achievements while others are just pebbles on a beach. I often wonder if they, too, remember that special day almost forty-five years ago. Wherever they may be, here are the names of my long ago classmates:

Dorothy Tobin, John Burg, Paul Dressen, Ralph Purdy, Kathleen Morgan, Jack Dickinson, Demetrius Kaponin, Eleanor Murphy, Luella Thill, Ardis Gouthier, Pat Condron, Harold Bollock, Jimmy Rounds, Robert Zimmer, Jack Cashel, Donald Pitts, Leroy Rowe, Jack Mullin, Bill Till, Mary Allington, Sheila Casey, Eileen Neises, Frances Schirmer, Phyllis Stenson, Lavonne Mackey, Florence Wolf, Dolores Lucas, Maureen Tobin, Frances Burg, Lorraine Judge, Sam Steiber, Earl Allington and Robert and Norma Barnes, my brother and sister.

The House on the Hill

Of all the homes that I have lived in I'm sure my favorite house was the spacious brown and white dwelling located at 522 South Main at the top of a wind swept hill. It stood like a fortress defying the elements of the changeable South Dakota weather, and remains today, a reminder of my past.

The nine-room house plus two porches (the front porch was surrounded by a latticed railing), a full basement and an extensive yard that nestled among a grove of Russian Olive trees. The interior was designed with hard wood floors

The house on the hill, 522 South Main

and woodwork. The beautiful spindled staircase climbed to the second floor where there were four bedrooms. We three girls shared a bedroom where the small closet was large enough for our limited wardrobes. One nail was sufficient to hold mine.

Mama and Dad shared a bedroom downstairs, with baby brother Jimmy. Whenever sister Neeney or I were sick we always were allowed to sleep with Mama so she could keep an eye on us.

Our living room furniture consisted of a sewing machine which sat in front of the large bay window, a library table, a few old rocking chairs and a day-bed which also served as a couch when company came. A Mrs. Burns, whom Dad often painted for, gave us furniture and I'll never forget the day when Dad brought home a pump organ that she no longer wanted.

The kitchen with a shelved pantry served as our eating quarters. Our company always dined in the living room where they could visit without a bunch of noisy kids annoying them. The kitchen table was another, but sturdy, castoff. A colorful oil cloth cover made it look presentable. On each side were two long pine benches where we kids sat, squeezed together like sardines in a can.

On the west side of the kitchen, next to the cellar door stood the enormous black iron and chrome cook stove, a reservoir to hold water hanging on its side. When fired up with wood and coal, it cooked all of our meals and warmed the house at the same time. A steaming tea kettle with hot water was a permanent fixture on the back of every range.

Mama's old faithful washing machine tried to hide in a corner near the stove. It was always covered with an old blanket to keep it from wear and tear. The kitchen also served as the laundry room. Our drinking water was stored in a gigantic cistern, adjacent to the back porch. It was filled a few times a year from a horse-drawn city water wagon driven by a Mr. Bill Dickinson. On wash day the water was hauled up from the cistern with a bucket and long rope, poured into the copper boiler and tub and placed on the cook stove to heat. I used to worry that Mama would get burned when she emptied the scalding water into the washer. When she yelled, "Gang way," everybody scampered out of the kitchen, including the dog.

To make matters worse, the black, sooty smoke that mushroomed from the stacks of the roundhouse often ruined a day's wash when the wind changed its course. "Which way is the wind blowing?" was an often asked question, or, "That damned roundhouse is going to be the death of me yet."

The family was getting weary of moving and so we learned to live within the gray shadow of the great Chicago Milwaukee railroad. We changed our outdoor activities when the billowing, black clouds of smoke spread across our property.

And then there were times when the roundhouse's smoke seemed to be in remission and only a few wisps of white smoke played with the wayward winds around the bottom lands. The rail yards were cleared and the main street of town was in perfect view. From our look-out on the hill, we could almost see forever.

It wasn't always easy to scrape up eight dollars for the rent money. Many times we kids chipped in to insure another month's stay. Dad's $48.00 a month (W.P.A. pay check) was only a drop in the bucket to cover the rent, fuel, and grocery bills. "Oh, we ain't got a barrel of money," was a favorite song of those times that we kids often sang to poke fun at our own predicament, or "Brother, can you spare a dime?"

"If things don't get better, I think we better hit for the coast." They say there is a lot of work out there in the painting business," I overheard Dad tell Mama. "How are we going without a red cent to our name?" Mama argued. "Just wish in one hand and spit in the other and see which hand holds the most." "Well, I'm not giving up yet." "There's more than one way to skin a cat," Mama said. "I've been thinking about renting out those two extra rooms upstairs. Another five dollars a month would come in pretty handy."

"Where will they go to a toilet?" I wondered. There were too many of us now trying to share the outdoor facilities.

The outdoor toilet or "biffy" was a most important building in any neighborhood. The small out-buildings were built with a two or three hole bench-like stool. A decor of calendars, pictures, magazines, catalogs and newspapers added a touch of home. Poor folks used printed pages for toilet paper. Mama tried to keep our privy as sanitary as possible with a lot of antiseptic and fly spray. The out-house was also an inviting target for Hallowe'en pranksters who pushed them over. Sometimes it was timed right when they were in need of a new excavation.

The "rooms for rent" sign was tacked to the corner post of the porch and we all sat back and waited for a nibble. Before you could say Jack Robinson, there was a knock at the front door and Mama opened it to find two seedy looking men standing before her. A noticeable aroma of alcohol filled the air. "The rooms have been taken," she quickly told them before they had a chance to open their mouths. I felt a little sorry for them as they meekly stepped off the porch and walked toward town. "I don't want any boozers or good-for-nothings under my roof. I'm not that hard up yet. Besides, those two couldn't afford a settin' hen, let alone money to pay rent," Mama said.

She was getting nowhere fast with her rooming business. A few fly-by-night tenants came and went, some owing her money. They were the rolling stones who gathered no moss, ever searching for a place of their own. There were more people leaving South Dakota than those who came in looking for any kind of job to put bread on the table. The drought was becoming a double threat to everyone. We were soon going to experience the devastating dust storms of the thirties.

It was becoming a nuisance to rent and then kick out the depression people. Mama was becoming a "hard hearted Hannah" and about ready to throw in the towel when she thought her luck had changed the evening a large, red delapidated truck pulled into our yard. Printed on the side in hand painted letters were the words, "Wild West Show." A handsome, dark-haired man, dressed in western attire, stepped from the cab and introduced himself as a Mr. F. D. Rockefeller. "Could he be related to the well known millionaire, John D. Rockefeller?" we all wondered at the same time.

Someone informed him that there were rooms for rent at the big house on the hill.

"We're only looking for a place to stay for a few months," he drawled, while signaling for a woman and small boy to get out of the truck. I thought his wife was real pretty and the dark eyed, freckled faced boy was dressed in cowboy clothes just like his dad. He held a small ukelele in his hands and plunked across the strings as he swaggered towards us. "My name is John D. Rockefeller," he said, rather proudly, "but everyone calls me Johnny." I must say we were all impressed with this show business family and I hoped that Mama would allow them to stay, more so when we heard the whinny of some horses in the enclosed truck box. We kids idolized cowboys and horses, and watched western movies playing at the local theatres.

The transaction was finally agreed upon after a two dollar bill was exchanged with a promise that the rest would be paid within a few days. After all, who wouldn't trust a Rockefeller?

We kids gladly helped our new tennants carry their boxes and bags up the stairs into their two-room apartment. Their meals would have to be cooked on a two-burner, kerosene stove. A makeshift sink consisted of a small table with a large galvanized pail to hold their water. I sensed their disappointment when Mama told them the bathroom facilities were outdoors. "Well, we will make out the best we can," Mr. Rockefeller assured his family as he carefully hung their gaily colored western clothes in the closet. Three pairs of leather, high-heeled boots with pointed toes were placed on a top shelf. "What I wouldn't give for a pair of cowgirl boots like that," I whispered to my little sister.

It was indeed an added thrill to watch the brown and white shetland ponies being unloaded and allowed to graze on the green weeds in the back yard before being tied up for the night. We were promised a ride on "Joker" the first thing in the morning. I was too excited to sleep that night.

The next morning Neeney and I were waiting for our rides at the crack of dawn. It seemed like an eternity before Mr. Rockefeller had the small saddle cinched and buckled into place and the leather reins thrown over the horn. I wondered about the steel bit clenched between the teeth. It looked cruel and painful. "O.K., who's first?" he smiled as he held out his arms. "Me," said Neeney. I was glad that she would have the first ride. She always had more nerve anyway. Neeney didn't need any assistance as she climbed into the saddle and "giddy-upped" the horse into motion. "There's nothing to it," she shouted while prancing around the yard.

Soon it was my turn and I must say I had second thoughts when the pony snorted while I was getting into the saddle. His furry body felt so warm and I could feel his muscles ripple. When he slowly began to move, with the leather saddle making creaking noises. Neeney and Mr. Rockefeller walked along on each side as I enjoyed my first real live pony ride. I imagined myself a cowgirl in the movies riding into the sunset, with my idol, Gene Autry.

All of the neighbor kids soon found out about our wild-west tenants and were constantly begging for rides on the two ponies. Little Johnny took advantage of a good thing and charged them five cents for one ride around the block. His folks needed every spare dime because rodeo people didn't make much money in those days. Rodeos were small potatoes compared with the rhinestoned extravaganzas of today. Performing in the hick towns across South Dakota netted only a few dollars for food and a few nights lodging in some small hotel. Yet we envied the life style of these "gypsies" who were here today and gone tomorrow.

Getting into show business was a dream of every boy and girl and especially for Little Johnny but we kids thought that he would never make it big after listening to him sing off-key, "Strawberry Roan." He bragged that he won first prize in an amateur contest at WNAX Radio Station in Yankton, S. D. "That kid can't sing worth sour apples," we told each other with disgust.

Yet Johnny was getting paid for his non-professional talents when he accompanied his parents to a few of the local saloons about town. The bar patrons enjoyed the pint-sized entertainer as he sang and yodeled all of the hillbilly tunes of the depression era. When we kids heard about all the money that was showered upon him, we turned a little green with envy. Neeney and I then practiced a little more often with our own style of harmonizing.

By mid summer our relationship with the Rockefellers was becoming somewhat strained. Mama was getting tired of the ponies and the manure they were spreading all over the yard. One day she found ponies tangled in her clothes lines, her laundry trampled into the dirt. And Mrs. Rockefeller was getting on her nerves with the racket she made with her three-inch, high-heeled shoes walking across the floor above our heads.

Little Johnny was becoming a smart aleck. He could repeat all of the off-color jokes that he heard in the saloons. "If it wasn't for that kid they'd starve to death," Mama fumed when their rent money wasn't being paid. "You tell that horsey set that if that rent isn't in my hand by next week, out they go," she firmly said to Dad. My dad was always too mild mannered and too chicken-hearted to hurt anyone's feelings, let alone kick someone out in the street. "Hold your horses, Ma," he pleaded. "Mr. Rockefeller promised to pay in full after the next horse show." "We'll see about that," said Mama. "I don't believe it."

It was hard for our mother to control her temper and not curse but when her face turned red, we knew it was time to vamoose. All that week she tried to remain calm, while keeping a watchful eye on the upstairs tenants. "If you give some people an inch they will take a mile," she complained.

It was on a Saturday night after we had all gone to bed with the chickens, when I was awakened by clumping feet on the stairs. It sounded like a herd of cattle. The next thing we heard was music being played in a fast "toe tapping" beat. "They must have brought some hillbilly hicks from the saloon," Mama said, bounding out of bed. After a few thumps on the ceiling with her broomstick, the music stopped. Just when we all dozed off again, the pickin' and singin' commenced. There was a good old hoe-down in progress at three o'clock in the morning, and we kids were now keeping time with "Hand Me Down My Walkin' Cane."

Although Dad tried to convince Mama that they were just having a little fun, she flew up the stairs, broomstick in hand and in no uncertain terms told the entertainers to keep quiet. She warned the Rockefellers to be out of her house by high noon the next day. And if they didn't pay the back rent she would take it out of their hide!

It was with mixed emotions I felt when we kids watched the rodeo people pack their few belongings into their old truck without a word. Mr. Rockefeller coaxed the ponies into their stalls and tied them securely while his wife hung cowboy suits with the fringed jackets in the cab. All the while Mama was watching the departure from behind the screen door. I'm sure Dad was trying not to be visible during these embarrassing moments. Just before Mr. Rockefeller started the engine, he stuck his head out of the window, smiled and said, "So long, kids, it's been good to know you. You all take it easy now, hear?" Little Johnny wasn't as cordial, as they were driving out of the yard he stuck out his tongue, then raised his thumb to his nose. That was the last time we ever saw the little cowboy.

A few years ago I found out that Johnny D. Rockefeller was killed in a plane crash while on a business trip for a country western music company. If he had lived I'm quite sure he would have been one of our top recording stars. He may have sung off key when only a five year old child but I truly believe he was the original rhinestone cowboy.

Swing Your Partner

The hard times of the 1930's were sometimes depressing but there were many outlets for people to enjoy themselves and to forget the cares of the day. One of the best ways to let off steam, relax and let yourself go, was to dance.

It didn't make any difference if a person had two left feet, was too skinny or too fat, too short or too tall, too young or too old, everyone loved to dance.

We kids learned the latest dance steps from the movies, the tap dancing of America's sweetheart, Shirley Temple, and the sophisticated routines of Fred Astaire and Ginger Rogers. The floor boards of our house were a make-shift stage as we practiced the latest steps to the beat of radio music. The older brothers and sisters never missed a Saturday night dance at one of the local ball rooms (Dreamland), or at barn dances which were gaining in popularity. One of the more popular dance bands was directed by a young man named Lawrence Welk who hailed from North Dakota. Passing by the Dreamland Ballroom, I often took note of the large posters with the bubbling champagne glass advertising an upcoming dance date. I was still a little bit young to enjoy the thrill of dancing on the smooth glass-like floor. I would have to be content

Dreamland Ballroom in the 400 block of North Main

to dance the fox trot with my brother, Bobby, or younger sister, Neeney, at home.

I couldn't believe my ears the day I overheard Mama and Dad discussing the possibility of having a house dance. It was another brainstorm of Mama's to make some extra money. There would be an admission fee at the door of twenty-five cents. In order to undertake a project like a public dance, there would have to be some good danceable music. "I know just the two guys I can get. Frank Nickles and Port Kinyon," Dad assured Mama. "Frank plays the fiddle and Port can really pick that banjo, and I know they can use the money."

"Well, I don't know, a banjo and a fiddle don't seem like much of an orchestra," Mama argued. "Who do you expect me to hire, Lawrence Welk?" Dad asked with a shake of his head. "You just get the two vacant rooms ready and I'll spread the news around town about the dance next Friday night. I'll bet we have a crowd."

Friday morning dawned, filled with great expectations about our "grand opening" social event of the season which was a few hours away. Mama had already made a list of some of the people she expected to come, mostly aunts, uncles, cousins and a few close neighbors. The strict Methodists who lived down the block wouldn't be caught dead at any dance, let alone ours. Mama had to make a rough guess as to the number of people who would come to a dance, a midnight lunch of sandwiches, and cake and coffee which would conclude the evening festivities.

The seating arrangements consisted of every borrowed chair or bench that we kids could find in the neighborhood. "The old maids and wall flowers will be the only ones sitting down," laughed our brothers as they hoisted each chair into place. "And you little kids will have to go to bed early because there will be only adults allowed." Dad had already promised me that I could stay up past my bedtime. He knew how I loved to dance and listen to him "call" for the square dancing. I could also help Mama and Aunt Carrie prepare the delicious lunch of minced ham and cheese sandwiches, marble cake and various kinds of home canned pickles. Carrie could transform a chunk of fat bologna into a gourmet's delight.

The first arrivals began to saunter into the yard as the twilight was turning into dark shadows. The street light on the corner was not ready yet to shine on us. "It's only a couple of bashful bachelors and that old lady McConkey who are just coming to nose," sniffed Mama while watching Dad sprinkling the corn meal on the floor to make it slippery.

"It's too early yet," Dad patiently replied, "the railroad men will be here about nine. It will take awhile for them to clean up and get dressed." Our anxiety was lessened to a degree when the two-man band arrived looking "bright eyed and bushy tailed." After introducing themselves to all they proceded to unpack their instruments from shabby looking cases. The "tuning up" was already music to my ears as I watched the long bow scraping across the violin strings while the banjo was plinked and plunked into the right key.

"What do you wanna hear, little girl?" the banjo player asked me. "Can you play 'Turkey in the Straw'," was my shy request. "O.K., Frank, let her rip," he yelled to his partner and the best toe-tapping music I ever heard filled the house to the rafters. The guests began to arrive, assured of having a high old time.

We soon lost count of all the customers jamming the make-shift dance hall, the kitchen, and the standing room only on the front porch. Brother Bobby, Neeney and I found a good place to observe the "hard times" generation from our perch at the top of the stairs. We snickered and made remarks about their appearance: the old maid with the long wrinkled neck, dancing with a short fat man whose bald head was shiny; the shy bachelor, Mr. Murray, looking uncomfortable in a too tight suit, trying to lead a gum-chewing grass widow whose painted cheeks matched her flaming red hair. Aunt Carrie trying to keep her dignity with her foot-stomping show-off husband, Uncle Pete. The railroad men looking distinguished in blue serge suits, standing on the sidelines trying to flirt with the prettiest ladies on the floor. Most of them were already "hitched" and were just amusing themselves on a layover in Mitchell.

"I wish Mama would dance with Dad just once. It would really make him happy," Bobby sighed as our attention was diverted to them. Dad tried to coax her onto the floor. Despite the excuse about being too plump and having sore feet, Dad never stopped asking her. Her refusal ruined many good times she could have shared with her fun-loving husband.

His look of disappointment showed in his handsome face as he walked away. Spying us kids on the stairway he motioned for me to come down and then waited at the edge of the dance floor. Asking the musicians to play something a little bit "mellow," my dad told the crowd, "Now I'm going to dance with my best girl." While everyone smiled their approval, I shyly followed Dad as he patiently led me through a waltz, "Over the Waves." I'm sorry I stepped on your toes," I apologized. "Just so you don't step on my heart, darlin'," he replied.

And so the band played on to the strains of "One Legged Joe," "Old Dan Tucker," "Coming Round the Mountain," "Strawberry Blonde," and "Missouri Waltz," sandwiched between the fast swinging square dances when I listened to the voice of my dad shouting out the "do si dos." By midnight the sweat-soaked dancers took time out for intermission to enjoy the free lunch or to take a nip of their own bottled refreshments that were stashed in a hip pocket or in the inside pocket of a suit coat. Although we kids were yawning and getting sleepy, the prospect of good food kept us awake and I still wanted to hear a few more songs. But Mama thought the hour was growing late and asked the musicians to play their last number.

It was indeed a successful house dance, a good time was had by all with a promise by Dad that there would be more of the same every Friday night. Neeney and I, with our half-eaten sandwiches in our hands, climbed up the flight of stairs and were ready to "hit the hay." The melodic strains of "Home Sweet Home" were still ringing in our ears.

"Good night, everybody, see you next week," Dad and Mama shouted to their departing guests. The doors were then locked, the lights were turned off and a quiet settled over the big house on the hill.

The Friday night dances were short-lived because of gate crashers who only wanted to stir up trouble among the dancing crowd. Although a few were bounced by my dad and Uncle Pete, they continued to harass the place by breaking a few car windows and other acts of vandalism. Finally Dad announced to his disappointed friends that the Friday night dances were abandoned, but he knew about a dance hall that could be obtained for a few dollars. The spacious hall belonged to the Knights of Columbus and was on Main Street above Feinstein's Clothing store.

And so began our Friday night fling at the K. C. Hall where the blue collared W.P.A. employes gathered to kick up their heels.

Dad was elected to a committee whose duties were to help maintain the hall, hire the entertainment and to collect admission at the door. He was also appointed to help "call" for the square dancing. It was a very important responsibility.

Getting ready always caused a flurry of mixed emotions, especially for Mama and Dad. Dad would rather dance than eat and loved to socialize with people whereas Mama was an introvert and preferred to stay at home. I'm sure she was often envious of his popularity. "You know you're welcome to come along," he told her for the fifth time as he carefully combed his graying hair and splashed on a few drops of after-shave lotion. "Well, if I were there, you wouldn't have a chance to dance with all the gay divorcees," she jealously commented. She realized her husband was a handsome man and was admired by some of the home wreckers about town.

But with a bunch of kids trailing along behind there wouldn't be much chance for a back street meeting.

Mama never showed her true feelings even while knotting his tie or brushing the lint from his coat. Her stubborn attitude might have sent him into the arms of another woman. I sensed that the love which they once shared was slowly slipping away. Only the more affluent people could afford divorces during those hard times. "We'll be home right after the dance," I promised Mama as I quickly shut the door and ran to catch up with my dad. Glancing back towards the house I could see her standing by her bedroom window, watching us as we headed for town to enjoy the dance. I often wondered if she was crying and was sorry she remained at home.

I could already hear the sounds of music as I climbed the long flight of stairs behind my dad and groups of people, young and old, who came to this place to have fun. Some would maybe meet that certain someone. Everyone was getting his hand stamped after paying the twenty-five cents admission charge. We were admitted free because Dad was the caller. (Sister Neeney didn't care much for this type of socializing so she stayed home.) So while Dad greeted his friends, I shyly peeked into the large hall to see what was going on.

Sitting and standing on a raised platform was a band tuning up their instruments. A guitar, drums, piano and a saxophone made up the combo. Their music sounded a lot different from the two-man band that played at our house dances. The jovial young man holding the saxophone was "Swede" Pierson whose popular band was well known in this area. The Kurtenbach brothers, Charlie, Ted and Pete, were the other members who played a "mean" banjo, guitar and piano.

64

Swede Pierson and his Band

All around the hall there were folding chairs to sit on and most of them were already occupied by the young and the restless, eagerly awaiting the music. Little boys slid back and forth on the corn meal that was scattered on the floor to keep it smooth. Most of the people were complete strangers to me and I was glad to see my sister, Evie, arriving with her girl friend, Margaret. (Margaret had a nice figure but her face would stop a clock.)

"Do you want to come to the ladies' room with us?" she asked, so I followed them into a small room crowded with women and girls. It sounded like a chicken coop with all the giggling and small talk. The aroma of cheap perfume offended my nostrils and one young girl was even smoking a cigarette. (That was considered unlady-like during the 1930's.) "Gee, I sure like your dress. Where'd ja get it, Monkey Wards?" "Are my seams straight?" "If I get a run I'll just die." "Can I borrow your compact?" "Do you like this new lipstick, it's called Taboo. Got it at the dime store." "My girdle is killing me." "I hope my finger wave stays in place." "Say, did you notice that handsome guy standing by the door when we came in, the one with the cute little mustache? I sure hope he asks me to dance." "I sure hope there are some guys here tonight who know how to dance. My toes still hurt from the last barn yard stomp I went to." "Oh well, as long as they can neck, who cares about their dancing." "We may spend the whole evening just being wall flowers." "Hurry up in there, I gotta go." "Hey, the music started, let's get out of here, time's a-wasting."

The teenaged girls of the depression generation left the ladies' room and I had the place all to myself. A faded mirror looked back at me from the wall. I was still just a little girl, too old for dolls and too young for boys. I was an in-between. But that night I felt grown up. I fluffed my curly hair-do that Mama fixed with the curling iron. My blue eyes looked bluer to match my polished cotton dress and the perky bow tucked into my light brown hair. My legs did look too thin encased in the white anklets. It would be nice to wear silk stockings and high-heeled shoes, I thought. Imitating the older girls, I wet my lips, flicked my tongue over my white teeth and walked out into the hall. Just maybe my Prince Charming will be out there waiting to waltz me around till the clock strikes twelve.

It didn't happen. I spent most of the evening sitting next to an old maid wall flower whose chances of attracting a man were pretty slim. There were other boys and girls my age having a great time gliding around the floor in perfect rhythm. Sister Evelyn was the belle of the ball even though one of her partners was scrawny and homely. My dad was too busy trying to please all the ladies who surrounded him after each dance. I didn't like the bleached blonde with the tight-fitting satin skirt who clung to his arm. "If Mama saw that, someone would sure get her hair pulled." I thought again about Mama sitting at home alone while my dad was having the time of his life.

I was beginning to feel melancholy but the foot stomping music of Swede Pierson revived me, even though no one asked me to dance. I can still recall those great songs of "Five Foot Two," "Marie," "Dinah," "Dark Town Strutters Ball," "Whispering," "Sweet Sue," "Sweet Georgia Brown," and the goodnight song, "Home Sweet Home."

Just before midnight as the crowd was beginning to disperse, I felt a light tap on my shoulder and when I looked up I saw my dad smiling at me. "Wanna dance, Kitty Cat?" He didn't forget me and my heart was happy and carefree again as we danced the final dance of the evening. The melody was "The Waltz You Saved For Me."

The K. C. Hall has long ago been converted into apartments where the traffic of the Main Street passed by. If by chance you stroll through the darkened alley some evening, perhaps you can hear the strains of music coming from the old dance hall. Can you believe with me that the ghosts of the depression folks are having a high old time?

Free Band Concerts

"COME ONE, COME ALL, BAND CONCERT COURTHOUSE LAWN FRIDAY NIGHT" was printed on the leaflet that was left on our doorstep by a small boy who was passing out the programs throughout the neighborhood.

"Mama, can I go to the band concert, I've never been to one before?" I asked while she was retrieving a batch of bread from the oven.

"It doesn't make any difference to me if you can get somebody to take you. I can't go over there and sit on that hard ground. Why, I'd never be able to get up again." Because of her weight it was always difficult for Mama to stand or sit long. "It's hell to be fat," she often remarked.

"I'll bet Evie will take me. I'll ask her," I said to my mother. "She has been to band concerts with her girl friends and I won't be any bother if I tag along."

"You get dolled up real nice and I'll take you along," my sister told me when I asked her.

I rummaged through the dresser drawer to find a clean pair of panties and white anklets. I was in luck; Mama washed that day. My one and only good dress with the purple flowers, trimmed with bias tape, would have to be ironed. "How do I look?" I asked Evie while she inspected me. "I wish you could do something with your hair; it always looks so 'scrippy'." I smoothed down my bangs till they almost reached my eyes. "Is that better?" I searched for her approval. "I think you'd better wear your 'tam.' It will hide that 'fly away' look."

At last we were on our way, with me bringing up the rear behind my big sister and her chums. I tried to keep my sandals from getting full of pebbles as we walked through the streets. It was a long hike from our place to the old courthouse.

When we neared our destination I could see a steady stream of townspeople and a few stray dogs converging around the square and settling down on the lush green lawn. Many carried small pillows and paper fans. The evening air was still muggy from the heat of the day and the mosquitoes were preparing to bite. (There were few repellants or anti-mosquito lotions then.)

After much searching and stepping through and over the crowds we found a good spot next to an old gnarled oak tree. I set myself carefully down and tried to cover my legs with

Bandstand on Courthouse lawn (first Courthouse constructed in 1883)

my dress, the mosquitoes were already buzzing. "Wanna piece of gum?" Evie inquired, holding out a package. I accepted her offer and chewed slowly while Evie and her friends made cracking noises with their gum.

"Here comes the Mitchell band," was finally heard as the black uniformed musicians climbed the steps that led up to the bandstand. I thought they looked just like toy soldiers with their brass buttons that marched down their jackets to meet the gold stripes on their trousers. The visored caps, trimmed with gold braid, all looked the same size but the men were short or tall, fat or skinny.

In quick precision they all sat down on wooden chairs in a semi-circle. On their laps reposed the polished silver and brass instruments such as cornets, trumpets, French horns and trombones.

In the rear a chubby-cheeked man stood in readiness sandwiched between a bass drum and cymbals. Coiled around another's neck was an enormous horn.

Evie giggled and said it was a "tuba played by a tubby." The musician was so rolypoly that the snug fitting uniform made him resemble a stuffed sausage.

Our attention was then focused on a short broad-shouldered man who approached the podium. Unlike the other

Mitchell Municipal Band — Joe Tschetter, Director

musicians he was attired in a cream colored uniform that made him look like a general. "Who is that man?" I whispered to Evie, noting the hushed silence of the assembled audience.

"That's Joe Tschetter, the leader of the band." "When he waves that stick the concert will start."

All eyes were glued on the dignified figure as he raised his baton, tapped it on the podium—and then it happened. Everyone began to rise from the ground and stand at attention as the music blared into a crashing crescendo.

My sister pulled me to my feet and told me to place my hand over my heart. "What for?" I questioned, never having attended a concert before.

"Because they're playing the Star Spangled Banner and we should show our respect for the United States of America."

While I held my hand over my heart—it was jumping with excitement—I sensed a feeling of pride that I never felt before. I peeked around at the people who were paying their respects and their eyes were directed towards the sky.

I looked up and discovered the American flag was fluttering into red, white and blue folds, reflecting the setting sun. Although I was only nine years old, I was proud to be an American and I understood that it was a privilege to be living in the land of the free and the home of the brave.

After many more soul-stirring marches that kept everyone moving their hands and feet in rhythm, the director made an announcement. "We are now proud to present Miss Phyllis Higgins and her school of dance." He bowed towards a very pretty lady who was dressed in the latest fashion. Standing near the rear of the bandstand were some little girls and a few boys, whose costumes were sprinkled with glitter-glatter that sparkled in the shadows.

"You better get up on your knees if you want to see everything," Evie advised me. "Those kids can really sing and tap dance. They will knock your hat off."

I couldn't believe my eyes when the first child appeared in what looked like a bathing suit, adorned with feathers and jewels. She was cute, and her dimpled cheeks were tinted with rouge. With a little help from her instructor, she danced through a halting rendition of "Peggy O'Neil." The crowd went wild with applause, begging for an encore.

The Danforth Sisters

Each act improved as the pupils wowed the audience with the hit songs of the 30's.

"Here comes the best act, I think, predicted my sister who was a self-appointed critic. "No one can top the Danforth Sisters. Now watch closely—you might learn something."

Indeed I did watch every move the little girls made, from toe-tapping routines to their sophisticated style of crooning into the microphone. Only on the silver movie screen had I ever seen beauty and talent compared to theirs.

"I wish I could wear clothes like that," I thought to myself, admiring the skimpy costumes that revealed their chubby bodies. I touched my skinny arms and legs that were laced with tiny blue veins and wished I had more flesh on my bones.

All good things have to come to an end, and the free band concert was soon over and we stretched ourselves upright and left the darkened square.

"Well, how did you like the band concert?" asked Mama as we entered the back door. (She never went to bed until all her brood was accounted for.)

"Oh Mama, you should have seen those cute little girls that were on the stage, just like in the movies. I sure wish Neeney and I could go to that dance studio and learn how to tap dance. Could we take a few lessons?"

Mama puffed on her hand-rolled cigaret, not wanting to answer. "You're just going to have to wait till we're in the money or learn to do it on your own."

"I'm going to 'hit the hay'. I've had a hard day. Turn off the light before you go to bed."

Sister Evie and I undressed and climbed into our cot that we shared with Neeney. She sleepily protested our invasion.

"Move over," I commanded as I pushed her to the edge of the mattress. In a few moments the household was back to sleep, all except me, I was putting my act together for my shining hour when I would sing and tap dance for adoring fans. In dreams a small girl sang and danced on the band stand, accompanied by her home town band.

The Medicine Show

"How would you kids like to see a medicine show?" Aunt Carrie asked one afternoon as we sat sipping fruit nectar on her front porch, shaded by the leafy vines of ivy that climbed up to the eaves.

"What's a medicine show? Do they show medicine?" questioned Bobby, making a sour face, just thinking about castor oil and other bitter tasting medications that Mama made us swallow.

"Not exactly," Carrie went on, "they sell some bottled medicine that is a good tonic for everything. But there will also be a free Punch and Judy show and an amateur contest. If you are interested be over here tomorrow evening at 6 o'-clock and I'll take you. And put on your best bibs and tuckers."

Everyone was congregated at Carrie's front door at the appointed hour. We couldn't wait to see this great extravaganza. "Hurry up, Aunt Carrie," we coaxed while she placed a large skeleton key in the door to lock it.

"I'm hurrying," she laughed. "Don't worry, we'll get there on time. It's only a few blocks from here in that vacant lot across the street from the ice company." There were also many neighbors and a few stray dogs beating a path to the free show that was advertised with hand bills.

From a distance we could see the light bulbs dangling from makeshift poles, and wooden planks resting on cement blocks for the local gentry to sit on. The grandstand was already filled to capacity with happy, excited people waiting for the master of ceremonies to appear.

"There's enough room on *that* plank," Carrie shouted above the noisy crowd, and she squeezed me in beside a plump lady who didn't budge an inch. She looked at me with irritation.

"Whew, we just made it," puffed Aunt Carrie as she boosted herself along side of me. Here comes the Medicine Man now. Isn't he good looking?" It was the swarthy master of ceremonies, dressed in a long, red swallow-tailed coat that bulged open between the buttons down the front. What were once white pants, looked grimy and wrinkled, tucked into a worn pair of patent leather boots. Tilted over one eye was a black stove pipe hat trimmed with a yellow band. His piercing black eyes glanced over the crowd waiting for them to quiet down.

"Ladies and gentlemen," he began, in a deep baritone voice, "you are welcome here this evening to enjoy one of the biggest little shows that has come directly from the vaudeville stages of New York City. Now before we begin, I want to inform you that our staff will be selling the famous Dr. Fitches' liver tonic plus the boxes of salt water taffy candy and the sweet smelling Queen of the Nile soaps and lotions. So be ready to buy when we pass among you. Thank you, and now it is my pleasure to introduce you to Goldie and her world-famous dog, Trixie."

From behind the white delapidated carnival truck a blonde lady bounded out, dressed in a red satin outfit that revealed more than her belly button to a gaping bunch of "honyakers" from the boondocks. A small rat terrier yapped along at her feet that were squeezed into a pair of high heeled pumps sparkling with decoration.

"Oh my," the fat lady beside me gasped, "if the sheriff sees that display of flesh she will be run out of town on a rail."

"That's the way show people have to dress," Aunt Carrie assured her. "They live in a different world you know."

"You can say that again," sniffed the woman, pulling her tight skirt over her bulging knees. I think she looks just like a shameless hussy."

The performer in the satin tights posed for her admirers, especially the men who yelled and whistled when she leaned forward. Her swirling mass of bleached hair was swept into a top-knot of curls that dangled from the crown of her head. Eyes of azure blue were fringed with black lashes, dripping with mascara. The pouting lips of crimson broke into a smile revealing the whitest teeth that I ever saw. Her complexion was like cream and a small mole on one cheek enhanced her allure.

"I sure think she is beautiful," I told Aunt Carrie. "I'd sure like to look like her when I grow up."

"Heaven forbid," again gasped the beefy woman. "That's enough of her. Let's see what the mutt can do."

I wondered why the prudish woman came to the show and I was wishing she would sit somewhere else.

The terrier was well trained for his part of the act and didn't make any mistakes in his routine—walking on his hind

74

legs and jumping through a hoop held by his pretty mistress. Applause concluded the canine act. It was now time for the hawkers to sell their wares and they quickly advanced with over-stuffed bags strapped to their waists. Eager hands held out their coins and a few dollar bills to purchase their "once in a lifetime" items that could not be bought at the local grocery or drug counter.

"Give me two bottles of the tonic and a box of taffy, Carrie requested and handed the man a dollar bill, "and keep the change," she smiled, knowing that the medicine show people had to make a living too, during those hard times.

"And now what you children have all been waiting for, Punch and Judy," the medicine man announced. He pulled a long cord that separated the curtains on the wood and cardboard stage that was constructed on the rear end of a truck. Suddenly two ugly heads appeared attached to small bodies with funny looking hands that waved to the crowd.

"That's Punch and Judy," laughed Aunt Carrie, waving back. "They are so funny. Just wait till you hear them talk."

"They're sure homely," I thought, studying the misshapen features with hooked noses and pointed chins. "They look like witches." I was hoping to see dimpled dolls with faces like Betty Boop.

The dialogue began at once with disputes and insults from the puppets who then proceeded to hit each other with tiny baseball bats and brooms, which reminded me of my parents' heated arguments.

During the grand finale, Punch and Judy kissed and made up after an appearance of an angel and devil puppet who helped them decide if they wanted to be good or evil. I'm sure the message that was intended was good food for thought for the attentive audience who hoped for a happy ending.

Last but not least came the amateur contest which caused a great stir. Everyone wondered who would have the nerve to get up and show their talents in front of the home folks.

"Why don't you and Neeney sing your Poor Little Girlie Song," Aunt Carrie suggested, trying to attract the attention of the emcee who was having a difficult time convincing an audience participation.

"Here is a crisp dollar bill," he shouted. "Come on, you jugglers, singers and tap dancers. Can any one tell funny jokes? What's the matter out there, cat got your tongues?"

A few uninhibited towns-people moved forward to sing a solo or duet while the jeering audience gave them the raspberry. Suddenly cousin Delmar, who really wanted the prize money, jumped up on the platform and announced that he was going to sing "River, Stay Away From My Door." All the relatives applauded wildly when he finished and the prize was handed over to my beaming cousin who stole the show, without too much competition.

The medicine show left town, along with Punch and Judy, and I never saw them again.

There was a new kind of road show that everyone was talking about, gaining in popularity throughout the midwest. It was called a carnival.

Shopping With Mama

"If I'm still alive in the spring, I'm going to go on a diet." Mama often made this resolution during the winter months when her bulging figure overlapped her apron. "If I wasn't so heavy I could wear some of those dresses that the W P A sewing rooms make. I don't know why they can't sew anything larger than a size 42." It was supposed to be a secret but Mama was a whopping size 52.

Finding a wash or good dress in any of the local stores was like looking for a needle in a haystack. So the yards of flowered and swiss dotted material usually came from the dry goods departments of the general stores. The bleached muslin and outing flannel were made into "queen sized" brassieres, underskirts and nightgowns. Mama was often kidded about her outsized dresses and lingerie as they billowed in the wind on the clothes lines. One of the other well-endowed neighbor women told her about a catalogue company that catered to pleasingly plump women. But their prices were beyond Mama's budget.

When spring did roll around it was time for Mama to make her annual trip to town to "shop for something decent to wear." If Dad obtained an extra paint job while "moonlighting" on the W P A he usually had a little extra money.

Mama knew that I loved to browse and window shop so I was the one that usually escorted her to town. (Besides, I was the right size for shoulder support.)

"I want to get an early start before it gets too hot," she told me as we sat together at the kitchen table. "You know how warm I get. "Why don't you use more talcum powder," I suggested, dunking a hard day-old roll into my coffee.

"Nothing helps," she replied, already wiping the perspiration from her face with the hem of her white apron.

"Why do we always have to live where the sidewalk ends?" I complained to Mama as we picked our way down the footpath towards Sanborn Street. (The fireweeds, heavy with the morning dew, wiped their drops on our clothes, and tickled my bare legs.)

"Because we can't afford to live like the Jones'," she answered, while losing her footing on a slippery rock. "Don't worry. Some day your ship will come in, as pretty as you are. There will be no problems." (Mama always said—when I grew up I would marry the richest man in town.)

Upon reaching Main street we still had to walk three more blocks to the K. & K. store. "They're having a sale on dress material so we'll go there first," she puffed while I switched shoulders to give my aching body a rest.

"May I help you?" a pretty clerk asked, watching us fingering the material and bias tapes that resembled a spring flower garden. Mama told the lady how much yard goods that was needed and how many spools of thread. I watched the dial on the clock-like gauge that measured the material unfolding from the bolt of cloth. (Mama measured a yard by holding the cloth from her nose to the end of her out-stretched arm.)

Mama laid her money down, and the large package was handed over to me to carry. "Now I want to go over to the Henry Field's Store and if we're in luck we may be on time to hear some good music, that is broadcast over the radio." (The Henry Fields store advertised their wares by a "hook up" with radio station K G D A, Mitchell.)

"Let's hurry. It's almost time—I don't want to miss any of those hillbilly tunes."

We arrived on time to see a local trio "tuning up" for their noon hour show, a group consisting of Ralph White on fiddle, Charlie Kurtenbach, guitar, and his brother Ted, on both banjo and guitar.

Although my feet were tired and Mama's corns were "killing" her it didn't keep us from toe tapping to the barnyard melodies of the Thirties—songs like "Comin' Round the Mountain," "My Little Rooster," "Turkey In the Straw," "Old Dan Tucker," and for a change of pace, the melodic strains of "Over the Waves," "My Darling Nellie Gray," or the all-time favorite, "My Wild Irish Rose."

"You should get up there and play your pump organ." Mama, I knew, always had a secret desire to be in show business. "Oh, I'd be too nervous," she blushed. "I couldn't stand all those strangers looking at me. But you girls should get together and practice more, because you're just as good as any of those cow girl singers at W N A X." (This was the Yankton station owned by the well-known Gurney family.)

"I'd just die, too, if I had to get up in front of that microphone," I agreed with her, following her through the aisles of canned goods in a well-stocked mercantile store, sandwiched between a furniture company and the telephone exchange.

Finding nothing "on special" we strolled west until we came to the corner of Third and Main where most of the clothing and dime stores were located.

"Just for fun," Mama mused, "let's mosey over to Baron's to see what the other half are wearing." (This was an exclusive shop.) Name labels were attached to every article of clothing in the store.

I knew that Mama would never carry a fancy box or sack with the name "Baron's" elegantly printed across the front, in gold.

The display windows were occupied by pencil slim mannequins who stood in fashionable poses. "I can just see me trying to squeeze into something like that," laughed Mama, pointing to a snug-fitting silk dress on a "nose in the air" dummy. "If you lost about ten pounds you could," I replied, trying to make her feel good, with a little exaggeration.

"Ha," she again laughed. "Well, let's go in. They can't charge us for looking."

I knew immediately that we were in the wrong place when I noticed that the well-groomed clerks didn't smile or say hello, as they gushed over the other customers who entered at the same time. I followed Mama across the soft, luxurious carpeting to the rear of the store where the suits and coats hung on satin padded coat hangers.

"Wow," Mama gasped, reading the price tags that dangled from the elegantly tailored garments, "they want an arm and a leg for these duds. Do they think people are made of money?" She then proceeded to pull one of the fur-trimmed coats off of the rack. I didn't want to say anything but I knew the coat was too small. I hoped it didn't come apart.

"We don't carry your size in these brands of coats and suits," a voice spoke, and we turned around. A lady who looked as "snooty" as the mannequins, gave us an icy stare through gold rimmed spectacles, her painted face frozen. Mama meekly handed her the coat and walked into the shoe department where the tiny, pointed toed, high fashioned shoes hung beside polished leather pocketbooks. "Mama could never get her 'number 10's' into those," I thought to myself. Mama always referred to her shoes as being "gun boats."

"May I help you, Madam?" a male clerk asked in a high pitched voice. His complexion was pale and he looked bored when he saw Mama. I think he was relieved when she answered, "No, I'm just looking. I'll come back in a few weeks." "Mama can sure put on a good act," I thought as she took her time inspecting the rich-looking merchandise that was lavishly displayed on two floors of the salon.

"I'd have to be a mouse to get into these," she joked, holding a pair of silk panties, trimmed with lace, across her large hips. Why, you can see right through them." I felt uneasy as another clerk stood by with a contemptuous look. By this time I was wishing that we were down the street where the dime store employees were friendly. "Hurry up, Mama, let's get out of here," I pleaded.

"I just want to take a peek at the jewelry, and then we'll go," she promised. So while she gazed through the glass showcase at the Tiffany-like "bangles and beads," I watched a matron of high social standing sniffing the bottles of colognes and perfumes that were displayed with expensive cosmetics. Names like Schaparelli, Madame Dubarry and Chanel were imprinted in gold and silver on the exquisite containers.

When I heard the clerk reveal the price of an ounce of perfume, I couldn't believe my ears. "That's about the cost of a week's supply of groceries," I figured. "Is there that much difference in the fragrance between a ten dollar bottle of essence and the heart-shaped flagon of sweet violets that Mama bought at a five and ten cent store?"

Mama was still enchanted by the brilliant ear-rings, hat and scarf pins made of rhinestones and silver or the gold inlaid bracelets, chains and lockets that were guaranteed not to turn green. I felt pangs of pity as I watched her, wishing for one of the shiny pins to make her plain-looking dress look more elegrant.

"Have you decided which one you want?" I asked Mama, making believe that we did indeed have a choice.

"I'll have to think about it," she smiled, lifting herself off the glass counter. We started to leave when I turned around in time to see two of the clerks laughing and talking in whispers. I knew that they were making fun of us and wishing that people, such as we, would do our window shopping on the south side of town with the "common folks."

"I wish we could buy Dad one of those fancy suits, I remarked as we peeked into the window of the Grigg and Becker clothing stores. "And look at those snappy looking shoes," Mama interrupted. "Boy, he could really dance up a storm in those."

When Dad could afford a pair of shoes they were purchased from some "work shoe" department.

We continued to walk south on the main street until we came to the J. J. Newberry store. Pushing open the swinging

Business buildings on East Third, later the site of the Commercial Bank

doors, we were greeted by the sight of wall-to-wall candy counters, delightful cosmetics that could be purchased for a few nickels and dimes, dolls and toys of every description, just waiting to be taken home. Pretty dishes, silverware, and cheap glassware in assorted colors and patterns gleamed on the shelves. (That same glassware is now called "Depression" and "Carnival" and is valued by antique collectors.)

"I'm going back to the housewares department," Mama said. "I need a few more cups and water glasses. You can look at the toys if you like."

I was like a "one-eyed cat in a sea food store," as I couldn't make up my mind what to buy with my pennies, wrapped tightly in my handkerchief.

I was torn between a small leather purse and a tiny celluloid doll, wrapped in a pink blanket. "I think the coin purse is nice," the pretty sales clerk said, snapping it open and shut. "Your money would be safe and sound in here." I stuck my finger into the leather pocket to test the depth. "I'll take it," I shyly replied, untying the money from my hanky.

Meanwhile Mama had found her way to the cosmetics counter where she was searching for the right shade of face powder, assisted by another lovely lady. (I'm sure the "million dollar babies" who worked in the five and dimes were chosen for their beauty along with their ability to make change.)

81

"I think this "Rachel" in the Lady Esther face powder will blend better with your olive complexion than any of the Ponds products," the helpful clerk suggested, "and did you see the new rouge that just arrived?" She handed Mama a dainty rose-colored box etched with gold leaves.

Mama opened the lid and softly touched the mound of rouge and applied it to her high cheek bones. "Oh, that does add something," admired the clerk. "I'll take a box," my mother flatly stated. "Now let's see, I need some talcum powder; I think I want another can of April Showers and I think that's about it."

Mama never bought any of the tubes of lipsticks, bottles of perfume, "dark eyes" mascara or the newest rage, the "Mabelline" eyebrow pencil. (The older girls in our neighborhood used burned match sticks to obtain the arched eyebrows and beauty marks.)

I was becoming fascinated with the world of glamour and could hardly wait to grow up so I could buy the red lipsticks of "Flame Glo," "Taboo" and other exotic names printed on the cardboard holders. Beautiful women with long flowing hair, vamps' eyes and pouting lips gazed out from the large posters surrounding the sweet smelling counters at all three of the local dime stores.

I had a great desire to be a dime store girl when I grew up, and to work in their salon of beauty.

Some of the sales clerks that I recall are Eleanor Rush, Doris Underhill, Velma Nolt, Doris Timmins, Vivian Lassegard and Madeline and Virginia Throckmorton. (I wonder what ever happened to those fresh faced beauties of the Thirties.)

"Are you ready to go?" Mama asked, standing near the doorway. "You can carry this sack of chocolates I bought for the kids." (She could never resist the bins of dime store candy.)

By this time my arms were piled high from our purchases but there was one more stop before going home. That place was Montgomery Wards.

We were greeted by each clerk as we walked past their counters, neatly stacked with the newly arrived spring merchandise. "I'm going to see if they have anything in my size," Mama said, stretching down her dress that was getting too tight around the middle.

A well groomed sales clerk greeted us. We knew and liked her for her friendly personality. She was Mrs. Emma Ainslei, one of the many personable employes of the store. I felt more relaxed in this atmosphere where more of the "blue collared" folks shopped for the cheaper but good quality items.

"You're in luck," Emma smiled as she led us to a rack of dresses made for queen sized ladies. "These latest fashions are in sizes from 44 to 52." "Why are all the big dresses black or navy blue with polka dots?" I wondered. "I'd like to see Mama dressed in a red, yellow or blue just once!"

"I think you've lost a little weight, Mrs. Ainslei said as she looked at Mama's wide back side. "Why don't you try on this pretty maroon in a size forty-eight?"

"Dolores will help me," Mama insisted, not wanting the clerk to see her undressed. So together we squeezed into a cramped dressing room that was hot and stuffy.

I tried my best to stretch the unyielding crepe material across my mother's broad back that was now wet with perspiration. "Can't you pull it down over my corset?" she panted. "It's too tight," I said. "I think you better try on a bigger one."

It was a struggle to pull the dress back over her shoulders again. I handed the rumpled frock to Mrs. Ainslei who was on stand by with another polka dot, sized 52. "If I can't get into this one I'd better buy a tent," Mama remarked. "I hope you don't grow up and become fat like me."

This time the satin-like dress flowed over her fleshy body and we both breathed a sigh of relief. "Go over there and look at yourself in that full length mirror," ordered the clerk, probably anxious to make a sale. "That sure slims her down, doesn't it?" she remarked to me.

Although my mother was a tall woman, five feet ten inches in her stocking feet and carried a lot of weight, she was still a handsome lady. I thought she looked wonderful in her navy blue dress, splashed with white polka dots. "All you need now is a string of pearls," Emma told her as Mama turned from side to side in the three way mirror. "My, you do look elegant."

Mama then looked at the price tag. "Hmmm, four ninety-eight. Is this the cheapest that you have? I shouldn't really splurge almost five dollars on a dress."

"You won't find another like it in town," Emma insisted. "That is a good buy. Do you want it?"

"Take it, Mama," I chimed in. "It looks real nice on you, makes you look thinner. It really does."

"Oh, all right, put it in a box," and a five dollar bill was taken from an almost empty purse.

"How about a new hat?" the sales lady pursued. But that would have to wait until another pay day rolled around.

The afternoon was growing late. It would have been easier if we could have taken the short cut across the tracks home instead of walking the many blocks around Sanborn street. But Mama couldn't climb down the cinder path that reached across the dry run creek.

"We better walk faster," I reminded her. "It looks like it might rain." I didn't like the looks of the billowing dark clouds that were gathering in the sky. "Let her rain; Lord knows we need it," she replied, panting.

It began to sprinkle just as we reached the bottom of the hill. "Home at last," I sighed. It had been a long day and I was tired and hungry. I pulled and pushed Mama along the weed-grown hillside.

The packages and boxes were placed on the dining room table and we both plopped down upon some chairs. "My feet are killing me," Mama moaned.

I pulled off the shoes from her feet, carefully. "I wish we owned a car so you wouldn't have to walk so far," I said sadly.

"If wishes were horses, beggars would all ride," she replied with a tired laugh. "I'm going into the bedroom and get out of this corset, I've had enough for one day." She limped into her sanctuary and closed the door.

This was only one of the typical trips to town that my mother and I shared together during the great depression years.

Fourth of July

Of all the holidays that were observed during my growing up years, I believe the most enjoyable was the Fourth of July, and I'm sure the nation was more patriotic during this period. Even though we were poor and yearned for the better things in life, America was still our native land and the greatest place on earth.

One of my earliest recollections about that glorious celebration was painful. While running around barefoot on July 4th, I stepped on a firecracker sizzling in the grass. I was not only scared out of my wits, my foot felt like it was on fire. Mama put my foot in a pail of cold water and told me to stay on the front porch away from the exploding firecrackers that were being tossed around in the yard. It was always a race between the neighbor kids to be the first one to shoot off a salute.

"Is your foot feeling better?" Mama asked, looking at the blister that was ballooning around my heel.

"A little bit," I answered, trying not to show tears.

"Well, I'll rub on some vaseline and wrap a rag around your foot. You'll be fine by tomorrow. But I don't know how you can go up town to see the parade. You can't walk on that burned foot," she said, looking at me sympathetically.

Just then Dad walked out onto the porch. He knew how much I yearned to see the parade. "I'll take you up in the coaster wagon. There's enough room for you and your sister. We'll prop your foot on a little pillow so it won't get bumped around."

"She will have to change her clothes. Everyone will be dressed up today. You can wear that new dress I made for you last week," Mama told me.

I limped into the house and hurried to get ready. I donned my pretty flowered print frock and pinned a blue ribbon in my hair. My brown sandals would have to be left under the bed. I would have to celebrate our Independence Day shoeless!

The ride to town wasn't too uncomfortable. Dad had oiled the wagon's wheels to insure a smooth ride. There was only slight bumps when it crossed the cracks in the sidewalk.

"Well, we're almost there," Dad shouted back at us. "Can you hear the band playing?" "Oh the monkey wrapped his tail around the flag pole," he sang to make us laugh.

Boy Scout Parade and Jamboree (1932)

Somewhere on the north end of Main Street, I could hear the thrilling sounds of our home town band playing a patriotic marching song.

We were lucky to have a relative who owned a cafe and grocery store right on the main street. We were privileged to stand there whenever a parade passed by. There was a wide porch.

When Aunt Christine saw my bandaged foot and surmised that it would be difficult for me to move much she suggested a solution.

"I'll bring out a step ladder and you can sit on the top. We can't let you stay in that wagon and miss the whole parade."

"Can I climb up there, too?" sister Neeney asked. "I won't tip it over."

"I guess there's room for two," Christine agreed, not wanting to leave her out.

From my perch above the heads of the crowds I could see down the street where the American flags were flapping in the wind in front of the business places. Red, white and blue bunting was wrapped gaily around the lamp posts. The sky was crystal blue with puffy white clouds and the sun was warm with a promise of a beautiful day.

"Hey, Dad, here comes the parade," I shouted as I watched the marching band coming closer with trumpets and horns glistening in the bright morning sunlight. A large flag was being carried by a uniformed man strutting in front. The crowd stood silent while the men and boys removed their hats and everyone placed their hands over their hearts. Our flag was passing by.

Behind the band a shiny black automobile moved slowly, with small flags adorning it. Decorations of red, white and blue bunting surrounded a sign that I couldn't read. Someone in the crowd said, "There are fewer men again this year. It won't be long until the rest of the Spanish American veterans are gone. God bless them."

Gazing out of the open windows were some elderly tired-looking men with white hair. They were the old soldiers of a war that very few people remembered. I returned the salute from a white gloved hand. As the car moved slowly down the street, a loud mouthed man remarked, "They're so old they don't even recall being in the army."

The next group of patriotic Americans were young boys dressed in natty looking uniforms with red handkerchiefs wrapped around their necks. They were the Boy Scouts.

Everyone shouted "hurray," waved and called out their names when a contingent of young soldiers passed in review. These men were in tan clothing with leggings wrapped from their knees to their ankles. Heavy boot-like shoes made loud noises as they clumped along the concrete street. The round iron helmets made them look threatening with the tight-fitting straps hugging their chins. I knew that they were men of war when I looked at the long guns that were across their shoulders. Extending from the barrels were sharp-looking knives—bayonets. They, too, were designed to kill.

"There goes some of the bravest men in town."

"We have a lot to thank them for."

"It's been quite a few years since they beat the pants off the 'Krauts'."

"Three cheers for the Doughboys."

"Hip, hip, hurray."

These remarks were spoken by a grateful crowd who came to salute the heroes from World War I. Mitchell had a lot to celebrate on that hot Fourth of July morning back in 1929. America was at peace. Everyone was sure that there would be no more lives lost on foreign shores. How wrong they were when they predicted an end to the hostilities in the world.

"Well, that's it," Dad said with a sigh as the last heavy cannon rumbled down the street.

"I'm so hot," sister Neeney gasped. "I want some pop."

Dad lifted me down off of my reviewing stand and set me back in the wagon.

"What kind of pop do you want?" he asked. "Strawberry, Grape, or Green River?"

"Strawberry," I replied eagerly. "It fizzes up my nose and makes it tickle."

"I want a bottle of Green River and an ice cream cone," my little sister insisted. She always made a fuss if she didn't get her own way.

"Be quiet, I'm just getting you pop for now. This afternoon I'll go to Reierson Bakery and buy a gallon of ice cream for the whole family," Dad told her. "Now stop yelling or I'll spank you."

During those years with no home refrigeration, ice cream had to be purchased at the last minute and then eaten quickly before it melted.

Most of the time our family celebrated the Fourth in our own back yard with a few neighbors and relatives. We couldn't afford to go to the horse, motorcycle and car races that were held at the Ruskin and Glenwood Parks and other places of amusement.

There was plenty to eat and drink and a few fireworks that were brought by Aunt Carrie and Uncle Pete. Mama mixed lemonade and fruit nectar in large glass containers. Chunks of ice clinked through the yellow and pink liquids that were stored in the ice box. By the time it was ready to drink there would be only slivers of ice to tantalize our tongues.

Dad and the boys carried out all the chairs, benches and stools, then set them beneath the shade of the cottonwood trees where "there is a little more breeze."

"It's going to be a scorcher today," Mama said, wiping the perspiration from her brow. "I sure hope it blows up a rain."

"Don't be silly, we don't want it today," Aunt Carrie interrupted. "It would ruin the fireworks display at the lake tonight."

"Now don't get too close with those firecrackers," Mama warned the brothers who were placing them beneath tin cans. "We've already had one accident today," meaning me.

Sister Neeney, who had the nerves of steel, was lighting the dangerous cherry bombs, a feat for men and boys.

"I think it's about time I get the ice cream," Dad announced as he looked at the flushed faces of his family. The temperature was around 110 degrees in the shade.

"You better hurry back," Mama warned, "or we will all melt."

As quick as a wink, Dad returned with two gallons of ice cream double-sacked in large brown bags. Already around the table stood seven anxious children with spoons and bowls in hand.

Mama quickly scooped up the melting portions of chocolate and vanilla and dropped them into our containers.

"You gave Buddy a bigger spoonful than me," complained Bobby, watching to see that everyone was given their fair share.

"I think Donnie has the most," another brother chimed in.

"I'm the oldest so I should get the most," replied our older brother, who we thought always got the best parts of the chicken, too.

"Now if you're going to fight about it, I'll give it to the neighbors," yelled Mama who was by now too hot and bothered to listen to their arguments. "Just eat and keep quiet."

Within a few minutes there were more expressions of misery from the children. Everyone knows that if ice cream is eaten in haste it makes for discomfort.

"Oh, my forehead hurts and my nose stings," everyone groaned about the same time, holding their hands over their faces.

"That's what you get for eating like a bunch of pigs," Mama reminded them. "I don't feel sorry for you."

"My head doesn't hurt, Mama," I told her cheerfully. "I stirred mine up and made it nice and soft to eat." Mama reached into the almost empty container and found another spoonful. She pushed it off with her finger into my bowl. (It paid to eat like a little lady.)

"It's just too hot for comfort. I'm going down in the cellar for the rest of the afternoon," Mama finally told her assembled kin folk. She arose from her chair, pulling away the sweat drenched dress from her body.

"I think we better head for home, too," Uncle Pete agreed. "I want to get ready to see the fireworks tonight. A few of the kids can ride out to the lake with us."

"Well, if I can get my old blunderbuss going they can all pile in, with plenty of room to spare," Dad said, thanking our uncle for the invitation.

We kids began to worry when the sun began playing hide and go seek among some threatening thunder clouds. To add to our concern, Dad couldn't get our Overland car to start.

"There doesn't seem to be much 'spark' in the old girl these days," replied Dad as we all looked underneath the hood at the aging engine. It didn't want to turn over.

"Don, you get behind the wheel again and adjust the choke and the spark. I'll try cranking her again."

After many turns of the crank that liked to kick back in protest, a sporadic "put put" noise arose from the vibrating car and we all gave three cheers for Father's genius.

"Tell your mother to get out here if she wants to go along. I have to keep her going now," Dad said as he pushed my brother aside and grabbed the steering wheel. Now the horn is dead. I sure hope no one gets in our way."

While Mama climbed into the front seat with Dad and us two youngest girls, the rest piled into the truck box of our pick-up.

"Throw that paint canvas in, too," Dad ordered. "If it rains you can all get under it. Is everybody in now? Hang on tight, here we go."

The overloaded car shot out of the yard in a burst of speed with a few backfires. I hung on for dear life as we careened down Edmunds Street and then headed north on the old cemetery road.

"I hope those guys behind me don't mind eating my dust," Dad shouted to Mama. "I'm afraid if I slow down, the car will stop. I can just see you walking back to town."

"You drive like those bootleggers in that gangster movie I saw last week," Mama laughed. "Can you make a bootlegger's turn?" I liked to hear Dad and Mama say funny things when they were in a silly mood.

After whirling through the winding roads around the cemetery, we came to a halt on the crest of a hill.

"I'll park here for now. Then when we leave we will be going down hill all the way. Well, you might as well get out and enjoy the scenery. It will be awhile before the fireworks start."

"I'll stay in here," Mama answered, already slapping at a pesky mosquito. "I'm afraid we're going to be eaten alive by the bugs and mosquitoes and who knows what else?"

"Well, we can't have our cake and eat it too," Dad snorted. "Come on, girls, let's take a walk down by the lake."

Sister Neeney and I were half carried through the high weeds until we came to the amphiatheater that was carpeted with lush green grass. Surrounding the outdoor arena were newly planted trees.

"Here is a good spot. We can see everything from here," suggested Dad, and we all settled down on the ground.

Across the lake on a small inlet called Radio Point, we could see the men readying the fireworks. At our age we had no idea what lay in store for us. The sun had disappeared behind the hills and twilight began to throw its veil over the water. Hundreds of people were sitting around the circular arena, watching the mini-display of sparklers that spit and fizzled.

"Look up there," Dad said, pointing to a brilliant explosion of Christmas-like splendor that lit up the sky above the waters. Each bomb burst, followed by a spray of twinkling lights proved to be more beautiful than the last one.

"Isn't that the prettiest sight you ever saw?" Dad asked, when suddenly we gazed in wonder at an American flag emblazoned against the purple sky. It was the grand finale of a most memorable pyrotechnical display.

When we arrived back at the car, we found it hemmed in by other vehicles of every description. Mama was sitting on the running board.

"How are we going to get out of here?" she asked in an exasperated voice. "I knew I should have stayed home."

"Now don't get your water hot. People can hear you." Dad tried to calm her down. "We will just have to wait, so we can roll down this hill without using the crank. I'll get you home in no time."

It seemed like hours before the other cars pulled away, leaving us ingesting their vapors and dust, and my mother blaming Dad for all of her discomfort.

Luck was with us after the road was cleared. Our old Overland took us all safely home without a huff or a puff or a hiccup.

Everyone scrambled out of the car and hurried into the house. Dad lifted me and my sister into his arms and listened to us chatter about our first glimpse of a Fourth of July display.

"Boy, we got home just in time," Mama said, holding open the screen door. "Look at that lightning, and it has started to sprinkle. Thank God for that! Maybe those fireworks had something to do with it."

As I lay in bed that night I wasn't afraid of the rolling thunder or the flashes of lightning that zig-zagged across the bedroom walls.

"The angels are celebrating the Fourth of July, too," I thought to myself. I said my prayers and went to sleep.

Golden Days of Radio

I grew up during the golden age of radio and from the time I was just a toddler sitting on my Mama's knee, I loved to listen to the various sounds, coming from the mysterious wooden box. I couldn't understand how the music and voices of people could be contained in it. Mama said it was just a miracle that most people took for granted. But she cursed when it became balky and the only sound was "static." The radio was pounded a few times until the stations came back on the air.

"I hope that radio works right tonight," Mama told Dad while turning the pages of the Radio Guide magazine. Kate Smith comes on at 7 o'clock." "When the Moon Comes Over the Mountain," she sang, trying to imitate her favorite radio singer who was also on the hefty side like Mother.

"You can sing just as good as she does," Dad complimented her, "but I think you out-weigh her by fifty pounds." "That's not funny," Mama fumed, throwing a magazine at him.

Although Mitchell was only a small city in an under-populated state, it was fortunate enough to have a radio station. Jack Verschoor, a local businessman, was the owner of K G D A that made its first broadcast on April 6, 1930. The transmitter or radio tower was located near Lake Mitchell on a small inlet known as "Radio Point."

The first studio was located on the second floor of the world-famous Corn Palace. The staff had to do a lot of arm twisting to persuade the area business people to buy a few minutes of advertising. To compensate for the empty programming a few local citizens who could sing or play an instrument were hired. Most of the hometown talent was poor.

The hole-in-the-wall station gradually gained the attention and the support of a sizable audience. Even in those early days a "Kiddie Hour" show was sponsored by some enterprising firm. We kids listened with undivided attention when the small fry of the town sang off key or tap-danced to "Peggy O'Neil."

"Why don't you girls get up there and sing that pretty song, 'Little Green Valley'?" Dad often asked sister Neeney and me. "You're just as good as those Underwood Sisters."

"They might laugh at us," I told my dad. Besides I'd be too scared to get in front of that microphone."

"It won't eat you," Dad explained. "I sure hate to see all of your talent go down the drain. You have to start somewhere."

Neeney and I could never muster up enough courage to make our debut on the home-town radio station, so no one ever heard our little ditties that we sang in perfect harmony. Yet Dad and Mama never tired of trying to push us into the spotlight of show business. Our ambitions surged again when we listened to the amateur contests that came over the airwaves from W N A X at Yankton.

This "biggest little station" in the midwest was becoming very famous throughout this area. It was owned by the Gurney family, well-known for their nurseries. They knew how to sell by "sure fire" commercials and entertainers that could charm the birds out of the trees with good old mountain music.

One of the most famous to be baptized into show business on this small radio station was Lawrence Welk and his Hotsie Totsie Boys. The Rosebud Kids, a family of talented children; Happy Jack O'Malley, a fun loving Irishman who played a squeaky fiddle; The Dean Brothers who could harmonize a sweet country song that brought tears; Ben and Jesse Mae Norman, husband and wife duo who yodeled and played the "Gittars" that made them loved by their devoted fans. And last but not least, George B. German, the singing cowboy and jokster whose voice reminded listeners of a bad case of laryngitis. His song books that included such melodies as "Strawberry Roan" and "Old Shep" sold like hot cakes to upstarts who yearned to be hillbilly singers on the Grand Ole Opry at Nashville, Tennessee.

Dad loved to listen to the radio early in the morning before the household was up. "Whitey" Larson was an early bird announcer who informed his midwest listeners of the latest events in the W N A X area. No matter how dire the situation, "Whitey" spoke in a voice filled with optimism.

Whenever I heard the pickin' and singin' of a good old country hoe-down, I sneaked out of bed and went downstairs. I always found Dad sitting by the kitchen table sipping on a cup of hot coffee, listening to the magic of a small table radio.

"You better bundle up good this morning when you go to school," Dad said, pouring a cup of coffee for me. "It got down to fifteen below zero last night." "I wish we could move to California where it's always warm," I sighed, shivering at the thought of walking the many blocks to school.

"I didn't think there would be classes today but there were no school closings announced by "Whitey Larson," said Dad, turning up the volume and twisting the dial. "Well, what do you know, I got Del Rio, Texas. Those other radio stations are getting better all the time, but they don't play enough good music," remarked Dad.

It was during times like these that we became familiar with the names of the cowboy bands and the hillbilly tunes that were more often than not sad and forlorn. There were the stories about unfaithful lovers, true love, death of faithful animals. But the songs I loved the best were about the hoboes and freight trains. The ballads were endless, "May I Sleep in Your Barn Tonight, Mister?" "Hallelujah, I'm a Bum," "Big Rock Candy Mountain," "Hanging Round the Water Tank" and hundreds more of the heart tugging songs.

There were many South Dakotans who practiced their guitar strumming, banjo pickin', yodeling and harmonica playing, in order to be a contestant on the W N A X amateur hour. We kids listened to the show every Saturday afternoon and secretly wished for an audition. We were offered that chance by a "shirt tail" relative of ours, Joe Bohr of Stickney, a good old country boy.

Joe was raised in a musical family who played everything from guitar to honky tonk piano. He often came to Mitchell to visit our Aunt Carrie and was very much interested in the singing talent of us sisters. He encouraged us to sing along while he strummed his guitar. "You girls are better than any of the contestants that I have heard over W N A X or even Nashville," he commented. "Why don't you go with me to Yankton to compete in those contests? I'm positive you will win with "You Are My Sunshine.""

We agreed at the moment that we would go but the thought of singing in front of an audience struck terror into my heart. When that day arrived, Mama told Joe that we decided not to enter the amateur show. He was very disappointed.

"Gee, I don't know what to say," he said, shaking his head. "Those girls have the talent if only they had the 'guts.' I don't understand it." He walked back to his car and drove away.

I watched him leave from behind a curtain and felt relieved that we were released from our commitment, yet angry at myself for not having enough confidence. "Why am I so shy and afraid to voice my feelings? Why don't I have enough nerve to sing in front of ordinary people?" Our promising career was nipped in the bud and we were destined to sing only behind closed doors. Joe never asked us to sing again!

As the years rolled by we soon tired of listening to music coming from the "sticks" so turned our radio dial to the networks where the soap operas, big time entertainers and comedians were heard. Personalities like George Burns and Gracie Allen, Edgar Bergen and Charlie McCarthy, Jack Benny, Al Pierce and his gang, Fred Allen and Eddie Cantor. The Major Bowes Amateur Hour was a favorite. There many of today's stars received their first break in show business. "Around and around she goes and where she stops, nobody knows," chuckled the kindly emcee, Major Bowes, who secretly wished that all of the contestants could be winners.

While the rest of the family enjoyed the rib-tickling antics of the comedians and the songs of such greats as Dinah Shore, Deanna Durbin and Bobby Breen, Dad loved the homespun humor of Lum 'n' Abner or the wise cracking chatter between Amos 'n' Andy, doing black face comedy.

"I sure get a kick out of those 'niggers'," Dad laughed, slapping his knee, not realizing that they were two white men.

"I think Fibber McGee and Molly are the funniest people on the air," Mama said, "and next to Kate Smith, I like Al Jolson. "When he sings 'Sonny Boy' I could just cry."

So the radio shows were rated by our family who thought themselves well informed critics. Sometimes there were a few arguments and fisticuffs as to where the dial would be turned. (Unlike today's generation who may own two or three T.V. sets, we felt fortunate to own one small radio.)

"I want to listen to 'The Shadow'," brother Don would tell the rest of us, and tomorrow night 'Inner Sanctum'." "Oh, those shows are too scary," we younger ones protested. "We're afraid to go to bed upstairs if the 'Creaking Door' is on the air." "You are just 'fraidy cats'," our brother shamed us. "It's just make believe."

I was always glad when Saturday night came and the older members of the family were gone. Then the radio belonged to us younger children. We settled down on a few fat pillows in front of the radio and tuned in for an evening of toe-tapping music or home-spun humor.

There was a choice between listening to the Grand Ole Opry, Louisiana Hayride and the National Barn Dance. Roy

Acuff, Minnie Pearl, Ernest Tubbs, Hank Williams, The Carter Family, Lulu Belle and Scotty and the fabulous Hoosier Hot-shots kept us entertained until we could no longer keep our eyes open. "You kids better hit the hay now," Mama suggested, swatting us on our backsides, "and don't forget to use the pail." It's on the back porch.

After warming ourselves near the pot belly stove, we raced up the cold stairway and jumped into bed. It took about ten minutes before I stopped shivering and then settled into a deep sleep beneath five or six heavy blankets.

The radio programs not only offered true-to-life stories for the adults, who couldn't survive without knowing how their idols handled their problems. There were also heroes and heroines for the youth of America to idolize.

I used to hurry home from school to hear the latest hair-raising episode of "Jack Armstrong, the All American Boy." I worried about "Little Orphan Annie and her faithful dog, Sandy, who were always knee deep in trouble. They were as real to us as the kids next door. Unlike the children of today who can see what the characters look like on T V, we had to imagine what was happening by their talk and sound effects.

Not only were we privileged to hear the great acts of radio and vaudeville but informed about the disasters that were occurring around the globe.

The Thirties were filled with history-making episodes from the kidnapping of the Lindbergh baby to the birth of the Dionne quintuplets, a rare event then which has since been duplicated by other multiple births.

When Bruno Richard Hauptmann was executed, we listened to the latest bulletins that told the world about the baby killer and his execution, which we felt he deserved. We all worshipped the father of the murdered child, Charles Lindbergh, or "Lindy" as he was fondly named. (Yet today there are those who believe that an innocent man was put to death.)

"Did you hear the news that came over the radio a little while ago?" gasped Aunt Carrie, trying to catch her breath, after running across the alley. "What news?" anxiously asked Mama. "Our radio conked out last night." "There were five babies born to a woman in Montreal, Canada. Can you believe such a thing? Just like a litter of kittens."

"Five babies, all at once," Mama exclaimed. "I think I have a house full." "Well, I'll go back home and listen some more," Carrie shouted, slamming the back door.

"What a time for the radio to go dead," Mama complained, looking at the silent "Atwater Kent" standing in the corner. "Every time there is some big news I have to hear it from the neighbors."

"I'll go uptown and get it fixed," volunteered brother Buddy, who didn't want to miss out on the latest chapter of Jack Armstrong who survived on a diet of wheaties.

"I won't have any money till the "relief" check comes and that won't be for another week," said Mama in disgust.

"Now I'll have to miss another episode of my favorite show," Buddy fretted.

"Don't feel bad," Mama consoled him, "Dad will have to go over to Carrie's to listen to President Roosevelt's fireside chat." Dad and the brothers were greatly interested in the sports figures of the day, including Bobby Jones, the golf champ, Jessie Owens, black athlete who could run like a deer, and their favorite of all time, Joe Louis, the Brown Bomber, boxing champ of the world.

Everyone was overjoyed when Joe boxed his way to victory during the many matches in his illustrious career. We kids winced and almost felt the blows when our hero was hit by an aggressive opponent.

"Give it to him, Joe! Knock his block off," we shouted into the radio when we knew that the Brown Bomber was ready to deliver the knockout punch, and keep his title.

When the roar of the crowd had subsided and our idol was again crowned the champion of the world, (he had lost his title once) it called for a celebration. Mama served a large dishpan filled with hot buttered popcorn to the "ring-side" fans around the radio.

One day while visiting my Aunt Carrie, I heard a group of singers, warbling about the lowly tumble-weed. I was enchanted by the harmony and the words about a lonely drifter who followed the tumbling tumble-weeds.

"Who are those cowboy singers," I asked. "That is the prettiest song I have ever heard."

"The Sons of the Pioneers," Aunt Carrie answered. "They come on the air every day at 11:45 over station K S O O, Sioux Falls. I think they are just wonderful, too."

"We can't get K S O O on our radio. It isn't new like yours," I sadly told her. "About all we can get is K G D A,

Mitchell, and W N A X, Yankton. But most of the time we get just static."

"Well, you just come over every day and listen to the Sons of the Pioneers at my house. You will love their other song that I think is just great. It's called 'Cool Water'." I fell in love with the Sons of the Pioneers a long time ago and have never forgotten the feelings of rapture, and a little melancholy when I listened to their heart-stirring melodies about the lone prairie. One of the Sons of the Pioneers left the group to follow his own career and became one of the best loved cowboy stars of all time, Roy Rogers.

Reading the "Funnies"

My earliest recollection of a newspaper dates from the age of four. After Dad had scanned the Evening Republican, he read the "funnies" to me. I vaguely recall the "Toonerville Trolly," a comic strip featuring funny little people in a funny little town.

In a few years I was able to comprehend the dialogue and was able to enjoy a chuckle or two while following the escapades of the "Reglar Fellers," "Pinhead and Puddinhead," "Skippy," "Felix the Cat" and the all-time favorite, "The Katzenjammer Kids."

The older members of the family were more interested in the cartoons about "Tillie the Toiler," and "Bringing up Father," featuring that lovable couple, "Jiggs and Maggie."

My attention was also being diverted away from the toddler comics to the heart-warming chapters of "Skeezix," the infant who was left on Uncle Walt's doorstep. We grew up with him in "Gasoline Alley," along with his relatives and friends.

I worried about my cartoon pals week after week but didn't know what love and devotion was until I met "Little Annie Rooney."

Annie was an orphan waif who ran away from an orphanage and its cruel caretaker, Mrs. Meany. She was pursued endlessly throughout her many travels, from the skid row of the bowery to the millionaire's mansion on nob hill.

I seemed to relate to the pretty little black-haired girl who was gifted with common sense and a fierce desire to help the under dog. Her faithful dog, "Zero," a constant companion, always warned her of impending danger.

Annie Rooney became like a sister to me and we shared our make-believe world. I don't remember the exact day that I said goodbye and can't recall if she ever found her blue bird of happiness or her pocket full of dreams. I was growing up and left my childhood in the pages of the past. I found a new love in a handsome fellow named "Tailspin Tommy." He was a tousled headed pilot who wore a leather helmet adorned with goggles and a white silk scarf. He and his sidekick, "Skeeter," barn-stormed, experiencing breath-taking adventures; they flew the "two wingers" into loop-the-loops and tail spins. Tommy was the all-American hero of the day when fliers and pilots were worshipped from afar.

But alas, Tommy was soon pushed into the background along with the out-dated propeller airplanes.

Aviation was changing into a jet age and the "funnies" had to keep abreast with the times. Along with the change a tall, dark and handsome stranger flew into my life. His name was "Smilin' Jack." Jack was a Clark Gable type of male who could make the ladies swoon with a wink. Although he was a romantic, he also taught young Americans all about the latest planes that were sketched in detail in his comic strip. We learned how to speak aviation slang, a new vocabulary spoken by the "fly boys."

During those years the characters in the comic strips played an important role among the young generation. Each member in our family found something in common with the personalities that arrived every day with the local newspaper.

We became acquainted with other cartoons when we discovered The Minneapolis Tribune and the Sioux City Journal. Their Sunday editions were filled with extra pages of fabulous colored pictures of new stars.

"I wonder if Dick Tracy will capture Prune Face," one worried brother debated while watching for Dad to bring home the Sunday edition.

"He always gets the villains in the end," Bobby assured him. He put "Steve the Tramp," "No Face," and "Flat Top" in the Big House. "I like Tarzan the best of all," brother Delmar chimed in. "I wish I could swing through the trees like he does." "I don't care what you guys think," Bobby continued. " 'Flash Gordon' and 'Buck Rogers' are smarter than any of those other people. You just wait and see, some day we will be flying in space, just like they do." "Oh baloney," the other brothers chorused, "that is really a fairy tale. Rayguns space ships, flying to the moon and other planets—you believe everything!"

Sister Evie loved the comics that showed the poor working girl, "Tillie the Toiler." So why wouldn't her favorites be "Apple Mary," "Winnie Winkle," "Ella Cinders" and that cute fashion plate, "Dixie Dugan." Dixie even offered paper dolls and cut-outs in her popular strip for the fashion-wise women of that era. Now sister Neeney who admired "brawn" instead of "beauty," chose the characters who showed spunk, who didn't take any lip. She thought "Popeye" was the greatest and was tickled pink when the pipe-smoking sailor blacked his enemies' eyes and made them see stars. She even liked spinach! "I am what I am, and that's all I yam," she often mimicked her one-eyed idol, shoving her pudgy fist under someone's nose.

Our father, who wouldn't be caught dead in a theatre, never-the-less enjoyed reading some of the strips such as "Andy Gump," "Moon Mullins," "Barney Google" and "Mutt and Jeff." He felt sorry for "Jiggs" who was always getting the worst end of it from his nagging wife "Maggie."

For some reason Mama related to the bossy, loud-mouthed "Maggie" and rolled with laughter when she saw that Maggie had again foiled her hen-pecked spouse. Just like Maggie, Mama didn't hesitate to throw a rolling pin while if angered.

"It's all right to read the funnies, but get interested in the news section as well," Mama often repeated. "You don't want to grow up being a bunch of dummies. You have to know what is going on in this big world." A newspaper was better than a history book as far as she was concerned. Mama never went past the 6th grade, but she was well informed and could discuss any issues. "If you want to know the meaning of the words, ask me," she said. Sometimes her grammar wasn't "up to par" but we understood what she was talking about.

Many of the current events of the Thirties weren't exactly good reading for young minds but we absorbed it all. Prohibition, bootlegging, gangland slayings, prostitution, gangsters and endless kidnappings, including the Lindbergh baby, that stunned the nation.

I see where there's been another kidnapping," Dad said. "A ten-year-old boy from Spokane, Washington. They want a king's ransom for his safe return." He held up the paper so we could see the picture of a bright smiling child. I read the story beneath the picture and I felt sorrow for the bereaved family. A few weeks later another photo was shown of the boy, this time lying in the blood-stained snow, murdered.

The kidnapping continued in a nation beset with greed, violence and the depressed who were turning to crime to make a livelihood. One day I read about a small girl who was found slain after being abducted. I began to be afraid and had nightmares about being treated in the same manner.

I told Mama about my fears. "Don't worry about being kidnapped," she scolded. "You're safe in South Dakota. Things like that don't happen around here. Besides, we are too poor; they only snatch the children of millionaires." (That was one consolation for being in the low income bracket.)

The F. B. I. were not only desparately trying to halt the kidnappings, they were also confronted with bank robberies that were sweeping across America. Names like Ma Barker, Karpes Gang, Baby Face Nelson, Pretty Boy Floyd and John Dillinger were in the news. Even though they were for the most part dangerous criminals who killed law men, they were idolized by some of a thrill-seeking public.

"Look here on the front page," said Mama. "Bonnie and Clyde, they robbed another bank in Kansas. Boy, they are two tough cookies. One of these days the G Men will get them." She cocked her finger as if pointing a gun.

Most of the gangsters and their gun molls were imprisoned. Some were shot down like dogs, such as Bonnie and Clyde, and John Dillinger.

A few became folk heroes and are still in books, movies and on T V screens. Today's youth look upon those early day criminals through the characterization of actors and actresses. They are glorified and portrayed as being unjustly condemned by the law.

It wasn't all blood and guts that splashed across the front pages. There were other interesting events that took place from the sidewalks of New York to the golden streets of Hollywood. There were many heroes to inspire the youth of America, including Wiley Post and Amelia Erhart, the courageous pilots who made aviation history.

We read (with a little bit of envy) about the Vanderbilts, Astors and Rockefellers who "languished" in ivory towers; of their undreamed wealth and how they spent their winters on some warm south sea isle away from the common people.

"What would they think if they had to live like we do?" I often asked Mama. "They're used to being rich, just like we are used to being poor," she answered in a matter of fact way. "The rich get rich and the poor have children. But the rest have troubles, too," she added. "It isn't all moonlight and roses."

"I could stand a few troubles if I was a millionaire," I told her, looking at a picture of some poor little rich girls making their entrance at a lavish debutante's ball.

I'm sure one of the most heart-warming events that occurred in those turbulent days was the birth of the world-famous Dionne Quintuplets. The five babies were born in obscurity, mothered by a young Canadian housewife. I scanned every newspaper and magazine to read and to gaze fondly at their pictures. I made scrapbooks to record their childhood activities.

We followed them from their first look at the outside world until they were no longer considered an oddity in a stranger than fiction happening. The five babies were showered with affection and priceless gifts from the rich and poor alike. They were taken away from their parents and literally owned by the Canadian Government. The charming little girls seemed happy in their secluded existence. Curious tourists watched their every move from behind enclosed fences and two-way mirrors. It was a fish bowl existence.

After the Quints were finally released from their sterile environment, where they were attended by nurses and doctors, they were helpless in the outside world. Soon the public learned of their unhappiness when a book was written by the Quints entitled "There Were Five." It was a revealing story about the confusion and heartache of their young lives. The name "Dionne" did fade into the yellowed pages of the newspapers and magazines for awhile, but new interest has been rekindled.

Today, collectors are paying good prices for anything that is related to the famous Dionne Quintuplets—Yvonne, Annette, Cecile, Emilie and Marie. They are again worshiped by a new generation who want to own a memento of the five little girls who were born without a separate identity.

Our family have been life-long subscribers to the hometown newspaper, "The Daily Republic." When I was growing up during the depression years it was called the "Evening Republican." At that time it was headquartered in an old building on west third street, next to the Carnegie Library. This widely circulated newspaper was owned by the Ronalds.

I always had a "hankering" to be a reporter on some city newspaper. How exciting to be able to meet the deadline with a "scoop" about some event that would shake up the country.

Mama loved to read the advice column that was written by the famed Dorothy Dix (fore-runner to Ann Landers). My mother liked to poke fun at the society page where only names of the local church and club women were mentioned. I'm sure she secretly wished that she belonged to the "upper crust" of the town and was not just a poor working man's wife. "Listen to this, my dawlings," she drawled, impersonating a socialite, "Madames Davison and Beckwith are having an afternoon tea in the rose garden this coming Tuesday at two P. M."

"There is to be a piano recital in the home of Mrs. T. H. Burns, Sunday evening. Students of Miss Olga Applegate will present music."

Mr. and Mrs. David Farnsworth hosted a sixteenth birthday party for their daughter, Elizabeth who will be sailing for Europe next month. "Do you think your name will ever be in the society page?" I asked when her act was over and the laughter died away. "I doubt it," she answered wistfully. "The only place my name will ever be found will be in the obituary column. I'm just an old pebble on the beach. Well, maybe I'll get my reward in heaven where money doesn't count."

Mama was right about her prediction. Her housework was never recognized as a fruitful achievement, and no one ever suspected that she was indeed as artistic and intelligent as the society ladies of the town. No one, that is, except a few close friends, her relatives and me!

Tribute to the W. P. A.

For the people who lived through the "Depression" the W. P. A. was well known. President Franklin Roosevelt initiated this new government program to provide help for the needy and the unemployed across the nation. Projects included professional service divisions and the maintenance and repair of roads, highways and sewage disposal plants. Dams, schools and court houses were constructed with the assistance of government funds. To save the land from future drought, thousands of trees were planted in shelter belts. They still stand today in silent memoriam of the dust bowl days.

Any adult member of a qualified household could apply for the many jobs and careers which were offered. Women were trained to work in the sewing rooms, where thousands of garments were made and shipped to all parts of the country. There were also mattress, furniture repair and upholstery shops where similar skills could be learned.

The National Youth Administration was designed to insure better futures for the youth of America. Young people obtained such jobs as city park supervisors and jobs in nursery schools. These nursery schools later developed into our public kindergartens. My sister, Evelyn, was an NYA employee, and I recall her monthly salary was thirteen dollars, but it went a long way in buying power.

Young boys were entered in early type vocationl-technical schools. A large steel building was constructed where motor repair and welding were taught to many future mechanics and machinists. Under the direction of Andre Boratko, the Federal Arts projects helped aspiring young artists, who designed and painted the murals in the courthouse and the art center. These paintings can still be seen in the lobby of the courthouse.

The former Carnegie Library has been renamed the "Oscar Howe Cultural Center" for the planner of this project and now a world famous Indian artist. His able assistant and fellow artist, William Lackey, became a syndicated cartoonist. Andre Boratko is now a successful portrait and mural painter in California.

Miss Ethel Dowdell, later to become Mrs. George Abild, was the state director of the professional and service projects for its duration of ten years. When the W. P. A. was phased out, she became a director of the U. S. O. in the South and she was also an instructor at Notre Dame Junior College during her long and useful career.

This energetic lady now makes her home in Mitchell and is not about to rest on her laurels. Her many interests are in the arts and literary free lance work. There is no end to her challenging outlets. Bicentennial research was her latest study, also the composing of a bicentennial song. I salute this lady for a life of dedicated concern for her fellow man.

Two more Mitchell women were very active in the professional and service divisions.

Irene Broderick was the director of the recreational division of the arts and projects in the city parks. The bookmobile and the mending of books was a branch of the library assistance project, and this was supervised by Eunice Navin.

People from all walks of life were sought to keep the wheels of rejuvenation moving. It would take many skills and know-how to bring the country out of the worst depression in years.

Dad's painting business came to a standstill during the worst years of the depression. Many houses in need of paint and repair were left to deteriorate. The jobs he obtained painting oil stations became few and far between. His health was also failing. The fumes from the paints, varnishes and murescos were infecting his lungs.

He became employed as a W. P. A. worker and obtained

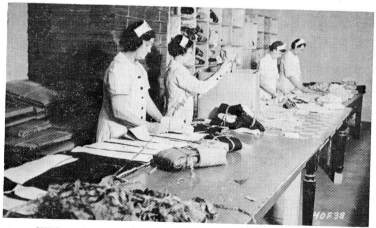

WPA workers preparing packages for overseas (Dora Creech, Florence Royalty, Sarah Andrews, Myrtle Wold).

an easier job in a mattress factory. There were numerous other duties, such as maintenance in the schools and packing garments at the sewing rooms. His last job was distributing commodities at the county store, which was located in the basement of the new courthouse, built in 1936.

Much needed foods were shipped to Mitchell, Beans, rice, dried peas, corn meal, flour, sugar, prunes, raisins, powdered milk, and lard were sacked, stacked, and placed on the many shelves. People arrived on foot, pulling coaster wagons and carts. A few lucky ones rode in cars and pickups. The commodities were handed out almost as fast as they arrived.

Fresh fruit in the form of apples, grapefruit and oranges was an extra treat for the hundreds of W. P. A. recipients. Mama used to change her hiding places where she stored the fruit and the best spot was beneath her brass bed. She didn't want us kids to overindulge.

The W. P. A. sewing rooms were located in the basement of the newly constructed armory building, next to the Corn Palace. Clothing from the W. P. A. sewing rooms were also dispensed from the county store. Garments were packed in the many cubicles throughout the store. There were overalls, pants, denim shirts and jackets for the men. For the women and girls there was a large assortment of blouses, slips, night-gowns and bloomers.

The clothing left a lot to be desired. A size numbered as ten would more likely be as large as a size fourteen and the material of the dresses was of the cheapest grade. The buttons were either too large or too small for the button holes. The dresses for girls were sewn in plain, drab prints, more to the style of older women.

I disliked wearing these clothes to school because a few of the girls from moneyed families laughed and poked fun at me. They knew my frocks were from the "House of W. P. A."

The pick and shovel crews of the W. P. A. projects were everywhere in this area. Men were hauled to the work sites in county trucks or a car pool (if their neighbor was lucky enough to own a vehicle). The pick and shovel were their trademark as these tools helped dislodge tons of dirt, gravel and clay from the earth.

These workers were often criticized for being stupid and lazy because they didn't have skills. They were accused of "leaning on the shovel." I recall a favorite joke about town, which was particularly true. A W. P. A. worker suffered a heart attack and died on one of the work sites. It was said that the undertaker made three trips before he found the right body.

The Works Progress Administration and Public Works Administration were all included in President Roosevelt's New Deal program. It was heavily criticized by the rich as a waste of money, good only for the free loaders and bums. However, this vital shot in the arm steered the nation out from the depths of the great Depression into a new frontier. Our family and millions of others were grateful for this helping hand.

The Welfare Lady

During the depression years there were numerous agencies established to provide aid to needy families. The Works Progress Administration (WPA) was one nationally sponsored program to help the millions of unemployed citizens.

My dad was employed by the WPA. His jobs were numerous, including working in the mattress factory and in the sewing rooms. When the depression began to dissipate, he clerked at the county store that was located in the basement of the courthouse. Because of his poor health (a double hernia and hardening of the arteries) he was exempted from the more rigorous jobs of tree planting and the other construction jobs of building public buildings and roads. His monthly check of $48.00 didn't help much in a family of ten people. The investigators visited our home a few times a year to find out if the family was still in need of federal assistance. "Here come those investigators again," Mama always complained as we watched the well-dressed case workers getting out of their fancy cars. "Maybe they think we bought a new car or ice box." The brown manilla portfolios were placed on the dining room table and the sheets of questionnaires were then read to Mama. "Was there any added income during the last six months?" "No." "Has there been any new furniture purchased?" "No." "Do you own a car?" "No." "Are there any children over sixteen working?" "Yes." "Do they contribute to the household?" "Yes."

After all the embarrassing questions were asked, the investigator often checked through the house to see if Mama was telling the truth. I always felt sorry for her because I knew she was proud and that pride was being hurt by the handouts that she had to accept from these total strangers, who acted as if the money was coming from their pockets.

"Everything seems to be in order and you will be eligible to receive another six months relief. Just sign your name here." I disliked the well-groomed lady, acting as though she was better than Mama, taking one last look around before she departed. "Some day when I get rich I'll buy Mama everything her heart desires." I promised myself. That pledge was never fulfilled.

Placing a piece of cardboard in our shoes often insured many weeks of extra wear. When a hole was worn through, another piece was inserted. We all tried to save on shoe leather, even by walking barefoot in the summer. Most of our clothing, dresses, underskirts, pajamas, overalls and some jackets were given to us through the WPA sewing rooms, but left a lot to be desired. The dresses were made in drab unstylish material and never seemed to fit properly. The men's and boys' shirts and jackets resembled prison attire. The other kids at school often poked fun at our "peasant" clothing. "Just grin and bear it till things get better," Mama encouraged us when one of us refused to wear a dress or pants to school. "It's not a sin to be poor."

"Why don't you go up to the city hall and see the welfare lady?" a neighbor asked Mama one day. "She buys extra clothing, shoes and sometimes overshoes for my kids." "I just don't know how I'm going to buy school clothes for seven kids this fall," sighed Mama. "With Dad laid up and all I just might give it a try."

But Mama lost her nerve and her pride wouldn't let her beg again so my sister, Evelyn, volunteered to take us four youngest children to see the welfare lady.

Everyone knew where the city hall was located, one block west of Main on Second Street. "Just go downstairs and turn to your left and you'll find Mrs. Williams in her office," Mr. Kirkpatrick, a friendly policeman, told us. What we didn't know was that she was also a police matron who was called

First City Hall Building, built in 1903

in when teen-aged girls got into trouble. Escorting delinquents to the State Training School was another duty of hers. (I was always afraid of anyone connected with the law.)

We timidly approached her cubby-hole office in one corner of the spacious waiting room. The door was suddenly pulled opened just when Evie raised her hand to knock. "What do you children want?" she asked without a flicker of a smile on her face. "Mama sent us here to ask for some clothes so we can go to school," stammered my big sister, trying to hide the fear in her voice. I felt a lump rise in my throat and butterflies in my stomach as I looked into her cold eyes behind her polished spectacles. I was becoming ashamed of looking for "hand outs" and I just wanted to run back home and hide from the world.

"Well, I was just on my way to a business meeting but you can come in and I'll see if you really need anything," she hurriedly explained. She removed her fur coat and sat down in a swivel oak chair. Shuffling some papers on a roll-top desk she scanned a long list of names.

We kids sat huddled on a small bench while Sister Evelyn told of our needs. My eyes began to wander around the cluttered room. It smelled like moth balls. The odor seemed to be coming from paper bags of clothing on some shelves. "She will probably give those used clothes to us," I whispered to Neeney when Mrs. Williams turned her back. I tried to admire the pretty green plants in the grimy basement window.

"I don't know if you children or your parents are aware of our limited amount of funds, but I am only alllowed so much money in my budget and I must not waste any of the taxpayers' money." As I listened to the lecture I again had the feeling that we were committing a crime and might as well be placed behind bars by this "police matron." The woman who was supposed to decide our needs seemed more like a prison warden who wouldn't care if our feet were bare.

I tried not to notice the wart on her upper lip and the red tint in the gray thinning hair. She looked directly at me and said, "I'm going to have to study this request. I'll let your mother know by next week what I decide." Four deflated youngsters walked out of the welfare office and back into a summer sun. None of us felt like talking as we headed for home across the railroad tracks.

The next week a penny post card arrived in the mail informing us that more money had been appropriated for the welfare department to help the needy families buy school clothes.

"Do we have to go back there again?" we asked Mama. "That lady doesn't like us. She's an old battle axe," Bobby commented.

"Police matrons just act tough. It's their way. Just think, you're going to have some nice new shoes, maybe those patent leather kind you've always wanted."

So, with a little more confidence we kids made the trip back to the city hall again. I felt apprehensive inside the immense stone building where people from all walks of life congregated—lawyers and judges, walking up the flights of stairs to the court rooms, to the townspeople and farmers who came on business. The dingy concrete walls were scribbled with names, pictures and dirty words. It smelled of stale tobacco smoke and the brass spitoons at the bottom of the stairways were splattered with tobacco juice.

The police headquarters were in the basement as well as the jail, where prisoners were locked up and fed only bread and water (we were told). We avoided the open door where we could see policemen standing near a high, desk-like counter. "Look at that big gun on his hip and that black thing sticking in his back pocket. It is a billy club," brother Bobby whispered to us. "When I grow up I'm going to be a policeman and boss everybody." (Little did we know that he would become a policeman in the Mitchell Police Department.)

We walked across the corridor to the office of Mrs. Williams, this time the door was open. She was sitting in a chair, her lap filled with colored balls of yarn. Two long sharp-looking needles were moving back and forth in a steady rhythm.

"Hello, Mrs. Williams," my brother Bobby greeted her cheerfully. "We got your card in the mail yesterday so here we are." I was expecting another curt conversation but she smiled and placed her knitting in a wicker basket. Mama always said that Bobby could melt a heart of stone with his beautiful brown eyes and his grin.

"You children wait out there and I'll get my coat. We have to go over to the J. C. Penney store to buy the clothing," she told us, while stuffing her purse with slips of paper.

"She's not so bad after all but I wish she would let us go by ourselves. People will know that we're with a welfare lady and getting our stuff free," brother Buddy complained.

The black patent leather shoes were on my mind as we four children followed the welfare lady out of the back door to the J. C. Penney store.

The store was decorated with colorful posters. Pictured with pencils, books and other school paraphernalia. "Scrappy," a cartoon character of a small boy, smiled down from the walls. Every counter was stacked high and bulging from the assortments of clothing for the back-to-school children. The clerks were busy helping the customers selecting some of the best merchandise that money could buy. Bradley Young, the manager of this well known store, worked right along side the clerks. Everyone knew him for his contributions to the town.

We followed our benefactor, Mrs. Williams, through the aisles until we came to the mens' and boys' clothing section. Overhead the money changers were gliding back and forth on wire tracks from the clerks to the cashier in the small office in the balcony.

"Hello, Mrs. Williams. What can we do for you today?" asked a handsome dark-haired young man, leaning over a pile of flannel shirts. "And who are your little friends?"

"These are four Barnes kids, and they need clothes for school, so we will start with the boys first. Remember now, nothing fancy, just cheap but long-wearing apparel." "How much are those overall pants with the copper rivets?"

While my brothers were being outfitted with their overalls, blue denim work shirts, wool socks and long underwear, I sneaked away to the womens' and girls' department next to the display of shoes.

The racks of pretty cotton frocks were ablaze with the colors of autumn. There were soft cuddly sweaters, some with embroidered flowers which were being chosen by little girls accompanied by their mothers. One of the better dressed girls, who was my classmate, asked, "Is that your mother coming there with your sister?"

"Oh no, that's my Aunt Mable who is buying our school clothes," I lied. I was hoping that her mother wasn't acquainted with the welfare lady and wishing that they would leave before they learned that our purchases were being paid for by charity.

"Let's see now, the shoes come next. Sit over there on those chairs." Mrs. Williams directed us to a row of hard back chairs. Boxes of footwear were stacked in neat rows all around the room. "What kind of shoes do you like?" the clerk asked me agreeably as he slipped off my worn sandal, exposing a large hole in the bottom. Before I had a chance to answer, the welfare lady snapped, "Those black oxfords on that table will be all right and they are priced within our budget." My heart sank. The clearance table held all the odds and ends of shoes that no one else wanted. "I think that brown pair will fit this other girl," she said, lifting a plain, masculine type shoe off the table.

I tried to act grateful to have a new pair of shoes after the clerk had them laced and told me to walk a few steps. "They're nice," I told the clerk, but my eyes were looking at the pretty patent leather slippers hanging out of their box on the top shelf.

"Do you children have any overshoes?" we were then asked. "No," we all replied in unison. My spirits rose. Maybe she will buy me a pair of those fleece-lined "Betty" boots with a zipper. But no such luck! We girls were given the black rubber four buckle overshoes.

These children tell me that they have a long walk to school so I think the two girls should have a few pairs of underwear and long stockings," she told the clerk at the lingerie department. "If you would buy me a snow suit, I wouldn't need the long-legged underwear and the stockings," I bravely spoke up, watching the bulky underwear being examined by the two women.

"I wonder if these poor families appreciate what the welfare and charities do for them," sighed Mrs. Williams to the clerk. "You'd think they would be more than satisfied. Wrap up the underwear and those dark brown stockings. I think that about takes care of it till next spring. Now you children take good care of these clothes because that's all you're going to get."

Mrs. Williams quickly made her exit and left us standing there, loaded down with our boxes and packages. As we moved down the narrow aisle toward the rear of the store, Mr. Murl Messerli, the kindly clerk, rushed over to hold the heavy door open for us. "If it were up to me, you kids could have had the clothes and shoes that you really wanted. Bye now."

"Bye," I answered as I carried my heavy package down the street, trying to keep up with my sister and two brothers.

"I am thankful for these clothes," I thought to myself. "They will keep us from freezing to death when winter comes."

"Hey, you guys, wait for me," I shouted to the rest of my family who were turning the corner by the library.

"Hurry up, slow poke, we haven't got all day," one of them answered. "The sun is going down already and Mama will be worrying about us."

The thought of the impending darkness that would soon envelope the footpath along the Round House pond prompted me to hurry. Mama was waiting on the back porch for us and I could smell the aroma of goulash simmering on the cook stove. "Wait till you see what the welfare lady gave us," I told her as we all crowded through the door.

Family Tree

During the years when I was growing up, large families were in the majority, especially among the poor who accepted each birth as a way of life.

It was not uncommon for a family to have between ten and sixteen children. Planned parenthood and abortion were almost unheard of. Very few mothers ventured outside of the home to seek a career. Their job was to bear numerous children until the change of life period began.

The neighborhoods that we lived in were usually overcrowded households but always seemed to expand for one more mouth to feed. I used to listen to Mama and the neighbor women gossip about some woman who was in the family way, or about an unfortunate teen-aged girl who was unmarried but pregnant, a fate worse than death. The girl became a disgrace to the family and almost forced to leave town. A few understanding, compassionate parents allowed their daughters to remain at home and helped them rear the child without a father. But her reputation was ruined and it was hard to live down a love affair that produced a baby with no legal father. "No matter who your father is, you're always your mother's child," was a phrase often heard.

Our family consisted of five boys and three girls, one child died in infancy and another by miscarriage. Mama often talked about a son named Russel who died at the age of six months, from the ravages of pneumonia.

There was a span of five and six years between the older brothers and sisters and us three younger members, brother Bobby, sister Neeney and myself. We were the late comers. Yet there was another addition with the birth of brother Jimmy. Mama was already forty-one years of age and my dad was past his prime at fifty-three.

Among an assortment of brothers and sisters there wasn't much physical resemblance between any of us. Some had features and hair coloring similar to that of our parents. It was evenly divided among the blue and brown eyes and the blonds and brunettes. We kids often argued about which side of the family was the best looking. Since I was one of the blue-eyes everyone decided that I took after my dad. Mama always told me that I was the picture of her sister, Theresa, who died in her teens.

We knew our heritage was German from our mother's

ancestry, and German, French and Irish from Dad's family tree, but Dad liked to tell everyone that he was a full-blooded Irishman. Sometimes he joined his Irish buddies to celebrate St. Patrick's Day at the saloon.

Two of my brothers were black-haired with eyes the color of burnished copper. They were often teased about having a little Indian blood in their veins.

I don't remember too much about my oldest brother, Donald, during my toddler years, only that I resented his bossing me around and tattling to Mama when sister Neeney and I played in the mud puddles or strayed from the confines of our own back yard. He often carried us, screaming and kicking to Mama who awaited with a switch to use on us for being disobedient. He became almost like a straw boss or a warden to make sure the rest of the family walked the line. It caused resentment among the other brothers and many arguments erupted because of his self appointed authority. When some of us tried to gang up on him he tossed us aside as if we were rag dolls. He was very strong. I soon learned it didn't do any good to complain to Mama or Dad and it was best to stay out of his way and not to ruffle his feathers.

Don grew up to be one of the most popular boys in high school. His athletic abilities gained him the respect and admiration of the whole town. Because he was handsome, he had more girl friends than you could "shake a stick at." This adulation caused him to become conceited and the rest of us had to give in to his every wish. It was difficult for me to practice brotherly love.

The second in line, brother Delmar, or Delly, was as different from Don as daylight from dark. Although he resembled our mother in appearance, his kindly personality was the same as Dad's. There wasn't a mean bone in his body. He became our protector and tried to keep peace in the family when squabbles broke out between us. There were many times when he got the worst end of it in a confrontation with his older brother.

"You big bully, why don't you pick on somebody your own size!" We younger kids hurled our insults at Don as he stalked away from Delly who was more often than not lying on the ground, nursing his wounds.

"He's just like an old mother hen, looking after her chicks," Mama often said of Delly when he searched the neighborhood, rounding up us kids to make sure we were all home before dark. He wasn't afraid of work and at an early age contributed most of his earnings to help out with the household expenses.

"Guess what, Ma, I got a job as a paper boy at the Evening Republican," he excitedly shouted one afternoon. "I'll help you pay for your new washing machine. And next summer I'm going to caddy at the Municipal golf course."

Delly kept his savings in an old sock and always loaned money to anyone who was in need of a candy bar or a ticket to the local movie house. The other children in the neighborhood often came to him for advice or just to listen to his funny stories and jokes.

He continued to pay "board" all through his high school years from his jobs as a pin-setter in Scharnweber's recreation parlors. "Bringing home the bacon" had real meaning for him. An extra sack of groceries was often set on the kitchen table, with packages of gum and candy for his little brothers and sisters. During all of my growing years there was never a harsh word spoken between us. A good relationship existed between a big brother and a kid sister.

Evelyn, or Evie, was six years old when I was born and I'm sure she helped out as a little mother in the care and feeding of her baby sister. From my earliest recollection she was either standing over a sink filled with dishes, sweeping the hard wood floors or hanging out the laundry. Since she was the eldest girl in a family of eight rambunctious youngsters, it was up to her to help keep the large noisy household in hand, especially during the times when Mama had to stay in bed due to her chronic back ailments and her bouts of bronchitis and pleurisy.

Evelyn liked to keep things neat and everything in its proper place. She would become infuriated if anyone walked across a not-yet-dry kitchen floor. A few of the brothers felt the wrath of her temper when she whacked them over the head with a damp mop. I, too, wanted to be as efficient as my big sister, so happily volunteered my services whenever she needed an extra hand. She often rewarded me by making a batch of fudge, and even letting me lick the pan.

The one chore that I disliked was helping to take the clothes off the lines during cold weather. I had to stand on tip toe to reach the clothes pins, unsnap them, and then pry loose the frozen articles of clothing. My hands would be numb by the time we reached the warmth of the kitchen.

The frozen overalls were propped behind the cook stove;

dresses, underwear and shirts placed on a wooden expandable rack and the bedding was hung on ropes strung across the kitchen. With all that moisture from evaporation in the house it's a wonder we didn't all come down with respiratory problems—or humidity may have been good for us.

Our limited wardrobes were ironed on the kitchen table. An old sheet served as an ironing pad. I thought it was fun when I was allowed to press the flat pieces, including pillow cases, Mama's aprons and handkerchiefs.

The dishwashing chore was endless and again I helped Evie wash and dry the mountains of dirty dishes, pots and pans. When the cooking kettles became encrusted from the spilled food, the heat and the smoke from the open coal-burning stove, we cleaned them by rubbing the bottoms across a pile of ashes or gravel. (We had never heard of a scouring pad.)

There was no need for a vacuum cleaner because there were no carpets on our hardwood floors. We girls scrubbed them on our hands and knees with rags and stiff-bristled brushes. The linoleum rugs only needed a light going over with a hand mop. The cobwebs that gathered on the ceilings and walls were swept down constantly. There wasn't much we could do about the black smoke that escaped from the two coal and wood burning stoves throughout the winter.

So keeping ahead of the housework was a never-ending chore for my industrious sister who never received an allowance or a thank-you from the rest of the family. It was only her duty.

When we younger girls blossomed into our pre-teen years it was Evie who tried to explain about the birds and the bees with her limited knowledge about sex. Somehow parents expected children to mature without knowing anything about relationships between boys and girls. That subject was taboo. I was even shocked to learn that beginning between the ages of eleven and fourteen my sister and I would have to wear something extra once a month. Mama never discussed the menstruation periods that came when a young girl changed into a woman. It was almost something to be ashamed of.

Although Evie allowed me to tag along with her to the movies, band concerts and gab-fests with her girl friends, that time did arrive when I had to stay behind. The bashful beaus began to appear at our door and she left me without a backward glance. I was jealous of her many boy friends and afraid she would marry and move far away.

"You just wait. Your turn will come," consoled Mama when she caught me peeking through the lace curtains as a suitor opened the car door and Evie settled down in a snazzy roadster with a rumble seat. "You should be glad that she is so popular."

Evie was blessed with soft brown eyes and wavy hair. Her complexion was olive-toned like Mama's. She was a very attractive girl except for one thing, her white teeth protruded. Sometimes she was brought to tears by a remark from a member of the family or an uncouth neighbor who called her "bucktooth" or by saying, "I bet you can eat corn through a picket fence." Braces would have ended many years of embarrassment for her but who could afford something so costly during the hard times?

Evie was still a picture of beauty every time Mama helped her dress for a dance date. Her luxuriant hair was set in the latest finger wave. A dab of rouge and lip stick added the right glow to her flawless complexion.

"Are my seams straight?" she shyly asked, turning around, revealing her shapely legs encased in a wispy pair of silk stockings. "You don't think my dress is too short, do you?"

"Now don't worry, you look fine," answered Mama, while she tied the sash on her flowered chiffon dress. "Just don't hump over. Stand up straight. You're not too fat. There's a lot of girls who would love to have your bust line. You will be the belle of the ball."

And she was. Her dancing partners were numerous. She was known as one of the best dancers around our part of the county.

It was usually around midnight when I would be awakened by the soft purring of a car driving into the yard. There would be the slam of a car door and I knew that Evie had come home from her night at the ball, just like Cinderella!

Mama was awake, too, and I could hear them discussing the evening's festivities. I often crept downstairs and eavesdropped on their hushed conversation.

"Well, did you have a good time? Did you have a lot of dances? Did you meet any new fellows?"

"Oh, yes," replied a tired young lady. "I danced with boys named Van Overshield, Jeming, Lewis, Hohn, and a guy in a blue suit, but I can't remember his name. And I've got a date for next Saturday night."

I was happy for her, yet a little envious because I now felt like an outsider. She was too involved with her good times to worry about me.

"Do you want to go with me and my boy friend to the wedding dance at Ethan tonight?" Evie asked, one day out of a clear blue sky.

"Oh, yes!" I cried. I knew and Mama knew that there wasn't a better chaperone in the whole wide world than my big sister Evie.

Bernard Alvin, nicknamed Buddy or whitey, because of his very light hair, was the fourth eldest child in the family and became tagged as the middle one. He was too young to have much in common with the older brothers and too mature for us little kids. It placed him in a position as a loner.

"That boy is stubborn as a mule and he'll never give an inch," Dad often commented when Buddy got into a scrap with another brother or neighborhood bully.

"He can sure stand on his own two feet. He will never take a back seat for anyone," Mama proudly answered. She wanted all of us to be tough and independent and to roll with the punches.

"The other boys call him Blinky and Four Eyes," I told Mama, trying to get into the conversation. Because of a pink eye infection at the age of six months, he was forced to wear glasses at an early age.

"Well, those bullies better think twice before they start calling him names because your brother can make them knuckle down and holler uncle," replied Mama, banging her rolling pin across a floured piece of pie dough. "He will go a long way in this old world because he's smart and ambitious. He makes just about as much money as the older boys at the golf course. No, he will never stay in this one horse town. I have a feeling that he will leave home at an early age to seek his fortune."

"Do you think I'll leave home at an early age, too?" I sadly inquired while watching her place the bulging apple pie in the oven.

"Oh, no. You will be here with me forever. Daughters don't wander very far. Besides, who's going to take care of me when I'm old and gray?"

That ended the conversation and I was happy with the thought of remaining in the safe confines of my home but

122

was also troubled about my brother, Buddy, who wanted to spread his wings and leave the nest at the top of the hill.

"Buddy" and I shared many good times together and there was always a bond of love and respect between us but his yearning to be free of family ties and a hankering to escape the confines of a rural town made him leave home at the age of seventeen.

I shall always carry the memory of the day he bid us all adieu. He placed his cheap cardboard suitcase on the back steps with his purple and gold school jacket lying on top.

"Well, this is it. Bye, Ma," he said, trying to keep a stiff upper lip. "I'll drop a card as soon as I get to Coeur d' Alene, Idaho. I'll look up Uncle Phil and maybe I can stay there till I get a job in the lumber mill. I can take care of myself around those lumber jacks. And don't worry, I'm not going to drink booze."

"I'm not going to worry," Mama lied, trying to conceal her emotions. "You just take care of yourself."

"And you, Kitty Cat," he said, pointing to me, "are going to write me letters and tell me the latest news back here. You can write better than the other girls."

"I will," I promised, following the family out into the yard where Buddy's friend waited in a loaded-down jalopy.

"Goodbye, goodbye," we all waved as the car backed out of the yard and headed toward the highway.

"Well, he's gone," is all that Mama said as she hurried back into the house, but I knew that her heart was saddened and she wanted to hide her tears behind closed doors. One of her birds had flown away and left an empty spot on the roost.

Robert William, or Bobby, was only one year older than me. The neighbor kids called us the Bobbsy twins because we were inseparable. I copy-catted my brother whether he was doing a good deed or up to some mischievous scheme. If a spanking was needed, we both got it at the same time. To escape punishment we often scampered underneath Mama's big brass bed but prodding with a broomstick soon brought us out. While Neeney and I tried to hold back the tears, Bobby's sobbing made the neighbors wonder if someone was being killed.

"I swear that child has bawled from the day he was born. He will cry at the drop of a hat. I don't know what will happen when he goes to school. He will have to learn to fight his own battles," Mama complained to Dad, who thought she was making a mountain out of a mole hill.

"I'll help him," sister Neeney quickly replied, doubling up her pudgy fist. "I'll poke those mean boys right in the nose."

"Little girls aren't supposed to fist-fight with boys," Mama answered. "It's a good thing Buddy will be on the same school ground."

Mama's anxiety about Bobby's "fraidy cat" personality was soon dissolved when her dire predictions didn't come true. He used his wits and schemed to get along with the school children, even a few bullies. Talking his way out of a bad situation often kept him from getting a black eye or having his nose pushed into the dirt.

"Well, I'll have to admit that Bobby is the best looking one out of the bunch. With that grin and those dark cow eyes he can melt a heart of stone," Mama bragged. "The teachers all like him and he is chosen to act and sing in most of the school programs."

We all were very proud when Bobby turned on the charm to the delight of the faculty and parents during the various festivities at Eugene Field, our "Alma Mater."

There was one time that I recall when Bobby's persuasive nature didn't help him one bit and he had to suffer the consequences, all because of a brass bed.

Mama's huge brass bed, adorned with large balls on each corner post, was her pride and joy. She kept it polished to a gleaming lustre. It also served as storage space beneath the heavy coiled springs.

"Who in the hell stole the brass balls off of my bed? I can't believe it!" I heard her shriek from the bedroom one morning.

We all raced to see what had happened. The once magnificent bed looked just ordinary without the poster ornaments. Who would do such a thing to the only good piece of furniture in the house?

"You don't suppose one of the boys took the balls and sold them for junk?" Dad queried, placing his hand on the bed post. "All the kids around here have been pounding up tea kettles, pots and pans and anything they can get their hands on.

"Well, I'm going to find out right now and everyone of

those boys is going to get a licking to make sure the guilty one is punished," raged Mama.

"Who do you think done it?" I asked my sister.

"I know it was Bobby. I saw him sneak into the bedroom this morning when Mama was visiting Aunt Carrie. He was carrying a hammer and a pair of pliers, but I'm not going to tattle," Neeney whispered back. "She would half kill him."

After a few minutes of the third degree on the brothers, Bobby stepped forward and admitted to the theft.

"I just wanted some extra money to buy you a birthday present," he grinned, trying to break down Mama's icy countenance.

"Don't you try to soft soap me," she fired back. "Where are those balls? My bed is ruined without those pretty ornaments."

"Down at the junk yard, pounded to a pulp," he answered, mounting fear in his voice.

Grabbing Bobby by the arm and throwing him over her well padded knee she proceeded to give him the licking of his life. The rest of us raced out of the house so we wouldn't hear his cries of pain. In a few minutes it was all over and a tearful Bobby emerged from the back door holding one hand over his rear. Neeney and I tried our best to console him while listening to his threats to run away.

"I'll run away and never come back. Then she will be sorry," he sobbed. "She's the meanest mother in the world."

"Be quiet, here comes Mama," Neeney whispered. "Maybe you're going to get it again; I think she's still mad."

"How would you kids like to have a nice slice of freshly baked bread with butter and jelly?" she asked. "Come on, Bobby, that means you, too." Mama was no longer indignant.

Bobby meekly followed the rest of us back into the house and sat down at the table. There weren't many words spoken as we chewed our food, only glancing at Mama and Bobby whose tear-stained face finally broke into a grin. (Mama was forgiven.)

"Can I have another piece of that good bread?"

"You sure can," smiled Mama, feeling somewhat remorseful about the spanking. But she was a firm believer in the old adage, "Spare the rod and spoil the child."

It is hard to describe the next child born one year after Bobby—because it was me.

"How did you ever get a name like Dolores?"

"It's a Spanish name, isn't it?" I often heard relatives and friends ask my mother. "How come she doesn't have a German name like Hilda or Johanna?"

"I named her after one of my favorite movie stars, Dolores Del Rio, that beautiful Mexican actress. And she was born on the eleventh of May under the sign of Taurus the Bull."

No wonder I grew up loving chili and Spanish music. I thought my name was pretty but Mama and the rest of the family always called me Lorsey or Kitty Cat. I loved to hear Mama tell about how tiny I was when I was a babe in my cradle.

"Why, she was so tiny and frail, all you could see were those two large blue cat-eyes, so I named her Kitty Cat. She is so shy and sensitive and thinks I don't pay enough attention to her, but I just don't have the time to cater to three small children with another on the way."

I was jealous of my little sister, Neeney, who "hogged" Mama's lap in the large rocking chair while I stood on the runners waiting for my turn to be coddled and fussed over.

About the only time she placed her hands on me was to brush the snarls from my hair or when she gave me a "spit" bath. I often felt she didn't love me as much as the other kids. And that was the reason I clung to my Dad for the affection that I couldn't receive from my mother.

"I think she's her daddy's girl," everyone commented.

SISTER NEENEY

"Are they twins?" This question was asked of Mama about her two small daughters who looked to be the same age. Being dressed alike from head to toe made us look like twins.

"No, Norma Jean is a year younger than Dolores, but is the same size and maybe a few pounds heavier. Dolores just forgot to grow." This response always brought a chuckle from the inquiring strangers. Sometimes I felt that I was the younger because Neeney was the stronger and most of the time had her own way. If she wanted something that belonged to me, she would scream until I gave it to her. When Dad brought home a sack of candy it was Neeney who got the lion's share. He soon tried to remedy the situation by buying two smaller penny sacks and then dividing it fair and square.

"Now you must learn to share with your sister. It isn't nice to hog everything," he tried to explain to her. "If you're not good, I won't let you have any more piggy-back rides or take you up town with me. I'll just take Kitty Cat."

This oft repeated lecture pacified her for a short time, and then she was back rummaging through my box of toys, tossing them about the room.

I always worried that she would "kill" my dolls by pulling off an arm, leg or even their heads. To protect them I carried them with me everywhere. It wasn't until she emerged from the toddler stage that we developed a better relationship. Also, I was beginning to find other little girls in the neighborhood to play with that suited my shy personality.

"I think those two kids have talent," one of our neighbors told Mama, after listening to us lisping through our version of "Mary Lou." "Too bad you can't afford to give them tap dancing lessons. Wouldn't they look cute in those little short dresses like the kids wear in the movies? You should teach them to harmonize. Who knows, in a few years from now— Hollywood, they could make you rich."

It wasn't long before Mama was coaching Neeney and me for our debut. "Now listen to me sing this song and when you have it down pat, I'll show you how to harmonize with the melody." Over and over the three of us sang while the older brothers and sisters listened and made comments.

"I think Lorsey should sing the high part and Neeney can handle the low part," Mama decided.

After many more weeks of pain-staking sessions we were ready to be heard by the relatives and close friends. "O.K., kids, let's hear you sing 'I'm a Poor Little Girlie' for Aunt Carrie and Uncle Pete," who happened to be our first audience.

Our voices blended into perfect harmony and then the giggling started. Mama was embarrassed by our undignified behavior.

"All right, let's start all over again," Mama said, giving us a warning signal with a glare.

"But Neeney makes me laugh," I protested, trying to muffle another snicker.

127

"Then turn your back to her," was the simple reply. "O.K., here we go again. I'm a Poor Little Girlie, my Mama's far away." Our mother sang along with us on the first stanza and then we knew there had better not be any more foolishness.

"And my daddy's a drunkard, and won't buy me no
    bread,
As I sit by the window and hear the music play,
It sounds like my mother, but she is far away."

"Oh, that was so beautiful," sighed Aunt Carrie, brushing a tear from her eye. "Josephine, you're some music teacher. Why, I had no idea they were so good."

"Here, kids," Uncle Pete smiled while he dug into his coin purse, "is a nickel for each one of you. Go get yourself an ice cream cone."

"Gee, just think of all the money we're going to make," I told my sister as we ran to the corner grocery store.

"Yeah, we can buy all the pop and candy in town."

"We will do O.K. if we don't laugh or get nervous."

"I'll remember, don't worry."

"Next week we're going to learn a new song called 'Sweet Jennie Lee From Sunny Tennessee.' I hope that one won't be so sad," I sighed.

"I sure wish Mama would teach us a happy song!"

JAMES PATRICK OR JIMMY

"If it's a boy I'm going to name him James after my brother, Jim," Dad said to Mama when she told him she was going to have another baby. "And I like the name Patrick. It's a good old Irish name. James Patrick it will be."

"I was so sure I wouldn't have any more children and I'm not a kid any more. I'll be forty-one years old in October," I overheard Mama tell her sister, Aunt Carrie.

"I wish it were me," Carrie sadly replied. "I always wanted more children after little Margaret died. How I wish I had a daughter but it's too late now. Now don't worry about what the neighbors think. There are women a lot older than you having babies. Just think what a comfort they will be when you get old and gray."

"Well, I hope the baby will be healthy, that's all," Mama

said, smoothing out the wrinkles of the dining room table-cloth. "I still feel that something is going to go wrong this time."

James Patrick came into the world on the cold night of March 28, 1931. The late-comer weighed in at 14½ pounds, large enough to have been twins. After weeks of touch and go from convulsions and respiratory problems, he developed into a seemingly healthy child with blue eyes and blond hair. He was the pride and joy of my parents and was adored by his brothers and sisters.

Mama continued to be concerned about his health and sensed that something wasn't quite right when Jimmy developed high fevers that left him listless and confined to his bed.

"He does have a little high blood pressure, but nothing to worry about," the doctor assured her. "I'm sure he will grow out of it, in time."

Now you kids keep an eye on him and don't allow him to play too hard," we were often advised. "You can't carry him around on a satin pillow," Dad reminded her. "He will be O.K. Just let him be."

"I'm afraid that he will die before he grows up," Mama continued, pulling back the kitchen curtain to watch Jimmy digging in a pile of sand. "It's all my fault. I was just too old to have another baby."

"It's all in your head; he will be here long after we're gone," he reassured her, laying his hand on her shoulder.

The years passed by and little Jim emerged from his teen-aged years and grew into manhood but Mama never lost her fear about his welfare. (His blood pressure was now under control with the use of drugs.) When her own life was in peril due to diabetes and a leg that had to be amputated, her last thoughts were for her youngest son who remained a concern to her.

"Please look after Jimmy," she whispered to me, "because I'm not going to be here after tomorrow. I'll never live through a leg operation. There are too many things going against me. Just remember what I told you."

The next day she died on the operating table.

There is a sadness when a member of a family dies, especially Mother, and it was many weeks before any of us were able to pick up the pieces again. With Jimmy, it seemed there was really nothing to live for and there wasn't a day that he didn't visit the cemetery to stand beside his mother's grave.

It was only five months later that I received a phone call from my sister. "I have some bad news," she cried. "It's about Jimmy."

"Was he in a car accident?" I anxiously asked. "What happened?"

"He died this morning from a heart attack." He was only twenty-eight years old. The doctor who examined him told us it was a stroke or heart attack that killed him but in my mind I felt he died because he lost his beloved mother.

I REMEMBER MAMA

"She's my mama."

"No. She's *my* mama."

Arguing with my baby sister, Neeney, over the affection of our mother is one of my earliest recollections. She was the most important person in the world to me.

Following her around the house and getting under foot, getting spanked and sometimes being allowed to sit on her lap when Neeney wasn't around was my daily pleasure. On these rare occasions I liked to lay my head against her warm shoulder and gaze into her lovely face as I listened to the creaking of the old rocking chair. A cloud of jet black hair coiled into a dolly puff at the nape of her neck. Nicely chiseled features and a flawless complexion were the envy of many women in the neighborhood. Perfectly shaped brows accentuated her pretty brown eyes that could change quickly with her various moods.

"Oh the moon shines tonight on pretty Red Wing," she crooned in a clear melodic voice as we rocked in rhythm to a song about an Indian maiden. "Well, that's all for now," she said, lifting me to the floor. "Mama has work to do."

As the years passed by, her once youthful figure began to expand from having too many babies and not having a properly balanced diet. Her bulgy stomach was now being concealed by a bibbed apron. "Oh, I feel like a stuffed sausage," she complained when she had to wear a corset. "This corset is killing me," she repeated often. She, too, had to endure the many jokes that were flung at her by relatives and friends who thought it clever to make fun of her being fat. "Fatty, fatty, two by four, can't get through the kitchen door," or, "If you get any bigger you will have to wear a tent." If it bothered her she never showed it. She tried to be good-natured about it. "Fat folks might as well be good-natured and get along with people because they can't fight and they can't run. You will notice," she mused, "you never see a fat old maid."

"As long as I have my cigarets, I'm happy," she said when she was depressed. "They give me a lift." She began to smoke at an early age when she and her brothers had to herd cattle for days on end. The brothers taught her how to light up and inhale the tobacco mixture. In the beginning, Mama rolled her own from a small sack of Bull Durham tobacco and a pack of cigaret papers. We kids liked to watch her place the white paper between her fingers, skillfully shake in the right amount of tobacco and then roll and seal it with a lick of her tongue.

"Blow some smoke rings, Mama," we begged as she puffed the clouds of smoke.

"Look at that one, just perfect," I marveled as the white rings softly wafted toward the ceiling, then dissipated into thin air.

"Let me try," brother Bobby insisted, reaching for the cigaret and almost knocking it out of her mouth.

"No," she snapped. "I don't ever want to catch any of you kids smoking. It's a bad habit and not good for you. Every time I smoke one of these, it's just another nail in my coffin."

"Then why do you do it?" I asked sadly, fearing that those weeds would really kill her.

"It's too late, I can't stop now. It's in my blood," she answered, snuffing out the butt in an ash tray. "Just take a fool's advice. Don't ever smoke cigarets. They are killers." Her warning about smoking left an indelible mark on me and my two sisters and I never took up the habit.

Mama was a great story teller and loved to recall her many escapades as a child in her home town of Wabasha, Minnesota. "My mother died when I was only two years old," she told me. "The same year our farm home burned to the ground. I was raised by a step-sister that I didn't like." I remember the first time I saw a Stanley steamer, I was scared to death. I had to walk miles to school in bitter cold weather. Had to go to church every Sunday. Church, church, church, I got tired of going there all the time. Maybe that's why I don't go now. Our family were strict Catholics and we really knew our prayers." Her stories were repeated so often that I knew them by heart.

"Wouldn't you like to go back and see your family again?" we often asked her when we heard so much about the kin folk who were strangers to us.

"No. They are all well fixed and have the world by the tail. I wouldn't want to hear them brag about all their possessions. They sure would have a laugh if they could see how I have to live. They warned me about coming to South Dakota. I suppose I'd be married to some rich land owner and wear a diamond on every finger if I had listened to my sister. Well, that's water under the bridge."

The only ties that held her to her roots were an occasional letter from a sister or niece, and the arrival of her home-town newspaper. Once a week the small newspaper arrived in the mail, rolled into a wrapper. Mama eagerly scanned the paper and then told us kids the home-town news. Although she was reluctant to visit the place of her birth, I had a feeling that she was putting on an act and secretly yearned for her to see once again her family and friends. More so when I watched her fold the papers and place them in a top drawer of the kitchen cupboard. Her eyes were often filled with tears.

"How come you're crying, Mama?" I would ask. "Did somebody die?"

"No! And I'm not crying. There's just something in my eye," was her only answer. I felt that she was an unloved child and was perhaps the black sheep of her family.

Maybe it was because we were poor that Mama seemed to feel that she didn't fit in with society. She chose to remain for the most part in her own home with just a few relatives and close neighbors to visit with. She did feel at ease with the neighborhood children who flocked around her back door. They enjoyed her hidden talents of singing the ballads of that time, her "barnyard shuffle," as she called it, or to hear her play the popular toe-tapping music on our old pump organ.

"Play 'You Are My Sunshine' again," was a common request. The kids joined in to sing the lyrics while some joined partners and danced around the room.

"She can play the mouth organ, too," I bragged, wanting everyone to know that my mother could entertain just as well as anyone that performed on the Corn Palace stage. I'm positive she often dreamed that one of her children would become a great star of stage, screen or radio. Movies was one of her passions and she always managed to squeeze a few nickels together to watch her favorite stars on the silver screens of the local movie houses. "Oh look, here in the movie ads," she motioned to my sister, holding up a section of the newspaper. "Fred Astaire and Ginger Rogers are coming to the Paramount in 'The Gay Divorcee.' We're going to have to see that one. And it says, 'Coming soon, Ruby Keeler and Dick Powell in 'Flirtation Walk.' Oh, I wish I could dance like they do." She whirled about the kitchen with a dish towel, then pulled it across her behind in a rhythmic motion of the "cha-cha-cha."

My dad didn't share in my mother's adulation of Hollywood movie stars. "I wouldn't be caught dead in one of those show houses," he declared. "All that make-believe, and you people pay your hard earned money so those people can live like kings out in California."

"You're just jealous," Mama teased, "because you're not as handsome as Clark Gable or Ronald Colman."

"Who are they?" Dad questioned, not ever having been inside of a movie theatre.

Mama's devotion to her idols never faltered and every Sunday afternoon she could be seen walking down the hill toward town followed by three or four of her off-spring. "You kids wait in the lobby and I'll get the tickets," she would say while she opened up her worn black purse. "One adult and four children," she said to the girl behind the glass enclosure.

"That will be fifty-five cents, please," the cashier smiled back.

Grabbing our tickets, we kids raced through the lobby and down to the very first rows to get our favorite seat. Mama usually sat in the last row where she could again relax and forget the cares of the day. For a few hours she could project herself into a make believe world and not just be a poor woman living on the wrong side of the tracks.

Mama's moods varied from one day to the next. Her feelings could change quickly from tranquility to explosive anger. She could also swear, but we kids became accustomed to her profanity.

"What got into you today?" Dad would ask when she

seemed to find fault with everything he had done, or lash out at us kids on the slightest provocation.

"You're never around here to discipline these kids, always afraid you are going to miss something up town. If I had somewhere to go, I'd leave all of you behind," she often threatened. Or, "I'm getting tired of trying to make ends meet. You couldn't make a living for a grasshopper." When the insults stopped and no apologies were made, Dad left the house and slowly walked down the hill towards town. Mama tried to relieve her frustrations by punching down the bread dough that was rising in the dish pan. We kids stayed away when she wanted to be alone with her miseries.

There were also happy times. Mama's cheery whistle could be heard coming from the kitchen where she was preparing one of her stick-to-the-ribs breakfast of flapjacks or corn-meal mush. On special occasions she made cinnamon toast or scrambled eggs with bits of browned bacon. We kids drank coffee with a few drops of canned milk and a little sugar. There were no fruit juices or bottled milk for a better diet.

Goulash was the main course at dinner time, with chili bean soup and home-made spaghetti on alternating days; and thick slices of bread smeared with oleo and syrup. "What do you kids want for supper, fried or mashed potatoes?" we were asked. She took a vote. It was either hamburger smothered in onions or a couple of fat rings of baloney with a large bowl of canned tomatoes to fill us up until the next morning. Pies, cakes and cookies were considered a treat and were served only on Sundays or when we had company.

Cleanliness is next to godliness was one thing she tried to instill in all of us. Soap and water were cheap. There is no excuse for anyone being dirty. My brothers used to worry that she would take the skin off when she scrubbed their hands and knuckles with a scrub brush.

"Here, let me get into the attic," she commanded while wiping out the grime from a reddened ear with a firm grip on us. "You don't want to have high water marks like some of these neighbor boys—or worse, lice!"

She was a little more gentle with us younger children, like a mother cat washing her kittens. A large dish pan was placed on an old kitchen chair while she sat on a stool with a Turkish towel thrown over her shoulder. Our hands and faces were washed with a cloth smeared with some antiseptic soap. She allowed us to go into the pantry to wash our privates.

"I think you boys are due for a hair cut. Those cowlicks

are getting too long," she decided. Hair had started to tickle their ears.

"Oh, darn," Bobby protested. "Just when I am able to make a nice wave in front you have to cut it off."

"You don't want to look like a sissy, do you? Hand me that pair of scissors and those clippers and get over here. And you better sit as quiet as a mouse or I may snip you."

I felt sorry for the brothers as they tried to hold still so Mama wouldn't gouge their scalps. Their eyes were kept tightly closed to keep the fine hair from getting in. "Now stop sputtering. I can't help it if some hair gets into your mouth. Keep it shut," she warned them.

"I'll sure be glad when we can afford to get our hair cut at the barber shop," Bobby moaned, gazing into the mirror at his closely cropped head that he thought made him look like a convict.

"Twenty-five cents a head is a lot of money," Mama reminded him. "Well, who is next?"

I watched my mother slowly age from a high-spirited young woman to an elderly silver-haired grandmother who never asked or expected too much out of life. Although she never liked to reveal her true feelings or demonstrated affection for any of her children, in my own heart I know she loved all of us. She never really failed any of us and she stood strong and unafraid when she knew her last days on earth were numbered.

"I'm ready to go now," she quietly told me the day before she died. "Somewhere I know there is a better place. I just hope that Dad is there to greet me. You can go now. I'll be all right." She laid back against her pillow and closed her eyes. I started to leave, then walked back and kissed her softly on the cheek. "I love you, Mama," I cried. It was the first time that I had embraced her since I was a small child.

"I love you, too," she murmured, raising her hand to touch my face. "Bye now. I'll see you tomorrow before you go to the operating room. Don't worry. You are going to be O.K."

The next day she was gone. Her once strong willed heart flickered to a stop while the doctors were fighting to save her life. Mama got her wish. I remembered what she told me. "If they take off my leg, I don't want to live and be a burden on the rest of the family. We buried her next to Dad on a snow-covered hillside in the Graceland Cemetery north of town. Her simple gravestone reads: Josephine M. Barnes, Born September 18, 1891. Died February 22, 1960.

DEAR OLD DAD

Unlike most of the other children in the neighborhood who addressed the head of the household as "Daddy," "Papa," or a sophisticated "Father," we kids knew our father as just plain "Dad." "Come to Dad," was one of my earliest recollections. I ran into the outstretched arms of a man who I knew offered me love and protection from my childish fears.

"My, you're getting bigger every day," he laughed as he swung me around in a make-believe waltz till we both became dizzy and collapsed on the floor. The fun and games continued with baby sister Neeney joining in.

"I got your nose," he playfully teased after squeezing our noses and then holding his thumb between his fingers and telling us our noses were there; or telling us that our heads were a little house with our forehead serving as the door, our eyes were the windows, the nose the doorknob and our mouths were the entrance. "Knock at the door, peek in, turn the knob and walk in. Oh, you're pinching my nose too hard," he laughed when we tried the same antics on him. "Well, that's enough for today," he remarked, smoothing back his dark curly hair that dangled over his blue eyes. "I have to get back to work." Reaching for his paint-spattered overalls that hung behind the door, he pulled them over his gray twill work pants and hooked the straps into place. Placing a white painter's cap, with the words "Dutch Boy Paints" on his head, he waved goodbye and walked briskly down Edmunds Street.

At the end of each day when the tall cottonwoods shaded the lane from the setting sun, my sister and I awaited our Dad's return, knowing there would be a penny sack of candy or a celluloid doll tucked into his overall pockets. His thin body straightened up from the weight of the heavy ladder and paint buckets that he had to carry, and he called to us as we rushed to meet him. Sometimes an old chair, a small table and a few pictures were brought home when his customers dispensed with unwanted items on their premises.

"Look what Mrs. Burns gave me today," he announced to Mama, throwing a pile of lacy curtains, a few feather pillows and other bedding on the dining room table. She thought that maybe you could use them. You won't believe this but she is giving me an old pump organ."

"An organ," Mama gasped in excitement. "It's something I've always wanted because we had an organ back home and I know how to play."

"Is Mrs. Burns rich?" brother Bobby inquired, looking through the rummage items.

"I guess she is," Dad answered. "They own a lumber company and I wish you could see their beautiful brick home. She even owns an electric car!"

"Must be nice," Mama sighed, gazing across the linoleum rug where the once colored patterns of flowers were fading away.

"I sure wish I had a truck to haul the ladders and paint pails to my jobs," Dad said. "I could save a lot of time and make more money before winter sets in. I've been promised two oil stations and the lumber company to paint next year."

"Get a loan from your brother, Mark. He is doing good in the grocery business," Mama suggested.

"I won't borrow money from relatives if I have to starve to death," he said with finality.

Dad managed to keep bread on the table during the summer months when the paint jobs were available, but during the long cold winter weather his wire-patched ladders, old brushes and canvases stayed in the woodshed.

"Why can't you get a job on the railroad or the highway department?" Mama often asked. "You have to have a year 'round job, not just a hit-and-miss job."

"You have to have a pull to get those jobs," was Dad's excuse. "I was born a farmer and I'm not cut out to be an engineer like Mr. Lawrence, or mechanic like Pat Kelley and Mike Flynn (two of Dad's Irish friends)."

"Jack of all trades and master of none," Mama complained, leaving Dad sitting at the kitchen table.

"Some day my ship will come in," Dad said to himself, watching the rain drops sloshing against the window pane.

When the autumn weather arrived with the cold rains and bone-chilling winds, Dad looked through the limited list of jobs that appeared in the want ads section of the daily newspaper. "Pin setters wanted. Inquire at Mitchell bowling alley," or "clean-up man wanted at Purity Dairy." Dad was forced to take manual jobs during his off season. Mama used to rub his aching back with liniment when he arrived home from setting pins by hand. Bringing home some of the left-over products from the dairy helped to stretch the food budget. The buttermilk gave Mama's flap-jacks a little extra flavor and the cold skim milk was delicious poured over a bowl of mush.

"Too bad you don't work in a meat packing plant. You could bring home the bacon," she often said, jokingly.

"I've found a new part-time job," Dad annouced one evening as he hurried to sit down to a cold meal that was still on the table.

"Where?" asked Mama, who was a little angry because he came home late for supper.

"Down at Navins saloon. They needed an extra bar tender two or three nights a week, and I applied."

"Well, that's just fine and dandy. Now you can have a high old time with your Irish buddies and forget all about me sitting here alone every night. Besides, I've heard that there is a lot of hanky panky going on there. What about those wenches that hang around there?" Mama stormed, glaring at Dad.

"Navins is a man's saloon and if a woman does come in it's only to rout out her husband. Besides, T. P. has been good to me ever since I worked on his hotel and he has helped me get other paint jobs. Where else can I get twenty-five cents an hour in the winter?"

"And all you want to drink," Mama finished, still not convinced about the job.

"You know I never get 'stewed.' If I drank like some of the boozers in this town, you'd have something to holler about. Shall I stay home and watch you starve to death?" And with that he left the untouched meal and stalked into the bedroom.

During these arguments between our parents we kids tried not to take sides but my sympathies were more with Dad than my mother.

I watched Mama slump down in a spindle-backed kitchen chair and lean wearily on the table while she pondered her next move, puffing on a roll-your-own cigaret.

She arose and went to the bedroom door. "I won't say any more," she promised. "You better take the job. I think I can borrow a couple of white shirts from Pete. He only wears them when he goes to a funeral. I just hope the neighbors won't see you coming home late at night."

Mama's jealousy proved to be mostly unnecessary. Dad arrived home soon after closing hours. She found she could catch up on her ironing or some other household duty that was left undone.

The left-over sandwiches, crackers and pickles from the free lunch that was served with the nickel glasses of beer were brought home in a carton. "Can I have a piece of bologna?" was a plea often heard from one of the brothers who was awakened by the chatter in the kitchen.

"Be quiet and get back to bed or I'll get the broomstick." This sent them scampering. Mama wanted to listen to Dad's tidbits of gossip heard behind the swinging doors of the tavern.

My dad's philosophy, "Behind every cloud there is a silver lining" continued throughout his life. He was never pessimistic like Mama who warned us from the beginning that life was mostly "hard knocks." He wasn't ashamed of his station in life and enjoyed being himself whether he was talking with a high-brow of the town or listening to a tale of woe from a loafer on the streets. Although he was christened Sylvester William, everyone called him just plain Bill.

The hard work and strain of climbing ladders, reaching the high places with his brushes and painting equipment left him an old man during the summer of his years. "If I can just manage to hang on a little longer, we'll be able to buy that house we've been wanting," he told Mama one day, rubbing his tired legs.

"You should let Dr. Ball check on those legs," warned Mama. "There's something wrong."

"Can't take the time. I have to have the Armour creamery painted by the end of June." He brushed off her concern.

And then it happened while walking home from work. Dad's legs gave out and a passerby had to help him the rest of the way home. The arteries in his legs were hardening with not much hope of recovery.

"Can't you do something?" Mama implored our family doctor after none of the medications helped to deaden the agonizing pain. "He can't take this much longer."

"There's nothing left," the doctor told her. That leg has to come off or he will be dead in a few weeks."

The hours-long operation was a success but Dad was left a cripple, confined to a wheelchair. He accepted this set-back with cheerful optimism and continued to help Mama around the house and to visit with his old cronies who came to call. After what seemed to be a few years of good health, he was dealt another blow with a succession of strokes that paralyzed one side of his body. From that time he was cared for by Mama who nursed him through endless days and sleepless nights. She listened to fits of rage unlike his usual tranquil personality. Sometimes he was lucid and talked about the good memories that he and Mama shared together.

"I'd sure like to see the old home place in Cresco (Iowa)," he often told Mama. "It's so pretty down there this time of year. I can just see the ice-covered Turkey River where we kids used to skate. You know, last night I dreamed that I was home with Mother and Dad and all the brothers and sisters; it was Christmas time."

On a cold winter night, November 18th, 1948, I sat near my father's bed and watched him struggling for breath before he lapsed into a coma from which there was no return. My heart was bursting with grief, yet relieved that the never-ending pain and suffering that lasted for over five years was finally over.

Because of costly doctor and hospital bills that drained the savings that my parents had managed to accumulate, there was very little money for a proper burial. The county would have to pay for most of the funeral expense, including an inexpensive gray metal casket. Although I was married by then, with a small child of my own, I had no funds to help out. One of my brothers and I did purchase a golden strand of rosary beads.

The next evening the mortician met us at the door and the family followed him through the soft carpeted funeral parlor. At the far end of the dimly lit room the casket awaited us. There were bouquets sent by relatives, neighbors and friends.

I stared in disbelief at the man in the coffin. The face that had been wrinkled from years of hard work and poverty looked much more youthful. His fingers held the rosary beads that he truly believed in. He looked serene in the gray worsted suit that had been packed away when he became an invalid. "He sure looks nice," Mama said.

After prayers were said and the tears dried, we all left the funeral home to await the final rites. The next morning I was awakened by voices coming from the kitchen. I could hear Mama say, "With everything else gone wrong, why can't Dad have a decent day for his funeral?" I looked out of the window and all I could see was swirling snow, drifting into the driveway. The stormy weather added to the gloom that prevailed in the household.

All too soon the black funeral limousine arrived and we were ready to leave. (There were a few laughs to break the

140

tension that was now hard to contain.) I remembered it was the first time we were all together since we were children, sitting around the table at supper time.

The Holy Family Catholic Church loomed majestically as we entered and followed Mama and brother Jimmy down the aisle. I was happy to see many of Dad's old friends and neighbors who braved the snowstorm to pay their last respects. Father William O'Brady stood at the altar. Although my Dad kept the faith, most of the family had forsaken the Catholic doctrine and were looked upon as outcasts (attending church only on Easter Sunday or during the Christmas season).

I expected Father Brady to show more concern and consolation for the bereaved family. I wanted to say from the pulpit that my father was a good man who loved his family. I was grateful for the years when he made sure that none of us ever went to bed hungry. God knew that our father deserved a choice seat alongside of the rich man whose family could afford to pay for the masses that were to insure their entry through the pearly gates.

The service was quickly concluded and the six pallbearers nervously found their places, then escorted the casket out of the church. With much difficulty the funeral procession made its way through the streets, escorted by a lone police car. A few bystanders looked at us with pity and curiosity, then went about their business.

A snow plow had cleared the road so we could enter Calvary Cemetery. The green pine trees stood out against the landscape that was white and dead.

On a wind-swept hillside my family huddled together beneath the canopy that tried to shield us. Along with the elderly black-robed priest we chanted again the final prayers for our departed father.

It was still hard for me to believe that in the casket lay the remains of my dad. I reached over to touch the crimson wreath of flowers that were laced with snowflakes. I then gazed up towards the gray cloud-shrouded sky and whispered "Goodbye, Dad. I hope and pray that you are at peace in God's paradise where the rainbows never end and the fields remain ever green."

School Days

EUGENE FIELD SCHOOL

I often thought that I spent most of my childhood walking to school in cold weather. The summers passed by too swiftly with never enough time to enjoy the great outdoors. I had mixed emotions in the fall. I loved going to school yet hated to give up my freedom.

We knew the school bell would soon be ringing when we saw Mama busily sewing on dresses made of flowered cotton material. The outfits were always made in the same pattern, plain and simple, with necklines and sleeves trimmed with colorful tape.

It was during the late summer of 1933 when our thoughts were centered on getting ready to enter the third grade at Notre Dame Academy. We kids enjoyed the private school where our teachers were called "Sister" instead of "Miss." The only drawback was the expense of sending three children to a Catholic-supported school. There was tuition to be considered and the books and catechisms were not free (plus the danger of crossing the Milwaukee Railroad tracks).

Most of the neighbor children went to the Eugene Field public school located on the south side of town. They were a mixture of religious backgrounds. After attending Notre Dame, I believed "only Catholics went to Heaven."

"I've made up my mind," Mama told us while sitting with Dad by the kitchen table. "You kids are going to Eugene Field. The public schools are not as strict about clothing, and it will be cheaper in the long run. You can even come home for dinner. It's only about five blocks from here. What do you think about that?"

Brother Bobby, sister Neeney and I all looked at each other and shrugged our shoulders. "We won't have to say prayers all day long in that school," Neeney said, already thinking about her liberation from strict rules. "And they allow girls to play soft ball."

"This is going to be the third school that we have gone to," I reminded everybody. We have already lived on four different sides of town. The neighbor kids were all glad to hear that we were going to be enrolled at their school.

The golden rod was yellow and the trees were beginning to shed their autumn leaves on that first day of school. Neeney and I were neatly dressed in our freshly starched frocks, white

Eugene Field School, built in 1922, still being used, located at 909 Court Merrill.

anklets and brown sandals. Everyone thought we were twins because we were in the same grade. Looking us over before we went out the door, Mama warned sister Neeney, "Now I want you to look the same when you come back. No rips or tears on your dress and no dirty hands or knees." Neeney loved to roughhouse with the boys, play marbles and even football.

We kids fell in line with the chattering, laughing neighbor children as they walked past our house. A few boy stragglers slowly brought up the rear, idly kicking stones. I tried to keep my polished shoes from getting too dusty from the dirt roads until we reached the street where the sidewalks began.

Sanborn street, running north and south, was a busy thoroughfare dotted with a few homes and grocery stores. These shops provided the school children with tablets, scissors and paste, penny pencils and had large glass show cases filled with candy and gum. Selling pop bottles to the grocery stores in return for pop and candy was an every day transaction among the school children.

Obeying Mama's orders to "watch out for the cars," we all cautiously crossed the main highway. This busy street has been renamed Havens Street. At last we were safe on the other side with our feet firmly planted on the new concrete sidewalk. "Wouldn't this be nice to roller skate on?" I joyfully thought to myself, although I didn't own good skates.

"There is our new school," I yelled, pointing my finger toward a red brick building with a tile roof. It stood on a slight incline, surrounded by a grassy court yard where a silver flag pole held a fluttering American flag high above our heads. The windows of the school rooms sparkled from the reflections of the morning sun. I thought it was a beautiful schoolhouse.

The school ground was swarming with children of every description. We searched our way through the groups of students looking for a familiar face. Meanwhile, sister Neeney and I were getting our share of stares. I was hoping she wouldn't say, "I hope you get your eyes full," but she was more interested in seeing if there was a soft ball game going on.

At last we found the entrance door on the west side and stood with our backs against the brick wall, watching the children enjoying their renewed friendship after a long summer's vacation. Since I was basically a shy child, it was difficult for me to get acquainted. "I hope the school bell rings pretty soon." I began to worry. I tried to look confident and nonchalant watching two little girls about my age studying me. Suddenly one of them came over to us and introduced herself.

"Hi. My name's Loretta. I'm in the third grade. What's your names?"

I smiled back at a chubby cheeked fat girl whose arms and legs looked out of proportion for the short skirted dress that she wore. (The name "Fatty" was bestowed upon her by the boys at the school.) "'This is my sister Norma and I'm Dolores," I shyly replied. "We're in the third grade, too." I felt that we had made a friend.

The shrill clanging of a bell stopped all the visiting and play activities and the children hurried to get into formation to enter the school. I took note of two strange looking boys running across the play ground. As they came closer, I was surprised to see that they were dark skinned. It was the first time that I had ever seen a black child. "Who are those kids?" I asked my new friend, Loretta. "Are they darkies?"

"Those are nigger kids, Harold and James Brooks," she said, "and they are both in our class."

The small boys, dressed in faded blue shirts and overalls, jumped into line, laughing and talking. (The only black people that I had seen were the men riding the freight trains that passed through Mitchell.) Their white toothy grins revealed that they were happy children and were warmly received by their fellow classmates.

"They don't have any shoes on," Neeney whispered, pointing to their bare feet, "and I think we're poor."

"They will wear shoes when it gets cold," Loretta told us. "Besides, they're kinda hard up and don't have a lot of money to spend on clothes. I already had a thumbnail sketch of my black classmates as they marched into the door ahead of me, their woolly heads bobbing up and down.

"So that's what a nigger boy looks like," I thought to myself. "I wonder if God really made them at night like Uncle Pete says." I was intrigued by them.

"Our room is at the end of the corridor, down there where Miss Kelley is standing." We continued to listen to Loretta as she pointed to the girls' bathroom, fifth and fourth grade rooms, giving us a grand tour down the marble floored hallway.

"Hello, Miss Kelley," Loretta politely saluted a small wavy-

145

haired lady standing near the door to our classroom. "These two kids are new this year. They used to go to Notre Dame."

"How nice to have them," she answered. When she smiled, her blue eyes crinkled with laugh lines and I noticed her slightly protruding teeth were white and shiny. I was always convinced that a person who smiled was warm and friendly and I immediately took a liking to Mae Kelley.

It didn't take long to readjust to the public school system. Our catechism lessons were replaced with the knowledge that we learned from books of every conceivable kind, including the stories about Indians, pioneers and about the wonders of the world. Miss Kelley held a captivated audience when she read aloud the hair-raising adventures of "Treasure Island," "Robinson Crusoe" and the heart-warming tales of "The Hollow Tree" stories and "Dr. Doolittle and Bertrum." Childrens' magazines were ours for the reading from the well-stocked shelves of the school library.

From this dedicated schoolmarm I learned how to overcome my shyness and to express myself in oral and written assignments. Although there were some smart-alecks who liked to put me down. I found that most of my classmates were gentle people who enjoyed my companionship. They came from all walks of life, farmers to townspeople. Their fathers were railroad men, grocers, lawyers, and businessmen. A few of the families gained their livelihood from the college classrooms of Dakota Wesleyan. Katy Roadman's father was the president of the well-known college located a few blocks south of Eugene Field. One of my closest chums was Connie Brown whose father was also associated with the University.

Most of the time we children were seated in alphabetical order until the students with poor vision or hearing difficulties were weeded out and placed in desks in the front rows. An occasional trouble-maker would also find himself at the front of the room close to the teacher's desk where she could keep an eye on him. If that didn't stop the bad behavior, the cloak room was the next step. The last resort was being sent to the principal's office to get the rubber hose—or so they said. I'm not sure anyone ever received this kind of corporal punishment but it made many a "Pecks Bad Boy" think twice.

I'm sure when we all look back on our good old golden rule days, we remember our classmates with varying degrees of affection or downright dislike. In every class there were the secret pals, the snobs and "snots," the know-it-alls, bird brains, egg heads, bullies, sissies, the teachers' pets and the morons who barely passed from grade to grade. How many can you remember?

The following are students that I recall when we were enrolled at Eugene Field during my four years of grade school and I hope you are all still around to read my book, wherever you are.

Maynard Anderson. A friendly blond, blue-eyed boy who liked to talk. Took a fancy to me and gave me gum and candy. His father owned a grocery store.

Arthur Bentliff. He could sing and play the ukelele. Blond and blue-eyed, all the girls thought he was cute.

Dale Caldwell. One of the tallest boys in class. Brown-haired with brown eyes, quiet, didn't seem to enjoy being confined to a desk all day long.

Ordell Forbes. He had the reputation of being the meanest kid in school. My sister Neeney tamed him one day by giving him a black eye and a bloody nose.

Lynn Beuhler. One of the smallest boys but his pleasing manners and friendly personality made him ten feet tall.

Hubbard Fellows. Quiet and studious, was troubled with a hearing problem.

Marjorie Fenton. A happy, talkative, well-dressed classmate. Enjoyed many gab fests with her. Her daddy was a railroad man.

Earl Hilton. The ideal student.

Mary Allington. One of our bosom buddies. Always lived in our neighborhood.

Betty Baumgardner. A very sweet blue-eyed miss who could sing like a nightingale.

Norman Mooney. God's gift to the girls. Had a dislike for the town students. We did battle with him with snowball fights.

Clarion Wilson. Another mischievous red-haired farm boy who liked to tease the girls.

Howard Sampson. Was strong and silent and big for his age. Sister Neeney and I admired him for his athletic ability.

Robert Westendorf. There's a clown in every class and he was ours. Liked to tell Mae West jokes.

Dorothy Goldhammer. Quiet as a mouse. A farm girl.

Norma Newell. Tiny, dark-eyed and cute.

Joanne Johnson. A country girl who was well-liked for her friendly personality.

Zelda Schmidt. Maybe I didn't like her name or her hair color.

Miriam White. A petite blonde who was always ready for fun and games.

147

Donna Dunbar. Her eyes were the color of violets and her hair hung down in ringlets.

Harriet Campbell. A pig-tailed "egg head."

Myrtle Smith. I really didn't know her.

Marion Hammond. Poor little rich girl. I envied her fancy clothes and standard of living.

Doris Young. She just sat in a corner and smiled.

Patricia Whipple. A catty trouble maker.

Loretta Kellogg. A charming little fat girl who knew how to laugh at herself.

Thelma Thoming. A curly-haired brown-eyed beauty.

Mary Ryan. "When Irish Eyes Are Smiling."

Gladys Lorenz. Loved attention and would do anything to get it.

Mary Lou Bergeson. Miss Personality. One of the most popular girls in class.

Katheryn Roadman. Teacher's pet.

Kenneth DeLapp. One of the brightest classmates. I had a secret crush on him.

Thurl Thomas. We all knew that he would succeed.

Paul Douglas. He dreamed of far away places with strange sounding names.

Richard Shearer. He was our Prince Charming. Had a "way" about himself.

Hugh McManus. Another heart breaker who set our hearts aflame.

Arthur Scott. Big eyed and wise as an old owl.

Brooks Brothers, James and Harold. Only blacks in our school.

Connie Brown. My best friend all through the grades. I treasure the memories of our good times.

Most of these students entered the third grade the same time as I did and we all learned to love and respect our Miss Kelley. She was very diplomatic and treated all students on an equal basis. Yet there were times when she lost her composure and had to shake some sense into an unruly pupil, usually a boy.

At that time teachers were allowed to slap, spank, and even pull hair if a student caused too much disruption in class. Today those infractions are tolerated. If a teacher was right or wrong in her judgment, her word was the law then and most of the children respected her.

Just about every student did try to get away with chewing gum. Many did so to show their bravery. The wad of gum was kept stashed in the mouth and then chewed rapidly when the teacher's back was turned.

"All right, who is chewing gum?" she would ask just about every day, and the teacher's trained eye would zero in on the guilty culprit. "Put that gum in the waste paper basket right now and you can stay after school and clean the blackboards and erasers." That was a sentence pronounced on many gum-chewing offenders.

"If I catch anyone throwing spit wads they will surely suffer the consequences." This was another misdeed not to be tolerated by the teachers. Yet the temptation was too great and the spit wad throwing was a never-ending paper war between the pupils.

Even I, little bashful girl that I was, succumbed to this diversion because of an innocent flirtation with a classmate, Earl Hilton.

He started the whole thing. I was minding my own business and engrossed in my geography lesson when I felt something softly hitting the back of my head. When I turned around all I could see were heads buried behind the books.

"Hmmm," I wondered, who is trying to attract my attention?" More spit balls began to fall on my desk. I finally leaned down and looked back just in time to catch Earl in the act. Two can play at this game, I decided, and began to tear up some tablet paper into small pieces, roll into balls, wetting them in my mouth and then placing my ammunition in my pencil box. It was fun throwing the wads in a mock battle until Miss Kelley discovered our outrageous behavior.

"You two stay after school tonight," she sternly told us. "The very idea. And you, Dolores, girls just don't do things like this. I don't know what has gotten into you lately."

My face began to turn red, as all eyes were upon me. I felt like a little devil who had just sprouted horns.

"I will never throw spit wads again. Now write that fifty times on the blackboard," she ordered us after we had picked up all the tiny balls from the floor. Remorse engulfed me and I felt miserable about what we had done. I didn't want Miss Kelley to think I was a bad girl. My arm was tired when I finally laid down the chalk and went to the cloak room to get my coat. Miss Kelley pretended to be finishing up her daily schedule as I sneaked toward the door, trying to hide the tears welling up in my eyes.

"Come here, dear," she said, holding out her arms. I'm sorry for punishing you, but those are the rules and that

149

applies to everyone. She placed her finger under my chin so she could look directly into my eyes.

"I'm sorry and I won't do it again," I promised as she tried to coax a smile from my tear stained face.

"Still friends, aren't we?" she laughed, placing her arms around me.

"Yes," I replied. I wanted Miss Kelley to be my friend forever. I never threw spit wads again. That is, not in Miss Kelley's classroom.

"And there were in the same country, shepherds abiding in the fields keeping watch over their flocks by night. And lo the angel of the Lord came upon them and the glory of the Lord shone round about them and they were sore afraid, but the angel said unto them, 'Fear not for behold I bring you good tidings of great joy, for unto you is born this day in the city of David a Savior which is Christ the Lord'."

Our class of third graders spoke this in choruses as we gathered around the giant evergreen tree in the gymnasium of the school for our annual Christmas pageant. From the first grade, taught by Miss Graves to the sixth, instructed by Miss Sundahl, all raised their melodic voices in solemn "Silent Night" to the rollicking happy tune of "Jingle Bells."

Then a hushed silence fell over the assembled school children as Miss Kelley opened up a large book and read us one of our favorite stories of the true spirit of the holiday season, "Why the Chimes Rang." It was a beautiful story read by a wonderful dedicated lady whose life work was to teach the young to reach out and find their own little corner of the world.

The story was ended and the book softly closed. The children smiled and tried not to notice the dainty lace handkerchief that Miss Kelley used to dry the tears that glistened on her cheeks. "Merry Christmas, boys and girls," she whispered as we all prepared to leave the auditorium.

"Merry Christmas, Miss Kelley, and a Happy New Year," answered the children, running up the stairs where each child received a large bag of candy.

"See you next year," shouted the children to each other as they left the schoolhouse to enjoy a two-week holiday. The old brick schoolhouse would stand silent in a winter wonderland until the halls would once again ring with the laughter of little children.

Buttons and Bows

From the time I was a small toddler wearing rompers until I developed into the bloom of adolesence, I wanted to dress up and look my best. I somehow managed to look presentable with hand-me-downs that made up my wardrobe. I realized that nice clothes and good manners were a status symbol in the society of the depression generation.

It wasn't until I enrolled in the third grade that I noticed that some of the children wore expensive looking clothing and leather shoes that seemed to fit better and not make creaking noises like mine.

I admired the pastel colored anklets worn by little girls. I somehow knew that I wasn't in style wearing long brown stockings held in place by tight elastic garters. When the winter weather changed to spring, I rolled my stockings below my knees.

I took note also that only a few of us girls wore oversized bloomers. I was embarrassed when some of the snooty girls whispered and giggled when I pulled them down in the doorless toilets. Later I waited till the bathroom was empty before I sat down, even waiting in discomfort.

"The other girls wear silk socks and pink panties," I told my mother, "why can't Neeney and I wear pretty things like that?"

"Because we can't afford to buy luxuries," Mama answered. "You will just have to make the best of it until times get better."

But one warm spring morning I received my heart's desire when Mama handed me a package with the name of a local store printed on it.

I quickly opened the sack and shook out the contents on the dining room table. I couldn't believe my eyes. There were three pairs of anklets in white, pink, and blue and three pairs of silk panties with a tiny bow attached to each brief. I raced into the bedroom to try on my luxurious garments.

"I'll show those girls in school," I thought to myself as I admired my svelte figure in the mirror. I felt a new confidence and a sense of liberation that could only be achieved by wearing silk, satin and chantilly lace.

I could hardly wait to get to school, then count the hours until the recess period. When Miss Kelley announced recess

I raced out of the room and down the hall until I came to the girls' bathroom. I found a place near the door. I waited for my classmates to arrive, especially Mary Jane, who was a "snot nose."

At the proper moment I raised my dress above my waist, then slowly pushed down my fancy underwear until they were around my ankles. While all eyes were focused on my strip tease I sat down like a queen on a throne.

A few of the girls stared in disbelief and some giggled. Mary Jane only looked at me with scorn in her dark eyes.

"Well, look who has come up in the world—Miss Fancy Pants. Did you get those from the W. P. A. or from the Welfare?" she asked, stepping on my toes.

"Mama bought these with her own money. Dad paints houses, you know. We have some money of our own." Words were beginning to fail me. Why did I always have to feel like second class just because we were a poor family?

"Look at the big cry baby cry," Mary Jane taunted while I tried hard to conceal the tears that were running down my cheeks.

"Oh, leave her alone," one of her chums told my tormentor. "She has never done you any harm. But if her sister Neeney finds out about this, you're going to get taken down and sat on. And speak of the devil, here she comes now."

Charging into the assembled group of girls my little sister made her sudden entrance.

"Are you picking on my sister again?" she demanded. "I'm getting sick and tired of you trying to put us down. We're just as good as your family. At least my dad isn't a drunkard like yours, and if your mother didn't take in washing you would starve to death. I should punch you right in the nose."

"Don't you dare hit me or I'll tell Miss Sanger," cried Mary Jane, looking at a small pudgy fist only inches from her nose.

"Just wait till I catch you off the school grounds, you're going to be sorry. I'll make you eat your words," Neeney promised her enemy. "You remember what I done to Ordell Forbes, don't you? He doesn't say much any more."

The girls' group quickly dissipated, glancing back over their shoulders. "I guess I shouldn't have shown my new panties. I just wanted them to know that we have nice things, too."

"It's going to take more than a pair of pants to get us in their high society, but I don't want to be like those two-faced snots. I have more fun playing with the boys."

"Why don't you play more with my gang; it's fun to play football," Neeney said.

I promised that I would spend more recess time in games that she enjoyed. Yet I would always yearn to be a little lady and to be accepted by my classmates who lived on the "right side of the tracks."

MISS BUTTERFIELD

My third year of school was coming to a close and I can honestly say that I was one of the brightest pupils in Miss Kelley's class. On the last day when we were handed our report cards there was no doubt in my mind that I would be promoted to the fourth grade. I was very proud of the "As", and "Bs" that I had earned during the past nine months.

"Did you pass?" each child asked the other as they scanned the cards. I felt sorry for the few who missed a grade. I wasn't always too sure of my little sister Neeney who found the confinement of school just too boring.

"See, I passed," she beamed, holding up a smudged report card for all to gaze upon. The below average grades were shameful, I thought. The teachers often compared our schoolwork and couldn't quite understand why Neeney couldn't turn in the neat and correct lessons as I did. Mama was sure that Neeney would some day get a scholarship for her athletic abilities.

Next year we're going to have an old "sour puss" for a teacher, some of the boys remarked, referring to the fourth grade teacher, Miss Edna Butterfield.

"She doesn't put up with any monkey business," we all agreed. "She had better not hear anyone calling her Miss Buttermilk or Butterfinger," I warned. All of us already worrying about next year. "Just because she doesn't smile like Miss Kelley is no sign that she isn't nice," I said convincingly, walking beside our neighborhood gang, all happy and relieved that there would be "no more pencils, no more books, no more teachers' dirty looks."

But the slightly stout, black haired, brown eyed, bespectacled "old maid" school teacher whom the students worried about proved to be as friendly as a pussy cat—stern look-

153

ing, but with a heart of gold. Her attire usually consisted of conservative suits, dresses and shoes with none of the frilly outfits and dainty pumps that our Miss Kelley chose to wear. Her manner was brisk and straight to the point and everyone knew that there would be no "pussy footin" around her. There wasn't anything feminine about her make-up. Old maids weren't supposed to have sex appeal anyway. And the tiny dark hairs above her upper lip gave her a masculine appearance.

"Looks aren't everything and beauty is only skin deep," I had been told by Mama who seemed to have a solution with words for every topic around the house. My relationship with Miss Butterfield proved to be a cordial one and it was a new experience in the world of art, created with a box of water paints. Our pictures came to life with the vibrant illustrations of the great outdoors, the sunsets and a multi-colored rainbow stretching across the pages of the paint books. She also admired my penmanship and the ability to compose poems and write short stories. How proud I felt to see my pictures and posters displayed on the walls of the classroom. Although I tried my best, arithmetic seemed to be my downfall and it was the one subject that I needed the most in life. Miss Butterfield consoled me by saying that she was sure that I would grow up to be a secretary because my penmanship was excellent. She chose me to write the class letters to our pen pals in far-away lands across the sea. My fourth grade teacher contributed much to my self esteem and I felt that I wasn't doing bad for a somewhat deprived girl. Most of the students from the lower income families who did have the brains and the talents seemed to remain at the bottom of the totem pole. Miss Butterfield was more than pleased with the nine months we spent together and I was promoted to the fifth grade. So was my little sister, Neeney, who sailed from one grade to another without difficulty.

MISS ESTHER GATSBY

Names like "lantern jaw," "crabby old maid," or "bitch" were applied by some of the school boys when they mentioned the fifth grade teacher, we will call Miss Gatsby. I did take note of the sour faced, frizzy haired woman who seemed to walk the halls with a superior attitude. She never returned my shy greeting or pretended not to hear. We were forwarned again by the older children who had been in her class. One boy told us, "She is rough and slaps you with a ruler. And if your hands aren't clean she sends you to the wash room. She washed out one boy's mouth with soap when he sassed her." "I'm really going to have to study hard next year," I thought to myself. "I don't want her to dislike me."

"She don't scare me one bit," laughed my devil-may-care sister. "She can't do more than kill you."

"I sure wish we could have Miss Kelley for our fifth grade teacher. Why can't they exchange grades?" I responded, slowly losing my complacency, and my wish to attend Eugene Field.

"Maybe there will be a new teacher. Miss Gatsby might get lucky and get married. Some teachers don't stay old maids all their life," Neeney answered, trying to calm my fears.

Miss Esther Gatsby did retain her position and all the stories that were told about her proved to be true. Being enrolled in her class turned out to be one of the unhappiest events of my school life.

It didn't take me very long to realize that she favored the students from the richer families who lived on the boulevards and tree-lined streets on the south side of town. Their mothers were in society—PTA presidents and on school boards. They seemed to spend more time at school than at home. The children from this type of background more than likely became the teachers' pets. Even during those hard times there were still prosperous families who could afford the luxuries of life. My W. P. A. clothing seemed a bit tacky compared to the dainty frocks, tweed skirts and matching sweater sets worn by the other girls. I envied the expensive polished leather shoes tied with shoe laces adorned with tiny bells. I made up my mind that I would show I was just as smart as they were with an almost all "A" report card.

Miss Gatsby showed her disapproval of under-privileged students by finding fault with their study habits. The slaps, hair-pulling and the use of the ruler across their hands only made the pupils more resentful. I still tried to maintain my contributions to the question-and-answer periods after history or geography lessons. She ignored my upraised hand. I began to feel like an outsider trying to break down the barrier that stood between me and this square-jawed teacher. I sensed that she realized my dislike for her when one day she rapped my knuckles with a ruler and made them bleed. She told me I was stupid because of my difficulty with a math problem. "I'll get even with you some day," I promised myself, "if it takes a hundred years."

And to my embarrassment, before the class she vented her meanness on my little sister, Neeney. "Norma, you get to the washroom and tidy up. How any mother can send a child to school looking like you is beyond me." I resented her insinuations about my mother's cleanliness. (Neeney's soiled face and hands came from playing football with the boys.)

"If we got the name, we might as well play the game," I surmised after listening to Mrs. Gatsby's cutting remarks about the uncouth underprivileged children in her class, and her asking why they couldn't behave like the well-bred boys and girls. I began to carry a chip on my shoulder, became argumentative and embroiled in a few scuffles and snowball fights that erupted on the school ground. There was one boy in particular I hated because of his remarks about my poor background. My chance to get even came one wintry day when the snow was just right for a good snowball fight. It would have to be off the school grounds and out of sight of the school personnel. Our plans were to make war!

"Are you guys ready?" Neeney shouted as we all prepared our ammunition for the big "push." It was to be a skirmish between the town kids and some "country hicks." The enemy were edging closer and I could see the boy whom I detested throw the first missle. One of my snowballs was packed around a small rock and I threw it with deadly accuracy at the bespectacled Francis and hit him in the face. (Most of the time I couldn't hit the broad side of a barn.) I knew instantly that I was in trouble when I saw the blood dripping from his mouth and his shattered glasses. He was half carried back to the schoolhouse. The battle had ended. Everyone blamed my sister, Neeney, for causing the casualty because she was a "straight shot." The next day Miss Thora Sanger, the school principal, denounced the snow fights and promised severe punishment for the culprits, vowing to find out the names of all who participated. I was never called to stand upon the carpet and the secret was never revealed how I got my revenge on that cold, snowy day.

I don't know how many years Miss Thora Sanger was the principal of Eugene Field School but I do remember that when I was a student during the 1930's, she was known to rule with an iron hand in a velvet glove.

The first time that I saw her I thought she looked like a grand Dutchess. She was a large bosomy lady who walked through the corridor with an air of authority. Her dark brown hair was regally coiled into a bun at the back of her head. Enormous brown eyes peered out from behind shiny gold-rimmed glasses. I thought her crepes and silk dresses were elegant, matching the rich looking leather shoes of tans and blacks. The small cubbyhole office located next to the library was her private domain where no one entered, except the teachers or members of the school board. It was, also a place where the incorrigibles were sent to have a choice of walking the line, or to be expelled from school. Miss Gatsby sent more than her share of students to the office of correction; most the children of the poor.

The double standard of justice caused ill feelings among the pupils who didn't have anyone to defend them against prejudice.

My resentment toward my fifth grade teacher reached its peak toward the end of the school term, which I thought was never going to end.

I was looking forward to the annual spelling contest because it was the one subject where I excelled and I was prepared. I was chosen to be the captain of one team and the daughter of a pillar-of-society family was the other. We each chose the students who we thought would help our team win. (I always felt sorry for the poor spellers who were chosen last.)

It didn't take long until the students were being eliminated by the misspelling of words. The other captain and I were the only two left in the contest. The accepted fifth grade words were becoming more difficult, especially the ones that Miss Gatsby offered to me first. I knew she was hoping for a win for Katy, but I was determined that I would be the victor.

At last the teacher gave me one of the hardest words that could be spelled two ways with a plural, but she only accepted my one answer and told me that it was wrong. The contest was over and I had lost to my now grinning opponent. The tears and anger were hard to hide as I watched Miss Gatsby proudly hand the honored certificate of "best speller" to the other girl.

My friends tried to console me as we walked home from school. They found a few choice names for the teacher. I was going to tell Mama about my defeat but I knew there wouldn't be much that she could do. She hardly ever interferred in school, let alone have a confrontation with Miss Gatsby who I thought had cheated me.

"Next year I'm going back to Notre Dame," I threatened as Mama listened to my tale of woe. "The nuns are nice to the kids and treat everyone fair and square."

"Well, we shall see," Mama answered. Her mind was more occupied by the piles of dirty clothes that lay on the kitchen floor, waiting to be washed. "Maybe your luck will change next year. I hear there is a new teacher replacing Miss Sundahl."

"Who told you that?" I questioned.

"Oh, the neighborhood gossip. She says that Miss Sundahl had a drinking problem and was fired. That's all I know about it."

"Anybody would be better than Miss Gatsby," I thought, gathering up my end-of-the-year school paraphenalia. School I thought by now was just a waste of time.

The following summer passed by quicker than usual as my days were spent baby sitting or acting as a hired girl for the mothers of the neighborhood, many of whom had to work to help make a living. Their husbands were either gravel haulers, W. P. A. workers or jack-of-all-trades employes. I was known to be dependable with the care of offspring.

The few nickels and dimes that I earned were saved to buy the necessities that were needed when I went back to school in the fall. For instance, $1.98 would buy a nice print dress or pair of shoes. Ten cents could purchase a pair of panties or anklets. Sometimes my older sister's coat was made over to fit me. The wide three-inch hem revealed the transformation. I yearned to own one of the gray tweed princess styled coats that were worn by some of the girls my age.

My feelings of insecurity and low esteem seemed to be magnified during that summer as I was growing into a long-legged, skinny twelve year old. I thought of myself as an ugly duckling. I wished that I was old enough to quit school and stay in our home where I felt safe from the people whom I thought looked down on us because we were poor.

"You're just as good as the rest of the kids," Mama often reassured me when she knew I was becoming fearful about entering the sixth grade. "I wish you would have more confidence in yourself."

Opening day arrived and my sister and I once again headed for the red brick schoolhouse and mingled with our classmates who had changed in appearance during the past three months. There were a few new faces in the crowd.

"Guess what," one of the more talkative children announced. "There is a new sixth grade teacher this year. She has a funny name like Wheel Dryer, and her first name is Gertrude."

" 'Gravel Gertie' we'll call her," one of the clowns of the class announced. I was secretly hoping and praying that she was going to be a nice, kind teacher no matter what her name happened to be.

The school bell clanged and beckoned one and all to enter the "halls of grade-school ivy." The sixth grade room was located on the second floor near the long stairway. I followed along with the laughing, carefree children and entered the door to our classroom. Inside the room, standing next to a desk, was a young, brown haired woman in a gray dress with white collar and cuffs. She looked plain and old fashioned.

When I walked past, I exchanged a shy "hello" and noticed her blue-gray eyes were beautiful and her wide smile revealed slightly prominent white teeth. At that moment I knew that my worries were over. Miss Gertie Weeldryer was going to be the most wonderful teacher that I ever knew. (To me a smile was as friendly as a dog wagging its tail.)

From the very first day of school her warm personality enveloped everyone of her pupils and we responded with an affection and a desire to reach new goals during our last year of grade school.

"There won't be any privileged students or teacher's pets in my class," she told the students. "You will all be judged on your own individual merits and I expect everyone to do their share to help make this year a fulfilling experience."

She spoke often about her own childhood on a farm near Chancellor (South Dakota) of wanting to be a school teacher ever since she was a little girl. Her eyes softened and sometimes became misty when she told stories about her family and relatives and how much she missed having them around. Living by the golden rule was her motto for life, and a belief that all were created equal. All should be proud of one's background no matter how humble. She repeated sentiments to instill new hope into the minds of the children like me, who were poor.

I was beginning to emerge again from my cocoon to become a more beautiful butterfly whose talent for writing poetry and short stories was being awaited by the world.

"You have a flair for writing," she often told me. "I wouldn't be a bit surprised if you turn out to be a famous writer. You must have confidence in yourself and never lose faith in your abilities. Promise me you will do that."

"I will," I told her, feeling more confident now that there was one person in the world who believed in me.

"I've decided to place you in the 7-1's next year at Junior High. Some of the most intelligent students from all the grade schools will be in that special division. If you continue to do excellent work you will have no trouble keeping up with the others. If you ever have any problems don't hesitate to come to me. And another thing, try to put a little meat on those bones," she smiled, squeezing my skinny arm. (Although I received free milk during my grade school years, I remained underweight.)

The last time I saw my favorite teacher was the day we received our report cards. I felt proud that she promoted me to the 7-1's. My sister, Neeney, didn't do quite as well. She was placed in the 7-2's, but was cautioned to study.

Everyone said their "goodbyes," and hurried out of the schoolroom. It was time for me to leave, but I couldn't find the words to express how much I appreciated all that my teacher had done for me. But I knew she understood when she took my hand and told me goodbye. There was something special between us.

"You're going to make it," she reassured me. "I'm not going to worry. Some day I will be reading about your accomplishments. Goodbye, dear."

There was a lump in my throat and I was afraid that I was going to cry. I hurried out the door and down the stairs. My grade school days were over and I wasn't a child anymore. I took one last look at the red brick schoolhouse and then hurried to catch up with the neighbor kids who were leaping with joy because school was out and a long fun-filled summer was coming.

I could write many pages about my beloved Miss Weeldryer and about the months that I spent in her classroom. She was a truly dedicated school teacher. I am now in the summer of my years just like the aging schoolhouse that still stands on the south side of town, only a few blocks from where I live today. I often pass by and take note of the happy school children on the playground. I recall when I was a child there and I see again the yesterdays and Miss Weeldryer above the crowds. She is waving to me to come back again to that golden season when we looked for the autumn leaves to press in our books to keep forever. How well I remember.

The day was chilly and the gusty wind was chasing the dark gray snow clouds across the sky. The dry leaves of red and gold were playing hopscotch across the tree-lined boulevards. It was fun trying to catch one of the elusive bits of foliage and there was much laughter coming from the small group being showered with the falling leaves. Reaching up into a rugged old oak tree, Miss Gertie found a perfect leaf and handed it to me.

"Remember me when you look at it many years from now," she smiled. Just like the treasured oak leaf so are the golden memories I have kept stored in my heart for Miss Gertie Weeldryer, the sixth grade teacher of Eugene Field School.

THE MUSIC TEACHER

"Do-re-me-fa-sol-la-ti-do-
do-ti-la-sol-fa-me-re-do."

I sang in a strained high pitched voice, trying not to hear the snickers that were coming from some of the students attempting to hide their own fear of singing the scale for Miss Valentine Preston, the music teacher for all of the grade schools of Mitchell.

"That's just fine," she said, giving my voice an above-average rating. My knees were knocking and my throat was dry as sand.

"I'm sure glad that's over with for another year," I thought to myself. Now it was my turn to listen while my classmates sang, some in sheer agony.

"He can't carry a tune in a bushel basket," Miss Preston commented on one of the boys who sounded like an alley cat sitting on a high board fence. There was one boy in particular who ruined the group singing by his off-key crooning. Robert was finally asked to just "mouth" the words during the school programs.

I loved music and could warble like a bird except all alone in front of the class. The voice tests were dreaded by most of the students, except Betty who could almost hit a high "C." Everyone was positive that she would end up on the stage of the Metropolitan Opera Company.

Music was Miss Preston's profession and she wanted the whole world to sing along with her. I thought of her as a minstrel lady when she waved her baton to direct a rollicking folk song. Her cupid's bow lips were rouged, her face double chinned, framed by a mane of wind-blown hair. Dresses with ruffled necklines and draped peplums clung to her short, but pleasingly plump figure that rose and fell with the rhythm of her singing.

Her shining hour came during the annual Christmas concerts that were held in the grade schools or at the Corn Palace where all the glee clubs and vocal groups assembled. She spent more hours patiently weaving a choir of melodic voices into a symphony of celestial music.

Our Christmas pageant was a night to remember. All the parents, relatives and friends were invited to attend. This was the only school function that Mama ever enjoyed. The limited seating section was always filled to standing room only.

Miss Preston approached the podium dressed in a gown of flowing chiffon, a comb of sparkling rhinestones nestled in an upswept hairdo. Looking very elegant, she bowed, turned to the first grade students and gave a signal for them to stand. While the proud moms and dads beamed, childish voices chorused, "Jolly Old St. Nicholas" and "Up In Santa Land." The six-year-olds usually stole the show with their bright-eyed enthusiasm.

Sister Neeney and I were dressed in our best "bibs and tuckers" on this special night. Mama found a way to scrape up a few extra dollars to buy new dresses. We were even chosen by Miss Preston to sing with a vocal group of girls the beautiful song, "Glory to God in the Highest." I wasn't a bit nervous as we followed our music teacher's direction. I peeked over at Mama sitting at the rear of the auditorium as usual. She looked as well groomed as the other mothers and the PTA president, and I was proud of her.

After each grade sang a medley of carols it was time for the grand finale and we all stood to sing the beautiful "Silent Night." The gymnasium echoed and re-echoed with the last word of "peace." We all sat down again. Miss Preston bowed gracefully to the audience while they applauded. The Christmas program had ended for another year.

The School Nurse

"Be true to your teeth or they will be false to you," Mama used to warn us kids so that we would remember to brush our teeth. There weren't too many toothpastes on the market at that time and they were expensive. Just plain table salt or soda was a good substitute but the taste was awful. I used to sneak a few gobs of paste from my older brother's tube. They could afford the foamy sweet-tasting cleanser. When I looked in the mirror I thought I had the perfect "Ipana smile" even though my white teeth were a little bit crooked. The only time anyone in our family or the neighbor's went to a dentist was to have a tooth pulled. The cavities were left until there was no other alternative.

I became accustomed to seeing many of the neighbors suffer from aching teeth because they couldn't afford to go to a dentist. Home remedies such as aspirin, cloves and even chewing tobacco were used to relieve the pain. Then there were stories of horror from those who did go to the dentist office. I used to almost feel the agony when they went into detail about a tooth extraction. A few of the men helped soothe the hurt by getting drunk before they went.

"I'm never going to go through that misery," I promised myself, rubbing some more salt across my teeth and gums.

"You better brush your teeth more often," I warned my little sister, Neeney, whose dental habits were as bad as her other personal hygiene, "or you will end up toothless like Mama and have to wear false teeth."

"My teeth will never fall out," she stubbornly insisted, stuffing a big "jaw breaker" into her mouth. "Candy is good for my teeth, no matter what that school nurse says."

One day while faithfully brushing above the kitchen sink I felt a twinge of pain and upon closer examination in the mirror I noticed a dark spot between two of my molars. The dreaded moment had arrived. My teeth were starting to go and in the following weeks the cavities grew bigger and bigger. I didn't want anyone to know about my problem, not even Mama. "Maybe it will go away," I hoped and prayed.

Miss Beth Olson, the school nurse, came to our school about every three months to check on the students' hearing, vision, teeth or any other problems affecting our health. I wasn't looking forward to seeing her this time because of my teeth but my appointed time arrived and I reluctantly went into her office with an odd feeling in the pit of my stomach.

She greeted me with a friendly smile, exposing gold inlays between her front teeth. The white starched uniform and cap made her look like a modern day Florence Nightingale.

"You can get on the scale," she said. "Let's see if you've gained any weight since the milk program."

I watched the metal indicator stop at the same numbers as the last physical. I was so skinny that if I turned sideways, I could hardly be seen at all.

"You're going to have to gain a few pounds to catch up with your height. I see you've grown another half an inch," she said, placing her hand on my head.

"Sit down on this chair. I'll test your hearing. Now close your eyes and let me know when you hear the ticking of my watch."

My hearing was excellent, she commented, while putting the dainty gold watch back on her wrist.

"Now let's test your vision. Stand over there and place this card over your left eye." So far so good, I thought.

She pointed to each letter that became smaller on each row but I could see like an eagle and she pronounced me O. K. She was saving the worst for the last.

Taking a wooden tongue depressor from a box and placing her hand on my shoulder and using the depresser she proceeded to look down my throat. "Nothing wrong there. What about the teeth?" I had thought of covering the cavities with my tongue.

Right away she noticed the decaying teeth and picked away with a sharp instrument. My jaws were getting tired and I noticed a look of concern on her face.

"Oh, my, that's really too bad," she whispered. "Those permanent molars will have to be saved. Don't your parents ever take you to a dentist?"

"We can't afford to go to dentists," I told her, trying to hide the mounting fear in my voice.

"Well, I have good news for you. Beginning this year there is a fund set aside for underprivileged children who can't afford dental care. I'm going to make an appointment for you next week with Dr. Buetell. He is a very nice man and he will fix your teeth as good as new. Isn't that wonderful?"

I tried to smile and appear grateful but I felt that she had just given me a death sentence.

I awaited my fate as the days and hours ticked away. "Why me? I brushed my teeth every day. My sister's teeth are solid as a rock," I moaned.

"It won't hurt a bit," my sister tried to console me as she blew another pink bubble from the wad of gum in her mouth.

"I wish you were in my place," I said angrily. "You never have anything happen to you." I was mad at the world.

There was no one to escort me on that last mile as I left the schoolhouse and walked the many blocks to the main part of town. I knew there was no avoiding this coming unpleasant experience. I had to face it. My knees began to quiver as I slowly climbed up the long flight of stairs in the old Western Bank building where Dr. Buetell was located.

"Come right in, the dentist is waiting for you," a pleasant voiced receptionist told me as I hesitantly walked through the door into a back room which was the chamber of horrors as far as I was concerned. I didn't know if I should sit, stand or lie down.

"Sit in that chair," she said, pointing to a black leather and steel contraption surrounded by fearsome hooks. "The dentist will be here in a minute. Just relax."

I felt so helpless and alone as I cringed in fear on the cold leather chair. I wanted to cry but I knew I couldn't do anything to upset the dentist who was going to improve my health.

"We need good solid teeth to chew our food properly," I could hear Miss Olson's voice repeating.

Suddenly a swarthy complexioned man emerged from behind me, wiping his hands on a towel. "Hello, I'm Dr. Buetell," he said, while a muscle twitched on his cheek. "You're Dolores Barnes, I see. I'll just tie this little towel around your neck and we'll see what the trouble is. Now open your mouth as wide as you can, and try not to swallow too much."

I tried to obey his instructions but sat as rigid as a board while he probed my teeth. I began to study his features through his fingers that were pressed against my face. His dark wispy hair was already wet from the perspiration that was in beads on his forehead. The penetrating black eyes looked like burning coals. When the grinding drill grazed my tongue, the pencil-thin black mustache gave him the appearance of a Simon Legree.

It was an agonizing ordeal for me. "Please let this be the last time," I prayed when the pain of the drill became too intense to bear.

"Just hang on a little longer. It will soon be over. - - - - That's it, rinse out your mouth and then you can go. Now take good care of those new fillings."

My face and jaws were stiff as I crawled out of the chair. The nurse handed me a new toothbrush with a sample tube of toothpaste, then waved me goodbye. I was never so happy to make an exit in my life.

The crisp, fall air felt clear and refreshing as I walked back to school to finish out the day. My teeth were as good as new and I was determined that I would never enter a dentist's office again. It would take wild horses to get me back.

But alas, throughout my life I found myself in the hands of many dentists, and no matter how hard I tried I couldn't preserve my pearly white teeth nor my dazzling smile. My little sister, Neeney, had the last laugh. Her teeth are still as solid as a rock.

The Police Story

"If you kids don't stay off of my property I'm gonna call the cops," a cranky old man often yelled at us when he caught us picking some lilacs from his bushes that bloomed along the sidewalk. "Cops take away little boys and girls that don't mind. Cops will put you in jail where they feed you just bread and water."

These dire warnings about the men in blue were often heard during my childhood, spoken by well-meaning relatives.

Scare tactics which didn't seem to bother most of the youngsters, drove fear into my heart. I didn't want the flat-foots grabbing me by the collar and hauling me off to jail.

"You better come down out of that apple tree before Mrs. Miller catches you," I told my little sister who was stuffing her pockets with the green fruit. "She will have you sent to jail." Stealing apples and cherries from the fruit trees around town was a temptation to many children.

"Oh, be quiet," she answered, "I'm not afraid of the cops. The birds eat all they want, why can't we?" "But she warned us to stay out of her yard," I continued. I didn't want my sister to be a "criminal."

When she had filled every pocket of her overalls, she jumped to the ground and climbed over the picket fence, next to the alley. "Oh! you had me scared to death," I gasped.

"Here, have an apple," she said, pulling a large one from a pocket. I accepted the stolen fruit even though I knew I shouldn't.

The apple did taste crunchy and delicious so I ate another one while we walked down the alley towards home. "I'm so thirsty from eating all those apples, I want a drink of water," Neeney remarked. "Let's get a drink from the pump." So we each took turns pushing up and down on the handle until our thirst was quenched. Refreshed by the cool water, we continued on home. Then the misery began.

"Oh, my stomach feels so full," groaned Neeney. "I don't feel so good." By this time I began to feel like an inflated balloon and had sharp gas pains. "I'm going to lie down in that cool grass," I told Neeney. "I don't want Mama to see me sick. She will make me drink that baking soda and water."

"I'm going to the privy," she answered. I soon heard groans and sighs of agony coming from behind the closed doors. She was sick.

When she finally emerged she was white and trembling. "I think it's the green apples," she moaned in a weak voice. "That's what we get for eating something that is stolen," I said. "God is making us suffer by giving us a good belly-ache."

Neeney and I lay in the cool grass the rest of the afternoon, suffering periodic cramps. By supper time we had recovered enough to sneak into the house and crawl into bed.

We had no sooner lain down when the bedroom door opened. It was Mama. "How come you kids aren't at the supper table, we're having weenies and sauerkraut and green apple pie for dessert. Mrs. Miller brought over a basket of apples."

As the time went by I learned that indeed the police did come and arrest citizens when they didn't obey the law. My own dad was "pinched" for bootlegging whiskey during prohibition.

There were also children and teenagers who were sent to the State Training School at Plankinton on various charges. Mostly runaways or children from broken homes. A few of our neighbors' children were sent to the school as incorrigibles.

"Did you hear about Margaret?" I heard Mama ask Dad one morning while they were talking over cups of coffee in the kitchen. "What about Margaret?" asked Dad, who was little interested in the neighborhood gossip. "Well, the cops and Mrs. Williams (the police matron) went over there this morning and whisked poor little Margaret away. I didn't know that she was considered bad."

Maggie was a fourteen year old girl who lived in a motherless home, only a few rods up the lane from our house. "What did she do, rob a bank? There's a lot of that going on around the country," Dad joked, scanning the newspaper.

"Don't be funny," snapped my mother. "Her old man locked her away. Said she was getting too boy crazy and he couldn't handle her any more. I feel so sorry for that poor kid. If her mother were alive, this would never have happened." "Well, Maggie no doubt will have to stay there for a while. That girl will know more than her prayers when she gets out of that place," predicted Dad.

"I wish there was some way we could help her," Mama sighed. "Mrs. Hogan told me that sometimes a minor child can be placed in a foster home and be released on probation." "Are you crazy?" Dad shouted, jumping to his feet. "I hope you're not talking about taking her in. This house isn't big enough for us, let alone another child. I'm putting my foot down. Just keep out of it. We don't want to get mixed up with the law again. Just mind your own business!"

Despite Dad's protests, Mama couldn't forget about the unfortunate case of "Maggie," who was placed in the school along with other miscreants from throughout the state. Secretly she and a parole officer were working on a plan to help Maggie who had no one else to turn to.

One day, out of the blue, a sleek looking black car drove into the yard and deposited Margaret on our door-step.

She was dressed in nondescript clothing and clutched a battered suitcase in one hand. Her crown of red burnished curls had been sheared, making her look like a singed chicken. We kids stared at the freckle-faced girl but didn't know what to say to her.

"Maggie is going to stay with us for awhile until arrangements are made for her to live in California with a cousin," explained Mama. "You kids make her feel at home now. Bobby, take her suitcase into the girls' bedroom."

It didn't take long for Maggie to become adjusted to our rambunctious household. She pitched in and helped with the daily tasks. Mama was paid a few dollars a month for the extra food expense. Maggie's father never came to visit his wayward daughter.

Just when we kids had accepted Maggie as a new member of the family, a letter arrived in the mail with a one way ticket to the west coast. She wasn't too happy with the news but knew that she had to abide by the rules of her probation. During the night I was awakened when I heard Maggie crying from across our crowded bedroom. I felt pity for her having to ride the train to California all alone.

It was with heavy hearts that we said goodbye to the little displaced girl who was embarking on a long journey to live with an unknown family.

"Take care of yourself and write once in awhile," Mama told her, trying not to show emotion. "You'll love California, you will probably never want to return to this old cold country again."

Maggie walked out of our lives and left behind the only real home she had ever known. At first the letters came on a monthly basis but as the years passed by they stopped. Was

Police officers, circa 1940. Top row, left to right: Leo Casey, Carl Hubert, Henry Stevens, George Carstens and Ada Williams (police matron and welfare lady). Bottom row: John Bauer, Herb Kellogg, Marcus Lau, Eltor Isaak, Walter Cunningham.

she happy, or sad, I wondered when I gazed at a fading snapshot of her?

"She lives in a different world now, with new friends and so many places to see," Mama explained when we asked why Maggie didn't write anymore. I just hope she's well and happy, wherever she is, and has forgotten those months that she spent in the reform school."

TRIBUTE TO THE MITCHELL POLICE DEPARTMENT

"Cheese it, the cops!" was a common teenage expression warning of the presence of a policeman in the vicinity. It was heard more often on Hallowe'en night, while the youngsters of the town were "tricking or treating," or soaping car and store windows or tipping over privies.

There were more than enough patrolmen on the force, but they had only one cruiser car, so they couldn't be everywhere at once. Walking a beat and wearing out lots of shoe leather earned them the nickname "flatfoot." Unlike the police of today (who ride in the modern patrol cars equipped with radios), their detail and duty was on foot. A few night watchmen were also hired to protect the business places.

170

Many nights a lone policeman could be seen walking the quiet streets of Main Street after the sidewalks were rolled up.

Most of the citizens were more law abiding during this period. Teenagers found more enjoyment at home with friends, family and neighbors, instead of hanging around on street corners. Money was scarce, so very few "hot rods" were owned by the young. Most youngsters were wary of the law. Who wanted to appear before a judge and be sentenced to the Training School? Kids then wouldn't dare call a policeman a copper or flatfoot to his face, or to spit on police and call them vile names. Not that the younger generation of the 30's wore halos. Enough got into trouble with the "long arm of the law" and were punished. There was more than enough drinking of beer and moonshine, but drugs were unheard of. The only repercussions they suffered were morning after hangovers.

Jailbirds and the town drunks were confined in the basement of the old city hall building. Stories of bread and water diets were often heard. Alcoholics were thrown into the "tank" to sleep it off. Today, an alcoholic usually receives sympathy and treatment.

Everyone knew that the police station was head-quartered on the first floor of the granite and cement structure, standing on the corner of West Second and Rowley streets in Mitchell. All the other city government offices shared this large complex.

Mrs. Ada Williams, the police matron and welfare lady, was located downstairs next to the rest rooms. Between our visits with her for our shoes and clothes and using the facilities, we became accustomed to seeing the policemen.

If there was any trouble with a delinquent girl in the home or school, she was reported to Mrs. Williams. Among her many duties, she was a chaperone at the Dreamland Ball Room. Many girls who were under the age limit of eighteen tried to escape her watchful eyes as she scanned the dance floor for minors. Many were escorted out the door quietly by the law.

We watched the police strolling back and forth to the City Hall reporting on and off duty. I must say I was somewhat apprehensive of their stern looks. Maybe because children heard too often, "If you don't be good, the cops are gonna getcha." I also believe the pistols buckled to their hips and the black "billy club" stuffed into their rear pocket convinced one and all to fly right.

"Slim" Carstensen, Mitchell police
officer during 1930's

Neeney and I usually gave them a wide berth as we passed them on the sidewalk. We took a good peek after their backs were turned.

For the most part, this job of upholding the law of the land was regarded with respect and commanded prestige. A rookie could work himself up through the ranks from patrolman to desk sergeant, perhaps chief of police, and then possibly be elected sheriff. Policemen then had to pay for their uniforms from their own pocket. The style and colors have changed with the times from the early 30's until today—from the khaki to the dark blue wools with gray shirts of the 40's. People can always readily identify a police officer by the metal badge on his cap and jacket. Salaries weren't really in the upper bracket. During the late 30's and into the 40's the pay was $100 a month. So it wasn't the salary that drew these dedicated men to this profession where their lives were in danger every day.

The many policemen whom I remember during my childhood have all passed away except for a few who have long been retired. They have been replaced by the "New Breed." The city hall with the police headquarters was demolished,

**Chief of Police Arthur Kirkpatrick
(in the late 1930's)**

replaced by a municipal parking lot where automobiles cover the footsteps of that long ago. Yet, when I walk along this old street, I remember the police as they were then. Here are the names of the patrolmen—desk sergeants, chiefs of police, deputy sheriffs and sheriffs, who served the City of Mitchell during the Depression years.

Emory Owens
Walter (Slim) Carstensen
William (Bill) Pattison
William Hale
Joe Julian
Charles (Art) Newman
Mark Lau
Leo Casey
George Carstens
Eltor Isaak
Carl Hubert
Clyde Palmer
Police Matron Mrs. Ada Williams
Tom Callan

Wood Smith
John Bauer
Arthur Kirkpatrick
Walter Cunningham
William Christopher
Burnice (Bill) Carrick
Henry Newlin
Leo Kirby
Hank Stevens
John Wenegar
Herb Kellogg
John (Jack) Tobin

173

In Our Merry Oldsmobile

When I was a small girl I often envied the neighbors who were lucky enough to own an automobile. The Widmann family who lived on the next block drove a shiny blue Essex with yellow wheels and running boards that connected to the fenders. Walt Widmann who was self-employed in the jewelry business was well off by our standards. Although he worked hard to support his family, he enjoyed taking the neighbor children along with his own to the bathing beach or just for a spin around the block.

"How about an ice cream cone at the Dew Drop Inn?" he asked while we cruised along north of Mitchell. "Oh goody," we all yelled at once as we watched for the small road-side drive-inn that sold soft drinks, ice cream cones and hot dogs. While we kids sat in expectation, Mr. Widmann returned with an assortment of cones in a paper tray. "Now be careful and don't let them drip on the seats," he remarked. I wouldn't dream of spilling a drop on the beautiful leather cushions. "I wish we had a car like this," I thought to myself, gazing through the sparkling glass of the windshield. The few automobiles that we did own from time to time were fit for the junk yard.

"This is sure a nice car," I shyly told our good-hearted neighbor. "It will do till we buy a new one," he answered, settling down in the comfortable upholstery. "Too bad your dad can't afford a decent car or truck to drive to work. I sure hate to see him carrying all that painting equipment by hand. Maybe I can help him find a good used car somewhere in town. Well, is everybody sitting down back there?" he called to the back seat drivers. "Here we go. Hang onto your hats." And away we went, leaving a cloud of dust swirling behind us.

"Who's beeping a horn out front?" Mama hollered from the kitchen, "go see who it is; it must be important."

In a few seconds Bobby came rushing through the door as if the devil was on his heels. "Hey, everybody, Dad's got a car," he gasped. "Hurry, come and see it." Sure enough there was a vehicle that had seen its best days, standing in the front yard. Dad was sitting behind the wheel with one arm resting on the open window of the door, looking as proud as a peacock.

"How do you like it?" he asked the whole family who had gathered around to inspect the old car. It looked like a million bucks to us.

Electric car of the 1930's. (There were two in Mitchell.)

"Is it really ours?" asked the boys, jumping up and down on the bumpers, and pushing on the horn button. "Ours and the Rozum Motor Company," Dad answered. "I only had to pay two dollars down and two dollars a month."

"That's a lot of money," Mama reminded him. "What if we can't make the payments?" "Don't worry, I'll never let this baby go back. In six months it will be all mine. Jump in and I'll show you how smooth she runs."

Before he had the words out of his mouth the car was filled to capacity with nine of us. We were having more fun than a barrel of monkeys.

"Is everybody in? Hang on now, we're off," Dad hollered to his passengers who were too excited to hear.

"Oh, look, all the neighbors are gawking at us," Mama smiled. "Bet they wonder how we can afford to buy an automobile."

"Hope they get their eyes full," Dad answered with a chuckle, "it's about time we have a little enjoyment." He pressed on the black horn that beeped an "ahuga" sound that scattered the neighborhood chickens and dogs.

"Where do you want to go?" he asked my mother, who was by now feeling a little elated with her new status symbol. "Out to the lake," she directed. "I haven't been out there since last spring when the water went over the spillway."

Our grand tour on the outskirts of town was an enjoyable

175

experience and we kids didn't want it to end. Upon arriving back home we just wanted to stay in the car until we were convinced that the old jalopy was really ours.

"I don't want to see any of you kids monkeying around with the dashboard, and be careful slamming the doors; someone might get a finger cut off. And leave that crank alone."

Dad's warnings went in one ear and out the other. During the first few weeks, brother Bobby started the engine and was rolling towards the oil station when a neighbor stopped the vehicle short of the gas pumps. Sister Neeney suffered the loss of a finger tip when she caught her hand in the door. There were other minor abrasions and one major catastrophe before our old bus ended up in the junk yard.

"When do I get to drive the car?" asked Mama one day, while watching Dad cleaning the spark plugs. "We've had it for two months now and I haven't been behind the wheel." "I don't think you know the rules of the road yet," Dad answered. "It takes a lot of know-how to keep track of the speed and give the right hand signals." "Oh, don't give me that malarky," Mama argued. "Any two-year-old can operate these modern day vehicles. I'll be careful and just take the kids for a ride out in the country where there's not much traffic."

"Oil Station" in the late 1920's. Station pictured was owned and operated by Ike Spears and Grace (Spears) Boone, by pumps.

176

"Well, all right, but remember to stay off the main drag. Go out on the cemetery road, the traffic is dead there." Mama didn't think his joke was very amusing.

Mama was having the time of her life as she maneuvered her way out of town, while we kids looked both ways at each crossroad. "Is there anything coming?" she asked, and we reported that the coast was clear.

"Boy, now I know how those race drivers feel," Mama exclaimed, with a look of rapture on her face. "I should have tried this long ago. I knew there was nothing to it.

The afternoon was growing late when we headed back to town and the needle on the gasoline gauge was almost pointing to empty. She searched her purse for a few coins to buy a gallon of gas at an oil station.

"Now don't tell Dad but I'm going to buzz a few blocks of Main," our mother told us, who by now felt like an old hand steering a car.

Everything went smooth as silk as she passed through each stop sign without an incident. Reaching the south end of town by the depot, we turned our touring car and went north again.

Nearing the Corn Palace we all looked out of the window to view the new decorations. Mama tried to peek at an angle through the windshield, forgetting about the steering wheel. "Look out," one of our brothers screamed, "your heading for that street light." Mama's reflexes were quick but she stepped on the gas pedal instead of the brake. We suddenly found our car draped around the iron lamp post. Streams of water gushed from the smashed radiator and gas fumes filled the air. We kids were thrown to the floor boards like rag dolls.

Fumed Mama, "Why didn't you kids warn me sooner? Did anybody get hurt?"

Along with my brothers and sisters, I climbed out of the damaged car that had started to attract a crowd. A stern looking policeman was among them. When I saw him I became very frightened and thought we would all be taken to jail.

"What happened lady?" the policeman asked in a gruff voice, "you're supposed to drive in the street, not on the sidewalk." This brought on a roar of laughter from the bystanders.

"I just wasn't looking where I was going," she tried to explain. "I guess I was going where I was looking." This remark brought more laughs from the crowd that formed a circle around us. I wish she wouldn't get smart, I worried.

After Mama had answered all the questions of the "third degree," the patrolman closed his notebook and ordered a man to call a wrecker.

"You people get into my car and I'll give you a ride home," he said. The disheveled group by now were feeling the bruises and bumps. I think he felt sorry for us.

"No thanks," Mama responded, "we only live a few blocks from here." I knew she would worry what the neighbors would think if they saw the police bringing us home.

"What in hell happened to my car?" asked Dad angrily that evening when he came into the house. "Did you run into a freight train? I knew I shouldn't have let you have the keys."

For once Mama was on the receiving end of a tongue-lashing and I felt sorry for her as she listened to Father's berating. He was usually as cool as a cucumber.

After Dad repeated the "I told you so's," like a broken record, Mama looked up at him and quietly said, "Well, have you got it all out of your system now? There's no use crying over spilled milk. It's over and done with. Kaput! I've had a rough day and I'm going to bed." She arose and slowly walked towards the bedroom, holding her hands to her wrenched back, a result of the smash-up.

Dad reached up into the cupboard, picked up his flash-light and walked out into the night, slamming the door behind him. He was going to take another look at the wrecked automobile that was once, but not for long, his pride and joy. I knew it would be a long time before we would be riding in another car.

The Flying Machines

"Mama! Mama!" we kids yelled through the screen door. "Come outside, there's an airplane coming. Hurry up or you will miss it." We scrambled back down the steps, not wanting to miss this exciting event.

Mama rushed out into the yard and, shielding her eyes from the sun with one hand, scanned the horizon. "There it is," she pointed skyward. "I see a little speck way up there by that big white cloud."

We all squinted into the wild blue yonder, listening to the drone of the plane's motor.

"I can't see anything," Bobby complained, "why don't they fly a little lower so we can get a good look?"

The tiny airplane soon disappeared from view and we all relaxed from the tension of watching an almost invisible object. Disappointment showed on our faces.

"Don't pout. There will be more airplanes flying over," Mama told us. "I heard there is going to be an air field built out west of town. Some day we can drive out there and maybe get a chance to get up close to one of the planes on the ground." In our wildest imagination we kids couldn't comprehend how anybody could fly a machine with wings.

"I wish I had wings like a bird," brother Buddy dreamily remarked. "I'd fly right over this town and look down on all the people. Gee, wouldn't that be something?"

"I'd like to live in the sky," I shyly suggested, and watch all the clouds drifting by and be able to touch them."

"If you lived in the sky, you'd be in heaven," Bobby informed me with a wise-as-an-owl expression on his face.

"I'd love to ride in a balloon and sail across the ocean," sister Neeney exclaimed. She was a daredevil.

Our thoughts took flight as we soared to far-away places that only children can imagine in their fantasies.

Unknown to us, Mama was eaves-dropping on our childish conversations. She opened the screen door and hollered, "You kids better come back down to earth now and get those weeds pulled out of the corn patch before your dad gets home." But we continued to watch, listen and hope for signs of an aircraft zooming overhead again.

One afternoon while playing beneath the cottonwood

trees we were brought to our feet by an approaching noise that sounded like an exploding washing machine motor. Just above the tree tops was a silver colored airplane flying so low that we could see the pilot in the cockpit.

Nothing could have been a greater thrill. We shouted, "Hi, Lindy," waved, then jumped up and down. (All pilots were Lindbergh to us.) To our astonishment he returned our greeting and dipped his wings. By this time the whole neighborhood was spellbound, watching the daring young man turning the plane, dive and do loops.

"Oh, I wish he would come down and give us a ride," we said. "He can't land. He has to have a runway. You wouldn't want to see him crash," one of the neighbor boys spoke up.

This air-minded boy's name was Jimmy French, whose knowledge of aviation was well-known among his friends. He was the envy of everyone because he often could fly with his family in their own aircraft.

"Why don't you kids come out to the airport some Sunday afternoon and see the new airplane? You can even have a ride for about fifty cents," he said. A half dollar during those hard times was a lot of money, but we finally persuaded Dad to take us to the airport.

"Now don't let those kids get too close to those contraptions," warned Mama. "Those propellers are just like knives when they start whirling. I read the other day that a man in Chicago got his arm cut off by one of those blades."

"Don't worry, Mama," Dad replied, "I know how to take care of things. I wasn't born yesterday, you know."

Mama waved goodbye with a worried look on her face while we happily bounced out of the yard in our old Overland.

Dad drove through town until we came to a winding country road, then proceeded on until we approached some pasture land. Surrounding the area were weather-beaten fence posts leaning between sagging strands of barbed wire. Sunflowers and milk weeds bowed and waved in the wayward winds.

"Maybe it's too breezy for the planes to fly today," worried brother Bobby while Dad gazed across the open spaces in search of the airport. "I think it's another mile north," said Dad, and gunned the engine, leaving a trail of smoke behind us.

After a few minutes of silence from a usually noisy bunch of youngsters, one of the brothers shouted, "Look over there!

"Tailspin Tommy" standing by his plane,
Mitchell Airport, sometime in 1930.

There's a plane circling low for a landing. Hurry up. The hangar must be over there behind those trees." Dad drove as fast as he could with all heads dangling from the car windows, so as not to miss anything.

Within seconds we spotted the wooden building at the end of a flat pasture. It looked like a large garage.

Everyone scrambled out of the car and ran to watch the exciting landing of the winged silver bird. The plane swooped around the field one more time, then came to a rolling halt where we stood. We were amazed to see a real airplane, only a few yards away. "Look but don't touch," a man told the gaping crowd.

The pilot climbed from the cockpit and jumped to the ground. Taking off his leather helmet and goggles, he waved and smiled to an entranced audience. Two men whom Dad called "grease monkeys" walked around the "two winger" and inspected the machine from prop to tail.

"Do you wanna take her up now?" he asked another flyer who was zipping up his leather jacket. "It purrs like a kitten. Boy, she is some plane."

"O. K. Everybody back away," warned the pilot. "We don't want anyone getting hurt." He settled down into the

181

cockpit then yelled "contact" to the mechanic who was hanging onto the propeller. After a few downward pulls the propeller started to whirl. "Hang on to your hats," yelled Dad as the rush of air blew dust over us.

When the smoke and dust cleared we watched the fabric and wire bird taxiing down the field and fly into the sky like a giant eagle. In a few minutes it disappeared into the fleecy clouds. My neck felt stiff and my eyes ached from the dirt that flew up from the wheels, but it was worth all the discomfort.

Our attention was diverted to a cabin plane that was being pushed out of the hangar by two men and a young boy. It was Jimmy French helping his dad and uncle wheel an enclosed two-seat plane onto the runway. The blue and yellow aircraft was newly purchased by the French family. "How lucky can a kid be?" we thought, watching the family climb into the cabin and close the plexiglas doors.

I listened to Dad and the crowd of onlookers discussing the adventurous flyers as they circled above us on "a wing and a prayer."

"It must take a lot of guts to fly one of those crates," a fat jowled man remarked, chewing on a stub of a cigar. "I wouldn't get up there for love nor money. No sir, not me."

"Me neither," another observer answered. "When I die, I want to be all in one piece." "Would you fly in one of those planes?" Bobby asked Dad.

"Why not?" Dad answered. "They say it's as safe as sitting in a kitchen chair. But they are too expensive for my blood. I can't even afford one ride around the field." Although we kids never got the opportunity to fly, it was still a pleasure to watch the few trail blazers test their skill and luck against gravity and the elements.

It was at the end of a lazy summer's day that I learned that high adventure did have a price to pay. Mama was busily setting the supper dishes on the table while I placed the silverware. We heard the back door open slowly and Dad walked in, his face as white as a sheet and his hands shaking.

"What's the matter with you?" Mama asked, looking into his distraught eyes. "A terrible accident happened this afternoon at the airport. There was a plane crash." "Oh, no," moaned Mama, "was anyone killed?" "Yes, the whole French family," whispered Dad, shaking his head. "Jimmy is dead?" we inquired again, not wanting to believe the horrible news. "Yes, little Jimmy took his last plane ride today," Dad said sadly as if it were his own son. "All of them killed instantly."

"I don't think anyone feels like eating supper now," Mama sighed, taking a deep breath. "Well, at least they all died together," she continued. "They're flying up there with the angels now." I couldn't hold back the tears when I saw my mother wipe her eyes with her apron. I walked outdoors so the other kids wouldn't see me sobbing. It was an emotional experience for a five-year-old child and I wondered why God allowed this terrible thing to happen.

The red sunset was turning into twilight as the mournful sounds of the hoot owl echoed through the trees. I looked up into the purple sky and thought I saw one twinkling star that gleamed brighter than the rest. (Mama always said when someone died there was another star added to the heavens.) "That's Jimmy's star," I thought. "I hope he is happy up there with his family."

The next day Mama and the neighbors were discussing the tragedy over the back fence, still stunned by the accident.

"I wonder what went wrong." Nothing like that ever happened around here before. Those new-fangled planes aren't much different than the first ones built by the Wright Brothers."

"I never did take much stock in those flying contraptions. They don't make them safe enough yet."

"Well, they were flirting with death."

"I'll bet there will be a big funeral. The whole town will be there. I wonder if they were insured?"

"Well, I'm not going. It will be too sad, especially when it's a child."

"Do you suppose the coffins will be open? I heard they were picked up in pieces. Oh, it's too terrible to think about."

When the paper boy brought the evening edition we all gathered around Mama while she unfolded the paper and laid it on the table. The French family were pictured on the front page and the headlines told of their death. Another photo showed the twisted remains of the once beautiful airplane.

I couldn't forget the laughing face of Jimmy, and there were many nights filled with dreams of planes crashing. Sometimes I awoke in fear at the sound of an airplane flying over the house. I lost my interest in air ships that sailed away with the winds. I now looked upon them as mechanical monsters that lurked beyond storm clouds. I made a vow that I would never set foot inside of one—and I never have.

The Dirty Thirties — Dust Storms

"If we could only get that Hoover out of the White House, I think the nation would be better off," Mama often remarked about the controversial president as she studied his stern face on the front page of the newspaper. "Something has to be done about the unemployment in this country."

I might have been young but I paid rapt attention to my parents when they discussed the problems of America "the beautiful."

"Who are those people?" I asked Dad, looking at a picture of elegantly dressed men, women and children waving from a luxury liner bound for Europe. We never took a trip ever out of town.

"They are the Vanderbilt and Rockefeller families who are millionaires and can afford anything that their heart's desire," my dad informed me as I sat on his lap while he read the newspaper. "They live in beautiful mansions on nob hill with maids and butlers."

"I'd like to be rich like that," I replied as he turned to the next page.

"Now here are some poor folks of America," he said, pointing to some gaunt people dressed in ragged looking clothing. "They are called Arkies and Okies because they live in Oklahoma, Arkansas and the dust bowl states."

"They sure look hungry," I remarked, noting the emaciated bodies of the children. "Why doesn't someone give them something to eat?"

"They are starving, so most of them are leaving their homes and farms and are moving to a land of sunshine where they can find better paying jobs, they hope. There is work in the vegetable fields and fruit orchards and the pay is five cents an hour. That's better than not working."

"Why can't we move to California?" I questioned. "It would be nice to live where it's warm and be able to pick fruit from the trees whenever we wished."

"It takes money to move that far away," Mama interrupted, "and we can't afford a settin' hen, let alone a trip to the land of milk and honey."

"Well, I still say that here is the man who is going to solve the problems in this country. He is going to help the poor." Dad held the newspaper that pictured a handsome man clenching a cigaret between his teeth. "This great man is Franklin Delano Roosevelt and he will be our next president," Dad prophesied. "He promises jobs and a new deal for everyone."

"They all say that," Mama sniffed, "once they get in office, it's a different story."

I didn't need anyone to tell me that I had the company of millions of Americans in the devastating era of the 30's. We were the "depression generation."

In the beginning only the southwest part of the country was a disaster area, but the devastation from the dust storms and soil erosion soon engulfed the Dakota lands. Farmers and ranchers were financial straits and were forced to seek government relief, because crops were damagd by the drought and grasshoppers. Livestock were starving. Baby pigs were slaughtered or given to the needy because there was no market for them. Water holes and stock dams were dry. The land was dying from thirst.

We kids often rode through the countryside with Dad and his farmer friend, Bob Moir, in his old truck. We observed first-hand the desolate appearance of a once fertile land.

Farm machinery remained idle among patches of fireweeds and thistles that were being fed to cattle. Weathered houses stood unpainted and in need of repair on homesteads now deserted by man and beast.

"Just look at those sagging fences over there," Dad said, shaking his head. "They're almost covered with drifts of dirt blown by the strong winds. I'd like to leave this damn country."

We kids tried to jump over some tumbleweeds as they rolled and tumbled towards us.

"You don't want to get any of those stickers in your skin," farmer Moir warned. "They can hurt and are hell to get out."

"I've got a good notion to get out of South Dakota," we again heard Dad try to convince himself, knowing that he was doomed to remain along with other Dakotans who couldn't afford to leave anyway. It was said about these people, "They didn't have a pot to pee in or a window to throw it out of."

So we all knew that the best thing to do was grin and bear it. Often the temperatures rose to the "boiling point." South Dakota was becoming famous as the hottest spot in the country. You could almost fry an egg on a sidewalk.

Mama found refuge in the basement where "old sol"

couldn't penetrate. There she would feel a little cooler. We kids found our oasis at the south side, Hitchcock Park and wading pools. Walking out to Lake Mitchell to enjoy the breezes over the water was one way to beat the heat. Sometimes the burning pavement blistered our bare feet and we were forced to walk in the sticky weeds where the sandburs made us jump in pain.

One of the most welcome sights during those scorching hot summers was the ice truck driven by one of the friendly ice men.

A white truck loaded with tons of crystal clear cakes of ice cut from the lake in winter, made the rounds about twice a week. Cards placed in the windows requested the amount of ice needed.

"Here comes the ice truck," was a shout heard throughout the neighborhood when it was spotted coming down our street. All the children crowded around to watch the iceman chop away the huge block of frozen goodness. When the chunk was separated it was picked up with a pair of iron tongs and thrown over the iceman's back. A heavy black rubber cape attached to his shoulders protected him from the cold water that began to drip instantly.

"Say, Mister, can we have those little pieces to chew on?" the thirsty children begged. What joy to suck the water from the dripping ice chips.

"Well, I tell you, I'm not much of a person to complain, but if this drought doesn't let up pretty soon, I don't know what will become of me," our farmer friend, Bob Moir, remarked one hot, sultry evening as he sat on our back porch conversing with the assembled neighbors. "There's nothing left on my place except tumbleweeds. I'm afraid I'm going to have to sell out. If the farmers can't make it, no one can." Everyone nodded his head in agreement.

"Why, you would think it was the harvest season already by the looks of the countryside. The grasshoppers are eating up the last of the vegetable gardens and field crops, too. We haven't seen the sun for days on account of the dust. This country is becoming nothing but a wasteland. They might as well give South Dakota back to the Indians." neighbors chimed in. We younger ones stood and sat around this somber group of people, listening to what they had to say about the "Dirty Thirties" and we began to worry about the future.

"You kids better hit the hay now and try to get some sleep. You boys can lie out in the yard where there might be

HARVEST HANDS
LISTENING TO
HOBO - ORATOR
MITCHELL, S.D.
STAIB'S
PHOTO.

Harvest hands looking for work. Picture taken in Milwaukee Railroad yards during the hard times.

a breath of air," Mama said, getting up from her chair and going into the house which seemed as hot as a blast furnace. There were no air conditioners in those days and not even an electric fan in most homes. The pesky mosquitoes that slipped through the screen doors added to our discomfort by biting us at night.

"This heat wave is bound to break pretty soon," I heard Mama say as she climbed wearily into bed. "Maybe tomorrow will bring some relief." That night I prayed real hard that God would make it rain, and bring back the green grass.

The next morning the sun came up in a sky full of dusty clouds and the air was still suffocating. Mama was up early to get her work done, before it became hotter than hot.

By noon the heat was unbearable and we kids were constantly drinking water. Buckets of water were thrown on the porch to cool things off. Flies swarmed on the wet boards. Mama's face took on a worried expression every time she studied the heavens, becoming heavy with foreboding looking clouds.

"I sure don't like the looks of that sky," she said, pointing to the northwest horizon. "I think we're in for a good one this time," she predicted. "You kids better stick around the place. Anything can happen on a day like this."

She didn't have to warn me twice because I was deathly afraid of storms. If I saw a tiny dark cloud in the sky I headed for home and ran into the cellar where it was safe.

The sky continued to darken in the middle of the day and the wind began to howl and to blow the dust in whirlwinds around the yard. The chickens were racing towards the coop.

"Hey, Ma, look. They've turned the street lights on," yelled one of our brothers, pointing toward the main streets of town, barely visible from our house on the hill. During all the excitement we didn't notice Dad coming up the hill and he was running fast. I never saw him look so strained.

"Hurry up and get into the cellar," he shouted above the howling wind, "or you'll all be blown away. You must be crazy to still be outdoors."

I was already halfway down the stairs as the rest of the family followed, some falling down in a mad dash for safety. I crawled underneath the steps where I crouched in sheer panic, paying no heed to the spider webs that clung to my arms and legs.

Approaching dust storm

"We better all say our prayers," Dad cried.

"Now don't get everybody excited," Mama sternly told him, "it will blow over in a few minutes. Just sit tight."

So we all "sat tight" in the darkness of the dusty cellar while the devilish winds struck with fury at our "fortress on the hill." Baby Jimmy began to whimper. I wanted to cry, too.

"This old house has withstood many a storm and will stand many more," Mama broke the tension with some comforting words. I could still hear the screeching winds throwing tree branches against the house and the breaking glass from the windows crashing across the floor.

"Please, God, don't let us get killed," I continued to pray, pressing my hands together. "Make the storm stop."

"Old Mother Nature is really mad this time," Mama's voice again tried to pacify her frightened family.

After what seemed like an eternity, the winds slowly subsided and then there was an eerie silence. It was over. We were still alive.

"Let's get the hell out of here and get some fresh air," Mama commanded. "This dust will suffocate us. Get that cellar door open and let's see if there's anything left up there."

There was another mad scramble up the stairs—children coughing, trying to rid their lungs of dust inhaled through the cracks of the cellar windows and foundation.

"Would you look at that?" Mama gasped, surveying the damage to the house. "I don't believe it."

Eight wide-eyed youngsters followed in her footsteps, stunned by the devastation. Pieces of glass were scattered everywhere. The kitchen curtains were blowing gently in the broken windows. Twigs and leaves from the trees were scattered on the floors which were muddy from the leaks in the ceiling; and more mounds of silt were piled on the window sills and in front of the doors.

"I guess we should be thankful we're alive," Mama sighed, "but this is enough to make a preacher cuss. This takes the cake for luck."

"I wonder if the chicken coop is still standing?" Dad queried as he stepped outside to study the damage. All of the neighbors were walking about the neighborhood to see if anyone was injured. Dad was happy that his flock of chickens were spared when he heard a neighbor complain that his chickens were blown away. Soon the worried faces broke into gales of laughter. Some of the incidents were amusing and all the folks were glad that at least there was a sprinkle of rain along with the dust.

The prickly tumbleweeds that were piled against the buildings would make a great bonfire, so the cleanup campaign began immediately. We girls got our mops and buckets to clean the house again after Dad carefully picked up all of the splintered glass.

"Well, they say, 'Behind every dark cloud there's a silver lining'," he told us optimistically as he gazed through the open doorway at a blue sky. "Look, kids, there's a pretty rainbow over in the east. That's God's promise of a better tomorrow."

We all stopped to gaze at the brilliant panorama that arched across the heavens.

"Is there really a pot of gold at the end of a rainbow?" I asked, "or is that just a fairy tale?"

"Well, I'm sure there is," he smiled, "and we'll find it some day. You just wait and see."

The hated duststorms continued to blow away the top soil of Dakota land but the strong willed people were determined to stay, with the help of the government. Shelterbelts were planted throughout the country to stop the erosion of the good earth. I don't recall exactly when the dust clouds disappeared finally and the land was slowly being blessed with showers. The parched earth responded again with bountiful harvests of corn and grain. The gardens flourished and the millions of tiny trees reached for the heavens to become anchors to hold the rich black sod.

The rain drops that saturated the thirsty ground sent forth an aroma that words fail to describe. Every time it rained, each drop was a penny from heaven for our garden.

Sometimes an extra heavy rainstorm filled the roads and ditches to overflowing, letting the neighbor kids and us have fun running through the mud puddles. Who cared if we were splattered from head to toe? It was cool and wet and it was water. The rains had come and all was well again with the world.

THE OLD WASHING MACHINE

From the time that I became aware of the activities around our house, wash day was an every other day chore for Mama. A washboard standing in a tub full of hot sudsy water was her only means of getting our clothes clean until Dad brought home a huge wooden washing machine one day. Although electric washers had been around for quite some time, it was a luxury for us to have this old appliance sitting on the back porch.

It was quite a sight to watch the first time Mama tried it out. We kids stood at a safe distance while Dad poured a boiler full of scalding water into the machine, closed the heavy lid with a movable iron gear on top and plugged in the "juice."

"There she goes," Dad laughed as the monstrous machine rattled and groaned and splashed some of the sudsy water down the sides. The wheels and gears were a fascinating sight as they revolved or worked back and forth. Brother Bobby, the inquisitive one, edged closer for a better look, only to be pushed back by a protective Mama.

"Don't any of you ever touch this washing machine, do you hear? You can be electrocuted or lose your fingers in those gears. This is not a play thing."

Her warning was loud and clear but it was still fun just to watch the "cement mixer" grinding away the dirt from our clothing.

Still, "When the cat's away the mice will play." The temptation to get closer to the washer was too much for me and my brother Bobby.

191

It happened upon another sunny wash day when Mama was more than busy trying to hang her wash on the line. She had placed two large chairs on each side of the washing machine to keep us kids from danger. We pretended to be busy at play, pushing each other in the tire swing.

"How do you like your new wringer washer?" a neighbor lady asked Mama, leaning over the fence.

"Just fine," Mama responded, shaking out the wrinkles of a pillow case, while holding a clothes pin in her teeth.

"Well, you certainly deserved one," the neighbor went on. "I don't know how you did it before with all those kids."

"This is our chance," we thought, as the conversation went on about how nice and white the clothes looked, and so on. We sneaked into the back door, tugged at the two chairs and finally dragged them out of the way.

"Shut the door," Bobby whispered as he playfully turned the lever on the wringer. It was dangerous—but what did a three and four-year-old know? Not to be outdone by Bobby, I decided to lie down under the vibrating machine and watch the fast flying gears and levers.

"Put a piece of paper in there and see what happens," Bobby suggested. Grabbing a page from a newspaper lying on the floor, I proceeded to shove it into the mechanism. Something seized the paper and my hand. I realized I was in trouble. When the machine stopped from a blown fuse, my hand was caught. I managed to pull out a mangled, bloodied mess and like a frightened, wounded animal, I ran and hid beneath Mama's bed. Brother Bobby was so startled he fell off the chair, hit the cord and unplugged the machine. He ran screaming out the door.

"Oh Mama, Lorsey got her hand cut off by the washing machine and she's dying under your bed."

Mama raced into the house and couldn't believe her eyes when she saw what happened. She followed the trail of blood that led to her bedroom. I'm sure I was more afraid of getting a licking for being disobedient than of the injury.

"Come out of there right now," Mama half scolded while I huddled close to the wall. "I have to get you to a doctor."

From my hiding place I could see many pairs of feet waiting for me. I felt trapped by fear and pain.

"Oh please, hurry up and get her out. She is going to be dead," brother Bobby wailed.

Mama stood waiting with a turkish towel when I tearfully crawled out. She wrapped it tightly around my hand. One of the brothers had already run down the block to a neighbor's to ask for a ride to the doctor's office. It was a worried bunch of brothers, sisters and a few neighbors who watched Mama, our neighbor and me drive out of the yard and down the street.

"Take me to Dr. Young's office," she told our driver, hanging onto my painful hand. "Drop me off in front of the Western Building. I don't know where Bill is working. It's always up to me."

"There, there, now, don't worry," Mr. Widmann soothed. "I'll wait right here and give you a ride back home."

Hurrying into the doctor's office, Mama asked for the doctor. The nurse quickly took us to the examining room where she placed me on a hard porcelain table. The towel around my hand was now saturated with blood and it hurt when the nurse pulled the towel away from my mutilated fingers.

Dr. Young shook his head after examining my hand and told Mama, "I'm afraid those fingers will have to come off. There isn't much left of them."

"No! I don't want that!" Mama said. "Isn't there another doctor in the building?"

"Dr. Warren is down at the end of the hall. Go and ask for his opinion."

Taking me in her arms again, she ran down the corridor until we came to a glass-paneled door with Dr. Warren's name imprinted in black letters.

His prognosis was more hopeful. "It's really bad but I think I can save those fingers," the kindly doctor assured Mama while he laid me on a small operating table. "It will take a lot of stitches and she will no doubt carry these scars for life. But that's better than no fingers."

An injection was given to numb the pain and my little fingers were slowly sewn back together again while Mama stood by with comforting words.

"There, you'll soon be as good as new," the doctor laughed with comforting words, wrapping a nice white bandage around my sleeping hand. "Now stay away from that washing machine. Just play with your rag dolls."

"I will," I half smiled, looking up at Mama to see if she was now going to scold me.

"I should have been more careful," she said. "It was all my fault. Come now, let's go home. I'll ask Mr. Widmann to stop at the drug store to buy you a big ice cream cone."

"Can I have cherry nut?" I inquired.

"Any flavor you want," she smiled, taking me by my good hand. "I want to thank you again, Dr. Warren," she said, reaching for her worn leather purse. "How much do I owe you?"

"Let's just say that this was my good deed for the day. There's no charge. I'm just glad that I was in my office today."

I'm sure he realized that there wasn't much money in her pocketbook, as I was first taken to the doctor who was hired by the county for the poor and underprivileged families.

I was the center of attention for many weeks, listening to Mama retell the story to relatives and friends who happened to pass by. My injuries quickly healed with not much scarring except at the fingertips that were left disfigured and nail-less.

"That was sure a close call," everyone agreed.

"Well, I'm getting rid of that damned old washing machine," Dad promised. "We're going to buy one of those new streamlined ones that have the motor enclosed and a wringer of soft rubber. If something does get caught, there is a safety release."

"I'll help pay for it with the money from my paper route," brother Delly added.

So a small down payment was made and a beautiful gray washing machine was brought home. It purred like a kitten and it was the only modern convenience that we owned. The first time that Mama used it, we were allowed to watch the metal dolly swish back and forth in a sea of white suds. Even though it was considered safe, I kept my distance, not forgetting my ordeal with the last one.

But the inevitable had to happen as curiosity got the best of brother Bobby again.

Mama had gone out the back door with a basket of clothes, leaving the rinse tub free for us kids to splash in. Bobby found a stray handkerchief that was over-looked so decided to finish the job.

"You know what Mama said about monkeying around with that wringer," sister Neeney and I cautioned.

Ignoring our warning, he placed the cloth in the wringer and zip, in went his hand. By the time it reached his elbow the fuse blew and he was hanging over the tub screaming his head off. Mama heard the commotion and raced back into the house to find little Bobby snared like a mouse in a trap. She quickly released the safety lever and Bobby pulled out a bruised black and blue arm.

"Let's see if there are any bones broken. No, I don't think so. You can thank your lucky stars that isn't a hard rubber wringer or your arm would be broken," she told her wailing son whose howls could be heard for blocks.

Brother Bobby didn't need a doctor's care and he didn't receive as much sympathy as I did. I believe Mama was becoming more than exasperated with her three mischievous youngsters trying to help with the laundry.

"All I can say to you kids from now on, is that if you don't want to listen, you're going to feel."

Holy Smoke

"Lady bug, lady bug, fly away home, your house is on fire and your children will burn." We children would repeat this dire warning whenever we sighted the tiny orange backed bug inching her way along the ground or clinging to a leaf on a tree. There was no thought about a male "lady bug."

More than often if we shouted long enough she would spread her tiny wings and fly away, which made us happy that her family would be saved from the ravages of fire.

The danger of our own home burning to the ground was an ever-present fear for me because of the coal and wood-burning stoves. During the long bitter-cold winters they became like blast furnaces to ward off the relentless icy winds that fought to enter our humble domain.

"You better watch those pipes, they're getting red hot," Mama warned Dad when he placed too much coal in the cast iron belly of the heating stove. "It wouldn't take much to make this old shack go up in smoke."

"Don't worry, I know what I'm doing," said Dad, objecting to her orders. He reached up and turned the draft on the tin pipe. In a few minutes the redness disappeared and the roar of the flames became comforting crackling noises. We kids often lay around the stove on pillows, watching the shadows dancing on the walls from the flames that waved through the isinglass on the door. These were moments of warmth and security and a time to dream.

But there were other nights when the household was awakened by the fire whistle.

"You don't have to get out of bed. It's not in this neighborhood," Mama announced. She had already been outdoors to make sure there were no signs of smoke or flames. "It's probably a false alarm anyway." She then re-checked our two stoves and climbed back into her large brass bed.

"What would you grab first if this house did catch fire?" my little sister asked with a tired yawn.

"My doll," I answered without any hesitation, patting my blanket-wrapped baby who always lay beside me.

"I'd run through the house to wake everybody up and then lead them to safety like the firemen do," she remarked, sitting up in bed, now wide awake with her thoughts of being a heroine.

"I'm going to be a fireman when I grow up, and slide down that brass pole. I could even drive that big red fire truck that we saw down at the fire station." Knowing my sister who was nicknamed "Tomboy," I had no doubts about her future in world of mechanics.

Talking about the numerous fires that took place in the small city of Mitchell gave the neighbors food for thought for a few days. A fire was big news!

"Where was a fire last night? I swear that siren wailed for half an hour," Mrs. Hogan gasped to Mama after walking across the field to our house. While she sat down on a kitchen chair to catch her breath, Mama gave her the details.

Gene Hill, the night watchman, told Dad that the old Savoy Hotel caught fire last night and all in it had to leave in their night shirts.

"I wonder how many married men were in there with those floozies," sniffed Mrs. Hogan. "Well, too bad it didn't burn to the ground. The town would be better off without those cat houses and saloons on the south end of Main street. They should set a torch to all of them."

"It seems the firemen are always on time to save the ne'r-do-wells but when a woman like Mrs. Good needed help, they arrived too late to save her. Poor soul, may she rest in peace."

"Yes, it was too bad she burned to death in that explosion," Mama agreed with her friend, "but those kerosene stoves are dangerous. I wouldn't have one in the house." "Well, one of these days every household will have an electric or gas range," Mrs. Hogan predicted. "Think of all the work they will save. No more smoke and soot and no ash pans to empty." "Yeah, that would be nice," agreed Mama, gazing at dingy walls.

We kids liked to watch Mama and Dad build a fire in the cast iron stoves. After placing some newspapers and small pieces of wood on top of the grates, a splash of kerosene was poured on the kindling. After warning us to stand back, a match was lit and thrown in. Then "poof"—instant inferno. Sometimes when the ashes were shaken down through the grates, an escaping glowing coal dropped on the linoleum rug. This caused a growing pattern of scorched spots around the stove.

Mama constantly warned us about playing with matches and if she caught anyone taking them from the match safe they were given a good licking. One of the fathers in the neighborhood touched his children's fingers to the hot lids

Fire destroying the Gale Theatre, on Main Street

of the stove if they tampered with matches. Still the long wooden matches found their way into the hands of the neighborhood youngsters who loved to watch the dancing flames turn a field of dried weeds into a blackened waste land. The "volunteer fire fighters" (mothers and fathers) often had to help smother a grass or bonfire that got out of hand. Gunnysacks soaked in water could be used to "beat out" a fire in no time. It was a bad situation when one of the outdoor toilets went up in smoke. The family was forced to use a neighbor's facilities until a new one was constructed.

Brush fires often came back to life during the night when the winds fanned the dying embers into glowing coals that found their way into dried leaves and grasses.

Every small town had at least one fire that everyone remembers, and I have my memories of the day the ice company burned to the ground.

The family had just sat down to enjoy a dinner of goulash —a delicious mixture of macaroni, tomatoes, bacon and onion. We were interrupted by the piercing wail of the fire whistle that rose and fell, filling our hearts with both fear and excitement.

The house was quickly emptied as we kids scrambled out

into the yard to look for signs of smoke. From our house on the hill we could see from one end of town to the other.

"There it is, see that black smoke," Dad pointed towards town. "Boy, that looks like a big one. I'm going to see where it is." He knew better than to tell us kids to stay home because we were as curious as he was and always wanted to be where the action was.

My legs were beginning to ache from trying to keep up with the long strides of my father. By the time we reached the main part of town other townspeople were also making an exodus to the north edge of town where the smoke was etched in black ribbons across the horizon. Like moths drawn to a flame, we converged around the area.

"Don't tell me the ice house is burning down," Dad said to a man who was hurrying alongside us.

"Sure as hell is," he answered as we all came upon a scene of billowing smoke emerging from the gigantic red barn that housed the summer's supply of ice. Policemen and

MITCHELL FIRE DEPARTMENT, 1901. Top Row, left to right: Fred Johnson, John Posey, Ed Schlimgen, Joe Vermilyea, Tom Briggs, Bill Duncan, Joe Swift, Roy McCurty, H. Swindler. Second Row: Art Wright, E. Halfhill, George Koehler, Otis Smith, John Stirges, F. Logan, Frank Parks, Clyde Kimball, Roy Perry. Third Row: A. Jackson, H. Carlson, N. O. Kingsbury, Bill Pratt, Jim Rogan, Bill Barber, Wm. Slade, Luke Williams, Joe Schlimgen. Front Row: George Liko, Frank Purty, Sig Schirmer, Ed Parcell, Jim Duncan.

volunteers were trying to hold back the crowd who wanted to have a ringside seat. The heat from the flames added to the heat of a summer's day. Standing at a safe distance we watched the stout-hearted firemen manning the hoses that sprayed the crumbling barn with streams of water. The melting blocks of ice turned the area into a muddy lake.

"This is nothing compared to the old days when we had to fight fires with bucket brigades and horse-drawn fire wagons," remarked an old white haired man standing next to me.

"Were you a fireman?" Bobby asked, half believing the frail looking gentleman, leaning on a crooked cane.

"I drove the wagon and it was pulled by a team of snow-white horses," he boasted, his fading blue eyes alive with memories of his youth. I thought that he must be close to a hundred years old because he was toothless.

"At the sound of the alarm, they were rarin' to go, pulling the steamer at a breakneck speed, with half the town following behind. Boy, we had some real barn burners then."

The old man cackled with glee. "The volunteer firemen were mighty proud of their fire-fighting machinery and horses. They entered fire school contests to compete with other departments."

There were "steamer" races and hook-and-ladder contests. The competition was tough. Banners and silver megaphones were awarded to the winners. The megaphones were used to communicate orders given during the noise and confusion of a big blaze.

I tried to be polite and listen to the tales that the old timer was relating, yet I kept my eyes glued to the burning barn that was slowly sinking to the ground.

He chuckled while placing a chaw of tobacco into his mouth and continued giving us the history of the Mitchell Fire Department. Most of the other bystanders moved away, not wanting to listen to stories about the good old days.

"One time we fire fighters were being criticized for racing through the streets of town. Someone might be killed. So the mayor ordered the men not to go over 15 miles an hour or they would be taken off the truck.

"Well, Sir, all went well until one day we had a real big fire. Obeying the new regulations, we 'mosied' down the street with the steamer.

Fire Station, located in the 200 block of East Second, now the location of Knights of Columbus Hall (picture taken in early 1900's). Horse drawn hose cart was manned by volunteers.

"When we came to one corner, the mayor was standing in the middle of the road, waving his arms like a crazy man. We almost ran over him before the horses were stopped. He was mad. 'Where in the hell were you?' he shouted. 'Don't you know my stable is burning up over there?'

"The very next day the speed limit was back to its original pace and our volunteer fire chief was again a happy man.

"I'll have to tell you about the chief," the old man went on, spitting some tobacco juice. "There wasn't a better man to handle the reins of a fast pair of fire horses. I can still see him driving that old fire wagon around the corners on two wheels. We fellows on the back end hung on for dear life. Now progress has ruined fire-fighting."

When the horseless fire engine appeared on the scene, it proved to be the downfall of the chief. He couldn't get the hang of driving a gasoline truck and had to turn over the job to a more mechanical-minded driver. The chief had lost his touch. I thoroughly enjoyed the story telling but told him I had to leave because the building was now a smoldering pile of water-logged debris. The old man said goodbye and went down the street, stopping now and then to observe the new breed of fire fighters as they loaded up their equipment on the shiny red fire trucks.

"Did you listen to that man tell about how he used to be a fireman a long time ago?" I asked my dad and a few local listeners as they rehashed the latest fire.

"Why that old geezer couldn't blow out a match, much less put out a fire," one fat man laughed. "He just hung around the firehouse and listened to the firemen talk."

I felt a twinge of disappointment when they said that the old man was "full of baloney and could lie like a rug." Somehow I wanted to believe the hair-raising tales that he told me when our local ice company was going up in smoke.

The first fire station in Mitchell was located on north Main street. A two-story, metal building, fronted by a paved driveway was later constructed on east Second street. Large enough to accommodate a horse-drawn steamer and an ever-ready team of horses, it served its purpose in its day.

In 1922 a new concrete and brick structure was built on the corner of West First and Rowley streets. In 1976 there was a 38-man operation, working in shifts, to protect the city of Mitchell from one of its deadliest enemies—fire.

Easter Time

When I was little I could always tell when Easter was just around the corner. The windows of the dime stores were decorated with flop-eared rabbits in every size, shape and form. There were tiny white and yellow "chicks" made out of fluffy cotton which peeped out from baskets filled with colored cellophane straw.

I yearned to cuddle one of the Easter bunnies with the pink ears and "shoe button" eyes. The only thing that Mama could afford to buy was a sack of the marshmallow filled candy eggs that came in every color. The chocolate eggs, chickens, and rabbits wrapped in tin foil were a little too expensive for her pocketbook.

"Just once I wish I could buy everyone in this family a new Easter outfit" (Mama's comment was made every year). "I just hate to go to church and see all those dressed up people." "They don't go to church just to see what everyone else is wearing," Dad replied, "they go to pray and to count their blessings."

"Baloney," Mama quickly answered, using this excuse to stay home. "They just go to show off. Well, I'm not going, I can pray just as good at home. Church is all right for those who can pay their way into heaven."

"How can you say that?" Dad gasped. "I thought you came from a strict Catholic family. You even have relatives who are nuns and priests. What would they think if they heard you talk like that?"

These debates occurred usually around the religious holidays when Mama discussed her views about religion and the hereafter. I listened intently and tried to decide for myself which one of my parents was right about salvation. This decision was never settled in my mind—not even to this day.

Our mother's pessimistic outlook on going to church was compensated for by our dad who never missed a Sunday service, rain or shine. He believed in the power of prayer although the little things he asked for never seemed to come.

I was never forced, but was asked if I wanted to accompany him and a few of the other children to mass.

Mama, who always declined Dad's invitation, nevertheless made sure that everyone's clothes were clean and pressed. Dad's white shirt with the frayed collar, and the blue serge pants, worn thin and shiny, were his stand-bys. His black shoes with the run-over heels could look almost new, with another coat of polish.

I tried to make the best of what I owned by adding a colorful belt or scarf to my wash dress ensemble. Sometimes I wore a bulky sweater over a layer of others to keep warm from the cold winds that chilled me. I hated the long brown stockings that bagged at the ankles and knees. No matter how tight I wrapped the elastic garters around my legs, the stockings still drooped. My head had to be covered, the church said, and this was done by wearing a flowered square of material tied beneath my chin in a knot. Instead of looking elegant on the Sabbath Day, I thought I resembled a peasant on her way to the fields.

Walking the many blocks through foot paths along railroad tracks, and on broken concrete, we arrived at the church unnoticed by the "upper crust." I envied their travel in comfortable automobiles that sparkled from the chrome bumpers to the windshields.

Finding an empty space in a pew near the back, I kneeled beside Dad and bowed my head in prayer. I was usually tired from the long walk and my legs would hurt from the rubber garters.

Dad opened up his prayer book, but I leaned back in the hardwood pew and watched to see what everyone else was wearing. When the Easter parade started down the aisles of the church I was all eyes, green with envy.

More than often the richer people flocked together with just a few of the common folk around. The front pews were soon filled with the professionals or the "pillars of society" who made sure that they were being seen by the other parishioners. They would never cheat or steal or covet their neighbor's goods (some folks were led to believe).

The prominent gentlemen were attired in tailor-made suits and overcoats with name labels from the best clothing stores. Their society wives were wrapped in mink and elegant coats from exclusive local stores. Shoes of the finest leather encased their feet. I envied them.

These were some of the leaders of society of Mitchell to whom most of us looked up. They were the doctors, lawyers, businessmen and bankers and families whose ethics were said to be beyond reproach. There were no skeletons in their closets.

I knew all of them by name only, but some of their children were my classmates.

"I wonder if that handsome man is really a woman chaser like Mama said," I thought as I watched him politely remove the mink stole from around his wife's shoulders. It was hard to believe that a friendly neighborhood grocer would pad the bills of his unsuspecting customers.

My thoughts and attention moved to the children of these people who never had to worry about where their next mouthful of food was coming from.

Little boys wearing coats and suits of corduroy and wool blends smoothed down their hair after removing visored caps of tweed and leather. They sat stiffly and well behaved with a look of angelic innocence.

The babes in arms looked like kewpie dolls in snug fitting "rompers" or dresses of satin and lace. Poke-bonnets, tied with pretty ribbons, covered their golden curls. We felt they were indeed born with silver spoons in their mouths.

The group that had my closest scrutiny were the little girls about my age (around ten years old). They were dressed in the latest fashions of pleated skirts with matching sweaters, black and white patent leather slippers, silk and rayon anklets in pastel colors co-ordinating with buttoned and bowed frocks. Easter bonnets of straw, trimmed with fruit and flowers, or the "off the face" and "sailors" adorned with feathers and streamers that hung down the back. I yearned for one of the princess style coats that hugged the body like a royal garment. A dainty purse and snowy white gloves would complete their ensemble.

I couldn't help but take inventory of my own clothes and I had thoughts of self pity. Maybe God did love only the rich folks.

"Does Dad resent those higher ups?" I wondered, noting the threadbare sleeve on his suit coat and hair that curled around his ears in need of a trim. Or does he give thanks for his blessings?

The good nuns and priests taught me that it was a sin to be envious of other people but I was growing weary of always being on the outside looking in. Was I supposed to feel guilty for my feelings of resentment toward others with possessions that I strongly desired?

After being squeezed into the pew with the other common people, listening to the sermon of Father Brady, it was time to leave. I was glad.

I tried to ignore the other little girls who stood around

205

the outside of the church, admiring each other's Easter finery and making happy talk. I just wanted to run away and hide like Cinderella, in my own little corner of the world.

Yet there were great Easter Sundays that were spent with my family, neighbors and relatives. There was also the annual Easter egg hunt that was held on the grassy hillsides near Lake Mitchell.

The City Fathers, local clubs and the Boy Scouts volunteered to hide the eggs among the grass, the trees and in gopher holes. What fun it was to find their eggs and sometimes collect an extra prize.

Our Easter Sunday was a banquet of roast chicken with all the trimmings, and plenty of colored eggs that Mama had painstakingly dyed the night before. The holiday was made more enjoyable when Aunt Carrie arrived with her gifts of large eggs made out of pressed paper that could only be purchased at the drug store variety counter. They were exquisitely decorated with rabbits, baby chicks and flowers. When opened we found jelly beans, candy corn and sugar-coated marshmallows.

Sometimes we had to cover our eyes while she hid the straw baskets of eggs and candy behind trees, under the porch or nestled in a flower bed of early blooming tulips.

If Easter arrived too early and the landscape was feathered with a frosting of snow, the eggs were hidden in the house by the older brothers and sisters.

The dresser and sewing machine drawers offered good hiding places as did the pots and pans in the cupboard. Needless to say, by the end of the day the floor looked like a mosaic carpet from the broken colored egg shells.

"Now don't eat too many of those hard boiled eggs or they will be coming out of your ears," laughed Mama. With a few sprinkles of salt they tasted delicious. Some of the kids threw half of the eggs away because they didn't like the yolks. The left-over eggs were peeled and mixed into the other ingredients of a golden potato salad.

One Easter Sunday proved to be happiest for me when I received something I had always yearned for—an Easter bonnet with all the frills upon it.

We watched from the kitchen window to await our Aunt Carrie's appearance. She lived just across the alley. Every year she tried to come up with something different from her bag of miracles to surprise us.

"Here she comes," sister Neeney shouted, and we raced out the door to meet her, trying to be the first to catch her around the apron strings.

"Now, wait just a minute," she would laugh, holding her gift-wrapped presents high above our heads. "They will be opened after the Easter Bunny comes." We knew that there wasn't a real rabbit who hid eggs around the yard, but our Dad and brothers were the "rabbit."

Not wanting to disappoint Aunt Carrie, we pretended to believe that we knew Peter Cottontail would soon be hopping "down the bunny trail."

After all of the eggs had been accounted for that were left mysteriously, Aunt Carrie distributed her gifts of love to her young nieces and nephews. The boys were given small glass toys in shapes of fire engines, dogs and telephones, filled with tiny colored beads of candy. Sister Neeney was tickled when she was handed a paddle-and-ball novelty toy wrapped in crinkly cellophane.

I wondered what was in store for me when I was given a white box tied with a pink ribbon.

Everyone gathered around as I quickly untied the bow and opened the lid. "It's a hat," I gasped as I plucked it from its bed of tissue paper.

"Oh, isn't it pretty?" everyone commented when I placed it on my head, then ran to look at myself in the dresser mirror. The bonnet was made of yellow straw with nosegays of violets circling the crown, lavender velvet ribbons just long enough to tie beneath my chin. "Now if I only had a pretty dress to match," I wished.

I ran back into the living room to show off my new hat to an admiring audience, especially to my dear aunt who was all smiles to see the household of happy children.

Till it wilted she wore it, till the ribbons and flowers were frayed and colorless. The sweet little bonnet was adored by an eleven-year-old girl who loved the pretty things in life.

Ladies of the Evening

Searching through the history of Mitchell, I found many old newspaper clippings about prostitution and jail sentences and fines levied against ladies of the evening, who lived in rooms or apartments in the various hotels along Main Street.

A few lived in splendor in homes richly decorated with lush furnishings and art treasures. These houses of ill repute were usually located away from the prying eyes of the public. No respected gentleman about town wanted anyone to know about his illicit relationships with women who were paid for their favors. When I was a child growing up during hard times I often heard about the world's oldest profession, which included black women as well as white. The blacks were referred to as "nigger wenches."

Everyone knew about a black brothel on North Main, especially some of the married women who wondered if their profligate husbands were having an affair with ladies of easy virtue.

"Mama says that old fat nigger lady that lives over by the railroad tracks is a whore," one of our boy schoolmates told us kids one day, during one of our many conversations on subjects that weren't for mixed company.

"She moved into that old cement place about two months ago and nobody hardly ever sees her—just sometimes when she goes to the corner grocery store. Mama sees men sneaking over there after dark."

"What do they do?" we innocently asked.

"They love each other up," he answered, thinking we were sure ignorant about the birds and the bees.

One day while cutting through the railroad yards on our way to school, we walked past the cement block house and got our chance to see the wench that white folks whispered about.

She was dressed in a long flowered skirt that reached down to her ankles. A white blouse bulged from a bosomy body. Her head was wrapped in a turban that made her look like Aunt Jemima. Hooped gold earrings dangled from side to side when she walked. She was carrying a tin bucket filled with chunks of coal that she picked up along the railroad tracks. She stopped when she saw us staring at her. Her glistening black face was unsmiling and her eyes narrowed to menacing slits.

"What yo' kids doin' on my 'prop'ty?" she asked. "Get away from heah'. Don't you ever come back around heah no mo.' Scat!" She moved towards us menacingly.

We were stunned at her outburst and ran away from her as fast as our legs could carry us. She was wicked and sinful as far as we were concerned and we vowed never to cross her path again.

Another street walker that comes to mind was a white woman in the autumn of her years. Age proved to be no barrier in her pursuit of male companionship.

"There goes old 'Nine O'clock Kate'," people said in disgust when they saw this skinny white-haired woman strolling down Main Street, probably searching for a customer.

She was no doubt a beauty in her youth, but the deep wrinkles now made her face resemble a mask. Her eyes were still blue that sparkled when she smiled and greeted the few people who believed that she was more to be pitied than censured.

We kids were accustomed to seeing her standing on a street corner or gazing into a store window at her reflection. Her red satin and black taffeta dresses were adorned with many ruffles and had shiny belt buckles. Strands of sparkling crystal beads cascaded over her withered bosom; her spindly legs were encased in black silk hose and her feet looked tiny in pumps of black patent leather. Kate always carried a lacy handkerchief and a black evening bag encrusted with cheap rhinestones. A fragrance of perfume filled the air when she sashayed by, in a futile attempt to appear young and desireable.

"How come they call her Nine O'clock Kate?" I asked Mama one day when gossips mentioned her.

"Well, the story goes that she was madly in love with a handsome man about town once but he fell head over heels for someone else. Charlie promised Kate to take her with him when he left for California, and was to meet him at the station in the morning. But alas, he had already skipped town with another girl. Poor Kate became the laughing stock of the town and the whispers behind her back drove her to a mental breakdown. So every evening she could be seen standing in the Milwaukee Depot around nine o'clock waiting for her lost sweetheart to appear. She soon realized that her lover was gone for good so she tried to atone for it by dating every Tom, Dick and Harry that came along. As the years passed by she became a 'lady of the evening' and could be nothing else till the day she died. She is more to be pitied than scorned," Mama said with sympathy.

After Mama told me the story about Kate's downfall, whether it was true or not, I felt sorry for this woman who roamed the streets. She should have been sitting in a rocking chair surrounded by loving grandchildren instead of being looked down upon.

It was on a blustery winter's day that I met old Kate. She was standing, huddled in the icy wind on a corner waiting for the traffic light to change. As we started across the slippery street she fell, hoping for a helping hand to lift her from the cold pavement. Although a few passers-by saw her predicament, they didn't want to be seen touching her.

"I'll help you," I said, placing my arms around her frail body and half carrying her into the warmth of a store.

I managed to seat her in the nearest booth to the door. She was shivering and trying to regain her composure. I began to feel uneasy when I noticed some customers and the waitress looking in our direction with curiosity. "Maybe they think she is my grandmother," I thought.

Kate finally looked up at me and smiled. I took note of her smoke-stained teeth and mouth smeared with lipstick. Crimson rouge was caked on her hollow cheeks, in sharp contrast to the fringed carrot-colored hair. The deep wrinkles that criss-crossed her face were imbedded with tiny flakes of white powder. I looked straight into her eyes which were old and tired.

"What's your name, little girl?" she asked in a husky voice. Then added, "I want to reward you for being so nice and helpful to me."

"My name is Dolores," I quickly answered, not wanting to spend any more time.

"My, what a pretty name." She fumbled in her purse with trembling fingers, withdrawing a quarter and placing it in my hand.

"Thank you, Miss Kate," I said, observing the purple veins of her hands. Arching her painted eyebrows in surprise she asked, "How do you know my name?"

"Well," I stammered, "I heard a man call you that one day on the street—when you walked by." I began to feel embarrassed and I was afraid she was going to ask more questions. Before she had time to open her mouth again, I lied, "I have to go now, I promised my mother that I'd be home soon." "Good-bye, dear child," she whispered. I turned my back on her and hurried through the door of the store.

Walking home through the snow along the Roundhouse pond I thought about my meeting with the elderly street walker. I remembered the stories and jokes repeated about her. Was she going to hell when she died or would God forgive her sins, as I was led to believe?

I pulled off a mitten and gazed upon the coin that had probably been earned by selling her body. I threw it as far as I could into the icy waters of the pond which lay along the Milwaukee railroad tracks.

"Guess who they found dead this morning?" Dad asked Mama as he kicked the snow from his shoes in the open doorway. "I heard up town that old Nine O'clock Kate was found frozen to death in her apartment. Guess she laid there for a couple of days."

Her obituary was in the paper that evening. "I always wondered what her real name was," Mama said as she scanned the news. "It says here that her name is Catherine Louise Richards, and she was born in Chicago. She was seventy-two years old. There aren't any relatives listed and she will be buried from a funeral parlor. I don't suppose she ever went to church. Well, who are we to judge? You remember what Jesus said to the people who were going to stone the harlot to death, 'Those of you without sin cast the first stone.' I'm sure God will have mercy upon her soul."

After the newspaper had been read by the family it was tossed into the wood box next to the cook stove. I picked up the soiled and wrinkled paper and laid it on the kitchen table. I wanted to read again the death notice of but a few lines, notifying the readers of the birth and death of one of the town's scarlet women. Nobody really cared and she would soon be forgotten. That is, everyone but me who grew up to write about Nine O'clock Kate who lived and died during the 1930's in Mitchell.

The Outcasts

Taking the shortcut to schools we attended often meant walking through or past the hobo jungles near the Milwaukee Railroad yards and into the wooded areas near the outskirts of town. Many of the towns outscasts or misfits found these "no mans islands" suitable for them and often built makeshift shanties from discarded cardboard and lumber found around.

We kids walked with a hurried gait past old Dirty Mike's shack next to the Omaha tracks, on the north side of town.

"He's sure a queer old duck," Mama commented about the man whose daily treks searching garbage cans netted him an assortment of rummage and food. Sometimes a sympathetic restaurant owner gave him a free meal in exchange for shoveling snow or washing dishes.

His garments were ragged overalls, a frayed suit coat and an old grimy black hat. What might have been once a handsome face was now covered with a graying stubble of beard. Bushy black brows arched above a pair of shifty blue eyes that darted from side to side as if he was looking for a hidden treasure somewhere.

Nobody seemed to know where he came from or why he chose Mitchell for his haven. There were rumors that he was a millionaire's son, an escaped convict hiding out, and that he was once an ordained priest.

The secret of the strange man who shunned the world was buried with him forever when he was found dead on the floor of his littered shanty, after a blizzard.

"Well, old Dirty Mike was buried today," Dad told Mama, with a touch of sadness in his voice. "He was buried by the county, in a pauper's grave, no doubt!"

"His worries are over," Mama answered. "I'd still like to know who he really was."

Another recluse who only wanted to be left alone lived on the south side of town nestled among a grove of cottonwood trees. His manger-like home was built out of logs on a hollowed out excavation, just large enough for him and his two bony horses. "He looks like he is part animal himself," people said when they chanced to meet him coming out of his jungle of high weeds and tangled underbrush. He earned a meager living hauling garbage from a few businesses. An old dilapidated wagon, held together with baling wire, pulled by a team of sway-backed horses, was his only means of transportation. "Here comes Shorty Born, the pig man," one of the school kids would shout when his wagon was spotted coming our way. Let's stand here until he goes by, if we can stand the stink." The slow plodding, spavined horses hung their heads close to the ground as they strained beneath the heavy harnesses to pull the creaking wagon filled with barrels of garbage. Swarms of flies buzzed around the refuse, biting the horses who could only shake their heads and swish their tails.

Sitting on a high buckboard seat was a hunched man whose knees were almost touching his face, partially obscured by an old dusty wide-brimmed hat. He glanced sidewise at us kids without a sign of friendliness. "I sure feel sorry for those poor old horses," I said as the group disappeared from our view. "He should be reported for cruelty to animals."

"Well, you don't have to worry about those horses anymore," Dad reported one day. "Old Shorty suffered a stroke and was taken to the Poor Farm. The horses, Dolly and Dick, were given to a farmer friend of mine and they will be as good as new. The Health Department burned Shorty's shack so you kids can play down in the hollow again. I don't think there will be any more bums camping on that city-owned property."

One chilly October morning while getting ready for school my brother looked out the window. "Isn't that smoke coming from the hollow?" Bobby asked, pointing his finger towards the white wisps of smoke circling above the tree tops. "Sure looks like someone moved in again to spoil our playground. I wonder who it is this time."

"We can't find out now or we'll be late for school," one of our chums shouted while we raced down the steep incline that led to the gravel pit. "We'll find out tonight on our way back home. We better bring along some big kids."

Late that afternoon our neighborhood gang returned to the cottonwood grove to see if indeed there were any squatters in our enchanted forest. Coming to a clearing where the autumn leaves were beginning to fall we saw an old cookshack on iron wheels. Surrounding the trailer house were boxes, baskets, wood chopping tools and an old wooden rain barrel.

"Gypsies," we thought, not wanting to venture any farther until we observed an elderly man sitting on a tree stump watching some chattering squirrels gathering acorns for the winter. When he heard our footsteps on the dry twigs he looked up and gave us a wide, toothless grin.

"Howdy, children. Did you come to welcome your new neighbor? My name is Sam. What's yours?" He arose and came towards us, extending a gnarled hand, while leaning on an old crooked cane with the other. Although he was the picture of old Father Time with long flowing white hair and a tobacco stained mustache, and no doubt possessed the innocence of a baby, we were warned by Mama to beware of strangers.

"Let's get out of here," we all agreed. "Maybe he is crazy. He might hurt us."

"Come back," he hollered after us. "I won't hurt you. I just want to be friendly, that's all."

"Don't tell me he came back to Mitchell after all these years," the neighborhood gossip commented when she heard us tell about Sam. "Why, that old 'floater' is worthless. He had a good woman and five children but never made a decent living for them because of his wanderings. His wife died years ago and I'm sure his relatives won't have anything to do with him. Now, he comes back to live off the county, no doubt. You kids better keep your distance from that old fellow. He never did have all his marbles. So old Sam Johnson has returned."

Mindful of these warnings we avoided the old man but he continued to shout a good morning to all who passed by.

Sometimes we would sneak by and watch him from a hiding place. If he wasn't chopping wood for the cook stove, he blew on a mouth organ. This seemed to delight the birds perched on the tree branches above his head. He had a strong vibrant voice that could be heard over hill and dale when he sang a sentimental ballad about far away places or songs like the beautiful, "I Dream of Jeanie With the Light Brown Hair."

"I don't care what people say about him, I feel sorry for him living there all alone with no one to talk to," I decided. "We should just go right over there and pay him a visit." The other kids were anxious to know more about this stranger, too.

One evening, just after supper time when the neighbor kids gathered near our doorstep, we decided to go down to the hollow and visit Sam. From our house on the hill we could see the flames from his campfire casting shadows on the giant cottonwood trees.

214

"Now don't be afraid. He won't hurt you," brother Bobby encouraged us, as we walked into his campground with faltering steps.

"Hi, Sam. We came to visit you." The wrinkled weather-beaten face was wreathed in a smile when he saw his company.

"Well, I'll be danged," he chuckled. "Come sit over here on these boxes by the campfire. The air is a bit chilly tonight and that big old harvest moon up there will be turning to gold in no time at all. I hope that big pile of wood that I chopped will carry me through the winter." He chattered away while we listened politely, but with one eye on the hatchet that lay at his feet.

The conversation soon changed to a question and answer period as each child asked Sam about his roots and where he lived during his wandering days.

The light from the campfire reflected in his eyes, now growing dim with age, and a sadness seemed to come over him when he told of being born here in Mitchell, of his parents, brothers and sisters; about his rolling stone years, his search for happiness, his ill fated marriage and broken dreams. "Now I'm just an old chicken that wants to come home to roost," he smiled, "and when I die I want to be buried next to my kinfolk at the old cemetery north of town. Ah, you kids shouldn't worry about an old fool like me," he said, wiping away a tear from his grizzled cheek. "Let me play a tune on my mouth harp before we say goodnight."

"Can you play 'Comin' Round the Mountain'?" someone asked, and the hand clapping began as we kept time to the music man.

Friendship bloomed between us kids and the eighty-five year old man who poured out his heart and soul about his love of nature, of his fishing and hunting expeditions from the ice-covered mountains in Alaska to the sun-kissed shores of Mexico.

"I think old Sam is getting too feeble to be living in that old shack alone. He should be in the county poor farm where at least he will have a warm bed and three squares a day," Dad remarked to Mama after taking a supply of groceries to him from the county store. "I wonder if he will wear the new clothes that the Salvation Army gave him. His mackinaw is getting pretty tacky and he is almost walking on bare ground in those shoes. Even though he is crippled by arthritis he still talks about making one last trip into the north country when he hears the wild geese flying overhead. He wants to fly away, too, I guess."

"I'm afraid his wild goose chases are over," Mama replied. "He will be lucky if he makes it through the winter. Some morning they are going to find him dead."

"Well, he insists on staying put so John Murray and I will help him keep the stove fired up and make sure his cupboard isn't bare. I took some sow belly and a sack of beans down there yesterday."

One day on a cold December morning I was awakened by a loud pounding on the back door. Then I heard Mama say, "Why it's John. What are you doing up so early? Come on in before you freeze to death."

"I wanted to tell you I found old Sam lying in the snow this morning and he is gone. I notified the undertaker so they should be getting him any minute. It's a funny thing, he had an old knapsack in his hands."

"He must have heard the call of the wild goose again," Dad said sadly as he poured himself a cup of hot coffee. "Well, the county will have to bury him. What little belongings he left behind don't amount to a tinkers dam and I'm sure there will be no relatives to claim his cook shack."

Sam Johnson was buried the next day with only my dad, John, and a few old cronies that knew him. The chaplain from the Salvation Army read the scripture, then took the body to the cemetery where it was placed in a pauper's grave, outside the confines of an iron fence.

The weather beaten cook shack was dragged out from the cottonwood grove and taken to the dump grounds where it was set afire along with the dilapidated furniture and musty bedding. Dad salvaged a few boxes of trinkets and mementos that Sam treasured. The picture post-cards were interesting as we could trace his life-long travels.

Many years have passed by since old Sam's departure. The cottonwood grove is now a trailer court and the nature trails and footpaths are now a gravel road. Nobody remembers the rolling stone who left no mark on the history of the town. But I remember him, especially during the long cold nights when I can hear the cries of the wild geese as they wing their way north. I'm sure old Sam is with them. His wandering spirit has taken flight into eternity, where his soul is at rest.

I'm sure my mother and father's dreams and hopes were that we children would grow up to be normal and healthy. And maybe one of us would make the family proud of some talent that would burst forth for all of the town to admire and respect. It never happened. Some of the children from the well-to-do families who could afford piano lessons and dancing schools, found their names in the local newspaper.

I recall Mama reading the latest achievement of a child whose I.Q. was above average and was destined to become a scholar in some outstanding university. It angered her at times that we remained unrecognized. Many times she became unreasonable and called us morons because we remained in the background in social or scholastic affairs. She didn't realize that she didn't set a good example for us. She didn't attend church, school or social affairs herself.

There were some children that were seen only on certain occasions, special church services or during Corn Palace week.

They appeared strange looking with large domed heads and mongoloid features. Their bodies were dwarf-like. When they looked at us from lifeless eyes, we wondered why they were born that way.

"How come those kids look like that? How old are they? Can they talk?" These and more questions were often asked by us children. Words like "goofy," "not all there," "looney," "crazy" and "feeble-minded" were used to describe the mentally retarded children. Unlike today, many were kept hidden away from the world. Some mothers were thought of as sinful and unclean because they brought a misfit into the world.

"You should be glad that all of your children are healthy and have good minds," Mama was often told by relatives, especially Aunt Carrie. "If I had a child like Billy Jones, I would be heart-broken." She referred to the plight of a local boy that some people called "the village idiot."

Unlike the few spastic children, Billy acted completely silly. He laughed and giggled at the antics of everyone else. He was oblivious to the teasing and taunts that the so-called normal folks liked to shout at him. Even small children were cruel.

His attire usually consisted of faded blue overalls that reached to the tops of his "clod knocker" shoes. A checkered work shirt (buttoned to the collar) and an oversized cap that covered his straw colored hair were all he ever wore. Although he was tall and skinny with the body of a young man, his mind remained in the babyhood. Children and adults both followed him around the streets of town to watch him. Billy was a funny looking scarecrow, who performed on his own little stage.

It was during the Corn Palace festival that Billy lived out his childish fantasies to be the leader of a band. He watched the local municipal band with uncontrolled excitement as it prepared to march through the streets along the crowded midway.

Pacing back and forth with hands thrust deep into his overall pockets, Billy behaved like a race horse at the starting gate. Although the local people knew all about the strange boy, visitors thought he was a clown, hired for the celebration. He was anxious to give on-lookers a good show, and to give himself a soul-stirring experience.

Joe Tschetter the band director, a show man in his own right, wasn't too pleased about the assistance of the "village idiot," but he always tried to keep his composure.

Billy waited at the corner and as soon as the orchestra was directly in front of him, he would leap into the formation and parade up the street with the band.

"How can the band play with that halfwit distracting their attention?" I heard an old maid school teacher ask, clutching an umbrella in her hand. "Why, he belongs in Redfield. The police should put a stop to his nonsense. Why don't his parents keep him in?"

"Let the poor kid enjoy himself. He isn't hurting anyone," responded a kindly-looking gentleman, waving to Billy as he marched happily by with the high-stepping routine of a drum major.

"Well, mark my words, one of these days he is going to get into trouble. You can't trust this kind of people," she sniffed, shaking her umbrella under his nose. "Why, he doesn't know enough to pound sand in a rat hole."

Billy continued to entertain (and sometimes offend) the crowds until one day his freedom was taken away from him and the "town clown" was seen no more on the streets of Mitchell.

Our neighbor, Mrs. Hogan, who knew everything that was going on in the community, informed us about the whereabouts of the half-witted boy. "They took Billy to the feebleminded school at Redfield for his own good. He was getting too girl crazy. It was a shame the way some of those girls teased and egged him on just to watch his reactions. Well, I hope they are all satisfied now. The poor boy, away from his family and locked up." She sighed and sipped on the cup of coffee that Mama placed before her.

"We all have a cross to bear in one form or another. God knows I've had mine. Well, that's life. We all have to take the good with the bad." "I'm thankful for one thing. My kids might be ornery at times and sometimes act like they don't have a brain in their heads, but they are normal and healthy," Mama told her friend who listened patiently, but more than often had her ears wide open for the latest gossip.

"Did you hear about Mrs. Whipple? Well, it finally came to it. She's taking in washing to put food on the table. Old Bill is drunk 24 hours a day. Wait till you hear the latest about Dr. Woods. He's divorcing his wife for that young floozie that waits tables. And poor Mrs. Cochran, they say she never sees her husband any more. He practically lives in a saloon. Never draws a sober breath. He was once the best lawyer in this town. These men nowdays—if they're not drinking, they're out chasing women." "I'm sure glad that my Hans is not a woman chaser." (Mama always said that Hans was too lazy to work and too honest to steal.)

"Well, what's the latest gossip today?" Dad always asked when Mrs. Hogan departed, after raking everyone over the coals. "She should be getting paid for writing a gossip column."

"That's about right," laughed Mama. "Telegraph, telephone, and tell Mrs. Hogan."

The Dog Catcher

"What do you know? Guess who got the job as the city dog catcher?" Dad asked as he scanned the local news in the daily newspaper.

"Hmmm, let me think. It would have to be someone who has an ornery streak in them," answered Mama, setting the dishes on the table for the evening meal. After naming a few of the local males who she thought had nothing better to do, she gave up, as Dad answered in the negative each time.

"Your brother-in-law, Pete, was appointed by the police department as official dog catcher of Mitchell, beginning the first of June. You better behave yourself, he is a lawman now."

"Let me see that," cried Mama, not believing what she heard. She grabbed the newspaper and laid it flat on the table. Reading the news of this earth-shaking appointment, she gave a sigh of disgust. "Well, there won't be any living beside him now with his new authority. I'll tell the kids to keep a sharp eye on their little dog, Rex. That's the first dog he'll nab."

"Oh, don't be too sure about that," Dad argued. "Pete isn't all that bad. Why don't you look for his good points?"

"Oh, no," snapped back Mama. "Just mark my words, he will get great pleasure putting away our dog. You know the old saying, 'Love me, love my dog,' but he don't love me."

The next day we kids edged over into Uncle Pete's yard where we saw him building a wire cage to fit on the back of his old pick-up. Our little mongrel pup, Rex, yapped along beside us, tied securely to a long piece of rope.

Pete stopped his pounding at our approach and took off his jacket and hung it on the fence post. "See this badge?" he asked importantly, pointing to a metal shield on his shirt pocket. "This police badge entitles me to pick up all the stray dogs in town and that means that mangy mutt right there." I reached for Rex and pulled him close to me. The dog seemed to sense the danger in Uncle Pete's threat.

"What do you do with the dogs that you catch?" brother Bobby finally got the nerve to ask.

"They are taken out to the dump ground and shot," he flatly said.

"Oh, no," I thought to myself as I imagined our innocent little dog lying in a pool of blood on a rubbish pile, dying in agony.

"Let's go home," I said to my brother and sister, not wanting to hear anymore. Brother Bobby gently picked up Rex and hugged him close.

"No one is going to hurt you," he whispered as the puppy licked his hands with a wet pink tongue.

Everyone in the neighborhood who owned a dog watched the new dog catcher, who acted more like a G-Man than just a city employe. As soon as he left, all the dogs, large and small, roamed at will, and upon his return they were pushed and pulled back into safe sanctuaries. Nobody wanted to tie up their pets as if they were some dangerous animal. Warned repeatedly by Mama, we kids were more protective of Rex because Pete was "laying" for him we thought.

One Saturday morning, arriving home from a Mickey Mouse movie, we noticed the door on the back porch was half opened. Rex had been left there for safe keeping. There wasn't hide nor hair of him.

"Mrs. Hogan must have forgotten to turn the latch when she left the sack of rhubarb. You kids better go and find him. He may have tried to follow you up town," Mama sounded concerned about our puppy's disappearance.

We kids were already sick when there was no response to our shouts echoing throughout the neighborhood. "Did you see our dog, Rex?" we anxiously asked neighbors and strangers alike when the afternoon grew late and there was no sign of our pet.

Finally we heard the dreaded news from an elderly man that lived on the bottom land near the railroad tracks. "I saw a small brown dog running back and forth trying to get across the creek over there by the round house pond and then a man came along with a big net on the end of a pole and snared him."

We thanked the old man and headed back up the hill. Tears were blurring my vision as I stumbled along the path matted with high weeds. Mama would know what to do if indeed our dog was in the hands of our relative, I consoled myself.

When Mama heard what we had to report, her face turned livid with anger. She wiped her hands on a towel and threw it on the sink. Looking up at the kitchen clock, she remarked,

"It's after five. He should be home by now. I'm going over there to find out if he took the dog and if he did I'll break - - - ." The words trailed off into a shaking of her fist.

We followed Mama as she stalked across the yard and up to the back door of Uncle Pete's house. The pick-up with the wire cage was parked near the garage.

"Maybe Rex is still in there," we thought as we anxiously peered through the enclosure. But we could see only darkness.

"This isn't a social call," Mama informed her sister Carrie when she answered the door. "Tell Pete to get out here, I have something to discuss with him."

When Uncle Pete came to the screen door, he quickly hooked the latch to insure a safe barrier between him and his enraged relatives. Before Mama had a chance to inquire about Rex, Pete got in the first shot. "Now you people know all about the city ordinance and I was appointed to uphold the law and I warned you and everybody else to keep their dogs tied up or I'd have to pick them up.

"You mean shoot them in cold blood?" Mama raged. "Is that what you done to the kid's dog? Where is our dog? You better tell me or I'll pull this door off the hinges."

The tears of anger and sadness coursed down our cheeks as we heard Uncle Pete admit that he shot and killed our little Rex. It didn't soften the blow when he said that he at least buried him.

"I hope you sleep good tonight, you low down rat," cursed Mama as the air turned blue with Mama's language.

"I don't have to listen to this," Uncle Pete shouted slamming the door on his accusers.

It took a long time for us to forget the loss of our little pal, Rex, and to forgive our uncle who we thought was the meanest man in Mitchell. But our lives were once again filled with the affection for animals when a neighbor brought over a cardboard box with the sounds of meowing kittens coming out of it.

"Do you kids want these baby kittens," Mr. Dunbar asked. "The mother was run over by a car yesterday and they need a new home and some loving care. All they want is some canned milk and a nice warm place to sleep."

"Oh, yes!" We all agreed to take the homeless kittens and gathered them in our arms with affection only little children can give.

"I want the little gray one," I decided, stroking the soft warm fur on the sleepy-eyed kitty who purred her feelings into my ear.

The litter of kittens left on our door step helped us forget our dog, Rex.

"At least cats don't have anything to worry about, because dog catchers just kill dogs," we all agreed as we watched our Uncle Pete driving down the street.

Baby Sitting

During the depression years the words "baby sitter" were unknown. Instead, the young girls who helped out with the children in a family were referred to just as hired girls. Not only did they diaper and feed the youngsters, but did household chores too, for a few dollars a week.

I began to sit with many of the babes in arms in our neighborhood at about the age of nine. "Dolores is so grown-up and trustworthy I don't worry about the kids when we're out late at night," the mothers often told Mama, and this made me feel proud and confident. I often pretended that the youngsters were my very own and I'm sure most of them developed a fondness for me.

In the beginning, sister Neeney went along for security when we stayed till near dawn. When the parents went out and celebrated at some night club that catered to the wilder crowds of the 30's. Most of the parents arrived home bleary-eyed and sometimes tipsy and arguing about some incident. "Now don't tell the neighbors about us coming home at this hour," the mother would say while she searched for a few coins in an almost empty pocketbook.

Mama was usually outside feeding the chickens when my sister and I walked into the yard, yawning and rubbing our eyes from our late vigil.

"Well, how much did you make?" she asked, throwing a last hand full of feed to the chickens. "We each got a dime," I answered, holding up a shiny coin which, during those hard times, was considered a good night's wage by poor children.

"Do you kids want some breakfast or are you too tired to eat?" Mama questioned, as we struggled to keep our eyes open.

"I'm going to bed," Neeney yawned, "and I'm sleeping till noon. So don't go waking me up in a few hours."

"What about church? Aren't you going with me and Dad?"

"Nope, I'd just fall asleep in the pew and then you'd be embarrassed.

"That's a good excuse," I sneered. "You just don't want to go. You're going to end up a heathen if you don't watch out."

I walked over to the cookstove, poured myself a cup of coffee and sat down at the kitchen table with Mama.

"Did the Reileys come home drunk?" Mama asked.

"Oh, no," I lied. "They were sober."

I loved the Sunday afternoons when the younger children wanted me to take them to the picture show. "Mama wants to know if you will go to the show with me today," said Donna Mae. "She will pay your way and give us some extra money for popcorn and candy."

"Well, all right," I answered. "Marlene, Sally and Artie are going along, too, so you be here at 12:30 sharp."

At the appointed time the moppets appeared on our back porch eager to go, dressed in their only good clothes. Although their parents were dirt poor, WPA workers' children were kept neat and clean, reflecting the love that was given them in lieu of the material things of life.

"My, you all look so nice," I told them as each one scrambled to grab my hand to be safe on our long walk to town. I tried to be diplomatic by changing off hand holding.

"Oh, I see you have your little family again," the cashier laughed as I laid our money down for the dime tickets. "These two are under six, so they should get in free," I said, pushing Artie and his sister, Sally, up front so she could see them. I herded my flock of lambs into the theatre where mellow music was coming from the stage which was adorned with a red velvet curtain. It was hard to decide where to sit but we picked the middle row of seats.

For a while there were only whispered questions asked during the munching of popcorn, until the screen burst forth with the giant-sized face of Mickey Mouse. The happy, excited children couldn't contain themselves. They jumped up and stomped their feet amid the squeals of joy. (What wouldn't I give if I could spend another Sunday afternoon at the movie theatre with my little friends of many years ago.)

Families moved in and out of the city with new faces of children for me to care for. I never had to ask my parents for pin money because I earned my own from the many hours of baby sitting.

One summer day a lady dressed in gray striped overalls with a red 'kerchief wrapped around her head, appeared at our front door. "I'm Mrs. Ainslee. I live over on South Rowley Street and I heard that you have a daughter who likes to take care of kids. I've been looking high and low for a girl to take care of my four. I work at Armour Creameries, picking chickens, and I need someone to come in and take over."

"Well, I don't know," Mama hesitated. "Dolores is only thirteen and has never done housework outside her home, but you can ask her."

I appeared when I heard my name being called, and peeked through the screen door where I saw a woman who was searching for a girl to help her. She looked me over, no doubt to see if I was strong enough. She spoke with a rather loud, irritating voice that was laced with slang words. I thought her bony-lined face seemed to reflect a cruel nature, as she gazed at me through a pair of rimless spectacles.

"I'm sure she will do all right," the woman convinced both Mama and me as I consented to be the caretaker of a family household. Besides, two and a half dollars a week was not to be sneezed at.

When I arrived at a rather run-down house early the following Monday, my employer met me at the door, surrounded by four wide-eyed youngsters ranging in age from about three to eight. I guessed right away the red-head, a boy of five, would give me trouble. "If you want to know where things are, just ask the kids," the lady said as she hurried out the door. "My husband and I will be home for dinner so scrape up something from the 'fridge'."

I already felt disappointed as I looked around the kitchen. It was in a state of chaos. The table where the children were eating breakfast was littered with dirty dishes and empty cereal boxes and lakes of milk running off onto the debris-laden floor. "Where do I begin?" I wondered, as I moved through the rest of the house, not believing how people could live in such a place. I began to rearrange the over-turned chairs and pick up the discarded clothing that was strewn from "hell to breakfast," as Mama might say.

Secretly I wanted to go back home and erase the whole scene from my mind but I didn't want Mama to think I was chicken. Besides, I would always have disagreeable work until I was old enough to "use my head."

The eldest child, a pale girl with red hair, looked me in the eyes, then asked, "Are you our new maid?" They must think they're rich folks, I surmised. Only millionaires have maids who wore frilly black and white uniforms and whose only duty is to answer the door bell. I felt that this youngster was going to order me around.

"Maybe things will look better after I clear away all the debris," I thought. I began to stack the dirty dishes, silverware, pots and pans into the sink.

"I'll help wipe," chirped the blond curly-haired three year old, climbing onto an old unpainted chair. The over-sized dish towel that she held in her hand had signs of tattle-tale gray. "If these kids are so anxious to help, how come this place looks like a shanty in old shanty town?" I questioned myself. I had just begun to scratch the surface of what I had to clean when I saw it was almost noon. There was supposed to be food on the table soon. I searched frantically through the messy "fridge" for something edible but found only an open package of wieners. The four shriveled potatoes I found had to be peeled and shredded into hash browns.

"Find me a can of vegetables." I boosted one of the boys to the high shelves of the pantry where the canned goods were stored. He handed down a can without a label.

"We kids tore all the paper off," he grinned.

"What did you want to do that for?" I asked.

"Just for fun," he answered, sticking his tongue through the empty space where two front teeth were missing.

I was lucky there was creamed corn in the can and soon the quick meal was on the table by the time the weary parents arrived.

"Just pull up a chair and eat with us," Mrs. Ainslee said above the noise of the children who were banging on the table with their spoons. Just dig in and help yourself.

"I was planning on running home for a quick bite," I told her, already feeling a headache coming on.

"Oh fiddle sticks. There's plenty here. Squeeze in between Betty and Bobby." I sat down on a rickety chair.

I tried to enjoy the meal but I felt like I was caught between the devil and the deep blue sea, with a talkative, uncouth mother on one side of the table and ill-mannered brats on the other. (And I thought our family was unrefined.)

"Boy, I'm going to get by cheap," Mrs. Ainslee cried, after noting the small portion of food on my plate. "But I have to watch my pennies. You never know when there is going to be a lay-off at the plant." Saying this, she plucked off a stray feather that she carried away from the "chicken pickin' " factory.

"Well, got to get back to the salt mines," she said, pushing back her chair and wiping her hands on her soiled overalls. "No rest for the wicked." Standing by the open door, she instructed me, "Put the two little ones to bed at one o'clock, but the others can play with the neighbors. See you after work. And she was gone.

I breathed a sigh of relief as I plunked down at the table and contemplated what was next. Little did I realize that before the day was over I was going to be baptized under fire on my new job.

The children were put to bed and, to my surprise, closed their eyes immediately. "They're really tuckered out," I smiled, pulling down the tattered curtain shade to keep out the sunlight. I tiptoed out of the room and closed the door. They aren't half bad, my first thoughts told me as I prepared to make the beds at the far end of the house.

When I finally completed the enormous task of reconstructing the household, I sank down in the worn upholstered rocking chair to rest. From the open window I could hear the wail of a fire engine, and farther off, the shrill scream of the fire whistle. "Hope it isn't our house," I thought as the sirens became louder. The house was soon vibrating from the rumble of speeding cars and trucks. I was suddenly jolted to my feet by a loud pounding at the back door. I opened the door to face a ruddy-cheeked fireman in full regalia. Over his shoulder I could see the flames from the barn that was going up in smoke. Panic gripped me. It was my employer's barn. What would they say? "I only work here," I stammered as the firemen asked about who lived there. "I'm just the hired girl."

"Is there a little red-headed boy living here?"

"Yes," I answered, wondering why he wanted to see him. "He's sound asleep right now but I'll wake him up."

"Oh, I think he's been playing with matches. The neighbor woman who turned in the alarm saw him lighting matches near the barn."

Bobby's look of angelic innocence soon gave way to the questioning by the fire captain, and he confessed.

"I started the fire but I didn't mean to burn the barn down," he said, sheepishly. "I sneaked the matches out of the pantry when our hired girl wasn't watching. She thought I was sleeping." "It's all my fault," I told the captain, "but I'll bet someone will get a licking when his mother gets home."

"I hope this has taught you a lesson," the captain said severely to Bobby. "It was only a barn this time but you may burn somebody if you ever play with matches again."

228

"Are you going to tell Mama on me?" a now frightened little boy asked with an innocent look, calculated to softening hearts.

"I have to tell, Bobby," I said, already feeling sorry for him. "If I don't, the neighbor lady will."

"I'm going back to bed and stay there all day and night," he promised as he walked towards the bedroom holding one hand over his rear expectantly.

Bobby's parents weren't too angry when they heard about the fire. "That old barn was just about falling down anyway," the mother said, after she surveyed the damage. "Well, I'm sure the old landlord has insurance."

"That kid should have his ears boxed," one of the neighbor women grumbled. "He could have burned down the whole block. I feel sorry for that girl who has to put up with those brats. I wouldn't have that job for love nor money."

"Just hang in there," Mama told me when I complained about the work. "Show those kids who is boss and they'll settle down."

So I reluctantly stuck to my guns while the work load piled higher and higher on my frail shoulders. The children's mother began to leave her weekend chores for me, when I arrived on Monday mornings. The ironing was added to my growing list of tasks. "You don't have to be fussy. Just do the best you can," she ordered, setting down a large wicker basket overflowing with clothes, that hadn't been pressed in a long time.

One afternoon when I was engrossed in an unpleasant task, angry voices came from the children's bedroom. Betty and Bobby were arguing about something that caused the little girl to scream. "I wonder what those two are up to now," I thought, and set my iron aside to make a check. When I opened the door a blast exploded that rocked me. Bobby was holding a shotgun which had just been fired. She was standing only a few inches from a hole in the wall where the pellets found their mark. I couldn't believe my eyes. Why did the parents leave a loaded weapon in the closet? Only a miracle saved Betty from being killed. He could have pointed that gun in my direction and blown me to pieces.

"This is the last straw," I stormed. "Lay that gun on the floor. You're going to get punished for this if I have to do it myself." My hands were shaking as I picked up the weapon and put it on the top shelf in the closet.

"I meant to put that gun away," the father apologized later when I tearfully recounted the close call. "I'm afraid you're not being responsible with those kids," the mother stated, taking a closer look at the hole in the wall. I recoiled at her remark and my shyness broke loose. I seethed in open hostility. I decided to tell them I was no door mat for their kids.

"Those kids need a good licking about twice a day. Too bad they don't have my mama for a mother. She would make them toe the mark. You can just find someone else to take care of your ornery brats, 'cause I'm quitting." There, I said it and I felt better.

"Aren't you ever coming back?" little Betty asked when I strode to the front door. "I like you, and we need somebody to take care of us."

"Never," I answered with a slight twinge of pity for the children who only needed a little parental discipline. My feet never moved more resolutely down the dirt road towards home. When I came to the large grove of cottonwoods, I glanced back at the place where I had worked so hard for every nickel I earned.

"I'll find another job," I told myself. "There has to be something better than being a hired girl.

Puppy Love

"Roses are red, violets are blue, sugar is sweet and so are you." This was a romantic verse often written in school children's books. My brothers teased my older sister about these sentimental words in her book. I felt sorry for her when they chanted, "Evie's got a boy friend." Shame on you, shame on you," while they rubbed their forefingers together as a sign of something naughty. Her tears often brought me to her defense with shouts of, "You're just jealous because you don't have a sweetheart." I vowed then and there that when I found my secret love, nobody was going to know about it. I was still too young to think about having a boy friend but I was beginning to shed my ugly duck image and was becoming a pretty young lady of twelve. The relatives told my folks that I was going to be a real heart-breaker when I grew up.

During the 30's the poor folks around where we lived often moved, always searching for better housing; or perhaps were kicked out by a cold-hearted landlord for not paying rent. Watching the loading and unloading of furniture and belongings became a favorite pastime for the neighbors. It was fun to investigate an empty house in hopes of finding something of value left behind. Even a light bulb or curtain shade was interesting.

There was one run down shanty across the alley from us that had more than its share of tenants.

"Have you seen the new neighbors that moved into the Brim house?" a neighbor woman asked Mama. "I heard that she is a gay divorcee with five wild boys. You know the old saying, 'like mother like son.' I'm keeping my kids away from that outfit."

After the neighbor left, Mama sniffed, "She has no room to talk. She better keep an eye on her own husband. He's always looking around for greener pastures."

The thought of a few more boys in the neighborhood intrigued us girls who were already thinking of a way to get acquainted. Pulling weeds from our garden, next to the alley, would give us a good opportunity to see if there were any cute ones in the new tribe. During the first few weeks the occupants stayed pretty close to home. There were mountains of chores for them, such as chopping wood, emptying the ash pans from the stoves and even hanging out the wash. Mama heard that the mother was employed at a produce company, breaking eggs. "I don't think those kids have time for anything," brother Bobby finally concluded, "but we can always ask. We could sure use some extra players for a soft ball team. Tomorrow after school we will start a game over on the side of the hill and maybe they will come over."

The scheme worked. One by one the brothers edged closer to our diamond and we in turn had our chance to introduce ourselves. They acted shy and not like hell raisers.

"My name is Bobby and these are my two sisters, Neeney and Lorsey," our big brother proudly told them. "What's your names?" We stood waiting for a response.

This is Donald, Bobby, Laverne and Sissy and I'm Floyd," spoke up a handsome boy who I figured was about my age. "We used to live on a farm but our folks got a divorce so Ma and us kids moved to Mitchell," he explained. "Gosh, he is sure cute," I thought as I observed the curly dark hair, tousled by the wind. He turned and looked right at me and I gazed into the bluest eyes that I had ever seen. I felt a blush and a strange wonderful feeling. I didn't realize that my heart had been awakened to a new emotion, known as puppy love.

I wanted him to like me, so the primping began immediately. My once buster brown hair style began to take on a soft curled look by using Mama's curling iron. I also began to find fault with my physical appearance. My pug nose turned up too much and my front teeth were too big, I thought.

"Your new boy friend has buck teeth, too," my older brother teased when he found out about my new love interest.

A transformation was happening to Floyd, too. The patched and faded jeans were being replaced with a pair of neat corduroy pants and ironed shirts when he appeared at our back door to see if I was around. His face, neck and ears were scrub-brush clean and his once unruly hair was now slicked with hair oil. Mama and Dad even approved of my romance and often mentioned, "Floyd is sure a nice, well-mannered boy." He almost became like a member of our family and entering into our inner circle.

Our friendship blossomed like the wild roses in green meadows, where we strolled hand in hand. We told each other our secret dreams and what we hoped to be when we grew up. Our ambition was to be somebody and to escape from the poverty of our childhood.

One summer afternoon, while we sat together under our favorite shade tree, Floyd declared his love for me. "I want you to have this ring," he said, placing a small white box in my hand, "and some day I'll buy you a wedding ring." I shyly accepted the tiny silver ring and slipped it on my finger. I felt grown up and almost "engaged," like the older girls on the block.

"I love you, too," I told him as he kissed me on my cheek. We became childhood sweethearts who vowed to love each other till the harvest moons turned pale.

But all good things have to come to an end and my world was shattered when Floyd sadly informed me that they were moving away to another state.

"Just remember that I'll come back some day and marry you," he promised, trying to hide the tears that glistened in his blue eyes. "Just don't forget me, please!"

I'll always remember that day when my friend and his family left their little shanty on the hill. I had already said my goodbyes and watched their departure from our back yard. I somehow realized that I would never see him again. My heart was sad.

As the years slipped away the puppy love episode seemed to have happened only in a dream and the face of my sweetheart faded from my memories. But now I often wonder what happened to the boy next door and if he remembers the vow that he made to a skinny, freckle-faced girl who lived in the big house on the hill.

Love Thy Neighbor

"Gee but I'd give the world to see that old gang of mine," is a line from a once popular song, recalling childhood playmates and bosom buddies or one's mortal enemies.

Although I was reared in a sizeable family with plenty of brothers and sisters, there was still a need to communicate with outsiders who appreciated me.

Juanita was the name of my first childhood friend who lived on our block between north Edmunds and west Seventh Street. Her family was considered better off than the rest. Mr. Lawrence was an engineer on the Northwestern Railroad. Playing with our dolls and enjoying our tea parties took up most of our waking hours. Nita even shared her wicker doll buggy, her prized possession, with me.

It was sometimes hard to follow the commandment, "love thy neighbor" with such an assortment of neighbors with different backgrounds. There were some back fence chewing matches and a few hair-pulling contests. It was decided within a few days whether a new neighbor was accepted or not. It was usually up to the children to make the first move and feel newcomers out.

"That old bag living next door in that cook shack won't even say 'hello'," Mama complained, a few days after a widow woman and her two sons moved into a modest trailer home just a few feet away from our fence line.

"Her kids aren't very friendly," brother Buddy agreed. "That little red-headed one sticks out his tongue, thumbs his nose, and calls us dirty names. Maybe, if we're lucky, they will move out again."

The McDonalds continued to live alongside of us with only icy stares exchanged between playing kids. One afternoon brother Buddy came running into the house with his shirt torn, blood splattered all over his overalls and his new glasses bent out of shape.

"What happened to you?" Mama gasped. "Stop bawling and tell me."

"Those two McDonald boys caught me over by the railroad tracks and beat me up," sobbed Buddy.

"Two against one is 'niggers fun.' Where are they now?" Mama wanted to know.

"Playing on a flat bed railroad car with some other kids,"

Buddy told her, peering through one shattered lense of his glasses. "I'm going over there and I'll break their necks," Mama stormed. "They have gone just a little bit too far." We younger kids followed with mixed emotions of fear and excitement.

The McDonald boys weren't aware of Mama's approach and when they noticed, it was too late. She grabbed the youngest one by the pants leg, dragged him to the ground and got in a few good licks across his buttocks. His brother narrowly escaped and alerted his mother who came on the run to protect her offspring. While we children watched, Mama and Mrs. McDonald circled each other to do battle. But the enemy had a weapon. She clenched her spike-heeled shoe in one hand. By now I was trembling with fright for Mama.

She might have been hefty but she was active on her feet and managed to out-maneuver her neighbor, taking the shoe away from her. Mother pushed her to the ground, then threatened to give her a dose of her own medicine.

"Don't hit me," Mrs. McDonald pleaded. "I'll tell the boys to behave. I'll make them apologize."

They stared at each other for a minute, then Mama loosened her hold, but had to satisfy one last taste of revenge. She hurled the woman's shoe across the street where it landed on the hood of a car at the oil station.

While Mrs. McDonald limped away to retrieve her shoe, we kids followed our victorious Mother back home. It felt good to know that we had a Rock of Gibraltar in Mama.

"If you aren't careful, you will have the law on your neck," Dad warned Mama when he heard about her wrestling match with Mrs. McDonald. "Why, she could get you for assault and battery."

"Oh, baloney," Mama scoffed. "I have a right to protect my own flesh and blood. I don't let people run over me like you do. You should stand up more for your rights."

"I don't want to get involved in any neighborhood fights." Dad shook his head in disgust. "There's enough of them right here in this house." He slammed the door behind him.

There wasn't a week that went by that a skirmish didn't erupt somewhere in our block and the youngsters decided which gang they wanted to be loyal to. The leaders planned the tactics of a snowball or rock fight. We little kids were told to keep out of the way when the barrage began. We cheered for our side, blasting away with our childish insults, "Liar, liar pants on fire, hanging on the telephone wire." "Tattle tale, tattle tale, hanging on a bull's tail," "Fatty, fatty, two by four, can't get through the kitchen door." Or one of the worst insults was to call out, "Your dad drinks whiskey and your mother takes in washing."

In a few days the very same children who were enemies before were playing together in all the fun games of depression times; games like "Pump, pump pull away," "Captain, may I?" "Red light, green light," "Punch the ice man," "Andy I over," "Kick the can," and one of the best night games, "Hide and go seek."

We had to have the eyes of a cat to pierce the darkness to find a hiding place away from the glare of the street light.

"Get out of here, you can't hide with us," one of the older boys would tell my little sister and me as he crouched behind the lilac bush with his girl friend. The "lovey dovey" sweethearts were always the last to come back to home base when the captain hollered, "Ole, ole outs in free."

I enjoyed the times when we just sat on the back porch and sang the favorite songs of that era, including the hillbilly music that was popular with the common folks. "Let's sing "Nobody's Darling," someone would suggest after we had shed tears over the forlorn love story of "Cowboy Jack," the lonesome cowboy, with a heart so brave and true.

"Come sit by my side, little darlin', come lay your cool hand on my brow. . . . Promise me that you will never, be nobody's darlin' but mine."

"I swear, you kids could sing all night," Mama interrupted as we began to sing "Little Joe, the Wrangler." "It's time to get to bed. You other kids go home now, it's late."

"Goodnight, goodnight," our farewells were exchanged as each group walked into the darkness with only the light from the silvery moon to guide them. As Mama was hooking the screen door, we could still hear the voices faintly calling, "Goodnight, don't let the bedbugs bite."

I'm not sure if any of the old neighborhood families will ever read this but, if they do, they will know they are among my memories of that long ago. There are a few who lived in our part of town, on the wrong side of the tracks: Allingtons, Bollocks, Kiepkes, Kinyons, Coopers, Goetchs, Lorenz's, Burns's, Snells, Bills's and Neugebauers.

236

My Crowning Glory

Unlike some of my little playmates who had long silky hair or curls of burnished copper, my locks were short and unruly and "dish water" brown.

"Will you please hold still?" Mama scolded, holding my shoulder, "I haven't got all the snarls out yet. You're going to have to learn to brush your hair so it doesn't always look like a rat's nest." I hated to have my hair brushed and combed. It felt like Mama was pulling it out by the roots. "She has hair just like her dad's, coarse and unmanageable. But I'm thankful that it isn't red. There are a lot of redheads on Bill's side of the family."

"Playing barber" often resulted in a licking when Neeney and I styled our tresses with a few snips of the scissors. Another time her hair and eyebrows were singed when brother Bobby held a match to them.

The latest hair styles of the day were discussed by Mama and various neighbor ladies who tried to keep up with the latest fashions in the movie magazines.

"How do you like my new marcel?" asked Marjorie, an over-weight girl who was more concerned about her hair than her ballooning figure. "Clara Bow wears her hair just like this. It's called the 'Vamp.' Kind of gives me that 'come hither look'."

"I think those spit curls are too cute for words," gushed another. "Wait till the guys around here get a load of you," Marjorie giggled, and then made a sexy pout with her rouged lips. (She chewed her gum with a snap, crackle and a pop.)

"I like the 'finger wave'," argued another. "It stays in for days." All you do is sop your hair with water, pour on some lotion and then wave the strands back and forth into little curves."

Mama, who never set foot inside of a beauty shop, listened to the "hen party," then stood up, placed her hand on one bulging hip and saucily remarked, "Well, I would like to be a bleached blonde, just like Mae West. Come up and see me sometime," she mimicked, swaying around the kitchen, patting her black hair. "I thought the ladies would die laughing," she said later.

"I wouldn't have the nerve to bleach my hair," fat Marjorie announced. "My folks would kill me. You know what they said about Rose Mapleton after she went blonde. Fast company! What some women won't do to get a man!"

"They say that new Henna rinse on the market really does the trick," spoke up Mrs. Hogan. "I'd like to try it on my hair. See how gray it's getting?" Everyone looked at her thinning gray hair with yellowish streaks.

"Don't do like old widow Walker," Mama advised. "She dyed her hair black and tried to look like a spring chicken. One day while she was fishing with one of her younger boy friends, it began to rain, and all that black mess dripped from her head and streamed down her face. Her friend didn't realize she was that old until he saw the white hair. Needless to say, he never asked her to go out again."

"Oh, Mrs. Barnes," laughed Mrs. Hogan, you can tell the funniest stories. I never know if you're making them up or not."

"Well, I don't have the patience to monkey with hair. If I go anywhere I just roll it up with the curling iron and let it go at that," Mama said. "They would have to hog-tie me before I'd go into one of those fancy beauty parlors. Besides, I can't afford to pay out two bucks for a permanent, like my two sisters-in-law do. Why, they can't even wash their own hair. Such luxury," she sniffed.

When I started to school I became more aware of the way other little girls took care of their hair. They had various hair-do's, from ringlets, down to the pigtails fastened at the ends with colored ribbons.

"I wish I had hair like Patsy's," I thought to myself, sticking my finger into her long, silky curl that dangled across my desk. Patsy, a sweet girl, was the pampered daughter of a prominent attorney.

"Mama, can you fix my hair like Mary Jane's?" I begged, gazing into the hand mirror at my short bobbed and banged look. "She has curls just like cork screws all over her head."

"There's nothing wrong with your hair," Mama protested. "You look cute with short hair. It makes your face look fatter. It's the Buster Brown style. All the child stars in Hollywood wear it."

"Shirley Temple doesn't," I corrected her. (Shirley Temple was the dimpled, curly-topped darling of the silver screen during the 1930's.)

I continued to wear the boyish hair-cut plus a few singed locks when I tried to fix my own hair-do with Mama's curling iron. Finally my problems were solved by my Aunt Christine who was one of the prettiest ladies in town. She had style and there was never a hair out of place on her titian waves.

"I can help out with the kids," she told Mama. "Especially the girls. I have made an appointment with Mrs. Clark, my hair dresser, to give all three of the girls a permanent wave for Christmas. - - - Dolores and Neeney are supposed to be there tomorrow afternoon. She is in the basement of the Larrison Drug store, with Harley Kirby, the barber." Even though my tomboy sister wasn't too thrilled with the idea, I could hardly wait until the next day.

At that time there were many beauty parlors in Mitchell. Some of the hair dressers operated from their own homes, while others, like Mrs. Berniece Clark, preferred Main street. Others that I can recall were Barrows, Ferguson, Fox, Steele, Realty, Lou S. Davis and the Lange beauty school where young women enrolled to learn the latest techniques for ever-changing hair styles.

"Here's where we go in," I told my sister as I patiently waited for her to jump over the railing of steps that led downstairs to a green door. "Why don't you stop piddlin' around and hurry up. We haven't got all day, and throw away that bubble gum." After "skinning the cat" once more, she reluctantly followed me.

We pushed open the door and found ourselves standing in a barber shop where a man sitting in a large white chair was getting a hair cut. The barber stopped with his scissors in mid air. "Do you kids want a shave and hair cut?" he joked. I shyly looked up into his friendly face and said, "Oh no, we're here to get a permanent. Isn't this a beauty parlor?"

"Oh, Berniece," he called toward the back of the shop. "You've got two customers out here."

A curtain was pulled aside and a very attractive lady with strawberry blonde hair peered out at us. "Come back here, girls," she smiled, her laugh making lines crinkle around her blue eyes. "We've been waiting for you." There was another operator in a snug-fitting uniform standing near a porcelain sink. Pretty bottles and cans sat on little tables; oval mirrors adorned the brightly painted walls. It looked like a mini drug counter.

Neeney was taken to the opposite side of the room and placed in a chair that tilted back. Mrs. Clark then placed a cellophane cape around my shoulders and proceeded to wash my hair. I was tipped backward into the basin with the cape around my neck feeling very uncomfortable. I was too timid to say anything when Mrs. Clark dug her fingernails into my scalp and began vigorously to wash my hair. The sudsy water splashed into my face and trickled down into my ears. My neck began to ache. I was miserable. "Just be patient," I told myself. "It will have to end sometime."

My little sister wasn't being as cooperative. "You got soap in my eyes," I heard her cry out. "How come we have to have our hair washed? Mama just done it yesterday. Beauty parlors are only for sissy kids."

Finally I heard, "That wasn't so bad, was it?" I shook my head "no" as she hoisted me back up into a normal sitting position.

"Now I'm going to comb your hair. You have nice thick hair. Then I'll roll it up on those metal rollers lying there on the vanity."

The strands of damp hair were wrapped tightly around the rollers and then fastened securely with clamps that were screwed into place. My head began to feel top-heavy from the many rows of bobbin-like curlers. I was afraid my neck would snap.

"Is everything all right?" I was asked again when she placed big gobs of cotton around my forehead, ears and the back of my neck. "Fine," I weakly murmured. I didn't know I had to go through all this discomfort to have curly hair.

"What is that awful smell?" I heard my sister ask, at the same time I detected it too. "That is neutralizer. It will help make your curls last a long time." The terrible smelling solution was dabbed on the metal rollers with a ball of cotton. "Keep your eyes closed," we were warned again. "Maybe that stuff will blind me," Neeney worried. I remained quiet and continued to suffer in silence with the suffocating vapors burning my eyes. "How much longer is this going to go on?" I wondered.

"Now don't be afraid. This machine is perfectly safe," Mrs. Clark told me. She pulled over a huge metal contraption that had long black cords with wide clamps attached to the ends. "I'm going to put these clamps on the rollers and then apply heat from this electrical wave maker. More pounds of weight were added to my already overloaded head gear. "Why did I ever consent to this?" I thought . . . When the current was snapped on and I prepared for my electrocution from the mechanical octopus.

"Hey, shut it off, it's burning my ears." The protests came from the other side of the room. "Mama didn't say it was going to be like this. Let me out of here." Her beautician ignored her protests. By turning myself ever such a little bit I could peek at Neeney in the mirror. I almost laughed out loud in spite of my own discomfort. She looked so helpless, like a fly caught in a spider web. She was never much for primping anyway, and to go through this session must have been torture for her.

My own head began to throb. I thought currents of electricity were going through my brain. My scalp felt hot and my ears were burning. Sizzling noises escaped from the rollers. I imagined myself a prisoner in a giant beehive. It was finally over. Mrs. Clark lifted a clamp from the curler, smelled the broiled hair and then said, "You're done!"

"Free at last," I breathed while waiting for the electric cords, metal clamps and rollers to be taken off my head. I reached up to feel the soft fat curls that bounced around like coiled wire springs.

"Oh no, I'm not finished yet," exclaimed Mrs. Clark when she saw me untying the cape. "The neutralizer has to be washed out and then I have to set your hair with bobby pins. After that comes the drying period and then the comb out."

"We will never be home by supper time," I protested. My patience was running out. "Does Shirley Temple have to go through this to look cute?" I wondered.

Mama told me there would be days like this and the only thing to do was to grin and bear it.

"You won't regret one minute of this," Mrs. Clark assured me, now hurrying to put the final touches on her kiddie curls. There was a new customer standing in the doorway, with hair looking pretty ruffled. "Can you give me a quick comb-out? I can't do anything with my hair," she complained. Her head looked like a big ball of "frizzies."

Finally, I was seated on a high-backed stool in front of an oval mirror and the last stages were completed. It felt good when Mrs. Clark swirled the mass of curls into corkscrew ringlets that dangled all over my head. It tickled when the curls were brushed and feathered around my face. I stared into the mirror at a little girl who was changing from an ugly duckling into a beautiful swan.

"Was that really me?" What a difference a new hair-do makes. I couldn't believe my new image.

"Well, what do you think now? Was it worth all the trouble?" asked Mrs. Clark, coaxing a bobbing curl into place. "Yes, I think it's nice," I replied with a shy smile. "Thank you."

Sister Neeney and I looked like carbon copies of each other when she jumped down from her chair. I thought she looked real cute and even lady-like when she picked up the hand mirror to gaze at herself. She turned from side to side to inspect the three hour transformation.

"Oh, I don't like it," she said, screwing up her nose. "It makes me look silly." She was too much of a tomboy to appreciate a little touch of beauty.

The street lights were casting a soft glow on the snow-covered Main street by the time we emerged. The voices of the newsboys could be heard as they stood on the corners, hawking the last editions of the paper.

"I'll never go back into that place again as long as I live," Neeney said. "I wish I still had my straight hair." I couldn't agree with her. I'd be willing to put my neck "through the wringer" again to look beautiful.

The rest of the family were eating at the kitchen table when we walked in the back door. There were expressions of surprise, laughter by some, and compliments from others.

"If they had black faces, I'd swear I was looking at two pickaninnies," one of the older brothers commented. He liked to be insulting.

"Shirley Temple, move over! Here comes the two new stars of Hollywood." This remark made me feel good and I was flattered. I peeked into the mirror above the sink to see if it was still too good to be true.

All good things have to come to an end, and vanity can burst like a bubble. After two weeks of preening and strutting around like a peacock, my head began to itch and it was time to wash my beautiful locks.

While I bent over into the sink, Mama washed my curls with loving care, then rinsed them and rubbed them down with a large scratchy towel until my hair felt soft and fluffy. That is, until I looked into the mirror.

I was shocked; what had happened to my ringlets that bounced when I walked? My head was covered with a tangled mass of frizzies. I thought I looked horrible and I wanted to cry.

Mama tried to comb the unmanageable fuzz, but soon gave up. "You will just have to let it be. It will grow out in a few months. Just be patient."

My hair-do that now made my head look like an oversized tumbleweed, would have been popular among today's weird hair styles.

I wonder why I didn't start a trend back there in the 1930's with my "Afro look."

Watch the Birdie

I don't know what I looked like when I was a baby because no pictures were taken of me. Not until I was about four years old did I find out that the strange looking black box that Aunt Carrie held in her hands could make magic.

"Now I want to take a family picture," she told Mama one day. "The kids are growing up without any pictures and I think it's a shame. Get everybody together and I'll find a suitable background in the bright sunlight."

It wasn't easy to round up seven children to get dressed in short notice, but it was finally accomplished with a few threats and tears. "I don't want my picture took," little Bobby protested. "I want to play marbles with Doodsie."

"Should I wear my hat?" sister Evie asked. "My hair isn't fixed."

"I think everyone should wear their hats and caps," suggested Carrie.

"I put them all away for the winter," Mama complained. "Heaven knows where they are now."

The heavy cardboard boxes were pulled out of their hibernation from the closet and Mama reluctantly dug through the blankets, winter coats and long-legged underwear. She came up with two wool caps and one round leather helmet that belonged to Bobby. The boys grabbed their headgear and pulled them down over their short cropped hair.

"Don't you think those winter caps will look funny when they're in shirt sleeves?" Mama asked.

"Years from now no one will notice the difference," Carrie smiled. "I just think that caps look more dignified."

"Well, the two little ones (Neeney and Lorsey) will have to look undignified because I can't find their stocking caps."

I was glad to hear this because I thought it was too hot already in the month of April to wear such scratchy headgear.

"Why can't you people get ready without acting like the world is coming to an end?" a calm and collected Dad asked his family. "It only took me five minutes to get dressed in my good clothes. How come you're wearing that big black dress, Mama? That won't show up on the picture."

"Because," Mama answered with irritation. "It is the

Lorsey at the age of five. In front of Aunt Carrie's home.

Big sister Evie, sister Neeney and I (Neeney on left).

only one I can get into—or did you forget that I'm having another baby in a few months?"

"That's all right," soothed Aunt Carrie. "I'll put the older kids in front of you so your front won't show. There's nothing to get excited about."

"All right, everyone follow me," waved Carrie, and we all followed her across the street. The background setting for our once-in-a-lifetime family photograph was a vacant rust-colored barn owned by a lumber company.

"You better hurry up," Dad warned. "I think Neeney is going to cry. I can't hang onto her much longer."

"I'm not going to look at that box," Bobby still protested, looking down at his feet. "I wanna go over to Doodsie's house."

"Just wait till this picture is taken; you are going to get it," Bobby was warned by our impatient mother.

The bright sunlight was shining directly into our faces and I just had to shield my eyes when I heard my aunt say calmly, "Now smile, everybody, and watch the birdie." Snap! I heard a click and it was all over.

"Now that wasn't so bad, was it?" Aunt Carrie grinned

as she prepared for another shot. "I just hope no one moved a muscle.

"I held my breath so hard that I couldn't smile," I confessed. "Will I look funny?"

"You could never look funny. You are as pretty as a picture," my dearest relative told me. She never failed to give love and comfort to us.

The picture taking session was ended with a promise by Aunt Carrie that she would bring the finished prints over to our house as soon as they were ready. It would take about two weeks before the rolls of film could be developed by the local photographer, Mr. Stair.

The long awaited day finally arrived and we kids ran to meet Aunt Carrie who was carrying a large brown envelope.

"Now hold your horses until we get into the house," she cautioned us. "These pictures have to be handled with care."

When everyone had settled down, the first snapshot was carefully laid on the dining room table for all to see.

"Oh, I look terrible," sister Evie said, covering her face. "My teeth stick out and I look like I'm smelling something awful."

"I think I look pretty handsome," our eldest brother proudly said.

"I'm the best looking," argued another brother. "Aren't I, Mama?"

"Look at Bobby," Mama said, shaking her head in disgust. "He didn't look at the camera after all. And Dolores had to hold her hand over her eyes. They are so bashful—sure don't take after me."

"That doesn't look like me. I'm holding my finger in my mouth," I shyly spoke up when I saw myself on the black and white picture. "Neeney looks mad at everybody." She was in Dad's arms.

"I should have worn a cap. My hair looks too short," brother Delmar protested.

Brother Buddy just beamed and said, "I look pretty good without my glasses."

"Well, don't get any ideas about not wearing them because you can't see much when it's dark outside," Mama reminded him. He was called "four eyes" by some of his unkind classmates.

"I have to admit Dad and I are pretty handsome on there," Mama finally admitted. They never had a wedding photo taken.

"I think we're all a pretty good looking tribe. But you know good looks run in my family," joked Dad as he took the picture from Mama's hand. "Yup, I can see that the kids have the look of the Irish."

"Now I'm going to put this picture in my photo album for safe keeping and years from now it will be a treasure to look at," Aunt Carrie remarked.

That one family snapshot, taken those many years ago, remained in the album to be shown only when we came to visit. After Aunt Carrie's death, the picture was given to me by cousin Delmar who knew how much I treasured it. Reprints were made for the other members of the family.

And so began my love affair with the one-eyed camera that was taken off the cupboard shelf with tender loving care. I was ready to pose and say "cheese" at the drop of a handkerchief.

You would think that Aunt Carrie was directing a movie in view of her patience and understanding needed to insure a perfect picture. Before the final take, our dresses had to be wrinkle-free, bloomers pulled up and our stockings not bagging at the knees.

"Now put your arm around Neeney," I was told when she wanted a snap of us three sisters. "Can you girls keep from squinting? All right, now hold still. Look into the camera." Snap! Unlike the sophistication of today's cameras that can take pictures instantly and under any conditions, the cameras of the 1930's needed a lot of sunlight and a statue-like pose.

Our shutter-bug aunt not only took snaps of her own immediate family, she found willing models among the circus and carnival people that included sword swallowers and lady wrestlers. Her kitchen walls were adorned with a variety of people who were a part of her generation.

By the time I reached the age of nine, I was an old pro in knowing which was my best side for a picture. I knew how to smile but not show my two rabbit teeth that liked to slip down on my lower lip. I learned how to relax and not frown into the glaring sun that seemed like a giant spotlight on my modeling career.

"You just wait and see. Some day you are going to be a beautiful model just like those girls in the Good Housekeeping magazine," predicted Aunt Carrie, while she tucked a large red bow into my hair.

Dolores, author of this book, and Neeney. Picture taken near Elks Lodge building on Main Street.

"Do you really think so?" I looked into the hand mirror at a pinch-faced, skinny child who I knew was not pretty. "Mama says that Neeney is the cutest one in the family. She will probably be the model and pose in all the magazines and newspapers," I sadly told her.

"Never," predicted my aunt. "She is too much of a tomboy. She would never get dressed in pretty frocks and sit still for any New York photographer. There now, you look perfect. Now let's go out on the sidewalk where I'll take your picture, holding a basket of flowers. This should be a good one."

One of the nicest pictures ever taken of me was taken on the day of my First Holy Communion in 1933. Harry Hersey, a local photographer, who recorded most of the town's history on film, was asked to take a communion picture. It wasn't easy to place each child in the right position and capture a look of angelic innocence from a group of tired, restless children. Although there were a few who were distracted from the instructions of the patient man hidden under the black cloth, the black and white glossy proved brother Bobby, sister Neeney and myself to be very photogenic. But there was a hitch. The pictures were just too expensive for the poor families to buy. That great moment was about to be lost forever for the lack of a few extra dollars. When our family friend, Maggie Connolly, heard of our plight, she gave us the money to buy the picture, and the family was most grateful. After over forty years, I made some reprints of that picture and gave them to a few of my classmates who couldn't afford them during the hard times.

Unlike today's fast-moving generation where people and events can be photographed and developed instantly by expensive cameras, it took time and patience then to record a family album to be treasured for future generations. I often wonder if the bigger-than-life colored pictures of this century will be admired by the space age generation or will their hearts have no thoughts of nostalgia.

Times have also changed about what should be photographed. It was once considered poor taste to have a young child photographed in the nude, no matter how innocent. In today's permissive society, children are being used to promote greed and pornography. So called art photographers are trying to convince the public that exploitation on film is not wrong.

In the beginning the silent majority were shocked to view the indignities and the immodesty of nude women who cavorted through the pages of girlie magazines. As time passed, the nudes revealed more, and undraped men joined in to reveal their masculinity in magazines for women. Nudity and profane language have crept into movie theatres and on T V screens, with the protests of citizens who want decency, and are just a voice in the wilderness. Arrests have been made, lawsuits have been filed, hearings have been held in the highest courts in the land. Yet, the pornography remains and a "Pepsi generation" wants the freedom of choice. They say if the prudes don't like it, they can look the other way. The liberated populace wants to hear, read and gaze upon anything and everything that once was considered immoral.

Were we the depression generation who were born into an era of virginity and modesty, and didn't know too much about the facts of life, too "old fashioned" to accept the liberal views of our children and grandchildren? They seem to accept the new morality without any guilt.

I certainly don't have all the answers. But I still like to remember those days of my childhood when I thought there was nothing so sweet and innocent as a baby's smile imprinted on a black and white picture.

249

The Doctors

"An apple a day keeps the doctor away," used to be a saying repeated to us kids, and we did indeed love apples or any other fruit that came by can, box, or barrel. Although Mama didn't know much about vitamins and minerals, she knew from natural instinct what was good or bad for us to eat. She used to brag about how healthy her kids were, and I'm sure some of the neighbors thought we were too ornery to get sick. There wasn't too much need for doctoring.

It was Mama who dug out the slivers from the fingers, feet and back sides. She bandaged the bruises and deep cuts from the broken glass and rusty nails, which often punctured bare feet. There was no need to call the doctor unless some infection was suspected. After all, Mama came from a line of doctors. Her father had been a veterinarian.

Unlike today's medicine cabinet, her few jars and bottles of medicine filled only a small corner of the kitchen cupboard. We kids feared the red bottle of iodine which caused much pain when splashed over our scraped skin. Mama eased our misery by telling us "Now you won't get lockjaw." To prevent more irritation, or maybe a loss of a limb, a bacon rind was placed on a wound, then bandaged with cloth strips torn from an old bed sheet or pillow case.

Another old standby to fight infection was a bread and milk combination, called a poultice. Whether the old home remedies were helpful or not, they were often the only means of health care for the poor people who couldn't afford a doctor.

We children had many "close calls" and I'm sure our lives were saved by our quick thinking mother.

One of our brothers put a stove bolt in his mouth and it lodged in his throat. Lucky for him, Mama was cutting out a dress pattern on the kitchen table and used the only thing within reach, a pair of scissors.

"Now don't you dare swallow or you will choke," she sternly warned him, noting his face that had already turned blue from lack of oxygen. Reaching down into his throat she grasped the still visible bolt and eased it out.

My sister's life was no doubt saved when Mama quickly induced vomiting. Evie drank kerosene from a tin cup that was carelessly left on a window sill.

Many of the neighbors consulted our mother about the childhood diseases in their families and she often made her own "house calls" to examine a sick child or adult with high fever.

"Mrs. Barnes, what is a good remedy for a ringworm in Earl's hair? I've tried everything in the drug store. Can you get rid of this carbuncle on my neck? Are cold or hot packs the right thing for a sprained ankle? What's good for a toothache, whole cloves or a pinch of snuff?" These neighborhood patients often entered or left our back door clinic.

Mama's own aches and pains were suffered in silence for the most part but she was struck down several times by complications of pneumonia and bronchitis. I feared for her life when I heard her choking and gasping for breath in the middle of the night. At these times she had to abstain from smoking.

"I believe I'm going into my 'change'," she remarked to Aunt Carrie one afternoon as they exchanged gossip about friends and relatives. "I'm just not up to par and if this hemorrhaging doesn't stop, I'll bleed to death! I can't afford to be laid up. Evie can't handle all of this housework."

"Too bad you can't afford a hired girl," Aunt Carrie sympathized. Well, you better get to a good doctor. I hear that Dr. Roer is the best one for female problems."

And so began Mama's bi-monthly trips to the doctor and I was usually taken along to help her. It was an arduous walk from the west outskirts of town to the pavements of Main street.

"Just a few more blocks and we'll be there," Mama consoled me, trying not to bear down too hard on my frail shoulder that offered support for her aching legs and feet. "It's a good thing there's an elevator in that building because I could never climb that long flight of stairs."

We limped into the building where most of the dentists, lawyers, doctors and other professional men were located. I tried to make happy talk as we rode in the slow moving elevator to the second floor. I didn't like the worried look in Mama's eyes.

"Have a chair, Mrs. Barnes, the doctor will be here in a few minutes," said the young lady in a white starched uniform. We sank down into the comfort of plump leather chairs that circled the waiting room. I glanced around at the other patients who sat leafing through magazines. They looked nervous and afraid, too, just like Mama.

251

I was jolted from the silence of the small group when the nurse called, "Mrs. Barnes, the doctor is ready to see you now," and Mama arose and followed her into another room. "Please, God," I prayed, "please let her get better." There was a lump in my throat that I couldn't swallow.

After what seemed like an eternity the door opened and Mama came out holding her coat over one arm. I looked into her face anxiously to see if the prognosis was good or bad.

She smiled and I was relieved. "Can you help me put my coat on?" she asked. I held the large wrap-around coat while Mama slipped her plump arms into the sleeves. I hugged her warm back when I straightened the fur collar around her neck. My prayers had been answered, at least for awhile.

The prescriptions were more than often filled at a nearby drug store. Bottles of pain pills and cough medicine were purchased for a few dollars, but it almost emptied Mama's purse.

"I think I have enough money left for a banana split and a fountain coke before we go back home," she laughed.

"Let's go over to Newberry's. Our spirits were lifted for awhile, sitting on the high stools in the dime store, refreshing ourselves, before that tiresome fourteen block walk in the heat of the noon day sun.

But as time went by the visits to the various doctors were made more often as there were doubts about Mama's deteriorating health. During these consultations the word "cancer" was mentioned and a gloom settled over the household.

"Well, I've monkeyed around enough with those other doctors," Mama announced one day in a fighting spirit. "I'm going to see Dr. Ball. He is a specialist in internal medicine." His office was located in a new building on Main street.

"No doubt he will charge more in those fancy surroundings," predicted one of our neighbors. "Well, if he has a good bedside manner, he's worth it. Now, take my doctor, Dr. Bobb. If it weren't for him, I'd be dead by now. Did I ever tell you about the time he pulled me through when I was practically at death's door after major surgery? Well, it was in the spring of '29." It was Mrs. Hogan, boring Mama and the rest of us with stories about her numerous operations and anxious to show her scars.

We kids soon became accustomed to the face of Dr. William A. Ball. It was a "Santa Claus face" with twinkling blue

Dr. William A. Ball, one of
Mitchell's early doctors

eyes, a thatch of white hair and bushy eyebrows. Unlike the sometimes impersonal attitudes of the other doctors, he treated us with love and respect.

"Here comes Dr. Ball," one of the brothers called to Mama, when his automobile drove into our yard. Behind the gleaming glass of the windshield sat the well-rounded doctor smiling at the children who gathered to inspect the bumpers, hood ornament or to stand on the sleek car's running board.

"Can I carry your bag?" someone asked, and it was handed over to the proud porter who carried it into the house, followed by the rest of us kids, and Dr. Ball.

"Have you been taking your medicine?" he asked Mama, wrapping a dark cloth around her bulging arm. "Let's see how that old blood pressure is doing." He pumped a rubber ball a couple of times and looked at a dialed gauge. "Hmm, still a little high. Well let's test your ticker and lungs." He then proceeded to listen through the funny looking contraption that he placed in his ears.

"Have you cut down on those cigarets?" he asked seriously, probably noting some disturbance in her heart and bronchial tubes. "You and Mr. Barnes should both realize that every time you smoke a cigaret it's another nail in your coffins." "I'm afraid that I'm addicted to them," Mama answered with shame. "I've tried to quit, I really have, but I can't."

"Now, you tell Bill to stay on that milk diet for his ulcers," the doctor said. "Bleeding ulcers are nothing to fool with. Has he made up his mind yet about having the operation for hernia? I don't know how he can work with all that discomfort."

"You're never going to smoke, are you?" He turned to me and placed his hand on my head. "I'm going to check you kids as long as I'm here so I'll start with you."

I felt timid when he slipped the metal detector part of the stethescope inside of my blouse and listened to my heart beat. But I wasn't afraid. We learned we had to love and trust Dr. Ball.

"I think this girl is germ proof," he finally decided after the checks of eye, ear, nose and throat were completed. "But she is too skinny. She must be the last one to the table."

I watched from the sidelines while my brothers and sisters tried not to gag when their throats were inspected with the tongue depressor. We were glad that he examined us with our clothes on. We were all modest.

"That tickles me," giggled my little sister when her chest and back were thumped by the doctor.

"You can be thankful that your children are as fit as a fiddle," he told Mama, placing the instruments into a black leather bag and snapping it shut.

"How much do I owe you?" Mama asked, reaching for her pocketbook that she kept tucked underneath her mattress.

"Oh, about two dollars, but if that will make you short, you can pay me the next time." The good doctor realized our family situation and that of countless others who never seemed to have the funds for the health care that was needed. Many of those charged house calls were never paid for.

"You come up to the office in about two weeks. I want to make some further tests on those lungs, maybe take an X-ray," he told Mama. He placed a neat black hat on his head and straightened the spectacles on his round cherub face that was as rosy as an apple.

We kids followed him out of the door and stood by while

he climbed back into his car, grunting a little until his body found the most comfortable position.

"You kids be good now," he chuckled, leaning out of the window to see if everyone was out of the way. "I'll be seeing you again one of these days."

"Bye, Dr. Ball," we all shouted as he drove down the hill, leaving a cloud of dust behind; leaving also an optimistic prognosis about our health.

There were enough doctors in this small city of Mitchell, fortunately, from the first frontier days of the 1880's until the year this story was written.

It took courage and dedication to treat such dreaded diseases as spinal meningitis, typhoid, diphtheria and pneumonia without the miracle drugs that came later. A good bedside manner was truly practiced by the doctors and midwives who kept silent vigils with their patients. House calls were made any time, either within the city limits or into the countryside. Thousands of babies were brought into the world without hospitalizing the mothers.

Mitchell became a well known medical center. Patients

Dr. William Delaney (on left) and Dr. William Ball, in front of first St. Joseph Hospital.

arrived by train, bus and automobile to receive the services of the skilled physicians and surgeons who were practicing there.

Two hospitals, Methodist and Saint Joseph's, provided the necessary accommodations.

Doctors were chosen because of their reputations as specialists in their chosen field, from the pediatricians and surgeons to the internists and eye, ear, nose and throat doctors. Personalities also played a big part in patients' choice.

Throughout the years most of the patient and doctor relationships remained on a trusting basis from birth to a death-bed vigil.

The doctors are but a few who served this community during the depression era, that I remember:

William A. Delaney, Byron A. and Clyde S. Bobb, Edward W. Jones, Harold Lloyd, Frank Boyd, Leonard and Frank Tobin, Earl Young, Daniel T. Gillis, Donald and Oscar Mabee, Robert Weber, Malloy, Shields, and William A. Ball.

MEMORIAL TO DR. WILLIAM A. BALL

Dr. William A. Ball was born July 22, 1877, in Hinsdale, Illinois. His family moved to Mitchell when he was four years old.

After graduating from Rush Medical School in Chicago, he began his practice in 1902.

During World War I, he served in the Medical Corps as a captain. While performing his medical duties in Mitchell, he was chief of staff at both the Methodist and St. Joseph Hospitals. He was a Rotarian and a member of the Masons for thirty-two years.

Dr. Ball specialized in internal medicine and gained the love and respect of the doctors and nurses who were privileged to work with him. He was affectionately called "Daddy Ball" by the many student nurses who heard his lectures on diseases and medicine.

The citizens lost a great doctor and human being when he passed away on July 25, 1949. A lifetime of dedication to his fellow men was ended, yet all who knew and loved him will long remember the "good doctor."

The Undertakers

Aunt Em was one of many elderly people who lived in our part of town. She shared a modest home with her son and family, which was not unusual then.

There was always room for grandma and grandpa. Children accepted their presence in their household. Few aged parents were sent to th old folks home on the edge of town.

"I wonder how old she is," was a question often asked when we watched grandma puttering around in the back yard, with gnarled hands clutching a crooked cane. Dad surmised that she was as old as the hills and was becoming "childish," and if the family didn't keep the gate locked, she would stray away, like a small child.

"I hope I never look like her," I remarked to my brother and sister when she cackled to us across the fence. "Why do people have to grow feeble and wrinkled, like dried apples?"

"We're never going to get old. We will always be kids," Bobby tried to convince us.

"Well, people have to get old before they die," I argued.

One sunny afternoon we noticed a gray coach-like car, with curtains on the rear windows, drive up to Aunt Em's house. After a few minutes, two men carried out a stretcher

H. Noble & Son, Funeral Directors, and their hearse (building now occupied by Salvation Army).

and placed it in the vehicle. The members of the family were crying and walking slowly back into the house.

When we told Mama about the strange vehicle, she remarked with sadness, "I'll bet poor old Aunt Em died. That fancy car was the hearse that takes dead people to the undertaking parlor. I'll run over there and see if there is anything I can do."

The next morning our kitchen smelled delicious from the fragrance of a cake baking in the oven. It was cooled and coated with powdered sugar frosting but we kids were told to keep our hands off. Someone was always picking at the icing.

"This cake is for lunch after the funeral," Mama said, placing it on top of the cupboard. "All of the neighbors bring food for the relatives and friends."

"It's something like a party," Neeney thought. "Can we go too?"

"No, no," Mama answered. "It's no place for you kids. By the time they take Aunt Em to the cemetery in another town, where she was born, and then come back again, it will be almost dark."

"Is she going to be put into the ground?" Bobby asked with interest. "Yes, but then her spirit will fly up to heaven and be with the angels." Mama was trying to explain about death and the hereafter to her wondering children.

As time went by we became accustomed to the funeral processions that passed us by on their way to the Graceland Cemetery, on the northwest edge of town. Often Noble and Broadbent undertaking parlors, one of best known, gave service and comfort to the bereaved. Sometimes the procession contained just a few cars; sometimes bumper to bumper with endless groups of mourners.

"Let's have a funeral," a neighbor chum remarked after we watched the last car turning off toward the cemetery. "I know where there's a dead bird. All we need is a matchbox and some cotton to make the coffin."

After rounding up a few wagons, tricycles and a scooter, we proceeded to form a funeral parade and buried our feathered friend beneath an old apple tree. A few real tears were shed during the sad ceremony.

"Did you hear about Mrs. Herdman? She died this morning," Aunt Carrier said sadly to Mama, about a next door neighbor and close friend.

258

"Oh, no!" Mama cried, "why, we're about the same age. What happened? I just saw her shopping yesterday."

"She just dropped over. One minute she was talking just like you and I are, and then gone, just like that," Carrie snapped her fingers.

How is Bob going to take care of all those little kids? Why, the youngest is no more than a baby."

"I don't know," sighed Carrie, who always worried about other people. "I'll try to help. The family is holding a wake at the house, so if you can get away, we can go over together and help with the children. It's going to be sad." She dabbed her eyes with her handkerchief.

When I heard this sorrowful story I realized that death was not just for the oldtimers. Mrs. Herdman was quite a young, vibrant woman, who laughed a lot when she visited Aunt Carrie's house. My heart was filled with compassion for the children that were left motherless.

"Do you want to go along to the wake with me?" I was asked, after other brothers and sisters declined Mama's offer. "I want to remember her as she was," Dad commented. He was never keen about paying his last respects to the deceased. "I attended enough wakes when I was a boy back home. Some of those Irish wakes were something to see." It was a practice then for the body of the deceased to be kept in the home while friends and relatives took turns keeping a vigil. Sometimes this was accompanied by drinking, dancing and celebration.

The autumn evening was chilly with a misty rain falling on the darkened streets. Reluctantly I walked along beside Mama, escorting her to the home of the woman who had passed away. Fear was gnawing at my insides, and my teeth began to chatter.

The bereaved husband, close relatives and neighbors greeted us at the front door of the large two-story house. Words of sympathy were exchanged. Then I followed Mama into the dimly lit parlor where flickering shadows danced on the walls. Two white candles glowed at each end of a metal casket. We joined a sad eyed group of people who were gazing down into the satin- lined coffin and talking in whispers. I edged closer and peered into the pale face of a woman who appeared to be asleep, yet was all dressed up in a pretty blue dress with a lacy white collar. A string of black beads with a gold cross was entwined around her hands. I had never seen Mrs. Herdman look so pretty before. A five year old child had no idea about a mortician's work.

"My, doesn't she look nice, so natural looking?" "Well, she didn't have to suffer; I'm glad of that!" "She was a good wife and mother. If anyone goes to heaven, she will." "Why did this have to happen? Why was she, of all people, taken away?" "It isn't fair." "Well, God knows best."

I listened to the comments of the grown-ups as they mingled and talked about the "good ones always go first."

"Do you want to have some lunch with the other children?" a friendly lady asked, pointing me to a round oak table in the kitchen. "We grown-ups are going to 'pray the rosary' when the priest comes." "How could anyone be hungry at a time like this?" I wondered.

"Our Father, who art in heaven," the voices rose and fell as the mourners prayed the last prayers for the dead. The now motherless children knelt down beside their father and bowed their heads. It was difficult for me to swallow a piece of hard cake as I sat on a spindle-backed chair. Some of the other children, unrelated to the woman who had died, whispered and giggled until they were noticed by one of the black-robed nuns, who placed her fingers to her lips. "You kids better be quiet," I warned them. "How would you feel if that was your mother?"

After what I thought was a very long time, the people arose and came out to the kitchen to dine on a variety of cakes and sandwiches and drink the gallons of hot coffee that brewed on the cookstove. I felt a tug at my heart when I saw the deceased woman's children bend over into the casket to kiss her. Wiping tears from their eyes, they slowly climbed the stairs and went to bed.

"I hope the sun shines tomorrow," one of the women remarked, pulling back the curtains from the stain glassed window. The rain that splashed against the panes added to the melancholy atmosphere.

"I hate to see anyone buried when it's raining." "I've heard it's a bad omen," another man added to the whispered conversation. "It's just another chapter in the book of eternity. The young can die and the old must!"

Mama finally interrupted the conversation. "Well, we have to go home now," she said to the bereaved father. "Thank you for coming," he answered, holding our hands in his own.

The black umbrella that was borrowed from Aunt Carrie kept us from getting soaked as we hurried home through the gloomy night. The streetlight at the end of each block guided our footsteps across the puddles of water in the broken sidewalks. Neither one of us spoke.

Dad was waiting at the front door when we finally arrived home, chilled to the bone.

"Who all was there?" Dad asked, sipping his coffee. "How did she look? Is Bob taking it hard?" "It's the same at every wake. Everyone feels bad for awhile," a tired and dejected Mama told my father. "But I feel there's real truth in that old song that goes, 'When I'm gone you'll soon forget me, when I've gone so far away.' I'm going to bed," she yawned and withdrew into her bedroom, shutting the door.

My little sister woke up when I tried to sneak into bed. She wanted to know what went on during a "wake." "What does a dead person look like? Like one of those dummies in the store window? Did they have a lot to eat?" "Yes, but I wasn't hungry." "Were the kids crying?" "Yes," I answered, trying to hide the catch in my voice. "I hope Mama doesn't die until we grow up. I wouldn't want a wicked old stepmother." "Neither would I," was my muffled answer from beneath the wool blanket that I pulled over my face. I didn't want her to hear me crying.

It took me a long time to recover from the trauma of viewing a dead person. Nightmares awakened me in the darkness of the night. I often dreamed that Mama was lying in her coffin among a bed of white roses. In the mornings I hastened to the kitchen to see if she was still there. "What are you staring at?" she would ask. "You act like you're looking at a ghost."

I couldn't tell her that I was glad that God was answering my prayers and allowing her to live with us until we were no longer little children.

THE FIRST FUNERAL IN MITCHELL

(This article appeared in the Evening Republican, Mitchell, S. D., in 1921.)

In 1880, a "nigger" appeared in Mitchell. He made himself useful, working in a saloon. He mopped the floor, cleaned the spittoons and drank most of the stock in trade. He was left one night in the back of the saloon; the next morning he was dead.

Great preparations were made for the funeral. The boys chipped in and bought a box that answered for a coffin. Tom Ball was the master of ceremonies.

A dray was utilized for a hearse. The funeral procession wended its way west to the school section, where a grave had previously been dug. There was no official burial ground. The box and the "Darkie" were placed by the side of the open grave. It was then that Tom Ball got in his work. "Boys, take off your hats." The crowd obeyed. Then Tom delivered himself of the following: "Boys, we know this nigger was a lamb of God because he had wool on his head. Boys, chuck him in."

The procession then returned to Mitchell and took "suthin." As a matter of fact, it is asserted by some of the oldsters who remember the incident, the negro referred to died of "delirium tremens" caused by an over-indulgence of spirituous liquors.

The only minister in Mitchell at that time refused to conduct the funeral services, but the "boys" were determined to perform the last rites for the Negro themselves.

Going to the Movies

"Mama, can I go to the picture show with Evie?" I recall asking Mother this when I was only about five. "She said she would take me if I helped with the dishes. Can I? I can get in free," I begged.

"Well, all right," Mama answered, "but you stick close to her because there will be a long line of people waiting to get in. I wouldn't mind seeing that show myself. It's 'The King and the Cowboy,' with Jackie Cooper and Tom Mix. Too bad I can't get Dad to go to one of those cowboy movies. Now put on your long underwear and stockings and a couple of sweaters. It is freezing outside."

I donned my cumbersome clothing and my wool mittens, happily. Aunt Carrie had knitted them for me.

"Wait, you have to have a scarf," Mama called, and she wrapped me into an endless piece of scratchy flannel with only my eyes peeping out. I could hardly turn my head.

"Bye, Mama," we waved walking out into an ice cold wind that pushed us down the snow-covered street. By the time we reached the theatre, I was half crying because of my frost-bitten toes.

"You wait in the lobby where it's warm," my sister said. "I'll get into line to buy my ticket. And, oh yes, take that awful looking scarf off your head. You look like a mummy."

After the frost melted off my eye lashes, I was able to see what a movie theatre looked like. I rubbed the toe of my overshoe against the red carpeting that ran the length of the mirrored lobby. I gazed up at the high ceiling that was painted in swirls of silver and gold. I was overjoyed with excitement at this new adventure away from Mama's apron strings. My attention was attracted to a popping noise coming from a wooden counter filled with candy and gum. I stepped closer to watch a glass-enclosed cage where exploded kernels of corn were flying about.

"That's real popcorn jumping around in that machine. I wish I had a nickel to buy a box," I thought, my mouth watering as the hot buttery smell filtered through the lobby.

"Well, I finally made it," my sister shouted in my ear. "That was sure a long line of people out there! Come on, let's hurry so we will get a good seat."

Forgetting the popcorn, I hurried into the semi-darkened theatre where rows and rows of seats were occupied by people, from kids like me to aging grandparents. Everyone seemed happy and laughter was everywhere.

"Quick, get in there. There's only two left on this side." My sister and I bumped into a half-raised plush seat that felt soft and warm against my still chilled body. I settled down and continued to gaze in awe at the crystal chandeliers that dangled from the high domed ceiling.

"Well, what do you think about all of this?" Evie asked, while offering me a piece of gum. "Isn't it swell?"

"It looks just like a palace that I saw in a picture book," I whispered. "Is that real gold on those walls? Where is that music coming from? When does the show start?"

"The music comes from behind those purple velvet curtains on the stage and the movie will start at one o'clock so just be patient and be quiet."

"All right," I again whispered, not wanting my sister to be upset with me. I knew that she was the only one who would take me to many more movies that I hoped to see.

Suddenly the beautiful curtain silently parted to reveal a gigantic paper-like screen and the theatre was flooded with bright lights and loud music. A man in a picture was turning a crank on a machine. It turned right at us and I became frightened of an expanding circle that came closer and closer. I placed my hands over my face.

"Don't be afraid," Evie soothed. "It's only the eye of the news reel camera. It shows and tells about things that are happening around the world. Now watch!"

I wasn't too thrilled to see moving pictures of floods, fires and the launching of a ship. I was glad that we lived in Mitchell, in our own little corner of the world.

"The news is over, you can look now," Evie said, pulling the fingers away from my eyes. "Look up there now. Isn't that cute?"

Prancing and playing leap frog across the screen were cartoon characters from the Terry Toons comics that were popular then.

"How come they can talk and sing?" I questioned, now giving them my undivided attention. "Are they alive?"

"They are drawn by people out in Hollywood," my wiser

sister answered, as if I should know about such things. Evie was an avid reader of movie magazines. Joan Crawford was her idol.

The cartoons ended with gales of laughter and the clapping of hands. I thought the show was over; I stood up to put on my coat.

"Sit down," Evie said. "Now the main picture starts and I don't want to miss a thing. Here's another stick of gum, now be quiet."

By this time I had to go to the rest room but was afraid to tell Evie that I didn't go before we left home.

The movie began and I was able to grasp the story about a young boy who was a king. His pal was a handsome black-haired cowboy who rode a white horse named Tony. There were hair-raising scenes that left me breathless, especially when they were trapped in an abandoned cave that was filling up with water.

It must have been the sight of the water that reminded me that I still had to go to the toilet. Finally I couldn't contain myself any longer, even though sister Evie was staring transfixed at the screen.

"I have to go pee," I whispered. "If I don't go I'll wet my pants. I gotta go right now!"

"Can't you hold it a little longer?" Evie asked. "This is the most exciting part. Just wait another few minutes."

And so I sat in agony awaiting the outcome between the King and the Cowboy and their arch enemies, the bad guys.

What a relief when I finally was able to relieve myself of my misery. Evie was waiting for me outside of the swinging door.

"Can I wash my hands?" I asked, noting the gleaming white sinks with hot and cold running water. "Such luxury," I thought.

"Go ahead, but hurry it up," she commanded. "I want to see the show all over again. That's the best movie I ever saw."

And so we did, and I must say I loved the "palace of make believe" from the first time I walked down the red carpeted aisle.

The next few years rolled by as quick as a wink and my

love for the movies never dwindled. Seeing pictures became a ritual that we couldn't live without. Some church goers condemned them as immoral.

"Mama, can we have three nickels to go to the Mickey Mouse show?" three younger members of her large brood asked. "There's a nickel show every Saturday morning at the Roxy Theatre. All the neighbor kids get to go."

"I swear you kids must think that money grows on trees. I don't have a penny to my name. Why don't you ask your dad. He sold some eggs yesterday."

"Hey, Dad, can we have some money to go to the Mickey Mouse show?" we begged our father who was feeding his prized flock of chickens.

He sat down a pail of chicken feed and reached into his overalls pocket. We all looked into his hand that held a couple of matches, a nickel and a few pennies.

"Well, I've got enough for one of you. Ask your brother, Delmar, for two more nickels. He got his pay this morning from the paper office.

And so we three little beggars sought financial aid from our big brother who always helped out in a pinch.

The extra money was given without any promise of us paying it back. We headed down the hill as fast as our legs could carry us and soon arrived at the theatre. There was almost a block long line of youngsters standing in a ragged formation. Standing tall among them were a few adults.

"You kids have to get at the end of the line," a red-haired boy ordered us when we tried to squeeze into a space in front of him. "The show will be over by the time we get to the ticket box," I complained to my brother. "We should have come earlier."

"I should have poked that freckle-face in the nose," sister Neeney stormed, narrowing her eyes into a slit. "If he wasn't so big, I would."

"Don't worry, boys and girls, the matinee won't start until you're all inside." We looked up at a well-dressed man with not much hair on the top of his head, but a wide smile on a friendly face.

"That's the man who owns the show house," a friend told us. "They say he doesn't put up with any ornery kids that don't behave. He throws them out on the seat of their pants."

"I'm sure glad of that," I replied as I watched two bullies engaged in a pushing game called chicken fight.

I looked up at the marquee that was all aglow with blinking lights. In large letters was printed, "Cartoons — 3 Stooges and Bob Steele in Smoking Guns."

Pictured on a colorful poster in the show case was a handsome curly-haired cowboy, hands resting on the two guns strapped to his hips. He was our hero, the good guy who always prevailed over his enemies—the crooks or the bad guys.

"Isn't he good looking?" one of the older girls gushed. "He is my favorite cowboy. You can have all the rest."

"Oh baloney," brother Bobby interrupted. "Tim McCoy is the best one of the whole bunch. He can ride a horse faster, shoot the straightest and can fight the best. So there!"

"Buck Jones has the prettiest horse and I think he is the best cowboy," argued another boy.

"You kids don't know what you're talking about," insisted a young woman holding a child. "That new star, John Wayne, has them all beat. He is all man!"

And so the argument went on about who was the best western star in the 1930's horse operas. It was a race to the finish line between Ken Maynard, Buck Jones, Tom Keane, Tom Tyler, Bob Steele, John Wayne, Lash LaRue, Whip Wilson, Wild Bill Elliot, Charles Starret, Hopalong Cassidy, Johnny Mack Brown, Randolph Scott, Dick Foran and a few other stars, some of whom were not popular long. I loved them all but I must admit that my special cowboy was the great Tim McCoy whose steel blue eyes could melt a smoking pistol.

Those hard-fisted, fast-riding and fearless-hearted men of justice were soon threatened by the new breed, the singing cowboys who could sing, yodel and twirl a lariat at the same time. They included the fabulous Gene Autry and his horse, Champ, Roy Rogers and the ever popular Trigger, Tex Ritter, Monte Hale, Rex Allen and another handful who couldn't compete with the popular Autry and Rogers who became world-famous. They were the kings of the westerns.

There were feuds among the small fry about which one of the two singing cowboys was America's favorite. I must admit my loyalty remained with Gene Autry, the yodeling buckaroo whose popular song, "Back in the Saddle Again" still lives in the hearts of his aging, dedicated fans.

What could have been a more exciting time for a child growing up in the 1930's than to attend the Saturday matinee. For only a nickel or a dime their world was turned into the days of the old wild west. Every boy and girl yearned to ride like their idol who chased the cattle rustlers or bank robbers over the sagebrush prairies. They prayed for his safety when he was attacked by a band of Indians who were mighty fierce in feathers and war paint. What a relief when their faithful sidekicks, played by such lovable characters as Gabby Hayes or Smiley Burnett arrived in the nick of time.

Although most of the westerns revolved around the same plot, and the six-shooters seemed to hold ten or more bullets without reloading, nobody really cared. As long as there was a happy ending for the cowboy and his faithful horse who rode off into the sunset, without even a kiss from a rancher's daughter, all was well. The children and grown-ups, too would be back again when Saturday matinee time rolled around.

In my home town there were three theatres during the depression years, the Paramount (formerly Metropolitan), the Roxy and the Lyric. The Roxy and the Lyric showed the quickies and the "B" westerns while Paramount offered the great classics from the large studios, Metro Goldwyn Mayer and 20th Century Fox.

So there was a choice in movies that were churned out during the 1930's. What a way for us to forget our troubles and chase our blues away.

The Saturday matinee at the Roxy theatre began at 10 A. M. Tensions mounted when the lovely black-haired Evelyn DuBois calmly seated herself in the glass enclosed ticket booth. Without a twitch or flick of an eyelash, she dispensed tickets from an endless roll.

The lobby was a treat for everyone. Besides the delicious popcorn and candy, there was a jungle menagerie with chattering monkeys and a sleepy-eyed lion named Duke.

It was always difficult to get into a front row seat because these were usually claimed by the earlybirds who had waited for at least an hour to buy a ticket.

"Where do you want to sit?" my brother asked us girls.

"About in the middle, was our usual answer, knowing that by curtain time our minds would probably change a half dozen times.

"Now hold onto my seat," I told my sister. "I'm going to the lobby to buy a snicker bar. Do you want me to buy you one?"

"No, I'd rather have five bubble gums," she said. She was famous for blowing the biggest bubbles in the neighborhood.

I passed by the owner who was patroling the aisles. "If you don't pipe down, out you go," was his dire warning. For some youngsters the anticipation and excitement was just too much to bear. They acted as if they had "ants in their pants."

Suddenly the lights dimmed and the well known face of Mickey Mouse flashed upon the screen, grinning from ear to ear. Whistles and cat calls broke loose and foot stomping, too, that made the floor vibrate.

After some cartoons and comedies with either the Three Stooges, Charlie Chase, Edgar Kennedy, Andy Clyde or others, the long-running serial began another chilling chapter of either "Tarzan of the Apes," "Jungle Jim," "Frank Buck," "Flash Gordon" or "Tailspin Tommy." The chapters lasted approximately a half hour and always ended with one of our heroes in danger of being burned alive, eaten by a crocodile, trampled by wild horses, or speared by Indians. Such suspense! We had to wait a whole week to find out how they would escape.

SHIRLEY TEMPLE

We kids talked about the movie stars as if they lived on the next block. We imitated their mannerisms, sang their songs and tried to tap dance like the moppets in the Our Gang comedies.

For instance, a movie was supposed to be an average type picture show about horse racing. We kids tagged along with Mama on a hot Sunday afternoon. The letters on the marquee

Shirley Temple

spelled out "LITTLE MISS MARKER." It started out to be a rather boring picture for me when a small girl, with bright eyes and cute dimples, appeared. Her head was covered with curls that bounced when she walked. She wore a very short dress, revealing chubby legs, and she had dimpled elbows.

"Isn't she darling? What a cute little girl. She is so precious. I have never seen anybody that pretty," were some of the murmured compliments coming from the audience, expressing their admiration for the charming miss.

"What is that little girl's name?" I asked my sister, Evie, who was a dyed-in-the-wool Hollywood fan.

"That's Shirley Temple," she whispered. "She's a new child star. I read about her in The Silver Screen magazine. She's only about four or five years old. Some people say she is really a midget."

Before that movie was over we were all in love with the gifted little girl who made us smile and shed a few tears. She was destined to be the best loved child actress in the history of motion pictures.

"Hey, look you kids," Evie shouted to us excitedly. "It says here in the movie ads, 'Coming soon, Shirley Temple in Baby, Take a Bow, at the Paramount'." It was another smash hit featuring the now famous Shirley.

"I wouldn't miss her show for love nor money," I told my brothers and sisters.

"I'd give my right arm to see her in person," Bobby said with a sigh. "I like the way that one little curl dangles over her eye."

The family was completely enchanted with Shirley, who could melt a heart of stone, with only a glance from her hazel-colored eyes.

Her pictures were usually shown for about three days. There were many times when we braved snow storms, blizzards and dust storms to reach the theatre where the sidewalks were packed with her admirers.

As Shirley's popularity grew, the nation helped celebrate her birthday in April. I recall receiving a piece from a giant birthday cake in the lobby of the theatre, where one of her latest movies was being shown.

Many times there was standing room only, with children sitting on the steps of the balcony. For the lucky little girls who could afford it during the depression, they could buy exact copies of her dresses, hair ribbons, jewelry, color books, dishes and dolls made in the image of the little darling of the cinema. Shirley Temple dolls are highly treasured today.

The young star became a million dollar actress during that turbulant era of poverty. Yet, even the disadvantaged spent money to enjoy for a few hours of sunshine. She appeared with the top stars of Hollywood from Lional Barrymore to the beloved "Bojangles," Bill Robinson, a black song and dance man. Who can forget the memorable list of movies that were made into the late 1930's: Curly Top, Now and Forever, The Little Colonel, The Littlest Rebel, The Stowaway, Heidi, Wee Willie Winkle, Little Miss Broadway, Dimples, Captain January, Baby, Take a Bow, and one of the last to be released, Rebecca of Sunnybrook Farm.

But time was running out for the precocious girl. She was growing out of her baby years and we had to face the reality that she was no longer a "cutie pie." Her movies began to earn less at the box office. She was getting too old to play the roles that called for an angelic little face and dimpled knees.

The gifted child that we all adored, faded away, married and started a new life. How we missed her! As for me, I have never forgotten the hours that I spent sitting in the darkened theatre watching Shirley weave her engaging spell around my heart.

TRIBUTE TO THE ROXY THEATRE

The Roxy Theatre was built in 1933, where an old garage had been located. The background and the story of this fine old theatre is interesting. (Jeff Logan, the son of Nelson Logan, related the history to me.)

During the depression, many business places were going bankrupt. It was a problem to borrow money from any source and building another theatre was almost foolhardy. There were already two theatres in this small city. Undaunted, Mr. Logan secured a contractor, hired some workmen, and started his big project. His employees were paid off with shares in a company investment. He had no knowledge of the theatre and movie business, but with the help of a few friends, Ralph Hurd and Cliff Noll, to name two, he met the challenge of this new venture.

It wasn't easy going at first. The other two theatres want-

Roxy Theatre (picture taken in 1930's)

ed to push him out. They belonged to a national chain of movie houses and had first choice of the top movies. Mr. Logan had to accept the low budget films and the reruns. He was learning fast and realized his theatre had stiff competition. His plan was to advertise and create extra gimmicks to catch the public's attention. He installed his own air conditioning system, which is still in operation. The theatre would be as comfortable as possible.

Another pleasing attraction was the usherettes. Pretty, young girls led the way to the seats, holding tiny flashlights. During these hard times, he decided to have a "drawing for dollars" every week. Each week it increased until someone claimed the prize. The crowds were large as everyone could use a few extra dollars. Drawing time was called Pirate Night. During one night in 1935, the unbelievable prize was $400, and the crowds filled the block in front of the theatre. Whoever held the lucky ticket that night must have felt like a millionaire.

Nelson Logan came up with another promotion stunt. He installed a powerful light beam, high in the air above the roof of the theatre, an idea which came from the floodlights of Hollywood. The powerful, revolving light could be seen flashing for miles. This was causing trouble, as planes were finding difficulty in landing at the airport with ths new beacon distracting the pilots, so the beacon had to be turned off, but it did bring a lot of publicity to the Roxy.

Mr. Logan soon came up with another attention getter. He created almost his own jungle in the lobby of his theatre. Everyone loves animals, so to everyone's delight, there appeared a huge cage full of monkeys and the king of the jungle, "Duke," a lion. Duke created much controversy. More so during the second World War when meat was being rationed. How to feed the giant cat? The problem was solved for a time when wild rabbit meat was substituted for other meats. This came to a halt when shotgun shells were hard to buy.

Poor Duke came to a very sad end. He was put to sleep by gas piped into his cage. His carcass was removed to a rendering plant outside of town, his hide joined cow and horse hides shipped out of state.

Another form of advertising was the "walking ad." Wooden or cardboard contraptions, or billboards, were worn over the shoulders of men and boys. They were hired to walk up and down the streets to advertise the show playing at the Roxy. Some of my brothers and neighbor boys earned their tickets by doing this work.

All in all, Mr. Logan gave the other theatres a run for their money. Luck was with him when he took only the low budget films from Republic and Monogram. Republic Pictures was gaining in status, with the ever-increasing popularity of the westerns. Millions of movie goers were making millionaires of the singing cowboys, like Gene Autry and Roy Rogers. Mr. Logan's home-owned theatre was making money, too.

The Roxy has been in business now for over forty years, bringing good entertainment to this area. I think Mr. Logan deserves a great deal of credit. He and his son, Jeff, are the sole owners of both the Roxy and State Theatres today. Most people will say "Thanks for the memories."

Next of Kin

"I don't know what she ever saw in him," is the way Mama described her brother-in-law, Pete Bohr, after they engaged in one of their many confrontations. "Caroline could have married the cream of the crops," Mama said. "But no, she wanted her Little Dutchman from Stickney."

"I get along with him," Dad said. "You can't seem to get along with any of the relatives. You're always picking away at them."

"Well, I don't let them walk all over me like they do you," she snapped. "Why don't you tell him off just once?"

We kids were better acquainted with Pete than with our other two uncles who lived in town. Because we all loved our Aunt Carrie, we had to accept her husband in the bargain. He was at least a head shorter than Carrie and was not particularly handsome. His light brown wispy hair was side parted above a wide forehead. He had steel blue eyes which danced with devilment. His teeth revealed that he "chawed" tobacco. We could see a bulge in one cheek. A brass spittoon was never too far away for him to practice his accuracy. He seemed to find great joy in teasing us kids with crude jokes or uncouth remarks about our upbringing. I tried to pull away when he wanted a kiss on the cheek in return for a piece of candy or cake. "I don't like it when he hugs me. His fingers tickle my ribs," I told Mama.

"He's just a 'clod'," replied Mama. "It's best to visit when he is at work, and that isn't very often."

Uncle Pete worked for an ice company located north of the Corn Palace. He later became a part-time shoe repair man and railroad employe.

"She must be blind if she doesn't know about his flirtations with the grass widows and divorcees in the neighborhood," Mama confided to her friend, Mrs. Johnson. "He really thinks he is God's gift to women."

"I feel sorry for poor Carrie. She works so hard to please him," Mrs. Johnson answered, with a shake of her head. "My Oscar would never do anything like that to hurt me."

"Get a load of that," Uncle Pete would say, gazing across

275

the alley at a new woman in the neighborhood. "Haven't you noticed?" he would ask my dad, who was busily stringing up a fence around the back yard. "I heard that one is game for anything."

"I wish you wouldn't talk like that around these kids," Dad protested, pointing to us. We were all ears.

"Look who's talking," Pete replied with a smirk on his face. "I'm sure they know more than their prayers by now. I've heard Josie (my mother) cuss and tell some Pat and Mike jokes right in front of your kids." And with that remark, Uncle Pete swaggered across the alley to get a better look at the curvaceous woman whom Mama called a rounder.

I often wonder how dear Aunt Carrie endured the behavior of her obnoxious spouse. "He is a good provider and is good to our son," was her defensive answer when she was told about some of his activities. "He just likes to sow a few wild oats. He will settle down one of these days. I'll never leave him. I promised to love, honor and obey till death do us part."

The chewing matches between Mother and Uncle Pete erupted off and on like a smoldering volcano and Dad sometimes had to act as referee. It was during one Corn Palace week that Uncle Pete got the last laugh on all of us and he was amused by our misery. Everyone was looking forward to the Corn Palace festival that was celebrated during the last days of September. It was also a good time for Dad to earn some extra money directing traffic.

It was with great anticipation that we followed Mama down the hill and across the railroad tracks, finding ourselves on the main street in the carnival atmosphere of a mini Mardi Gras.

"You kids can have one ride on the merry-go-round but then we're going to that good show at the Roxy theatre, "All Quiet on the Western Front," Mama said, as we pushed and weaved our way through the visiting throngs. "This is only Monday night and you will have the rest of the week to run up and down the streets."

Bobby, Neeney and I reluctantly left the noisy midway to accompany Mama to the theatre.

"Here's fifteen cents, you can each have a box of popcorn."

"I hope there is a Mickey Mouse cartoon or an Our Gang comedy," Bobby mumbled. "This show isn't for kids anyway."

"Get in there and sit down," Mama warned, "or I'll leave you standing out here in the street."

I was enjoying the World War I movie and a box of fluffy, buttery popcorn. Neeney managed to beg a chocolate bar to boot.

"Oh, I don't feel so good," my sister suddenly cried, holding one hand over her mouth. "I think I'm going to throw up."

"I'll go tell Mama," I said. I dragged her up the aisle, trying to find Mother in the darkened theatre.

Mama was upset, to say the least, to have to leave during the best part of the movie, but she took Neeney to the ladies' room where Neeney lay on a leather couch, a sick girl. As she placed her hand on Neeney's forehead, Mama knew her little daughter was ill.

"Don't tell me you have the measles," she cried, taking note of the red splotches appearing on Neeney's face. "I'll call a taxi. You had better not walk home."

The next morning Dr. Ball was called and he confirmed that Neeney indeed had a severe case of measles.

"That means you will all have to be quarantined till she is well. Measles could spread like wild fire among the children."

"Do you mean we can't go up town anymore this week?" I asked.

"That's right. You're not supposed to leave the premises. Only Dad who has to stay on the job. He will have to find some place else to stay."

It was a gloomy day for all of us. The Corn Palace festival would have to continue without us.

It was a sad group of children who watched the Health Officer tack up the pink signs on the sides of the house, which read, "Measles. This property is quarantined." There were a few rules on the signs in small print.

"Of all the luck," Mama complained under her breath. "This is the worst."

No one seemed to notice our Uncle Pete standing near the edge of our quarantined property but when Mama saw her old enemy, she lashed out, "I hope you get your eyes full. This should make you happy."

"Well, I like that," Pete answered, placing his hands on his hips. "I was going to ask if there was anything Carrie and I could do to help, but now all I can say is that I hope that damned sign stays up there for six months."

"Get into the house, you kids," she ordered. "Looks like we're in for a long siege. At least we won't be bothered by stupid relatives."

"There's sure been a great change in Pete since Carrie's illness, though. He waits on her hand and foot," Mama commented. Aunt Carrie's long illness with diabetes was taking its toll on her health. Her vision was slowly fading. During her last remaining years on earth she couldn't have asked for a more devoted husband than the man she married.

After her death, the once belligerent "Mr. Know It All," the pain in the neck, Uncle Pete, sought friendship with and consolation from his once alienated sister-in-law, my mother. Mama was at that time making her home with her daughter, Evie. Time was marching on for the both of them and for him the days were dwindling down to a precious few. It was time to mend some fences.

"It gets mighty lonesome in that old house," he began one day nodding across the field toward the modest dwelling where the yard lay tangled with ragged weeds. There wasn't a trace of the moss roses that once bloomed in every color. "I sure miss my Caroline. There's not much to live for any more," he continued, pulling out a handkerchief. "That woman was a saint. I didn't deserve her."

Trying to help him through his melancholy moods, Mama would rekindle the memories of some of their best feuds from the days gone by, which now could be talked about without anger.

"Remember that time you penned up one of our run-away pigs and decided to keep it for the damage it caused to your garden? And the time you gave me a black eye on Christmas Eve?" he laughed, slapping his knee, now crippled with arthritis. "Boy, we were some humdingers. I don't know how you folks put up with us. I wish we had it to do all over again, don't you?"

"Not on your life. I wouldn't go through those years again for love nor money," Mama replied.

Re-living the past seemed to be good therapy for both of them, now slipping into their autumn years. They were both sorry for the hurt that they inflicted upon each other.

"Well, I might drop by again tomorrow, Josie," he smiled, standing in the doorway, not really wanting to leave.

"O.K. I'll have the coffee pot on," she replied. She arose from her chair and cleared the table.

Standing alone again in the silence of the kitchen with only the ticking of the clock, Mama heaved a big sigh and said, "Yes, I guess those were the good old days after all."

COUSIN DELMAR

"If that kid had sense he'd be dangerous," some of the neighbors said of my cousin, Delmar, the son and only child of Aunt Carrie and Uncle Pete. "He is always up to something. If it isn't one thing it's another."

I was fond of my cousin, who grew up near us. When we moved from one neighborhood to another, so did his family. He always dressed in the latest styles from little boy sailor suits with the sailor hat to corduroy knickers. "He is the sunshine of my life," Carrie often told my mother, laying a hand on his dark wavy hair. "Don't know what we'd do without him. It's funny the way things turned out. You were given all your children and we just have Delmar. It isn't right to raise a child alone."

"You can have half of mine," Mama teased, always trying to make a joke out of that particular subject.

"Now don't get your clothes mussed up," Carrie would say, watching Delmar running outdoors to play with his rough and ready cousins. Sometimes my brothers were peeved when his suggestions about fun and games proved to be better than theirs. "He sure thinks he's a smarty pants. I think he is

Aunt Carrie and Delmar Bohr

just a big sissy," one of my brothers would say. "He still thinks there is a Santa Claus." The laughter and ridicule never seemed to bother Delmar. He never lost his composure. I'm sure he realized that he was no match for four brawny cousins.

"I'll play with you, cousin Delmar," I would say when he shied away from the wrestling matches of the roughnecks. "We can have a tea party and play with my dolls." Not wanting the other boys to see, we nailed together a table made out of an apple box, found some stools to sit on, then pretended to have a great feast. "I wish I had you for a sister," he told me shyly. "I like you the best of all my cousins." We had a close relationship that has lasted all through the years.

Because he was an only child, he received more than his share of love and material things in life but still yearned for the attention of the neighborhood kids and sometimes created outlandish schemes to hold their interest. April Fools Day, I believe, was created just for him.

"What are you doing, making fudge?" I asked him, watching a pot of hot chocolate bubbling on the cookstove.

"Yeah, April Fools fudge," he chuckled. "See those little chunks of black coal in that pan. I'm going to cover them with this goop, add a few raisins, then place the candy in this pretty box. Boy those kids are sure going to get fooled when they bite into these 'delicious chocolates'."

"I don't know," I warned him. "You better be ready to run. You might get your block knocked off."

"Well, what is April Fools Day for, but to play tricks on people? This is going to be fun. Now don't tell your brothers about this."

I betrayed his trust and told my brothers about the trick but said not to reveal the source. As the morning progressed I knew the jokster was having success by the sounds of laughter coming from his back yard. I also noticed some of the children were spitting out the coal and chocolate concoction with threats like, "I'm going home and tell Ma on you and she will come back and box your ears good."

"April Fool! April Fool!" Delmar taunted, from behind a latched screen door.

The days weren't long enough for all the schemes and tricks that my kissin' cousin kept up his sleeve. It was during the worst drought of the dirty thirties when the grasshoppers were invading the land that there wasn't much anyone could do to stop them. Sitting one afternoon on the back cellar door, Delmar came up with the idea of making grasshopper soup. The day before, he tied kernels of corn to a long string, allowed our chickens to eat, then pulled the food from their gullets.

"Now you kids pick up all the hoppers you can find and throw them into this copper boiler, but make sure you put the lid back on."

I wasn't too crazy about this idea. I thought the hoppers were detestable with their defiant eyes and prickly legs. Sister Neeney, who was never afraid of anything, had no qualms about holding them in her hand.

"Spit 'tobacco juice' or I'll kill you," she shouted, picking one from a fence post. "Can you see that 'tobacco juice' coming out of its mouth? He understands what I'm saying."

I shuddered and turned away. "I'll watch but I can't

stand to pick them up." The boiler was quickly filled to the halfway mark with the creepy, crawling, hopping mass of insects.

"Now the final touch. Instead of water I'm going to pour gasoline over them and they will soon be dead," explained Delmar to gullible bystanders who wondered what he was going to do.

The gasoline that Delmar sneaked from his dad's garage was poured into the boiler, then the mixture was stirred with an old broomstick.

"Now what are you going to do with that stinking mess?" I asked, holding my nose.

"We're going to give this goop to your dad's chickens. They will just love it. Now help me lift this boiler over to the fence and we'll dump it over."

Cousin Delmar was right. The hunger and curiosity of the chickens made them gobble the ready-made meal. In a few minutes every morsel was gone.

"Now watch," said Delmar, with a sly grin. "Those chickens will soon wish they'd never seen a grasshopper. Suddenly the prized flock of leghorns began gasping for air. The fumes were interfering with their breathing. Some were running wildly around the fenced-in yard searching for an escape from their discomfort. Cousin Delmar was beside himself and laughed till the tears rolled down his cheeks. In all the confusion, none of us noticed Dad coming out of the house. He had heard the commotion going on in his chicken coop.

"What in heaven's name have you done now?" he shouted at our cousin, surveying the erratic behavior of his feathered friends. "Why are they so excited? What is going on here?"

Delmar gave them some grasshopper soup made with gasoline," we all tattled at once.

"Where in the hell did you ever get such a crazy idea? Don't you know that it will kill them," fumed Dad, shaking his fist under Delmar's nose. "Your folks are going to pay for this, I'll see to that. You've ruined my good laying hens, you little jackass. If I was your dad, I'd give you the whaling of your life. Now you get off of these premises and I don't want to see you step foot in this yard again. And as for you kids," he turned towards us with exasperation, "I would think you'd know better. Now get into the house. Your mother is going to hear about this." Dad never had the heart to inflict the deserved punishment.

"Do you suppose cousin Delmar will get a licking when Dad tells what happened?" I asked my brother, Bobby.

"Naw. He can do anything and they never lay a finger on him. He has never been paddled in his life. I wish Mama was like that. She hits us with most anything." I was already feeling the pain.

The chicken incident was soon forgotten and cousin Delmar decided to be angelic for a while and change his devil horns into a halo. "Uncle Bill, can I come over and play now?" he asked my dad pleadingly.

"Well, all right. But no funny stuff." Everything was going smoothly as we engaged in a game of marbles.

"Mama and Dad are having a house party tomorrow night but I'm not supposed to say anything because your folks aren't invited," said Delmar, letting the cat out of the bag. "You know how your mother always picks a fight with my dad. She is a real brawler."

"You mean your dad starts the arguments," I shot back, "especially when he has his snoot full."

"Our mama and dad don't drink beer anyway, so ha! ha! ha!"

"We can choose our friends but not our relatives," he remarked, and then picked up his marbles, shoved them into his pocket and walked down the alley toward his home.

From behind the lace curtained window, Mama watched the assembled guests walking past our house and entering her sister's back door. "It's not Carrie's fault," Mama apologized. "She has to go along with whatever he decides. He is nothing but a bow-legged little Dutchman."

Dad was just amused as he, too, took a peek from the kitchen window. "It's about time for supper. I'd better call in the kids." Standing on the back porch he hollered, "Supper time," like a sea captain through a bullhorn. From all directions kids came on the run. We were hungry from a long afternoon's play and the aroma of fried hamburger and onions made our mouths water.

"Where is Jimmy?" Mama asked. "I thought I told you kids to keep an eye on him. You know he's only four years old."

"There he comes now. He must have been over to Aunt Carrie's," Dad sighed with relief. "Probably invited himself to the party. Carrie probably gave him a nice lunch."

"Look at him," Mama exclaimed. "He keeps staggering. "I hope he's not having one of his dizzy spells again."

We all ran with Dad who picked up little Jim in his arms after he had stumbled to the ground. "He's not having a spell, I smell beer. Someone has been letting him drink beer," Dad angrily shouted.

We all repeated at the same time, "Cousin Delmar."

"I'll skin that kid alive," Mama threatened. "This is one time that he has gone too far."

"Tomorrow. Do it tomorrow," Dad shushed her. "Let's take care of Jimmy first. We can't let him go to sleep. He will have to walk it off to get that stuff out of his system."

After the walking and talking to wear off the effects of the alcoholic beverage, Jimmy was pronounced normal again and we all breathed a sigh of relief.

Memories were short in those days. One crisis moved into another. Tempers flared for the moment and then were forgotten. Cousin Delmar was slowly changing from a prankster as he matured. "Cousin Delmar wants to take us fishing. Can we go, Mama?" we begged her. "He has some extra bamboo poles and a whole can of worms."

"Now it's fishing," she snorted. "Where in the world is he going to catch fish? In the round house pond?"

"Out in the Jim River. It's not very far to walk," we waited eagerly for her to say yes. "You kids can't swim. Who would pull you out if you fell in? No, it's too dangerous. I can't depend on your cousin."

"Oh nuts," brother Bobby responded. "You know we're not babies anymore. Other kids get to go fishing. Cousin Delmar has promised to watch us real close."

"I'll bet," Mama laughed. "He will probably use you for bait."

"She will give in if we keep begging," Neeney whispered, "let's try a few tears."

And so we did. Our mournful cries of protest finally did cause her to throw up her hands in disgust and say, "You can go, but you better be back before the sun goes down. I'll pack a lunch of minced ham sandwiches and a few cookies into a sack, and you better take a jug of water. It's going to be a long old hike."

It was a merry bunch of youngsters heading east out of town on a bright sunny morning. I carried the lunch ever so carefully so as not to mash the food. By noon we reached the grassy banks of the James River and plopped on the ground to rest. The water looked blue and refreshing as it lapped against the river banks. Nestled among the tall grasses and groves of trees were hundreds of wild roses from bright pinks to deep reds. But they had sharp thorns.

"Did you ever see anything so peaceful and beautiful," I sighed, lying on the cool grass and gazing up at the blue sky. "I could just stay here forever."

"Well, enough day dreaming," Cousin Delmar laughed. "There's some yellow-bellied bullheads in there that I'm going to catch. Hand me that can of juicy worms."

My brothers and Neeney proceeded to pick out the wiggling angle worms and place their hooks through them.

"Oh, I just can't do that," I shivered. "That's awful. I can't look at those squirming things."

"You're sure a fraidy cat," Neeney taunted. "I'll bait your hook this time but you are going to have to learn to do it yourself."

The lazy afternoon passed by all too quickly. The fish were biting and flip flopping all over the river bank. Cousin Delmar strung them on a long line, and secured them in the shallow water to keep them fresh. All I caught was a small sunfish that was left behind to die.

Smacking his lips, Bobby grinned, "Boy, I can taste them already. Won't Mama be tickled to see all of these fish?"

While the rest of the group gathered their gear together, I searched around for a bouquet of wild flowers to take home to Mama. I was always trying to earn a bit of affection.

"I told ya I'd get the kids back home safe and sound," Cousin Delmar shouted to Mama while she watched from the back porch, as we approached home. "And you should see all the fish we caught. You won't believe it."

"Oh my goodness, that is a mess," she marveled as her nephew held up the strings of fish. "Take them out to the old tree stump and I'll clean them right away. I'll have to get a pail of water and a sharp knife. I'll have them ready for the pan in no time."

I wasn't too anxious to watch the bisecting of the fish. I felt a twinge of pity for the bullheads who were barely alive, swimming about in an old bucket.

"Now all you do is crack them over the head with this hammer," Mama instructed us, while we kids stood around the tree stump which made an excellent chopping block. "Then you cut off the head and slice the belly down the middle with a sharp knife. There, like so!"

I felt squeamish as I watched Mama pull out the innards. "What's that balloon thing?" I inquired.

"That's a floater. All fish have those," Bobby picked it up and squeezed it between his fingers.

"Next I take this pair of pliers and pull all the skin off and then throw the fish in that pail of cold water. That's all there is to it," she laughed as the water splashed in her face.

That night the fried fish were placed on a tin platter and set on our oil-cloth-covered kitchen table. "I'll divide these fish so everyone has their share," Dad announced, as he placed a crusty morsel on my plate. "There are some small bones in the meat so be awful careful you don't get one in your throat."

"Yeah, they say if one gets stuck in your throat, you're a goner," one of our brothers responded, reaching for another fish.

Later I looked around the table at the mounting piles of skeletons from the bullheads but my fish remained intact.

"Do you want mine?" I asked my brother Bobby. "I don't feel very hungry tonight; besides, I don't want one of those sharp bones in my throat. From that day on I never really had an appetite for fresh water fish. I eat mine from a can.

AUNT CARRIE

"Here comes Aunt Carrie," I shouted to my little sister as I stood looking out of our bay window at the newly fallen snow, "and she's got a big package. I wonder what she's bringing this time."

"I hope it's a toy for me," she said, pushing me aside for a better look. "Carrie likes me best."

"I'll bet it's for me," I yelled as we both rushed toward the door to let her in.

"Now you kids just be calm," she said, holding the package high above our heads. "There's a little bit for everybody this time."

"Here, put it on the dining room table," Mama told her, leading the way through the house.

Carrie chatted on. "You know, since we moved into the Beckwith building, I have found more things that people throw away. Wait till I show you what I came across this morning." (Uncle Pete was the janitor and handyman in the apartment complex and had access to all the discarded trash.) Holding up a dress of gray and red material, she held it up to my shoulders, then searched for my knee to see if it was the right length. "Well, what do you know. It just fits," Mama said in wonder. "And look at those red crystal buttons on the bodice and cuffs. Who would throw away an expensive dress like that?"

"That's not the half of it. Lookee here," said Carrie, setting a pair of black and white leather shoes on the table. "There's not a button missing from these high tops. Aren't they good looking?"

"Can I have them, Aunt Carrie?" I asked, hoping that they wouldn't be too small. I always yearned for a pair of high button shoes. Sitting on the floor, I hastily pulled on the ankle boots till they felt snug around my legs. "See, they fit," I cried excitedly.

"Don't count your chickens before they hatch," Mama advised. "Those buttons have to be hooked into the button holes. Get me that button hook out of the sewing machine drawer."

I held my breath while Mama closed the gap between the soft folds of leather.

"Please let them fit," I prayed. "If they were too small, Neeney would be the owner of the fancy footwear."

"Now see if you can walk in them," she ordered.

"They fit perfect," I laughed, walking back and forth across the hardwood floor, feeling gay, in the latest style of the day. "Thank you, Aunt Carrie," I told her. "They are just what I've always wanted."

"Ha, ha, I got a new dress, too," sister Neeney reminded me as she turned around in a brown tweed, trimmed with a red collar, belt and cuffs, and a matching pair of bloomers that hung down to her knees. For some reason she always looked better in overalls.

"I want you girls to wear those dresses when you come up town tomorrow because I want to take your picture. Some day you will want to know what you looked like when you were little kids," Aunt Carrie said, reaching for her coat.

The next day the snow had turned into slush from the warm rays of the sun. I worried that my fancy shoes would get wet and shrink.

"Don't worry," Mama said. "Mr. Widman is giving us a ride right up to Carrie's doorstep. What would we do without such a wonderful neighbor?"

Aunt Carrie found a dry spot for us to pose, on the south side of the Elks building where the bright sunlight glared into our eyes and made us squint. "Can't you smile just a little bit," she coaxed my sister, who never was enthusiastic about having her picture taken. When Aunt Carrie thought she had the right angle, she told us, "All right now, hold real still and watch the camera." "Click." Another history-making snapshot was taken and we all gave a sigh of relief.

"Is that really me?" I gasped when we were shown the small black and white picture. "I think it turned out pretty good," our aunt said, "even though your eyes were shadowed by your bangs and Neeney didn't smile. I'm going to put this picture in my photo album, along with the others, for safe-keeping, but you can look at it whenever you come over." If it hadn't been for our dear aunt, there would not be any of those once-in-a-lifetime pictures that I treasure today.

Unlike my mother who possessed for many years a statuesque figure and good looks, Aunt Carrie never would have stood out in a crowd for her beauty. Her mousy hair blew wispy from a head that seemed too small for her round shouldered body. A prominent stomach made her look plump. Slightly bowed legs were too thin and out of proportion. But no matter what she lacked in outward appearance, her inner beauty sparkled in her blue eyes.

"I just can't believe you two are sisters," was a common comment from people who compared Aunt Carrie and Mama. "I guess I'm the ugly duckling in the family who just forgot about growing into a beautiful swan," was Aunt Carrie's ever-ready answer. From the time that I was a babe in arms I loved this wonderful lady as if she were my own mother.

"One of these days I'm going to steal Dolores away from you. I could teach her so many things that you don't have time for. If my little Margaret had lived, they would be almost the same age. You don't know how lucky you are to have three daughters." These remarks were made to Mama by her sister who yearned to have a little girl of her own.

"I'd like to live with Aunt Carrie in the daytime and with you at night," I said compromisingly to Mama, not wanting to hurt her feelings.

"You just learn all you can when you are at her house. She is very artistic and creative. She will teach you how to bake cookies and cakes, to embroider those pretty pictures on pillow cases and you will learn how to grow a flower garden. To repay her you can help with the housework." And so my apprenticeship began at an early age in the quaint little house on the hill where the morning glories grew around the back door. Spending part of my time in such a pleasantly cluttered home was almost like living in a dime store. Aunt Carrie treasured the souvenirs, trinkets, novelties, premiums and prizes that she bought or won at local carnival or medicine show games. Pictures of stars from the WNAX Radio station adorned the walls. Radio Guide magazine kept her in touch with the soap operas that she listened to every day.

"We will have to be quiet," she shushed me. "Ma Perkins is on now." She twisted the radio dial to WNAX, Yankton. I pretended to enjoy the episodes that became the heartbeat of American women. Her face revealed the joys and sorrows of her radio family. I learned the names of her favorite shows from Myrt and Marge to One Man's Family. When the morning soaps were over, we finished our household chores, listening to the beautiful music of the Sons of the Pioneers that came from the KSOO Radio station at Sioux Falls, South Dakota. Plus a young man who played the accordion like a wild gypsy. His name was Myron Floren.

Saturday morning was pay day. Carrie insisted that I accept a quarter for being her helper. The money came in handy to splurge at the Mickey Mouse show, Saturday morning at the Roxy Theatre. "Have a good time now," she shouted as I raced to join my brother and sister who were already heading down the hill towards town.

Aunt Carrie was not only a friend in need to our family. Her compassion for others extended throughout every neighborhood that she lived in whether the people were "Sunday go to meeting" folks or among the town's "ne'er do wells."

"Why do you want to help that old good for nothing wino?" someone would ask when they saw her leaving the tumbledown shack near the railroad tracks.

"He's a very sick man and needs someone to care for him till he gets back on his feet," answered the Good Samaritan. "Some good homemade soup and a few loaves of bread won't put me out of business."

"Well, I think you're wasting your time on that bum," insisted her critic.

"You're wrong, so wrong. There is good in everybody and no matter how useless their life style seems to be, I can still see a little good in a person.

Her "love thy neighbor" creed continued throughout her life, with many all-night vigils at the bedside of dying friends. She offered shelter to displaced families, remembering the shut-ins with a special cake or a bouquet from her ever-blooming flower garden. The world was indeed a better place because Aunt Carrie was there.

The years slipped away and I was no longer a little girl but a married woman with a child of my own when I received a letter from Mama telling me that Aunt Carrie was seriously ill and was not expected to live. "She wants to see you before she goes completely blind," she wrote. "Come as soon as possible."

It was with a saddened heart the afternoon I went to the hospital to see my Aunt Carrie for what was to be the last time.

She was lying motionless in a metal bed that was enclosed with railings to keep her from falling out. The rays of sunlight coming through the window reflected from her pale face. Her once blue eyes were already faded and sightless.

"Hello, Aunt Carrie," I greeted her. "This is Dolores. I've come to see you." She turned her head towards my voice and broke into a beaming smile.

"Oh, I'm so glad that you could come." She clutched my hand and held it to her face. I could feel coldness that was creeping into her.

"I'm getting along just fine and I'll be back home before you know it. I've got so many things to do before Christmas. Even though I can't see any more, I can still keep busy. I worry about Dad (Pete) over there in that house alone. He says he really misses me."

"You better rest now," I whispered, noting the strain in her voice, "and I promise that I'll come to see you Christmas Day." As I kissed her on the cheek, I felt the tears that were trickling down her face and I, too, cried. Her wish to celebrate another Christmas wasn't to be, and she passed away on a cold wintry day in mid-December. She now lies on a hillside in Calvary Cemetery, beside her husband, Peter.

Yes, I'll always remember my Aunt Carrie for what she was—a beautiful person and, wherever she is, I'm sure she is making someone happy by placing a little rainbow around their shoulders.

Aunt Christine and Cousin Leland, Kinfolk

There were other kinfolk living in Mitchell besides Aunt Carrie, Uncle Pete and Cousin Delmar, who were on Mama's side of the fence.

"Your two brothers are as different as daylight and dark," Mama remarked about Dad's brothers, Frank and Mark. "There isn't a better man who ever walked the earth than good old Frank, but I don't care for that hot-tempered red-headed Mark. I don't know how Christine puts up with him. If I were her I'd kick him out before he drives away all the business from the cafe. Can't you do something about his drinking?" Mama pleaded with Dad.

"I've tried to reason with him but he won't listen. He can't seem to shake the demons. If Mother and Dad knew about this they would turn over in their graves."

"Well, if he keeps monkeying around in that kitchen he will be in *his* grave," Mama assured Dad. "They say Christine chased him down the alley the other day with a meat cleaver."

Such conversations by our parents were taken with a grain of salt by us kids who were used to the stories about relatives and neighbors. We learned to like or dislike the neighbors by our own intuition.

I was fond of Uncle Mark even though his breath smelled of alcohol whenever he waited on us kids at the candy counter of their grocery and cafe. "Do you want the jaw breakers or the golf ball suckers for the extra penny, or shall I throw in a couple of lemon drops," he patiently queried as we pondered. His homely wrinkled face was flushed when he arose from a squatting position behind the glass counter. The bulging brown paper sacks of candy were given to us by trembling hands.

The Barnes Cafe and Grocery Store was located directly across from the Corn Palace and was noted for delicious home-cooked meals and famous barbecued hamburgers, costing only a nickel. A limited line of groceries satisfied the needs of the surrounding neighborhood. Charging grocery bills came in handy when there wasn't any cash on hand but the debt was sometimes hard to pay off at the end of the month.

Mama fumed when we kids brought home grocery slips that were overdue. "I think Uncle Mark is cheating, overcharging on the bologna and hamburger. I'm sure he's laying an extra finger on the scale."

"Well, why don't you go yourself?" Dad suggested, not wanting to hear more about his brother's larceny.

So shopping at the grocery store was usually left up to us kids who were more than willing to go for the extra treat of an ice cream cone or candy bar given to us by Aunt Christine. She knew it was tough sledding for our family. If there were left-over meats, or vegetables, or day-old bread, they were placed in a paper-lined box and sent home with us.

"She is sure a great beauty," was what most people said after they saw my Aunt Christine for the first time. And when she spoke in a delightful accent they could tell she was from one of the Scandinavian countries. Sweden was the land of her birth. Her figure, in freshly starched white uniforms, was well endowed and the curves were all in the right places. Her outstanding features were her emerald green eyes, fringed by long dark lashes. A quick wink at one of her male customers made them think they were something special. Ringlets of auburn red hair swirled around her head and dangled into little kiss curls that framed a face with a peaches and cream complexion.

"I wish I had her pearly teeth," Mama often remarked about her sister-in-law's "toothpaste" smile. The white, even rows of teeth flecked with a few tiny gold fillings were kept in perfect condition. Aunt Christine was well aware of her beauty and when it was enhanced by a little help from the drug store or the beauty shops, who could ask for anything more?

"Well, if I could afford to have a henna rinse once a month and buy all of those cold creams, I'd look pretty good, too," Mama sniffed when someone made mention of Aunt Christine's allure. "Why, I'll bet she has half the men in town in love with her," another gossipy neighbor said. "Just about all the railroad men from the Omaha line eat their meals there. She certainly has what it takes."

I was too young at the time to understand why Aunt Christine and Uncle Mark decided to end their marriage but

I'm sure it was his drinking problems and jealousies that arose in their daily contacts with small town folks. One day, out of the blue, Uncle Mark, or Red, as he was fondly called, left his wife and son and the town of Mitchell, never to return until the day of Aunt Christine's funeral. He wanted to see, once more, the beautiful Swedish girl who won his heart so many years before.

After Uncle Mark's departure (a good riddance as far as we were concerned), the Barnes Cafe flourished despite the hard times. Aunt Christine, along with her only child, a son, Leland, or "Little Red," were well off and we liked to brag about our "rich relatives." Our cousin was the "spittin' image" of his father, with a million freckles to boot.

"I'm sure glad that none of my kids have red hair," Mama repeatedly told Dad, knowing that there were many carrot-topped Irishmen in his family tree.

Leland was a well-mannered, unspoiled child who had a sense of humor and quick wit that proved to be a great asset in the business world. His inquisitive mind and inventive genius helped him to promote new ideas to advertise their cafe, only a stone's throw from the "World's only Corn Palace." Many tourists beat a path to his door when they took note of the hand-painted signs that advertised refreshments, post cards, and the coolest spot in town, made possible by a home-made air conditioner. The small wooden building fronted by a plank board porch became a hangout for the youth about town. They were attracted by the mouth-watering hamburgers sprinkled with slices of onions and juicy dill pickles; the tangy bottles of orange pop or the double dip ice cream cones in any of twelve flavors. Besides gab fests with cousin Red were fun.

The place was jumping with joy the day the juke box was installed at the rear of the store. It was a happy day to be able to hear the latest songs of the day from records revolving on the turntable. While the lights flashed in a rhapsody of rainbows, we were in juke box heaven.

"Oh, please play that record 'Coconut Grove' again," we begged our cousin as he stood waiting to place another nickel in the slot.

"Now I'm going to play 'Oh Johnny,' sung by Wee Bonnie

Baker, with Orrin Tucker's Band. Be patient and I'll play all of the records free, and then it will take money to hear this music."

Success seemed to come easy for Red and his mother but there were endless hours of hard work for them to compete with the "Greeks" down town. "You can't take it with you, so we're going to spend it," was their motto. "Their luxuries included a modest cottage on the shores of Lake Mitchell. During the depression years this was looked upon as the height of living. A sailboat, the only one of its kind, and a magnificent convertible automobile in flaming red were among their luxuries. The Chamber of Commerce often asked Red to drive his magnificent Oldsmobile to carry the many dignitaries who came to town for social or political purposes. Sometimes we kids didn't go for the idea of Republican candidates riding in our relatives' car because we fancied ourselves dyed-in-the-wool Democrats.

"I heard you kids booing and giving us the raspberry as we drove by," he laughed, after parking his car along the curb and taking off the white banner that read, "Vote for Landon and Knox." "You never know, Alfred Landon just might be the next president of the United States and Frank Knox who rode in my car today will be his vice president."

"Never in a million years," we jeered. "No one will ever beat Franklin Delano Roosevelt. Never, never." We showed him our red, white and blue Roosevelt buttons. We defied anyone to challenge our idol who was for the underdog.

"Here, do you kids want these sunflower badges that were left in the car?" he again teased. The sunflower was the emblem of Kansas, the home state of Alfred Landon, who lost later to our hero, Roosevelt.

"You can throw them away," we answered.

"How would you girls like to sell fireworks?" cousin Red asked Neeney and me one afternoon as we twirled around on the swivel stools by the food counter.

"Oh yes," we replied in unison, "that would be fun. Where are you going to get them?" knowing that the few fireworks that were available each year had to be purchased from out of town suppliers.

"Well, a man from Sioux City was in here the other day and we made a deal. Ours will be the only fireworks stand in town and I've bought a hundred dollars worth. The Fourth of July is only about a month away so if you want the job, it's yours. I'll give you free meals, buy you each a slacks outfit and pay a dollar a day. You can go down to the store this week, pick out your clothes and put it on my bill. And by the way, study up on your arithmetic because you will have to make change."

What kid wouldn't jump at the chance to sell fireworks? A job like that was made in heaven. No doubt the older brothers weren't asked, because their long summer days were spent at the municipal golf links as caddies.

Becoming familiar with the fireworks and their prices began a few days before we were to start selling. The small wooden shanty, adorned with red, white and blue bunting, had already been built by our "Handy Andy" cousin.

The boxes of crackers, Roman candles, sky rockets, pinwheels, snakes, spit devils, torpedoes, cap-guns and caps spread across the floor resembled an arsenal. "This is the new Gene Autry cap-gun and belt that will sell like hot cakes," Red told us while spinning the chrome-plated toy weapon around his forefinger. "They sell for seventy-five cents. I've made a price list of everything so you won't have trouble remembering. And one final warning, don't let any kids into that stand. They may have a lighted punk or cigaret and the whole works could blow sky high." This final statement made me have second thoughts about working in a firecracker stand.

Neeney and I were at our battle stations as the early morning sun peeked over the Corn Palace. The holiday fun-seekers were arriving in droves to check out our wares. After a few timid greetings of, "What can I do for you?" I soon felt like an experienced clerk, and became an expert at demonstrating the Gene Autry gun that every child wanted. I could "shoot from the hip with the speed of a striking rattle snake!"

"Is this guaranteed?" "Give me a package of those ladyfingers." "Do you have any free punk?" "Do these Roman candles really work?" "What can I get for a penny?" "Are those spit devils too dangerous for a five year old?"

Many of the eager youngsters unraveled the firecrackers

around the stand and began to shoot them off right under our very noses. Others were trying to escape the burning, sputtering spit devils that proved to be a menace to a bared foot. (Many of those early days' fireworks have been banned.)

"If you do that stunt again I'm calling the cops," our irate cousin, Red, warned one boy who threw a lit firecracker into our powder house. During that time there was no city ordinance about fireworks and the tiny gunpowder explosives were shot off from one end of town to the other. There were some serious burns and a few people were maimed.

By mid-afternoon the shelves of our one-man stand were almost sold out except for a few rolls of caps and cap-guns that weren't firing right. Neeney and I were more than exhausted from our first try in dealing with the public. Cousin Red was all smiles as he totalled up the profits.

"Since you kids worked so hard and didn't make any mistakes, I'm giving you an extra dollar and those rolls of caps and the guns for you to keep." Imagine me with my very own Gene Autry six shooter. How lucky can you get.

"How about a helping of fried chicken with all the trimmings?" Aunt Christine shouted from the kitchen. Neeney and I eagerly accepted her invitation.

Like all temporary things, the fun of these days we shared with our relatives came to a close when Aunt Christine died at the early age of forty-two years. It was the first time that a death had occurred in our clan and I was deeply saddened. We couldn't believe that the fun-loving, vibrant woman was dead.

"The doctors found that she was riddled with cancer and couldn't help her," a grief stricken Leland told my parents a few days before she passed away. "Ma just thought the pain was from that minor car accident."

Before she died there was one last request—to be buried from the Catholic church. Because of her divorce she was excommunicated from the sacraments of the faith that she adopted when a young girl. Her wish was granted. The solemn short service was performed at the Holy Family Catholic Church.

The loving relationship that was shared between a mother

and son ended and cousin Red was alone for the first time in his life. He tried to pick up the pieces by continuing the business with my brother, Delly, as a partner but it didn't succeed.

"It's no use. I just can't seem to hack it anymore. I'm going to get away from here and start somewhere else," he told Mama one day. "I've brought you all of Ma's belongings. They are out in the car. I'll bring them in." The fur-trimmed coats, feathered hats, satin and silk lounging pajamas and robes were carefully laid on the bed. Strings of pearls and rhinestone jewelry bulged from large velvet jewel boxes, as well as a vast assortment of bottles and jars that contained expensive face creams and lotions. "You can have these, too," he said, and handed Mama a mirrored tray, glittering with cut glass perfume bottles.

"Oh my," Mama gasped, "are you sure you want to give all her beautiful things away?"

"Ma would want you to have them, because she always knew you appreciated the finer things in life but never could afford them, so here's a sample. I'll be leaving as soon as I sell the property and I don't suppose I'll ever come back. There's nothing left in this town for me since Ma is gone."

Cousin Red was true to his word. He never returned to the scenes of his childhood on the sidewalks of north Main Street.

Today the former Barnes Cafe building still stands there. It has been remodeled since the 30's but the ghosts of the past remain. When I walk by I can visualize the cafe and grocery sign hanging from a wrought iron hook. I also see a pretty red-haired lady dressed in a white uniform. She is waving to her customers and saying in a Swedish accent, "Come on in, everybody. There's good food on the table."

Dear Hearts and Gentle People

There was hardly a time that our house wasn't overflowing with company. Besides our neighbors—the ones who could borrow a cup of sugar when needed—a few close friends and relatives always joined in the week-end festivities.

"Is there room for one more?" Uncle Frank asked as he surveyed the gathering clan, sitting on every available spot in our sparsely furnished home. There were never enough chairs so we youngsters usually sat on the hardwood floor.

"Get up, give your chair to Aunt Mabel," Mama would order one of our brothers, who was playing solitaire on the dining room table. "I was just about winning the game," he protested. "Do as you're told," Mama warned. "Get into the kitchen with the other kids and listen to the radio. That 'Little Red School House' program should be coming on."

Uncle Frank politely pulled back the chair so his wife could sit down. She was his second wife, and they always acted like a pair of "love birds."

Aunt Mabel liked to wear fancy clothes, and was usually attired in the latest fashions, from feathered hats that perched on her marcelled hair to the dainty pumps on her feet.

"Another new dress," Mama marveled as she touched the ruffled collar. "Where did you get it?"

"I buy all of my clothes at Geyerman's. Can't seem to find anything suitable at the cheaper stores."

Uncle Frank beamed as we all admired her matched outfit. I often heard Mama (with a bit of envy) tell Dad that Frank worked his fingers to the bone just to please Mabel.

"I bet they never have a fight like Mama and Dad," I thought, as I watched them.

They lived in a cozy apartment where Uncle Frank was the hard working custodian. Next to my beloved Aunt Carrie, I liked Uncle Frank the best of all our relatives. He was kind and young at heart, and wouldn't hurt anyone's feelings.

There was always a full pot of coffee simmering on the back of our cook stove, canned milk and sugar sitting on the kitchen table. The "depression cake," that was milkless, eggless and butterless tasted delicious frosted with a thick layer of powdered sugar.

More than often, a few of Dad's Irish cronies came to call, faces still flushed from the night before. They were known to bend their elbows at the local beer parlor.

"Now keep this under your hat, I don't want the little woman to know," Mike warned my mother, taking a small flask from his vest pocket. "You know she doesn't allow spirits in the house."

"You're safe here," Dad laughed, who more than once rescued his fun-loving friend from hot water.

The amber colored bottle was placed on the table and then passed around for those who wanted a little "nip" (always for health reasons, of course).

"Oh! Oh!" Mama cried, peering out of the window, "here comes old lady Hogan. Every time she sees a car drive into the yard, she has to come over to see who it is. Quick, put away that whiskey. She will tell around that we're running a 'speak-easy'."

"Oh, I see you have company," a trying-to-look surprised Mrs. Hogan told Mama. "Well, I won't stay long. Just wanted to borrow your hot water bottle. Hans came down with the chills last night." (Mrs. Hogan always over-stayed her welcome and often threw a wet blanket on get-togethers.)

"Why do you answer the door?" asked Irish Mike later. He resented her invasion of privacy. "Pretend you're not at home."

"With eight kids running in and out, how could I do that?" Mama answered.

"Say," interrupted Pat, "did you hear the latest joke about the salesman and the farmer's daughter? Well, this salesman was driving through the country and he came to this farm house and - - - -

"Just a minute," Dad said, "I don't want the kids to hear this." He closed the dining room door. On the other side of the sliding doors six pairs of ears were pressed to hear the punch line. Today those same jokes would be considered mild. I'm sure we kids learned a lot about the birds and the bees when we heard these knee slapping stories. Other tidbits of information were given to us by the neighbor kids who eavesdropped on their parents. The word "sex" was not mentioned, but "you know what" suggested the same meaning.

"Ma, here comes Maggie," brother Bobby shouted, tapping on the bay window. We all looked out to see a tiny white-haired lady stepping out of a taxi.

"She never misses a Sunday, Mama laughed as she walked to the door. "I wonder if she will preach, or cuss, today."

Laden down with sacks and packages, and a gallon jug of tavern beer, stood Irish Maggie, a long time friend of the family. She was a domestic, who had worked at Saint Joseph's Hospital from the time she arrived from Ireland, many years before. She was in the winter of her years but in spring in spirit. Her age was a well kept secret.

"Well, don't just stand there. Help me with this stuff," she ordered one of my brothers, then proceeded to work herself out of a bulky fur coat and three layers of sweaters.

"Can't be too careful," she said, "the hospital is full of flu and pneumonia patients these days."

She soon made herself at home, like a visiting grandmother. We kids sometimes resented her when she thought we needed a few manners, or a little more religion. She never failed to bring along a supply of the Catholic Messenger for us to read. Mama said she was both saint and sinner because she liked to carouse and was a divorced woman. The taxi driver often had to wait in front of the tavern while she danced and Irish jig before leaving with her jug of beer.

Although we often had home brew in the basement, it didn't taste as good as the amber colored beer that Maggie bought up town. She dispensed it in small quantities, like an aristocratic hostess at a society tea. She saved the biggest share for herself, which often made her woozy by the time the glass container was empty.

"Come on, Josie," she said to Mother. Play some music on your organ. Do you now the Irish Washer Woman?" Mama always obliged with us kids keeping time from the sidelines.

With her many petticoats "hiked up" to her knees, the dance began and Irish Maggie was like a young Irish lass, stomping, whirling and clicking her heels. When her energy was finally spent, she collapsed into a rocking chair.

I helped pin back into place the long silver strands of hair that dangled from the bun at the top of her head. Her blue eyes sparkled and her cheeks were flushed like a rose when she looked at me and said, "Thank you, child, you're an angel."

Mama knew that Maggie would then become melancholy and her thoughts would take flight to the land of her birth. Organ music was played, mellow and sweet. "I wandered today to the hill, Maggie, to watch the scene below, the creek and the rusty old mill, Maggie, where we used to walk long ago." Mama's voice was loud and clear and we kids joined in to harmonize the rest of Maggie's favorite song. "The green grove is gone from the hill, Maggie, where first the daisies sprung, but to me you're as sweet as you were, Maggie, when you and I were young."

There would be silence for a few moments. Then Maggie would arise and walk into Mama's bedroom, holding a handkerchief to her eyes.

"She will be all right in a few minutes," Mama consoled us kids, who were feeling sorry for her. "She's got a 'crying jag.' Too much to drink."

If it was company time during the winter months when the days grew short around mid-afternoon, it was soon time for lunch and we kids were hungry for some of the store bought foods.

"One of you kids can go to the grocery store and get some minced ham and an assortment of cookies. I don't want those cookies half eaten by the time you get back," she warned. "Oh, yes, and don't let them give you the butt end of the meat." One of the brothers raced down the hill to the corner grocery store where we bought our food.

Sister Evie and I usually helped Mama prepare the quick snack for the dear hearts and gentle people who looked forward to a homey lunch with our family.

"Let Lorsey put the cookies on the plate. She has a way of making them look pretty," Mama told Evie. "You slice the onions and pickles. I'll cut the meat as soon as I sharpen the knife on this crock."

When the stacks of sandwiches, slices of cake, relish trays and the steaming pot of coffee were placed on the dining room table, Mama called, "Come and get it." If we kids were lucky we squeezed in at the table. Otherwise we found a spot in the kitchen, away from the talk in the dining room.

"Oh, everything tastes so yummy," Aunt Mabel said, taking a dainty bite from her sandwich and closing her eyes. "What did you put into this delicious filling?"

"Just plain minced ham with a little salad dressing," Mama answered. She enjoyed receiving compliments on her culinary art.

The platters were soon clean, and we finished with a cup or two of steaming coffee from the gray enameled pot. "That really hit the spot," smiled Uncle Frank, searching his vest pocket for one of his favorite cigars. Aunt Mabel opened a silver case and brought forth a smooth white cigaret. Her husband reached over and galantly lit her cigaret. (Dad never did that for Mama.)

Mama and Dad "rolled their own" from their bags of loose tobacco. The dining room was soon engulfed in a cloud of smoke.

"Why do people always have to smoke after they eat?" I asked my sister, as we finished the dishes. "It burns my eyes. I'm never going to smoke when I grow up," I said. (And I didn't.)

It was the end of another day for people who enjoyed the little things in life, such as a few hours of companionship. My dad, who loved to be surrounded by friends and relatives, was always willing to share what he owned—a cup of coffee, a loaf of bread, a heart full of good wishes.

Lake Mitchell

"Water, water everywhere, but not a drop to drink" is an old quotation which must have referred to salty oceans but not to our fresh water state.

The James River that winds along the outer limits of Mitchell, was not adequate during the early days to supply the water needs of this growing community. Water was obtainable from artesian wells, strategically drilled.

It was during the early twenties when plans were developed to construct an expansive reservoir for water, which would serve this small, but fast growing little city. It was decided to build a man-made lake a few miles north of the city limits.

I was but a toddler of three when Lake Mitchell was completed in 1927, so it seemed to us it was always there—a clear blue sparkling body of water surrounded by a treeless landscape. I fondly recall the first time I enjoyed a cool dip in the big pond. I was a skinny little kid of five.

Dad came home early one sweltering afternoon with a small package, which he handed to me. I was becoming accustomed to shiny trinkets and penny dolls, but this one was wrapped with cord. As I eagerly untied it, I gazed upon something bright red. Mama lifted the garment into the air and I was thrilled to see my first bathing suit. There was another one just like it for sister Neeney. It didn't take us long to discard our clothes and slip into swimming outfits. Dad told us we were going out to Lake Mitchell to try out its waters.

We hopped into our old Overland with the box on the back and away we went, straight north and around the winding road by the golf course. During the 1920's the swimming beach was located on the west side of the lake where the amphitheater is today.

Dad couldn't get the car door open fast enough. We rushed out and down the grassy hill as fast as our legs could carry us. What a joyful experience it was to jump and splash and pretend like we were really swimming. I think Dad and Mama enjoyed it too as they sat near the shoreline and watched to see that we didn't "go in over our heads."

I fell in love with the lake, and through my childhood years spent many hours enjoying the bathing beaches, which were re-located every few years. During the thirties, the "old swimming hole" was on the north side of the largest part of the lake. It was called Spears Bayside Beach.

It was "no sweat" for us and some of the neighbor kids to walk the long distance over the hot pavement north of the city. We used to stop and rest on the old concrete bridge, which crossed the dam and spillway. Once in a while, a salesman or farmer offered us a lift. We girls enjoyed the comfort of the cushioned seats while the boys rode the running boards.

It's hard to describe the exhilarating feelings that engulfed us when the cool waters splashed against our skin. While teenagers and adults swam out to the raft and diving boards, we younger kids remained in the safe confines of a roped off area, surrounded by large floating barrels. Water wings and rubber inner tubes were inflated so they lazily floated on the water. I loved to lie near the sandy shoreline, listening to the happy voices of the swimmers and to feel the tiny waves lapping over my toes. Sister Neeney, who was always braver than I, spent most of her time out on the raft where she swam, dived or belly flopped with the best of them. I was too timid and also too modest to parade around in my "almost birthday suit." One of the lifeguards that I recall was a handsome, bronzed young man named Hal Dean, who kept the vigil on his fellow bathers.

The lake not only offered scenic beauty and recreation but also fresh, soft water for the city. Living in a cottage on the grassy slopes surrounding this beautiful lake was enjoyed by a few. Only the more prosperous could afford a small motorboat or sailboat, which skimmed over the water, and by a few. Only the more prosperous could afford a motorboat or sailboat, which skimmed over the water, and churned it into pretty white-capped waves.

Tons of ice were cut and chopped during the winter months and stored in the huge barns and warehouses of the Spears and the Anderson ice companies. The ice was sold during the summer months.

Time changes everything and my childhood playground is not the same after five decades. Today the lake is almost surrounded by yards, homes, cottages and cabins. Ramps have

Lakeshore Drive north of Mitchell. At that time, Highway 37. (Spears Beach in top center of picture.)

been installed to accommodate the high-powered motorboats. Water skiers are common-place. It is almost impossible to find a good fishing spot. Like everything else in our fast-moving society, privacy has disappeared. There are still sun-kissed sunbathers and swimmers, but the lake waters have become contaminated like that of other lakes and streams. Our drinking water contains huge amounts of chlorine and other chemicals to help purify it. As this is written the old lake is drying up. There may have to be new techniques to insure the water supply for the city.

Many moons have come and gone since I first laid eyes on this lake near our town and I hope it remains for many years to come. Recently I drove out to the "old swimming place" to see how it had changed from the small inlet that I once knew.

The winding beach road was scarred with pot holes and shifting sands. Weeds and grasses waved high along the foot-paths and bathing area. Deteriorating cement foundations looked forlorn where the bath houses and concession stands once offered us privacy and a cold bottle of pop or a candy bar. Green, slimy moss clung to the foaming water along the shoreline, which I remembered as a sign of the end of sum-mer and the start of school. Mama called these "dog days."

While I stood and gazed across the lake with nostalgic memories, I could almost hear again the squeals of delight and the shouts of laughter echoing across the bay, the sigh-ing of the wild rose bushes and towering cottonwoods along the shoreline. Did I imagine that I saw the ghosts of the "de-pression generation" happily bathing or swimming or was it only reflections on the waters?

The Wages of Sin

If the majority of people are judged by the cars that they drive, the way they dress and by the neighborhoods where they live, no doubt our family would have received a zero during the depression years.

Although most of our neighbors were as poor as church mice, there were some who thought themselves above the rest of us and often revealed their true feelings in one way or another.

One particular family was a "holier than thou" group, considering us downright heathens because we weren't regular church members, as they were.

I used to cross the street so I wouldn't have to walk on their sidewalk. Mrs. Dooley was always sitting on the front porch reading her Bible. She looked at me through rimless spectacles and spoke not a word. "If she's going to be living in heaven, then I don't want to go there," I thought to myself. She was surely an old crab.

One day while out in her flower garden that spilled over our fence line, she overheard one of my brothers speaking rather roughly. "Take it to the Lord in prayer," she shouted, looking skyward. "Forgive those who are possessed by the devil."

She enjoyed spreading the word of the gospel and did so for anyone that would listen. But Mama didn't want to hear about doom's day just yet. "Just because I don't go to church is no sign that I'm going to hell," she often remarked. "I'll get just as far as some of those hypocrites who run to church all the time."

Those she called Holy Rollers continued to hold prayer meetings at the Dooley home and we could hear the shouting and crying clear over to our house. "Shall We Gather at the River" and "Bringing in the Sheaves" were two of their favorite hymns, sung with gusto. "They will raise the dead," fumed Mama, trying to get some sleep. "They're only doing what they believe in," Dad offered. "They mean well. Mrs. Dooley is a good Christian woman."

"I notice Brother Jones spends more time next door than

the other members of the congregation. I wonder if they are really reading the Bible or if there is some 'hanky panky' going on," Mama suggested, while peeking through the curtains at our next door soul savers.

"Why don't you 'live and let live'?" Dad answered quietly.

"I just don't like her because she thinks she's so high and mighty," replied Mama. "I'd like to move somewhere else, away from those fanatics."

Mama's suspicions of Mrs. Dooley proved to be right and she could hardly wait to tell Dad the same juicy gossip.

"I told you I was right about the old hypocrite. Mrs. Hogan told me that Dooley came home earlier than expected the other day and found his wife and Brother Jones doing 'you know what.' Dooley is going to file for a divorce. How about that?"

"Well, what do you know!" Dad replied. "You could have fooled me. That just goes to show that you can't tell a book by its cover."

The episode was soon forgotten and I never did know what happened to Mrs. Dooley who we suspected lost her virtue. Anyway, we moved away from that part of town but there was always a mixture of faiths sprinkled throughout each neighborhood.

The Salvation Army succeeded in saving a few sinners whose lives had been in the grip of John Barley Corn.

One of our God-fearing neighbor ladies was married to one of the town drunks who seldom drew a sober breath. I felt pity for her when I watched her push, pull and drag her sodden husband up the hill past our house. We said he was "four sheets to the wind."

At one time they lived in a tar paper shack near the main highway. Bertha took in washing to make ends meet, and more than often, Tom stole her hard-earned money to buy whiskey.

"He'd sell his shoes for a bottle of booze," some of the kids used to tease and taunt. Tom usually was headed for town for another binge at one of the saloons.

"Did he always get drunk like that?" I asked Mama, while we watched him take one step forward and two back.

"Oh no," Mama answered, shaking her head. "I remember when he and Bertha got married. They made such a handsome couple. She couldn't have asked for a better man. Then for some reason he started to drink and hasn't been able to stay sober."

"Does he get so drunk he really sees snakes?" brother Bobby asked, shivering.

"He tries to shake snakes off his arms and pant legs," Mama explained. "His brain has been softened by alcohol. One of these days they're going to find him dead, unless he changes. "It will take more than a miracle to dry him up."

"Big Bertha," his wife, often stopped by to visit and get warmed up before facing the cold winds that blew in from the northwest.

"What is that woman doing out in this blizzard?" Mama wondered, watching the tall, raw boned lady feeling her way into our yard. "She is as crazy as Tom. She will catch her death of foolishness."

"Can I stop for a few minutes," she gasped, when Mama opened the door. "I have to get up town to buy Tom some medicine. He's real sick. I don't think he will last through the night. Can you loan me two dollars till Saturday? I'm afraid the drug store won't charge it."

Mama would search her pocketbook for a stray dollar bill. Between the rest of the family, a few more coins were collected for the husband's needed medication.

"Why don't you call a doctor?" Mama asked. "There must be something they can do besides putting him in a straight jacket."

"The doctors won't have anything to do with him any more," she sobbed. "They said that he belongs in Yankton with the rest of the crazy people."

"Why don't you see the Salvation Army captain?" advised Mama. "I've heard great things about those people. They feed and clothe the sick and the needy and will help anyone. They helped us out when things looked black."

Bertha stopped sobbing, wiped her eyes and blew her nose. "I guess it won't hurt to try," she said with a choke in her voice. "I can't just stand by and watch Tom go to pieces. Why do they sell whiskey to poor people?"

We were all troubled by the plight of Tom's courageous wife who stood by her man despite his addiction to alcohol. She was devoted to Tom.

"Would you stay with Dad if he was always drunk like Tom?" I asked Mama. "I probably would," she answered in a somber tone. "I've stuck by him through everything else, 'til death do you part,' the marriage vows say. They also say 'through sickness and health' and I suppose that includes drinking booze."

Weeks passed and we saw nothing of Tom and Bertha.

"I don't believe my eyes. Here comes Bertha and Tom and they're all dressed up," Dad shouted to the rest of us, and we all ran to the window. "Is Tom drunk again?" someone asked. "No, I don't think so. He walks perfectly straight," Mama answered, heading for the door to let them in.

We all gazed in awe at the transformation that had taken place in Tom, once so seedy. He seemed clear-eyed and sober, with a smile from ear to ear.

He was dressed in a pin-striped double-breasted suit, white shirt and dark blue tie. His shoes were polished, he wore a snap-brim hat cocked to one side, and his hair was now trimmed. He was the picture of a man about town.

"I hope I haven't shocked you folks too much," he grinned, exposing some separated teeth, "but I've turned over a new leaf. From now on it's going to be smooth sailing for me and Bertha. With the help of the Lord, I'm going to help others who have fallen by the wayside."

"He has found himself with the help of the Salvation Army and its dedicated workers," Bertha said. "If it weren't for them, we could never have made it." "Praise the Lord," Tom chimed in, sounding like a born again Christian.

"As soon as the weather warms up, I'm going to drive a gravel truck for the WPA," Tom told Dad, "and then we're going to strike out for Washington state. They say there's a

311

lot of jobs out there in the shipyards. I used to be a pretty good carpenter, you know."

"Well, Tom," Bertha smiled at her reformed husband. "We better get going so we don't miss out on the evening service at the 'Sal'." We all watched as they walked down the hill and across the railroad tracks to join their brothers and sisters in prayer.

"Do you think Tom will stay on the wagon?" Mama asked Dad. "Something tells me that he will," my dad answered, being the optimistic soul that he was.

"What does that mean—'stay on the wagon'?" we kids asked.

"It means that a person isn't going to drink alcohol any more."

"I hope Tom stays on the wagon the rest of his life," I prayed that night as I thanked the Lord for giving me a dad that never got drunk like some of the other fathers who lived nearby.

Tom and Bertha left Mitchell, along with many other hard pressed residents who sought to escape the poverty of this dust bowl state.

I don't know how many of them struck it rich in the west, Oregon, Washington or California. We often wondered if Tom succeeded in his hope of living one day at a time and was granted the strength to overcome the weakness that caused him to be labeled the "town drunk."

Tribute to the Salvation Army

Although we children were baptized Catholics, we often went to church with neighbors of different faiths. So once in a while we found ourselves in the citadel of the Salvation Army, then located on North Main street.

The captain, who dressed similar to a soldier, wore navy blue uniforms with stand-up collars. A visored cap of navy blue, trimmed with red cord, was worn over his silver hair. He was a handsome man in the autumn of his years.

Two of his assistants were young women who looked somewhat distinctive—not just like church leaders. We kids thought they were old fashioned, out-of-style.

Dark blue dresses, in a modest design, almost reached their ankles. Black stockings and shoes made up their identical outfits, plus the oval blue bonnets that almost concealed their faces. There wasn't a trace of makeup on their almost flawless complexions.

The few times we kids joined the congregation in prayer were during their annual Christmas programs for the needy children of Mitchell. I believe the toy and a sack of nuts and candy prompted us to attend, more than to find salvation.

During the thirties the Salvation Army didn't have the respect and the appreciation of society that it does today. They were often ridiculed as "beggars."

Undaunted, they pursued their goals and tried to obtain funds from every source that they could find.

The small brass band, comprised of the Captain and his helpers, played on the street corners for anyone who would listen. It was hard times for many but coins were always obtained from a few generous citizens.

One of their band's favorite places to play was on the corner of west second and Main street in Mitchell, a few doors away from a saloon. I'm sure the good people of the Army were hoping to save a few of the drunks who sometimes listened for a few moments, then staggered on down the street.

Sometimes a yokel jokester couldn't resist trying to be

funny when the Captain asked if they were looking for salvation, would say, "No, I'm looking for Sal Jackson." This amused his uncouth friends and bystanders.

The origin of the Salvation Army was in England, from where it gradually spread into the far corners of the world.

A small contingent of officers and volunteers arrived in Mitchell in 1889. A local businessman, Gus Swanson, offered them the use of a small building until their own headquarters were constructed on Main Street. This old building still stands.

Their work was cut out for them, and not a single person was turned away if in need of food, shelter, or a place to worship. The first captain was a man named Schroeder, followed by many new replacements in the Corps. Names like Marinus Bouters, Bert Locker, Bernie Carlton, Katherine Clark and Charlotte Reynolds are recorded in the history of the Mitchell Army. They came, served, and then transferred to new towns or cities where they helped the needy and underprivileged people, wherever found.

Today the dignified uniforms have been somewhat changed from the heavy wools to a lighter dacron material. The familiar bonnets have been slightly restyled and the skirts are shorter. But unchanged are the ideals and their compassion for other human beings. The words that illustrate their faith in mankind are: "He's not heavy, he's my brother."

Earning Spending Money

The boys and girls of the Thirties were an ambitious breed. They all pitched in to help defray the expenses in a household. If a teenager had a job and earned a few dollars a week, part of it was given to the parents.

There were so many little things to enjoy, such as the movies and soft drinks, and so many tantalizing trinkets in the dime stores. So, if a child wanted the better things, he had to get out and scratch. A buffalo nickel looked mighty big during the depression years.

Since our brothers were older than my sister and I, their working days began before ours. We were living then on West Fourth Street. The boys found jobs at the Municipal Golf Course near Lake Mitchell. It was about a three-mile hike to work, so they would leave early in the morning, sometimes before the sun began to shine. This was during summer days of soaring temperatures that might climb up to 105 or 110 degrees.

They were called caddies, and carried on their youthful shoulders heavy golf bags, while they watched players hit golf balls into the wild blue yonder. Golf at that time was a wealthy man's game. The players were probably doctors, lawyers, and other businessmen, who could afford the luxury of taking a day off. It was a status symbol to be a golfer.

I believe the caddies were paid about twenty-five cents for a round, and most of the golfers gave them tips. I recall a Dr. Shields, who was most generous. He rewarded my brother, Whitey, with a new pair of glasses. He realized Whitey's eyesight was poor when he couldn't find most of the elusive balls. Mama always said, "Whitey couldn't see after four o'-clock, and was blind in the dark."

Caddying was hard work, yet it had many rewards. The boys all learned to play a good game of golf. Brother Buddy once won a Junior Championship and received an all-expense trip to Minneapolis. My, the family was so proud of him, when his name appeared in the local newspaper.

Realizing the kids were poor, these moneyed golfers helped them out in other ways. I can recall the boys counting their day's earnings and mentioning the people who were extra generous. Names like Doctors Delaney, Shields, McGreevey; or Peg Frazier, Mr. Wedehase, Leo or Tom Harmon, Louis Russell, Fred Tinan, Doctors C. S. or B. A. Bobb, Shorty Noble, Shorty Broadbent, or Judge Seacat. Lorn Arnold was the manager of the links then.

Neeney and I also put in our tour of duty at the golf course. Although we were only seven and eight years old, we often carried sacks and pails of lunch out to the links. Sometimes we took a shortcut through the cemetery. We loved to walk on the beautiful green grass and get sprinkled with water from the whirling hoses that supplied the greens. It was so tranquil and quiet on the links, with only an occasional shout of "fore" echoing across the fairway. We found the clubhouse a cool oasis, where we enjoyed our frosty bottles of strawberry pop.

The caddies paid us a penny for each golf ball we found and it was fun to search through the wild mustard weeds to find the white "dimpled pills." By the time we returned to the club house, our overall pockets were bulging. The battered balls were placed into a long wooden box with stiff brushes and cleaned. The golfers bought back their good as new balls from the bag boys.

Other caddies were all friendly to us girls. They didn't mind the intrusion of two little tomboys who wanted to make some extra pennies. Some of the other caddies, who walked the many miles around the Municipal Golf Course, were Cousin Delmar Bohr, Don and Robert Westendorf, the Kiepkes, Shearer and Kiner brothers, and others.

The Municipal Golf Course has been renamed Lakeview. What was once considered a rich man's sport is now enjoyed by many. The caddy boys have been mostly replaced by motorized golf carts, which can carry more than one golfer around the links. (I don't profess to know much about this game or its value as relaxation and competion. I only remember the pleasure I enjoyed as a child at the old golf links near the blue waters of Lake Mitchell.)

One of the other occupations open to young boys was the advertising business. During this time, movie theatres thought of a unique way to let the public know what was playing. So, the "walking ads" were invented. Movie posters were pasted on a two-sided cardboard sign, which was placed over the shoulders of a boy, who was to carry it. He was to walk up and down through the business district for a certain time. My brothers walked for the Paramount, Roxy and Lyric Theatres, carrying signs. They received passes, which were the same as money, as all kids of the Thirties idolized the stars of the silver screen.

Picking cockleburs from weedy corn fields was another way for town boys to earn extra cash. I am sure this was one of the more undesirable occupations. I recall the neighbor boys gathering at our place to await the arrival of the truck to take them to the country. One of the farmers they worked for was a Ed Wynande, a prominent land owner.

Searching for pop bottles was something every child could do in the summertime, too. It was great to uncover a coke or root beer bottle from a pile of debris or in a ditch. Mama often took us kids to the edge of town, where the side roads were a treasury of discarded bottles. Our favorite place to investigate was "Lover's Lane," a narrow winding road north of the city limits. Young couples and old (who were still young at heart) liked a little privacy in this sanctuary to "pitch a little woo." Empty milk bottles were also a prized find. Kids often swiped the glass containers from the pantry, then sold them to buy a ticket to the movies.

I'm sure the recovery of junk was one of the most profitable ways to make "pin money." All of the kids in our neighborhood were learning the difference between copper and brass, tin and iron, zinc and aluminum. A small magnet was carried in every boy's hip pocket. This instrument would reveal the difference in the metals. A hammer was all-important to pound down the junk into lumps so it was easier to separate in gunnysacks.

Searching roadside ditches, creek beds, alleys, ash piles and the dump grounds would bring forth a bountiful supply of discarded tea kettles and coffee pots, copper boilers, and gaskets, aluminum pots and pans, zinc fruit jar lids and parts of brass beds. Those articles today would be an antique collector's treasure.

They were all dug out and hauled into the back yards to be pounded down and sold to the salvage yards. A couple of pounds of junk on the scale might bring a few dimes or a quarter, depending on the metal. Copper, aluminum and brass received top priority.

There were often pots and pans snitched from the family kitchen to add a few more pounds to a kid's junk sack. This happened one time when one of my brothers went too far in his quest for "precious metals." Mama spanked him.

My earning power increased around my age of ten as I have mentioned. Little girls who sat with children weren't called "baby sitters." The words "hired girls" were used as there were extra chores to do, such as washing dishes and sweeping floors. How times have changed!

For one thin dime I sat the entire evening with a bunch of noisy youngsters, not much younger than myself. The parents more than often came home when the roosters were crowing and I had to walk home alone at dawn. The extra nickels and dimes were spent on the movies or for some colorful ribbons in the local dime stores.

At the ripe old age of eleven, I worked outside the home, caring for two small boys, Dale and Gordy Creech. I also prepared noon meals, which normally consisted of boiled wieners or fried hamburgers, a can of corn, or tomatoes and mashed potatoes. I received seventy-five cents a week and I felt mighty rich with my earnings, which I shared with the family.

Mama called me the "jack of all trades," as I was also very efficient at the task of fixing hair. The neighbor ladies discovered I liked to fuss with the finger wave and French braid, so they soon asked for me. On the week-ends I was up to my ears in wave set, bobby pins, curling irons, scissors and clippers. The women wanted to look their best for Saturday night when everybody went out on the town. Most of the celebrating was done at barn dances, chicken shacks, and beer joints.

Planting Our Garden

During the Thirties just about every family planted a garden to supplement their food supplies. For the low income families who lived partly on relief and worked for the WPA it was a luxury to buy groceries in tin cans and paper boxes.

The staples that had to be bought from the grocer's shelf were flour, sugar, lard, canned milk, coffee and spices. Bottled milk and fruit juices were outside our budget. Bologna, hamburger and liver were about the only meats that our family could afford. Dad began to plan his garden when the March winds were still blustery and snow flurries chased each other over the landscape. While some of the neighbors ordered their supplies from Gurneys at Yankton a famous seed house, Dad purchased his seeds, onion sets, tomato and cabbage plants locally.

It was fun to tag along with Father to the vegetable, fruit and seed stores, near the railroad yards.

Boxes of golden oranges and baskets of ruby red apples made our mouths water.

The proprietors often gave my sister and me a juicy winesap to munch on while we sat on an empty orange crate.

"You've got enough seeds to cover the whole side of the hill," Mr. Ledford, the seed man, laughed as we carried the bulging sacks of seeds and sprouts out the door.

"Don't forget, I've got ten mouths to feed," Dad called back over his shoulder. "This is just a start."

"I sure hope we get some rain this spring," Dad said hopefully to Mama as he gazed across the dried brown weeds and grasses that lay dormant on the hillside. "Another year of this drought will finish us all."

"We didn't do too bad last year," Mama replied. "If it doesn't rain we can still water the garden from the cistern. You better get hold of Bill Stevens and his team of horses to get the plowing done early this year. Hey, look over there. There's the first robin." She wet her finger and pressed it into her palm for good luck. The red-breasted bird paid them no mind but hopped away in search of a nesting place.

We were sitting at the breakfast table listening to the birds serenading the neighborhood, when the sounds of creaking wagon wheels broke up the concert. Quickly pulling back the curtains, we saw two brown dray horses hitched to

319

a weather beaten wagon. "Whoa," yelled a man dressed in work clothes sitting on a buckboard seat. The horses snorted to a halt, then shook their heads as if wanting to go on.

"I said whoa," he shouted, jerking on the reins and making them chomp on their bits. He reached for a leather whip but didn't use it.

"The plowman's here," brother Bobby shouted to my Dad who was mixing some paint in the basement.

The man had unhitched the plow horses from the wagon by the time Dad went outside, with four kids right on his coat tails.

"Can we watch them plow?" The strong-muscled animals were munching on some fireweeds.

"If it's all right with Mr. Stevens," said Dad, looking at his friend for an answer. "It's O.K. by me, just so they keep a safe distance from the horses," the man replied, giving a clicking sound from the side of his mouth. "Giddyap, horses," we followed the command and accompanied the plowman down the hill where the frost-free ground was soon to be churned into a vegetable incubator.

Mr. Stevens hitched the horses to a heavy-looking plow, with a sharp iron blade that gleamed like polished silver. The reins were wrapped around his neck while his hands gripped the wooden handles. He worked the plow into position and gave a shrill whistle. The horses began to pull.

We patiently sat on a knoll, watching the man and his team crossing back and forth across the field while the fluttering birds swooped down to steal an unsuspecting worm or bug from behind the plow.

"Let's take off our shoes and socks and walk in those furrows," suggested sister Neeney to my brother and me.

"Mama says it isn't warm enough yet to go barefoot, we might catch a cold," I warned her. "You know what happens when we catch cold. We have to drink that awful tasting cough medicine."

"She don't have to know," answered Neeney, slipping off her shoes and throwing them aside. "I want to see what that dirt feels like between my toes."

My brother and I usually gave in to our sister's whims so off came our footwear and we plunged into the freshly overturned earth. I sat myself down on the bank along the furrow and dug my toes into the cool soil. My feet felt free and easy and back to nature, released from confinement.

"This does feel good," laughed Bobby, kicking damp clods of dirt into the air. "Let's see who can throw a chunk the farthest with our toes." We were soon embroiled in fun and games, unmindful of our clothes and hair becoming caked with "Old Mother Earth."

"How are we going to wash off this dirt?" Bobby finally asked, looking down at his grimy overalls, rolled up to his knees. "Boy! Mama will give all of us a good licking." "Let's go over to Mrs. Creech's house and wash up by the pump," I suggested. We took turns pumping the long iron handle that forced cold water from the spout.

"You kids look like a bunch of ragamuffins. Were you playing in that plowed field?" Mama asked when we appeared at the dinner table with high water marks on our arms and legs. "I'll never get that ground-in dirt out of those clothes. I shouldn't even give you any dinner for being naughty. Get into the bedroom and change your clothes before I get the broomstick."

"I didn't think she'd know we were playing in the field, did you?" Neeney asked. She had tell-tale rings of dirt around her eyes.

"We can never fool her, so we might as well always tell the truth," I answered, stepping into a fresh pair of bloomers.

The western sky was turning pink from the dying sun when Mr. Stevens came into the yard. He had put in a long day from sunrise to sunset, and he appeared tired.

The weary horses were glistening with sweat, and foam was bubbling from their mouths. "Can I have some water for me and my horses?" he asked Dad, wiping his grimy face on the dusty sleeve of his shirt.

The pails of water were quickly drawn from the cistern and poured into an old wash tub for "Dan and Dolly" who thirstily plunged their noses into the water. The pesky flies caused their hides to quiver and their tails to switch angrily in an effort to brush them off. When their thirst was quenched they looked at us with gratitude in their soft brown eyes.

"Boy, that tasted good," said the plowman, handing the dipper back to Mama. "Well, I done pretty good today, I just about plowed up the whole hillside and bottom land. But it was so hot it just about done me in."

"How much do we owe you?" Dad asked. "Oh, about a buck and a quarter," he answered. "The two bits is for the dragging." Dad reached into his denim shirt pocket and pulled out a crumpled dollar bill, sprinkled with bits of tobacco. Searching through his overalls, he brought forth a couple of stick matches clinging to strings of lint.

"By golly, you will just have to wait till next week," Dad said in embarrassment. "Mama must have picked my pockets."

"Why don't you give me a couple dozen of eggs," Mr. Stevens then suggested, "then we'll call it fair and square."

The transaction completed, Mr. Stevens and his team of faithful horses went out of the yard and clippety-clopped down the street. The rest of us went back into the house to prepare the seed potatoes for the next day's planting. It would be Good Friday, what for some reason was thought to be the right time to insure a bountiful crop of "spuds."

It was back-breaking work, chopping and raking the large chunks of dirt into a fine-ground seed bed for our vegetables. Dad measured and dug the long rows from the top of the hill to the bottom with a hoe.

Stakes were placed to designate where the planting would begin. We kids tried to spread the seeds evenly and not get too many in one spot.

I was often forced to run for cover when I looked into the beady eyes of an even more alarmed garter snake. "They won't hurt you," Dad remarked, watching the striped little snake winding its way toward a patch of fireweeds. They're a big help for our patch. They eat the bugs and other insects." His tolerant remarks about creepy things didn't stop the shivers from running up and down my spine.

After all of the rows of seeds and hills of cucumbers and pumpkins were planted it was now the "watching hour," to catch the first glimpse of greenery that came out of the ground. It was also time to pray for rain.

Neeney and I often lay on our stomachs to search for the tiny fingers of the carrot tops breaking through the hard crusts of the ground.

Dad and Mama walked along their hillside garden awaiting the birth of the young sprouts. Sometimes it seemed like they willed them to leave their dark wombs in the earth and emerge into the dawn. They were a man and a woman with green thumbs who were instilled with the love of watching things grow. This was one time that they were at peace with each other.

By early summer the garden patch was green with long rows of tender leaves hanging with pods, sprouts or blossoms. Hiding beneath their tops were red and white radishes, golden carrots, the turnips and rutabagas, which would grace a kettle of soup.

The tomato plants and pumpkin vines bloomed in flowering glory, fortelling the coming of delicious food.

Like all home-grown plants and foliage, the garden had to be nurtured with tender loving care to keep the weeds and insects away from the budding sprouts. While Dad pushed the three-pronged cultivator through the rows, we kids searched for potato bugs and cut-worms. The insects were thrown into a tin pail filled with kerosene, where they quickly perished.

There was one worm that gave me the creeps—the tomato worm that waved its tiny head, with a fierce looking horn. Sister Neeney would grab one by the tail and watch it writhing in protest at being taken from its leafy home.

Most of the time we were worried by the unrelenting drought, and although there were a few showers early in the spring, we had to rely on our water supply stored in a cavernous cement cistern near the back porch.

The blue skies of a promising season usually turned to a dusty haze towards the early part of the summer and we desperately searched the heavens for some needed moisture.

What joy when the dusty clouds were chased away by cascades of refreshing rain that drenched the wilting garden turning it into a new shade of green.

As soon as a shower was over, everyone ran to inspect the garden, along with all of the other neighbors who planted along the hills and bottom ground near the round house pond.

"Well, it's only a sprinkle but it's better than nothing," Dad remarked as he walked through the plants, glistening with precious droplets of water. "If only they could hang on a little longer, we may have a lot of vegetables. I think we will begin the water bucket brigade to keep on the safe side. That old sun isn't going to show us any mercy this summer."

The dented cream cans, tin buckets, cooking kettles, and any vessel that would hold water, was put into use to save our garden from the inevitable drought. Wagons, carts and wheelbarrows carried the irrigation system to the fields.

Sometimes our brothers would get chided when they misused the precious water to drown out a ground squirrel.

I felt pity for the tiny animal when it finally ran out, soaked to the skin and badly frightened. I was pleased when the boys sometimes decided to let it live.

During the hot summers our cistern had to be refilled two or three times because of the water needed for the garden. Sometimes it went to waste bcause the blazing sun dehydrated the parched land faster than we could supply it with cool water.

Another enemy who joined forces with the sun were the hot south winds that swooped down like fire-breathing dragons to squeeze the last drops of moisture from the withering vegetation.

"It's only the last part of June and you'd swear it was the harvest season the way everything has burned up."

I would hear Dad say to Mama, in disgust, "There won't be much in the cellar this fall - - - why in the hell doesn't it rain?"

I felt sorry for my dad who worked "like the devil" for his pay and always hoped for a big crop to insure some extra food on the table. All he asked for from heaven was a few drops of rain.

"Please, God, make it rain," I prayed every night before I shut my eyes and fell asleep. Not often, but once in awhile, I was awakened by the pitter patter of rain drops falling lightly on the weathered shingles of the roof.

In the morning I could look through a bedroom window that was washed clean of its film of dust. The tree tops and lilac bushes waved in the early morning breeze, refreshed by the shower that fell during the night. How beautiful the earth was then, sending fragrance and renewed hope of better days to come.

I looked towards the eastern sky and said simply, "Thanks for the rain, God."

The Grasshoppers

Along with the yearly droughts that brought infestations of flying and crawling insects, by far the worst to arrive was the grasshopper. Grasshoppers swooped down like vultures to claim remaining vegetation that was partially devastated by dry weather.

We kids soon became accustomed to the ugly sticky-footed creatures in their speckled skins. Their large bugged-out eyes seemed to glare at us. "Where in the world did they come from, and why were they placed upon this earth?" we often wondered. "Were they sent from outer space to destroy our grass and crops?"

These insects were cursed by young and old alike. All of us had to constantly brush them aside or stomp on them.

"Tell them to spit tobacco juice or you will kill them," Uncle Pete told us kids. We believed his stories about the intelligence of the hoppers.

"There's a new spray being tested by the government; it's supposed to be better than lime or Paris Green," Dad said, as he read to the family from the front page of the evening paper. "I'm going to buy a couple gallons as soon as we can get it in Mitchell. We need all the help we can get." "They're getting so bad they're beginning to chew on the clothes when I hang out the wash," Mama added. "They won't stop at anything," Dad warned. "Every year they get worse."

And so the battle lines were drawn between us and our enemy, the spring-legged grasshoppers. It was a fight to the finish. I don't recall if it was the insecticide that drove the invaders away from this part of the country or there was a remission of drought. It did finally come to pass that the noted insects crawled, hopped and flew away to another place.

Canning Time

No matter whether the harvest season was bountiful or barren, we still needed a cellar full of canned fruits and vegetables to last throughout the long cold winters of the great depression.

Sometimes the vegetables had to be bought from roadside stands like those of Barney Gaetze and Dan Sullivan, two local dealers who sold from their own gardens and the shipped in produce from other states.

Early in the summer most women in the neighborhood began to search for the empty jars that were stored away in the dusty basements. There were exchanges made of the quarts, pints and crocks between Mama and Aunt Carrie.

"Can I use your twenty gallon crock this fall?" asked Mama. "Dad wants to make some sauerkraut." "All right," answered Carrie. "Are you going to need those little half pint jars? I want to make some grape preserves. I hope none of them are cracked."

Then we kids were sent into the musty cellar to retrieve all the empties. I couldn't stand the creepy spiders that spun their wispy webs across everything. "Go get the broom," I told my brother, "I'm not going into that dark corner until those spiders are chased away."

Mama inspected the jars for nicks and cracks, then placed the good ones in the sink to be washed in a hot sudsy bath. When Mama couldn't remove the residue with a rag on the end of a stick, I had to finish the job. My hand was small enough to reach the bottoms of the jars.

"You kids better get over to the garden this morning and pick the peas," Mama told us when we all sat around the table for breakfast. "Everything is ready to begin canning, and I want no piddlin' around, do you hear?"

"Bobby always throws peas at us," I tattled, looking at my mischievous brother, who was tipping the cereal bowl to his lips to drain it.

"Those girls eat all of the tiny peas from the pods," he complained.

"Now shut up and get busy," she ordered. "I want a couple buckets of peas within the next hour or there will be hell-a-poppin'."

Bobby pulled our old coaster wagon up to the back porch, the buckets were thrown in and we were off to the fields, with sister Neeney and I taking turns riding on it. Sometimes we tormented Bobby by dragging our heels on the ground.

We kids toiled like eager beavers, picking, then pulling our heavy laden wagon of vegetables up the hill. The spikes of icicle radishes were pulled even if they were pithy. The string beans and beets needed a little more time to grow into their skins.

"I hope Mama doesn't make any more of those 'icky' green tomato preserves," said Bobby, making a sour face. "I hate it when she makes me eat preserves on pancakes. I'd like to throw these green tomatoes away."

"Don't you dare," I shouted, stopping the wagon. "Mama says she's going to can everything she can get. Aunt Carrie even makes pickles from the watermelon rinds. She doesn't waste anything."

"I hate those pickles, too," Bobby continued. "I just like dill pickles, sauerkraut and tomatoes—everything sour!"

"Too much sour stuff isn't good for you," I cautioned him. "Mama says it will make your blood turn to vinegar and you will shrivel up." "Oh, baloney," Bobby laughed. "She just makes up those stories to make us mind."

Throughout the long hot summer, Mama's "canning factory" was in production, like an assembly line. The copper boilers and wash tubs bubbled and steamed atop the cookstove which was fired up like a roaring inferno. We canned many jars of tomatoes, corn, beans, peas and pickles, to be opened in the fall and winter.

My arms and shoulders would ache from the constant shucking, paring and coring that was needed to prepare the vegetables. A few times my hands were burned by a hot tomato that didn't want to shed its skin.

While sitting on the floor, with a pan of tomatoes in my lap, I often felt sorry for my mother who had to slave away steadily. I can still see her tightening the lids on the jars with sweat pouring down her face. A wipe from her stained white apron removed the perspiration. She reminded me of a mother squirrel, storing away every possible morsel of food for the winter.

Sauerkraut-making was Dad's department, along with the small cucumbers that were placed in a brine-filled crock.

We kids enjoyed shredding the green heads of cabbage, that flew in all directions. Dad placed the mounds of crisp goodness into stoneware crocks, a salt solution was poured into a mixture to make it ferment. A weighted object was then placed on top to press the cabbage into juicy kraut.

"Boy, this is going to taste mighty good this winter with a pan full of spareribs," Dad said, smacking his lips.

"I like weenies better," Bobby chimed in. "I like the juice," I added. "My mouth is watering already."

It was with satisfaction that Mama and Dad surveyed the shelves that bulged with the canned goods. In the bins covered with sand and gravel were carrots, rutabagas and turnips. Onions and spuds were placed in gunnysacks and stored in a cool place.

"I'm not going to worry when the snowflakes fly," Mama predicted. "There's enough down here to feed a threshing crew."

"That's what you said last year," Dad reminded her. "Don't you remember the cupboard was getting bare by the first of March?"

Mama was not like Old Mother Hubbard, who went to the cupboard and found nothing. We children never went to bed hungry. We may have been poor, and without the luxuries, but our parents made sure there was always food on the table. And we helped.

The Melting Pot

I'm sure people of just about every nationality could be found in the Mitchell area from the start. Some of the outlying towns gathered in cliques, and looked upon other nationalities as outsiders. My home town of Mitchell adopted all of the migrants, no matter what far-away shores they came from. The first funeral held in this city was for a black man who died in one of the saloons.

He was described as a "lamb of God," because he had wool on his head, by a well-meaning white man, reading the eulogy over his grave.

"You will never go hungry if you marry a Greek, nor want for clothing if you marry a Jew." This I often heard Mama tell the young neighbor girls in discussions of love and marriage. Every girl's dream was to marry a tall, dark and handsome man with money.

"Did you ever hear about any of those people marrying outside of their faith? I haven't," Dad corrected her. "They don't mingle with outsiders."

"Who asked you?" Mama would snap. "You're not supposed to be listening to woman talk."

"Marry an Irishman," Dad kidded the sweet sixteens, "and you will never go wrong."

"That's a laugh. All they do is run to church, let their homes go and raise hell." So Mother argued, putting down Dad's heritage.

Sometimes Father would get angry and lash back with profanity belying his usual tranquil personality. The combination of an Irish father and a hot tempered German mother resulted in disputes about the blood that ran in their veins. Sometimes Mama would joke about our heritage and say "the Irish and the Dutch, they don't amount to much."

Some of the more prosperous citizens in town were shopkeepers of Greek or Jewish origin. They were a hard-working class who were proud of their accomplishments and had a great love for their close knit families. I thought they looked wealthy and wise, and handsome, with olive skins, black eyes and pearly white teeth. A few of the business families that I recall are the Sam Saxes, Delly Beckers, Chris Bozekes, Feinsteins and Georgopoulos's.

"How come there aren't very many 'niggers' in this town?

Just Mr. Williams, the coal man, the Brooks and Cooper families, and the shoe-shine boy?" we kids would ask when we listened to the grown-ups discussing the ethnic groups in Mitchell.

"Because they don't belong here. We don't want them in this town. They are only for shining shoes and sweeping out the pool hall," spoke up Fat Leo, a local bootlegger who joined in the backyard gab fests, even though he was greatly disliked.

"They have just as much right to live here as you or I," Dad corrected him, in defense of the black people. They don't cause any trouble. What harm have they ever done to you?"

"What about that 'nigger' who shot and killed his brother-in-law in that night club last year? They all carry a knife or gun, you know."

This obnoxious, red-necked Swede continued to disparage the negro race, feeling superior with his Scandinavian heritage. We girls kept our distance from him. He liked to pinch us and tickle our ribs if he had the chance. He was married three times but his wives all got rid of him.

Unaware of the prejudices in the deep south, we kids only knew about the black people, from the image projected in the newspapers and on the movie screen, or from bits of information from our elders.

We were led to believe they were happy, fun-loving people who enjoyed being servants, and who sang and danced and loved to bury their face in huge slices of watermelon. We thought it fun to sing the comical songs of that era that made fun of black children as stupid. "Three little nigger boys, black as tar, tried to get to heaven in an electric car." Or, "Eenie, Meenie, Minie, Mo, catch a nigger by the toe; if he hollers, make him pay fifty dollars every day." "I know something I won't tell—three little niggers in a peanut shell." We also were delighted with the Tar Baby and Little Black Sambo books that lined the shelves of the library.

The few black children whom we became acquainted with in school were accepted without any prejudice from us or the ordinary folks of the town.

Another minority group were the "Russians" or Mennonites who lived in their own commune along the James River. They were criticized by many of the local people because they had a different philosophy, usually spoke a foreign language and dressed in quaint clothing.

We kids often saw the Russians unloading their produce at the grocery stores and vegetable stands. The men dressed "funny," with somber looking black suits, and hats and beards that made them all look identical. The women and girls shyly peeked at us from behind their calico bonnets, matching their ankle length dresses.

"Wouldn't you hate to be a Russian?" sister Neeney asked, watching the truck load of Mennonites driving away. "Those kids can't listen to the radio or even go to the movies."

"I'd run away if I had to live like that," Bobby commented. "I'm sure glad we can do anything we want, well almost everything."

"Maybe they are happy to live like that and think we live wrong," I suggested about the Mennonites, who came to America to escape oppression.

All through my growing-up years I listened to ethnic jokes about Swedes who were 'Norwegians with their brains knocked out'." The Irish and the Dutch who don't amount to much, the Scotchmen, too tight to pay a nickel to see 'Christ turn a hand spring,' the Germans who still pledged allegiance to the Fatherland, the Jews who profit by over-pricing.

I began to wonder what type of people did follow the golden rule. Were they all riddled with flaws, or were these misconceptions? I knew my family was far from being an ideal unit. We were just the poor.

"Rich man, poor man, begger man, thief, doctor, lawyer, merchant, chief. I would count the buttons on my dress, trying to foretell the kind of man that I would marry. (How young and foolish I was to believe fairy tales, superstitions, astrology and old wives tales.)

I made up my mind that if my future husband was destined to be poor, perhaps he would be a fun-loving handsome Irishman like my dad. (Would you believe I married a Scandinavian?)

331

Main Street

During the Thirties, there were still many business enterprises, despite the times, in every building on Main Street, from the drug stores to second-hand and harness-maker's shops on the side streets. Even though times were hard, most shopkeepers managed to keep their heads above water. Many were born and reared with a proud pioneer heritage, having parents who settled here when the town started in 1881. Others arrived from foreign shores to seek their fortune in this small melting pot. Going into the many shops, stores, and office buildings, we kids became acquainted with friendly merchants and professional people—the backbone of Mitchell.

Along with the chain and neighborhood grocery stores, there were the fruit and vegetable stands, owned by hard working home gardeners. There were wayside peddlers scattered through the town, their stalls filled to capacity with everything from mouth watering watermelons, in season, to luscious apples heaped high in crates and baskets. Some folks would obtain a better bargain with a little "Jewing down." Some of the home grown fruits and vegetables which were bought and sold, were grown in the Hutterite Colonies, along the James River. A few of those early days roadside businessmen we remember were Henry Moore, Dan Sullivan, and Barney Gaetze. Barney's Market is still in business, owned and operated by a son, Forrest.

The "warehouse district" was located west of the Milwaukee depot on Railroad Street. It was then a bustling street where coal companies, feed and seed stores and the wholesale houses obtained most of their supplies from the railroad. We kids often watched the railroad cars being unloaded alongside the huge storage buildings. The apples, oranges, and grapefruit that sometimes rolled out of the baskets and broken crates were eagerly retrieved by scrambling youngsters who loved the fresh and sometimes forbidden fruit.

How tempting the golden stalks of bananas looked as they dangled from the iron hooks, a mouth watering delight for kids who were always hungry. I recall school boys entering one warehouse and coming out with a noticeable bulge beneath their jackets. "Snitching" became commonplace. I'm sure the foreman sometimes wondered about the missing bananas.

Across the narrow dusty street from Krueger's warehouse was Bauer's Produce Company. This is where the farmers sold their eggs, cream and poultry. It was a busy and noisy market place. We kids were most interested in the squawking chickens that were transferred from the trucks to wire cages.

Sometimes the frightened birds broke away from their handlers and scurried across the railroad tracks. In hot pursuit were two or three boys, along with my brothers, trying to capture a fat hen or sometimes a fleet-footed turkey. If they were agile enough and captured the elusive prize, it meant an extra pair of drumsticks on the dinner table. It was "losers weepers, finders keepers."

After all these years the old warehouse district still stands except for the Porteous Elevator, the coal bins and the Mizel Salvage Yards. The weather-beaten buildings, adjacent to the railroad yards, were once an important part of the industrial section of town. Although I like to recall all of the good times of my childhood, I also remember the harsh, cold winters, when our legs were our only way to get from here to there. Passing through the warehouse district was a dreary trek when the winds blew coal dust into our faces, already numb from the cold. I was often crying by the time I reached the schoolhouse. My hands and feet would have to be rubbed back into circulation.

Maybe it helped me to use a grand imagination and to

Western Building, Mitchell. J. C. Penney Company on ground floor, Main Street.

333

Scene on Mitchell Main Street (picture taken in the late 1920's)

fantasize about my future. Some day I would leave the ice and snow of South Dakota, and move to a sunny spot in a warm desert. My dream never came true that way. I'm still living in the unpredictable climate of this great state of infinite variety, and probably always will.

"If they want a blue suit, turn on the blue light, and if they want a green suit, turn on the green light."

Jewish merchants who operated the clothing stores on Main Street were jokingly supposed to have this slogan. So we would see customers examining a suit of clothes or overcoat outside of the local business places. Under natural light they could detect a flaw in the color or material of the garment.

But there were many fine local clothing stores for men and boys. To name a few, there was "The Toggery" "Beckers," "Sam Saxe," and "Griggs." Good business suits, topcoats, hats and general apparel were sold there. The blue collar workers, farmers and railroad men, more often purchased their sturdy work clothing from the Louie Lifschultz. Famous brands of shirts, overalls, and jackets were sold at a reasonable price there.

The more exclusive stores that catered to the aristocratic ladies of the town were Baron Brothers, Butterfield's, Feinstein's and Geyerman's. There were other stores, whose merchandies was less expensive, such as The Hollywood, Style Shop and Jarold Shop. Their merchandise was priced closer to the budgets of the average working girl.

We kids delighted in observing the changing styles as clerks dressed and undressed the silent dummies in the display windows. Another of my ever changing childish dreams was to grow up to be as elegantly gowned as any of the gorgeous models in the fashion magazines. I think I wore out the pages of the mail order catalogues, picking out my favorite frocks, shoes and bonnets. Mama called these catalogues "wishing books."

Along with the dress shops, men's wear, and children's stores, there were the shoe repair shops in Mitchell. Three of the most familiar to me were owned by Omar Hilligos, William Brokopsky and Toy Courey. During the depression, shoe leather was carefully conserved. Boots and shoes were re-soled many times. Steel plates or "clips" were fastened to the heels and toes. The sounds of clicking and scraping footwear could be heard on the sidewalks as people walked down the street.

Early day photograph of Mitchell's Main Street

School teachers hated the shoe plates for their racket, and for marring the wooden floors in the school room. Tap dancers loved them for the extra "clickity clack" it added to their dance routines.

My memories bring back Toy Courey, a young, ambitious man, who was literally tied to his shoe repair benches and machines. He nailed and glued many half-soles and heels on to our worn shoes throughout the depression years. Mountains of boots, moccasins, shoes, and leather goods awaited him daily. Sometimes I thought of him as the little old shoemaker who repaired shoes at midnight while the town was asleep.

Many of the people that I mention in this book have died and are perhaps forgotten. I hope to preserve their memory and to pay them a tribute here.

The Staff of Life

If anyone ventured into our kitchen and observed the many loaves of homemade bread baked there twice a week, it would seem that we lived on bread alone. It seemed to me that Mama spent half of her life up to her elbows in a pan of bread dough.

It was fun to watch while she measured the flour, water, salt and yeast, then mixed them into a sticky fermenting mass. Covering the pan with a clean cloth, Mama placed in a warm spot for the dough to rise.

"Mama, the bread is blowing up and running over the pan," I would remind her when her attention was on some other household chore. She would place the ballooning dough on the table, and punch it down again for a second rising.

Sometimes she allowed me to jab a few times into the soft mixture that felt like a flabby belly.

The neighbor kids could always tell when the golden crusted bread was taken from the oven. They smelled the fresh baked aroma.

"Your bread tastes better than my mama's," was the usual compliment coming from a small band of hungry children as they ate thick slices of bread.

"If we eat the crusts, can we whistle better?" "Can I have another piece with some jelly on it?" "Jelly?" Mama gasped. "Do you think this is the Ritz?"

We kids enjoyed our bread smeared with syrup and oleo, or sometimes just melted lard when the pantry was nearly bare.

"I want 'dibs' on that slice," they would say when someone asked for an equal share.

Even the little gray sparrows gathered around the back porch to pick up crumbs. They flew away to the safety of the clotheslines when a feisty rooster appeared on the scene to grab his share of the tidbits.

"Now don't waste any of that bread," cautioned Mama. "There are starving children somewhere." I don't know how we could have helped those hungry children by not wasting our food! Sometimes Mama's philosophy was far-fetched.

I didn't realize that there were other kinds of baked goods besides Mama's stick-to-the-ribs loaves until one day I sampled a slice of bread that came from a paper wrapper. It was light and smooth in texture and the taste was delightful.

"My mama buys this bread from the bakery down on Sanborn street," a neighborhood chum said, while we enjoyed a snack from a table littered with dirty dishes and empty catsup bottles. "Since she started to work at Armour's, picking chickens, she don't have time to bake bread." I was glad that my mama remained at home and kept our house nice and clean, after I looked over the unkempt house of my chum.

"I'm going to ask Mama to buy this kind of bread," I remarked, easing another slice from the colorful package. But when I told Mama about the delicious bread that felt like it was made from air, she just laughed and said, "That boughten bread is too expensive and it takes too much of it to satisfy a person's hunger."

We would have never been treated to the "factory-staff of life" but Mama became crippled with rheumatism and could barely raise her arms. Her home bakery had to be closed down until she recovered from her winter ailment.

"Send one of the boys down to the bakery to buy some of that day old bread," she would call one from her bedroom. "There's some change in the sugar bowl." When my brothers wouldn't want to run the errand, Neeney and I offered to go instead.

"Now here's a quarter," Evie remarked, holding up the coin that had to go a long way. "You ask for Mr. Art Reierson when you get down there. He's the boss. Tell him you want this much worth of day-old bread."

Making sure we understood, our big sister helped us get bundled into our winter clothing. She placed the quarter inside of one of our mittens, then let us out into the cold whistling wind.

Neeney and I jumped and crawled over the snowdrifts as we went down the hill towards Sanborn street, three blocks away. Upon reaching this street we headed towards a large wood and concrete building. It was the bakery owned by Art and Oscar Reierson, two brothers whose products were known for their famous "Butter and Egg" and "Kreme Krust" labels. Also for the delicious ice cream that could be purchased in "13 different flavors."

Together we pushed open the squeaking wooden door and found ourselves in the warmth and fragrance of a bakery

Reierson Brothers Bakery and Grocery Store, on Main Street

building where the ceilings seemed to reach the sky. Down at the farther end we saw some men in white removing bread from slots in the wall. The loaves were lifted out on long wooden paddles and placed on tables.

One of the bakers saw us and yelled, "Hey, what do you kids want?" "We came to see Mr. Reierson," I shouted back. "We want to buy some dry bread."

He laid his paddle aside and walked through another door. In a few minutes he came out, accompanied by another man, also dressed in white. The baker pointed towards us and Mr. Reierson approached with a smile on his rather pale face. "He's bald headed," whispered my sister, noting his shiny dome under the lights. "I hope he likes us."

"Well, what have we here?" he asked, looking at the two little strangers that came in from the cold. "Is this a social call?"

"Our mama got sick and can't bake bread no more, so we're supposed to buy some day-old bread with this quarter," I explained nervously. "We can't afford to buy fresh bread."

"That's too bad about your mother," he said with sympathy. "I'll see what I can do for you. Follow me back to the bread racks." We trailed after him until we entered another room that was stacked with colorfully wrapped loaves of bread.

"Wow, look at all the bread," Neeney remarked, marveling at the sight.

"Do you girls like cupcakes?" Mr. Reierson asked, handing each of us a daintily wrapped package of miniature cakes, covered with swirls of chocolate and vanilla frosting.

"Thank you," we answered in unison, looking up into the bakery man's face. He had already become our friend.

"Now you just sit down there on that bench and eat your cakes while I find some nice loaves of bread." He left us to look for some day-old foodstuffs.

"Umm, umm, aren't these delicious," sighed my sister, savoring the devils food cake that left her teeth smudged with chocolate.

"They sure are," I smiled, picking off the icing and eating it first. Wish Mama would make little cakes like these."

When the last of the crumbs were wiped from our mouths Mr. Reierson had reappeared, laden down with loaves.

"Do you think this will be enough for a quarter?" he asked, with a twinkle in his eye. It was more than a bargain, I thought, counting the eight loaves of sliced bread. We handed him our quarter.

"I'll carry the bread out to the door for you," he said, so we followed him back through the bakery, practically stepping on his heels.

We held out our arms while he stacked the loaves almost up to our noses. He pulled up our coat collars around our necks and then opened the heavy door. The icy wind was waiting for us.

"Come back when you run out again," he laughed, watching us until we crossed the street to safety.

"He's sure a nice man, isn't he?" I remarked to my little sister, while stepping into her footprints in the deep snow.

"Yeah," she answered. Next time I'm going to ask him for one of those radio rolls that I saw on the rack—the ones covered with caramel frosting and cinnamon.

Our arms and legs were aching and the bread was squeezed slightly out of shape by the time we arrived back home.

Mama was watching for us and opened the cardboard covered stormdoor. We stomped the snow off our feet and came in.

"Look at all the day-old bread we got," Neeney shouted, tossing the loaves on the kitchen table.

"That is sure a lot for only a quarter," Mama agreed. "We should have thought of this a long time ago. Sliced and everything. It should make good toast. I'll make some right now."

Mr. Reierson's bread tasted delicious after Mama toasted a few slices in the wire toaster that lay on the hot lids of the cookstove. A cup of hot cocoa added to the mid morning snack. I felt as contented as a squirrel who had a supply of nuts stored away for the winter.

"Now you won't have to work so hard baking bread all the time," I told Mama, pouring myself another cup of cocoa.

"I'm glad of that," she answered, trying to stretch the pain from her aching arm. Maybe I can be a lady of leisure from now on." (I knew it was only a joke.)

Through all kinds of weather Neeney and I continued to hippety hop to the bakery shop to bargain for our weekly supply of bread. The employes became used to seeing us traipsing through their floury domain. They allowed us to watch the complete process of baking bread (if we stayed out of their way).

There were eight cavernous ovens that could accommodate 300 loaves each. During this period a one pound loaf sold for only a nickel, the "Pullmans," a few cents more. Bread, buns, rolls and other pastries were wrapped about midnight to insure the freshness and good taste for the morning deliveries. The Reierson brothers employed approximately twenty-five persons whose weekly wages were above average. They worked hard for forty cents an hour.

Not only were the Reierson brothers famous for their delicious baked goods, but their ice cream was popular too. Their many heavenly concoctions, made with pure sweet cream, were mixed in huge pasteurizers once a week.

The out-of-town cartons were packed in special containers to keep them frozen. A gallon of ice cream sold for seventy-five cents, wholesale, then for only eighty-five cents a gallon could be purchased at retail. Not to be out-done by a local "pop" factory, Reiersons bottled their own tangy orange drink, "Green Spot." They also operated a retail bakery and grocery business.

This thriving enterprise had its beginnings in 1912, and continued until 1946 when it was sold to Joe Langenfeld. It was later resold and became a cheese factory, which as this is written is a progressive business, owned by a Mr. Dee.

Yes, time has made a few changes here and there around my home town but I'm glad that most of the old business landmarks are still standing, including the old Reierson Bakery building. We still live only a stone's throw from the old place.

Yet whenever I pass by I don't see that giant mouse whirling around on a piece of cheese, advertising the "Mouse House." I see the old friend from my childhood, Art Reierson, standing in the open doorway, watching my sister and me carrying home our daily bread.

The Grocery Man

During my growing-up years in Mitchell, the townspeople enjoyed a one-on-one relationship with the local business people, from the much needed druggist to the friendly neighborhood grocer. There was a relaxed atmosphere and time for chit-chat. We kids became acquainted with the proprietors of the shops and stores, most of whom catered to patrons who had to charge.

One of the first grocery stores that I remember belonged to my Aunt Christine Barnes. It was on North Main Street, across from the famous Corn Palace.

It was fun to tag along with Mama or Dad when they purchased a few staples from shelves stacked with boxes, bottles and cans. While Mama watched to see that she received a full three pounds of hamburger, we youngsters pressed our noses against the candy counter.

"Hurry up, you kids, make up your mind what you want; I haven't got all day," Mama urged. She was always in a hurry to return to her never-ending housework.

It was quite a decision to make between the tempting displays of candy, peanuts and bubble gums.

"Gee, those cherry golf ball suckers look good, but the caramel all day suckers will last longer," I whispered to brother Bobby, whose brown eyes sparkled in anticipation, as he gazed at the boxes of colored jelly beans and lemon drops.

"Can I have a nickel to spend?" he asked Mama, who was growing impatient.

"I should say not," she would respond. "Only two pennies' worth." "I'll take a strand of black licorice and a bubble gum," he finally decided. "Let's get some of those candy cigarets," Neeney suggested. "We can pretend that we're smoking, just like older people." I agreed with her—a thrilling idea.

Three happy children skipped alongside Mama as we journeyed back home. The black strand of licorice made Bobby look like he was chewing tobacco.

Neeney and I enjoyed our smokes of candy cigarets, holding them between our fingers in grown-up fashion.

"Isn't this fun?" I remarked, blowing into the wind after biting off a tiny piece of licorice.

"Just stick to candy cigarets. The real ones will put you

in an early grave," Mama warned her children, although she never practiced what she preached.

The family wasn't too happy when we moved from the hub-bub of the city to the outskirts of town. These were the "Boondocks." But luck was with us. There was a small weathered building near our fence line, occupied by a grocery store. In no time at all there was a well-worn path from our house to John Crampton's Grocery.

Hanging on to Mama's apron strings we kids followed her when she went to the store to purchase supplies.

"Give me three cans of milk, two pounds of lard, a sack of flour, three cakes of yeast, five bars of soap and a couple pounds of weenies," Mama requested while Mr. Crampton wrote down the items in an account book, stopping now and then to wet the end of the stubby pencil.

"How about some nice fresh eggs? Just came in this morning," suggested the grocer.

"No thanks, We have our own chickens that keep us well supplied with both meat and eggs."

"Can I charge these groceries until the end of the month?" asked our mother. My husband works for the WPA and only gets paid once a month." My heart stood still, because a few grocers had refused to give us credit.

"You certainly can," answered the kindly grocer, who realized his customers' hardships. "And I even let little kids charge candy and pop, if they are good." We had already studied the candy counter across the room. It beckoned to our taste buds.

"Hippity hop to the candy shop to buy a piece of candy; one for you and one for me and one for Sister Sandy," sang my sister and I as we skipped through the grass on an errand for Mama.

Sometimes it was for a can of cocoa or an extra bar of soap. The request was written on a piece of paper, and sometimes permission to buy an all-day sucker or some bubble gum.

Mr. Crampton always greeted us with a smile and a heart full of patience as we debated at the confection counter. He seemed to wear the same outfit year in and year out—a well-worn pair of dark trousers with a white butcher's apron tied around his middle. His white shirt was neat as a pin while a fashionable bow tie adorned his starched collar. Gold rimmed spectacles hung down over his nose, his soft brown eyes looked out at us kindly. He seemed to us like a friendly Dutch uncle.

One sunny summer's day, while sitting on the front porch of the store, we took note of a huge red metal box being carried up the steps by two husky men. Printed on the red container was "Coca-Cola" in large white letters. We followed the mysterious box into the store. Mr. Crampton had decided to install a pop cooler and fill it with all flavors of pop, including Coca-Cola, Green River, strawberry, orange and cherry pops. Pails of crushed ice were poured over the bottles where they nestled together in an ice cold bath. From that day on in summer Mr. Crampton wore his shirt sleeves pushed up to the elbows. His arms had to be free to go into frigid water to retrieve the bottles of pop.

Mr. Crampton catered to many poor families, with a few that made a good living, employed by the State Highway Department. The machine sheds, garage and main office were located across the street from the grocery. The employes took their lunch break every afternoon at Crampton's, refreshing themselves with cold drinks, candy bars or pieces of fruit. We kids became acquainted with the sweat-stained workmen who liked to chat or tease us a bit.

Mike Flynn or Pat Kelley could always find an extra buffalo nickel or an Indian-head penny hiding in their overall pockets for our out-stretched hands.

"Now we can buy one of those big nickel candy bars!" Neeney exclaimed, holding the larger-than-life coin that we were supposed to share. A choice had to be made as to size, texture and taste of the many candy bars Mr. Crampton had on display.

The popular bars were Hershey bar, plain or nutty; the chewy Baby Ruth, the crunchy Butterfinger, the scrumptious Milky Way or Snicker, the tasty Three Musketeers, Cherry Hump, Chicken Dinner or Amos 'N Andy. Because the Power House looked large enough to satisfy two appetites, it was most often chosen.

Our confectionery heaven with its marvelous treats soon added another dimension, when we were tempted by chocolate covered ice cream bars and frozen popsicles.

"What won't they think of next?" Mama laughed when we rushed home to show her the colored ice on a stick that melted so quickly.

Our friendship with our grocery man almost came to a

bad end through no intent of our own, and thereby hangs a tale.

Late one afternoon, just before supper time, my sister and I, along with a neighbor boy, Ordell Forbes, strolled by the back porch of the grocery store. Stacked into a neat pyramid were three cases of eggs that we thought were being discarded because they were spoiled. We didn't know that a farmer had just left them.

"As long as Mr. Crampton is throwing away these rotten eggs, let's take them over behind our barn and break them," Ordell proposed. "I've always wanted to smash eggs."

"Oh, won't that be fun?" we both agreed, grabbing hold of each end of the case and lifting it to the ground.

It took a lot of huffing and puffing to carry the heavy crates of eggs about a half block down the alley. Our old red barn was soon covered with a yellowish layer of smashed eggs, the ground littered with broken shells. It was great fun while it lasted and we laughed until our sides hurt. Little did we realize that our "omelet spree" was vandalism, and there was going to be **trouble.**

That evening when the last of the supper dishes were being cleared from the table, an urgent pounding was heard at the front **door.**

"Oh, hello, John," Mama greeted Mr. Crampton. He looked flustered and was shaking, standing in the open doorway. "What brings you here this hour of the night?"

"This is not a social call, Mrs. Barnes," he replied, with a strained voice. "Do you know what your two daughters done this afternoon? They and that little Ordell Forbes stole three cases of my eggs and broke every single one of them."

"Oh no!" I gasped, as I looked at my sister who was already hunting for a place to hide behind the cookstove.

"You two kids get in here right now," Mama stormed. "I never thought you would do such a thing. Shame on the both of you."

We slowly approached our accuser, quaking with fright. "We thought the eggs were rotten, because they were on the back porch," I tried to explain. "We didn't mean to break good eggs."

"Ordell said they were no good," sister Neeney chimed in. "It was his idea."

347

When Mr. Crampton saw how terrified we were, and on the verge of tears, he calmed down and said, "Well, I guess it's partly my fault. I should have brought them inside right away - - - I believe your story but that Ordell is old enough to know better. If he was my kid, I'd skin him alive."

Mama was upset about the incident and determined to teach us a lesson. And so two little girls went to bed that night crying in pain from a licking at the hands of their unforgiving mother. When the sobbing subsided and we lay in the darkness, anger and resentment towards Mama began to engulf us. "She never listens to our side of the story," Neeney whispered hoarsely. "Every time we do something we have to get a licking. "I know it," I answered, trying to muffle my voice. "I don't think she loves us any more." I pulled the blanket over my head, turned my still burning buttocks towards the wall and tried to go to sleep.

It was a long time before I could look Mr. Crampton in the eye and not feel guilty. But time heals all wounds (and spanked bottoms) and soon we were close friends again.

John Crampton moved his thriving business on the fringes of West Fourth Street to the north end of Main Street. As the years passed by, we lost touch with our old friend. We moved into new neighborhoods, but there was always a corner grocery store to welcome newcomers.

Many of the family-operated stores had their living quarters in the rear or in the basement of their building. They were often interrupted during meal time or even later by a customer who needed some emergency supplies. Babies could run out of milk during the night.

A few of the grocers didn't want to take a chance keeping too much produce and perishables so had in stock only the necessities. Milk, eggs, butter and meats were stored in wooden ice-box type coolers. The choice of available meats was mostly hamburger, wieners, minced ham, bacon or cold meats. If there was steak or pork chops, we didn't know it and could not afford it anyway.

I was always afraid Mrs. Curtiss, a store owner, would sever a finger as I watched her slice the chunk of bologna with a razor sharp knife. She would carefully wrap our "25 cents worth" into a neat package and tie it with string. Sometimes she threw in the butt of the meat end for a good measure on the old brass scale.

It was a treat to buy a bottle of homogenized milk which was too expensive to have delivered regularly.

"Where's that empty milk bottle that was in the cupboard?" our mother would often be asked. Milk bottles were sold or traded back to the stores by us kids, who sneaked them out of the house. The milk and pop bottle exchanges often left us with enough money for a Saturday afternoon movie.

Dad tried to pay the grocery bill every month but more than often the balance overlapped into the next month. I didn't like it when Mrs. Curtiss asked us kids, "When are you folks going to get this bill paid?"

"Mama said next week," I fibbed, wanting to add some penny candy to our charge account, before she cut off our credit.

"That grocery store is robbing us anyway," Mama fumed when we brought the stack of charge slips home. "They are either padding the bill, or you kids are charging without my permission - - -

And another thing, when we pay the bill they never give you kids a sack of candy, like Mr. Crampton used to do. They must be out for the almighty dollar these days."

Mama finally decided that charging groceries wasn't in our best interest so decided to try the cash and carry stores on Main Street. One of the first chain stores was the "Red Owl." The wise old bird with one eye closed was their emblem.

I followed Mama through the portals of the Red Owl

Red Owl Store in Mitchell in 1929 (candy bars, three for ten cents!)

store first at about the age of ten, and I must say it was an exciting sight. After buying at the corner grocery, we thought this ultra modern shopping center was too good to be true. "Now remember, I have only five dollars to spend, so don't go picking out any "Snackadi," Mama whispered to me aside.

After carefully choosing a few cans of vegetables, a box of detergent and a pail of lard, she edged her way to the meat counter, stacked with meats that I had never seen before.

"Did you ever see so much meat in your life?" I asked Mama, looking fondly at a ring of liver sausage.

"What can I do for you, madam?" a clerk greeted us. He was standing behind the gleaming white glass meat enclosure, dressed in immaculate white clothing. A black bow tie looked too tight around his bulging neck.

"I haven't decided yet," she answered, trying to act as though she could afford to buy the most expensive cut.

"These lamb chops look great, don't they?" he suggested, tilting the tray for her to get a better look. "These two-inch steaks are ready for the grill." As I stood there I had no idea what he was talking about. Our meat was either fried in an iron skillet or boiled in a kettle of water on the hot lid of our coal-burning stove.

"Well, I think I'll just take two pounds of hamburger and two rings of bologna today," Mama finally told the butcher. He gouged out a pile of hamburger and slapped it on a piece of waxed paper. He eyed the sweeping dial on the scale, wrapped the package and sealed it with a piece of gummed tape.

"There you are, madam," he half smiled, handing over the packages of meat that were more often purchased by folks who had to save money.

"I can't chew steak anyway, with these false teeth," Mama laughed as we prepared to have our few groceries checked out.

Standing next to a chrome-plated cash register was a sophisticated young lady dressed in a red and white uniform that held in her well endowed figure.

It didn't take her long to add up our bill and hand back a few coins in change. Pointing to a display of cigarets, Mama asked the clerk the cost of one pack. "Fifteen cents," she was told. Mama handed the change back to the clerk and took the cellophane-wrapped package of "tailor mades."

Eslie Meyer and son, Claude, in their home-owned neighborhood grocery store.

"Do those really smoke better than the ones that you make with Bull Durham tobacco?" I asked, trudging alongside my mother on our way back home. I hated cigaret smoke.

"They sure do," she answered, taking another puff on the weed. "Just like that ad says, they give me a lift. But don't you kids ever get started on these things."

After inhaling a few more drags, she threw the cigaret to the ground, hoisted the sack of groceries into a more comfortable position, and we proceeded up the hill.

Mama's "roll your own" cigarets were soon replaced by the better tasting, milder, finer tobaccos in "tailor mades."

Camels, Lucky Strikes, Old Golds, Philip Morris and Chesterfields were brands smoked at our house. Mama found that she couldn't live without them. She smoked till the day she died. I believe that they helped my parents to an early grave.

It remained difficult for our folks to save enough money to buy groceries with cash. So we went back to the independent merchants.

By charging groceries to those needing credit, the small grocers managed to keep their heads above water. Yet it began to be a losing battle to compete with the fast service super markets that began to spring up.

351

Those of us in the summer of our years recall the neighborhood grocery stores wistfully. I'm sure we can all remember where our particular stores were located and recall the names of the people who owned them and worked there.

All I have to do is drive through the streets of my home town now and I can remember the stores.

There is a lumber yard on the spot we patronized where John Crampton's once stood. Hanneman's has been converted into a TV appliance shop. Young's grocery has been remodeled into a cozy bungalow where the family still lives.

Ptak's family grocery store is now a boutique. A ceramic shop stands on the corner of South Sanborn where Hurry's catered to the public. I could continue with names like Spratford, Rubin, Worthing, Oliver Hegland, Sam Lesser, Goldammer, Jensen, Raskin, Applegate, Curtiss, Kelley, Cummings, Wider, Stucke, Meyer, Storm, Gormley, Clustka, Cremer, Bauer, Donavan, Welner, Haskett and the Barnes.

A handful of family grocery stores still remain in the older neighborhoods where once customers beat a path to their doors. If you look close enough there are still visible signs of a once busy store. Fading along with the dying buildings are the names of the families who were the proud proprietors. A sagging door, held together by rusty hinges, once knew every kid and grown-up on the block. An old thermometer that told us kids the temperature hangs bent and broken. It once advertised the popular soft drink of that era, Coca-Cola. The wide windows are stained with age. Remnants of a striped awning still cling to a creaking iron canopy. Be careful, don't stumble on the broken sidewalk that is crumbling like the people who once walked over it in their youth.

Stop a minute and gaze into the windows. If you have a good memory and imagination you will see again the long forgotten grocers that you knew in your childhood, when we all were a part of the hard times. Time slips away.

Down Town

Although times were hard and money was scarce, there were many restaurants in Mitchell doing a flourishing business. They seemed to be everywhere, from the sidestreets to the main drag. Some were just counter diners, while others boasted of being the elite in dining service.

Dad and Mama always walked on by. They had no need for the homecooked meals nor could they afford to buy a thick, juicy steak. While tagging along, trying to keep up with them, I used to peek into the cafe windows and observe the customers sitting at small tables with luncheon cloths in colorful patterns. "You need good table manners while dining out, and you have to know how to use the right fork," Mama told us, just in case the opportunity should ever arise.

There was one special "burger joint" where Dad stopped on occasion to enjoy a hamburger, topped with slivers of raw onion and a fat slice of dill pickle. Patrons perched on stools and sat in wooden booths drinking beer from glass mugs. In a corner stood a popcorn machine filled with fluffy white corn. A handsome man with dark hair and a pencil-thin mustache scooped up popcorn, filling a box, then poured butter over it. While I sat by Dad, munching on the warm, salted popcorn, he sipped a glass of cold beer, while swapping jokes and gossip with the other patrons.

I loved to stop at this place, where people seemed to enjoy themselves, talking to the man who was frying the hamburgers. Dad called him "Chris" and I soon learned his last name was "Bozekes." Chris's Inn, located next to the Elks Lodge, was almost a landmark on the streets of Mitchell. Chris's mouth-watering hamburgers were sold by the hundreds for only five-cents during the depression era. He was one of the Greeks who migrated to America with the ability to succeed in business.

The Barnes Cafe, owned by my Aunt Christine and Cousin Leland, was friendly competition to the Hamburger King, Chris. Their specialty was a secret recipe for the newly created barbecued hamburgers. The meat was cooked at low heat in a huge electric container. The taste was out of this world. Kids and grown-ups alike plunked down their nickels for this kind of steamy burger covered with onion slices and dill pickles. Another nickel went for a tangy bottle of orange pop, and their lunch was complete.

The Barnes Cafe was located across the street from the Corn Palace. Aunt Christine, an attractive red-haired woman, who spoke with a Swedish accent, was known for her home-cooked meals at reasonable prices. Many of the employes from the Omaha Railroad line ate at this small cafe. It was always cool inside during the sweltering summers. Cousin Leland installed his own air conditioning system. His was also one of the first restaurants to advertise these with the sensational new neon lights.

School kids liked this place as a hangout more so after the first juke box was installed. I recall the rapture on the young people's faces as they watched the swirling colors of light cascading from the music box. They put nickels in the slots and the latest tunes burst forth in fantastic rhythms. I recall songs like "Oh, Johnny, Oh" and "You'd Be Surprised" by a new girl singer named Wee Bonnie Baker who sang with Orin Tucker's band.

Some of the Greek families of Mitchell owned and operated downtown cafes. Their children worked alongside the hard-working parents to provide the public with everything edible from "soup to nuts."

The hot dog was made famous in Mitchell by the Frisco Cafe, on North Main. A steaming wiener placed between a fresh bun, with an added spoonful of a secret sauce, a creation of George Georgopoulos. During Corn Palace week, thousands of hot dogs were sold for only five cents each.

Dad Corker and wife in their cafe and confectionery shop, circa 1929

The Oriental Chocolate Shop, Virginia Cafe, and The Legion were three more restaurants with Greek owners.

Hoon's Cafe, owned by Nellie Hoon, specialized in home-cooked meals within reach of the working man's pocketbook. Farmers and townspeople alike voiced their approval of Hoon's "rib sticking" dinners, as they walked out patting their stomachs.

The Little Tavern was located on South Main, near the Milwaukee Depot. A rotund, jovial man, Louis Russell, served steaks, lunches and snacks, and if requested, a schooner of foaming beer. His son, Louis, Jr., later operated the famous Louie's Steak House, on the corner of East Havens and Highway 37.

For the more elegant diners, the Navin and Widmann hotels offered spacious dining quarters, with linen table cloths, sparkling silverware and a tea rose for a centerpiece. Many traveling salesmen found this service to their taste.

"We're going to dine out tonight," was never heard around our house. It took a lot of money for a family to eat at a fancy restaurant. The hamburger stands were more suitable for our pocketbook.

Ella and Margaret Conlon were the earlier proprietors of The Navin Cafe, later another well liked dining establishment, The Lawler Cafe. Politicians, businessmen, civic organizations and clubs found the spacious banquet room of the Lawler suitable for their meetings and conventions.

I'm sure the "coffee break" was popular during the Thirties. Everyone downtown found their favorite spot to relax and have a cup of "java." The luncheonettes, coffee bars, hamburger joints, breakfast nooks—were mostly on Main Street. There were no "drive ins" then, where folks could come by car in rough dress. Curb service was not yet offered. I recall only one "drive in" during the Thirties—the Dew Drop Inn—dismantled a few years ago. It was a forerunner of the modern fast-food cafes that now dot town and countryside. Other small cafes were Welch's, Bender's, Tiffany, Corker's, Crippen's, Checkerboard, and The College Inn. Many others came and went over the years. New buildings or stores now stand where once the names of early days proprietors were printed on the windows, and colorful awnings adorned the front of their restaurants.

Main Street seems to be dying a slow death. The modern malls on the outskirts of the city are taking away its business. An epitaph may be written, in memoriam to what we once called "downtown."

A Tribute to the Mail Carriers

"The mailman is coming." I heard this announced often when I was young. My first remembrance of postmen in Mitchell dates from around 1928, when we still lived on North Edmunds Street.

Our mailman was Martin Donavan, a slim, long-legged, friendly man with a wide-mouthed grin. We used to race down to the corner of Seventh and Edmunds, and wait for our mail. He soon ambled into view, wearing the blue-gray uniform of his occupation. We used to have an argument about who was supposed to carry the letters home to Mama. Mr. Donavan was diplomatic and solved the problem by allowing us to take turns.

As I remember, we didn't receive a great deal of mail or packages—a letter or post card now and then from Dad's relatives in Cresco, Iowa, or from Mama's kinfolk who lived in Wabasha, Minnesota. The joyful New Years and Christmas cards, which arrived during the holidays, were opened eagerly and placed where all could see. Once a month, Mama received her home town paper, The Wabasha Herald. While we kids hovered around the kitchen table, Mama scanned the paper for the latest tidbits of news. I often wondered why she wiped the tears from her eyes as she re-folded the paper and placed it on top of the cupboard. She never wanted anyone to see her wax sentimental.

Our favorite postman didn't come to our house any more after we moved to the west side of town. Our home was then out of this carrier's district, so Dad had to pick up our mail at the post office. I noticed "General Delivery" on all of our letters from that time on.

Later we moved back into the city limits, but there were no sidewalks, so no home delivery. And so began our treks to the grand old post office, which was then located on the corner of Fourth and Lawler Streets. There were a few different locations for the post office, until the Federal building was constructed in 1909. The first floor not only served as a post office, but was also a wonderful place to rest and get warm during the cold weather. During the sweltering summers, the cavernous structure retained a cool temperature inside.

The long windows had comfortable sills to sit on while waiting for the mail to be sorted, and placed in the patrons' boxes. A woman clerk, wearing a leather apron and a visored cap, distributed the enormous stacks of mail. A wrought iron

Federal Building, built in 1909 (once the Post Office, later School Administration building)

cage protected the window where she peeked out at us kids with a smile. Her name was Emma Splitt. Sometimes I think she was as disappointed as we were if a certain letter we wanted failed to arrive on time. That all-important piece of mail was an envelope, tan in color with a green check visible through an opening. It was our "meal ticket" from the government, a WPA check for $48 that arrived once a month.

I often wished we could have afforded one of the many lock boxes which lined the walls from top to bottom. We kids curiously observed the business and professional people reaching in and taking out loads of mail and packages that were important to their business.

At the far side of the lobby were parcel post and money order departments—bee hives of activity. Lewis Erickson, Glen Smith, Guy Foreman, and James Potter were a few of the dedicated employes we remember, working for the civil service. During the Christmas rush, extra people were hired to meet the demands of extra work. Boxes, bags, and parcels, large and small, were weighed and tagged for delivery to destinations all over the world.

During the Thirties, all mail and parcel post arrived by train. Trucks picked up the mail from the depot in large canvas bags. It was sorted by postal workers and mail carriers who often labored far into the night.

Mailmen had to be a special breed and had to be physically fit to stand up under many miles of walking. The bulky leather shoulder bags weighed approximately thirty-five pounds when full. At one time, there were three deliveries a day. The blue-gray military-like uniforms were bought and paid for by the postman. If a young man applied for this position, the age limit was from eighteen to thirty-five years of age and the applicant had to be "as healthy as a bear."

We youngsters became acquainted with two others in the post office during the depression years. A rotound, friendly man with carrot top hair always waved a cheery "hello" as he moved through the marble tiled annex and stairway. Everyone called him "Tom." He was Tom Callan. After retirement, the position was given to Tony Rozum. The gold letters on their office door spelled out "Post Master."

I have watched many postmen over the years who carried mail through hail and high water for the citizens of Mitchell. Lest we forget these dedicated men, here are some: Art Dortland, Joseph Hanna, Frank Worthing, Frank Coughlin, Leopold Vernig, Patrick Brennan, O. F. Kieser, James Traupel, Harold Eberhard, George Earls, Martin Donavan, and Lewis Murphy (who holds the record of serving forty-seven years on his route). It makes me wonder how many shoe soles were worn through, and how long his feet hurt.

A Tribute to the Barbers

"Shave and a haircut, six bits," wasn't just a few words to finish a song during the Thirties. Haircuts were only fifty cents. Shaves were an extra twenty-five cents for those who could afford it. If other families cut their hair at home as we did, the barbers really would have ended up in the "poor house."

The home hair styles were sometimes a sight for sore eyes. Some of the boys at school resembled convicts with their shaved heads. Others had a lopsided cut, which made their "cowlick" or "rooster tail" stand upright.

My brothers tried to manage their unruly locks with a few drops of greasy hair oil, which cost only ten cents a bottle. But they had the plastered down look. If a boy forgot to wash his head, the dirty oil mixture would work down onto their shirt collar, giving them a grubby appearance. Some of the young men adopted the "pompadour" which was very popular. If a boy was cursed with "flop" ears, they took something away from his charm. The majority of the men and boys conformed to the style of the short or cropped hair. Sideburns were seen only in the movies or on some "drug store cowboy" about

City Barber Shop, circa 1916, on North Main Street.

town. There were very few mustaches and not much long hair except on the musicians with the dance bands. A few sports "Romeos," or traveling salesmen, wore the small, pencil-thin mustache or "cookie duster," supposed to give them sex appeal.

Hair grooming aids were few, compared with today. Wild-root, Fitches, Kreml and other cheap greasy "kid stuff" brands of oils, and different tonics sat on the shelves in the barber shop. They not only promised a well groomed look, but were supposed to prevent dandruff, falling hair, and itchy scalp. (I often wondered why most of the barbers were bald.)

Some men were able to enjoy the luxury of a shampoo and shave along with their hair trim. Youngsters liked to peek through the window at Riggert's Barber Shop and watch a customer "getting the works." The customers looked comical to the kids, lying back in the barber chairs with their noses sticking out from a steaming hot towel. We thought men were courageous to allow the gleaming sharp razor to shave their throats. (It was no place for the shakes.) I'm sure the gossip of the community was repeated many times in these establishments. Oh, to be a woman in a corner and listen to the behind-closed-doors secrets of men.

A citizen didn't have to look far for a barber shop. During the late Thirties, there were forty-two tonsorial houses in Mitchell. They were located in hotel lobbies, beauty parlors, side streets, and in homes. The familiar red, white and blue barber poles were, for the most part, on Main Street. To-day those wooden posts with the swirling stripes are highly prized by antique collectors.

Riggert's Barber Shop is the place where I watched my dad getting his hair cut. At that time there were four chairs, and during Corn Palace week, five. The farmers and blue collar workers usually reserved their barber dates for Saturday night. It was a familiar sight to see four or five barbers working at the same time, while the men and boys sat on long benches waiting their turn. The teenagers wanted to look "spiffy" for a big night on the town or at a country barn dance.

Riggert's Barber Shop was owned and operated by George and Herman Riggert. Many barbers worked for the brothers over the years and some of them were Al Church, Bob Thread-gold, Chris Knutson and Cliff Saukerson. Harley Kirby was an owner of his long established barbering business, which had its beginnings in 1887. Mr. Kirby had the distinguished record of being a barber for over fifty years in South Dakota.

Many of the young "hair cutters" at the time went into the barbering business on their own after serving an apprenticeship under a master barber. Some other barbers were Bill Rush, Niblick, Nobis, Ted Ebel, Woodman, Bill Goetch, Grover Wagner, Fred Harper, Jack Hillary and Jack Carr.

The barber trade has changed drastically from the Thirties until the year this was written. There is a new kind of barber or hair stylist, as they like to be called. The long, straight razor has almost faded away into oblivion and has been replaced by the "electric shave," mostly at home. The familiar highway signs advertising Burma Shave were dismantled many years ago. Longer hair, sideburns, and mustaches are "in" today. Men are not too inhibited to visit a beauty salon to have facials, manicures, permanents and other hair styling.

Only a handful of the old time barbers and their shops are still in business. When I pass by I often wonder if there is a red, white and blue barber pole in heaven, where the pioneer "hair cutters" of Mitchell have finally retired. The "Shave and a hair cut, six bits" is gone forever.

The Barnyard

"This little piggy went to market, this little piggy stayed home; this little piggy ate all the meat, this little piggy had none; this little piggy said 'wee, wee, wee,' all the way home."

Dad used to repeat this little story while he wiggled our toes, before he tucked my sister and me into bed.

We enjoyed the songs and stories about "My Little Rooster" and "Old McDonald's Farm," where all of the livestock sang and danced in the barnyard. He often wiped away a tear when he talked about his own boyhood, where he grew up on a farm in Iowa. He herded cows along the Turkey River and rode his pony across the green meadows. Dad was always a sentimental country boy.

As he could no longer live on a farm, he changed our back yard into a menagerie of sorts. Besides his mixture of Rhode Island Reds, Plymouth Rocks and Leghorn chickens, he accepted the runts from a sow's litter, and now and then a nanny goat.

Mama wasn't as impressed by the orphaned animals and often had to "put her foot down." One day Dad brought home a baby goat. "What did you bring home now?" asked Mama as we all gathered around the truck where Dad and farmer Bob Moir were seated.

"It's the cutest thing I ever saw. Just wait till you see it," Dad grinned while unhitching the tail-gate on the pick-up.

"I don't have to see it. I can hear and smell it," said Mother, petulantly. "It's either a sheep or a goat. We kids could hear a muffled "ba-a-a" coming from a large cardboard box.

Dad set the box on the ground and pulled out a black and white baby goat, holding it in his arms. It was shaking from the fright and the cold. "Well, what do you kids think of this little fella? Shall we keep him?" Who could resist the lovable animal, in need of a home and affection. Mama just looked on in disapproval while we kids petted and coddled the little stranger.

After a few tears, Mama relented and allowed Dad to bring the "kid" into the house where he was placed on the open oven door to warm up.

We all took turns feeding Billy from a bottle with a nipple borrowed from our baby brother. Our visitor pranced around the kitchen, much to our delight and to Mama's dismay.

"I'll build a wooden stall for him in the chicken coop," Dad said. "He can run around the yard with the chickens. You kids can lead him around on a rope if you want to take him for a walk."

"Little Billy" was great fun while he was a kid but goats do grow up and we soon realized that he was getting too belligerent. He didn't like being pulled around by a leash so he humped up and braced himself, and wouldn't budge. The nubbins on top of his head sprouted into sharp pointed horns with which he "butted" everything in sight. It wasn't safe to go to the privy for fear of being chased back to the house.

"You kids keep that goat off the porch," Mama stormed, sweeping away Billy's droppings. "The straw that broke the camel's back" came the day when Billy chewed up Mama's nightgown that was hanging on the clothesline.

"That does it," Mama stormed. "That goat is going back to the farm." In a way, we kids had to agree with her. We couldn't change the stubborn animal, no matter how hard we tried.

Farmer Moir came back to re-claim the kid who had grown into an old man with a scraggy beard on his chin. It was with mixed emotions we felt when Billy walked up the ramp and into the old truck. He peeked out at us kids through the slats, gave a short bleat, then proceeded to dine on a pile of alfalfa. He was just too anti-social to settle down in town. The wide open spaces would be the best place, where there were no barricades to fence him in.

"So long, Billy," we shouted. "It's been good to know you." The truck took him away and we never saw him again. We never learned if our friend Billy lived to a ripe old age or if he became "goatburger."

During those hard times in the Thirties, no four-legged animal or feathered fowl was safe from a few who were too lazy to work but dishonest enough to steal.

Some roamed the country side, stealing chickens and rustling cattle. Steers were slaughtered and the meat sold right from the trucks in this area. Many farmers kept watch over their herds at night and more than once a thief received some buckshot in his rear end.

"I see where they arrested three Mitchell men for cattle rustling, and two from Ethan for stealing chickens," Dad read from the paper. "I'd better padlock the chicken coop tonight.

I have enough trouble with rats, let alone some two-legged ones. I wish we could buy a side of beef or pork. I get tired of eating chicken all the time. Why don't I take those runty pigs that Bob Moir doesn't want?"

"Don't tell me anything about hogs," Mama interrupted. "We had enough of that billy goat, remember! The subject was dropped and nothing more was heard about turning our back yard into a pig sty—until a few weeks later when the idea again was proposed.

"Who's doing all that pounding in the back yard? Is Buddy working on his tree house at this hour of the morning?" Mama asked me, while I watched her kneading dough in a large mixing bowl.

I looked out the back door and could see my dad stretching a roll of woven wire between some trees, next to the alley.

"Looks like Dad is building a fence," I reported to Mama. "Maybe he's putting up a pig pen. Well, I'll put a stop to that right now," Mama said. She tipped over a chair in her fast exit out the back door.

I followed my mother through the knee-high fireweeds, with blood in her eye. Dad saw her coming and was prepared for a piece of her mind. He made sure the wire fence stood between them.

"Now, Ma, you can holler all you want but I'm going to get a few baby pigs from Bob Moir. I can get them cheap because they are 'runty.' By fall we will have plenty of bacon and pork chops to sell, and plenty left over for us."

"What about the pig smell? There's enough flies around here now. Besides, the neighbors aren't going to like this."

"I already talked to them and they said it was all right as long as the pigs don't break out and run into their yards and gardens." I watched and listened to my parents argue about raising "meat on the hoof."

"Well, have it your way, but I warn you, if those hogs break loose, there will be hell to pay. That dinky fence couldn't hold a rabbit."

Dad finished tacking up the barricade while Mama walked back to her kitchen, with a doubtful look.

The piglets were unloaded the next day amid clouds of dust and squeals of protest. We kids thought they were cute even though their reddish bodies were scrawny, and their tails had no curl. They scurried into the high weeds in search of food and a muddy place to wallow.

It kept Dad busy watching over his pig farm and making sure they couldn't root beneath the fence and escape. Their slop consisted of buttermilk mixed with feed and a little corn that Farmer Moir brought to town.

"You kids keep an eye out for these baby porkers," Dad instructed us. "Keep them away from the fence line. It was asking the impossible because the pigs paid us no mind. After being slapped with a switch or a broom stick, they soon went right back to making tunnels.

After many weeks of "pig patrol," one day we kids deserted our post to join the neighbors in fun and games. A blood-curdling shout brought us to attention when we saw Mama running towards us. "Hurry up and get home, the hogs are loose." She managed to chase one into Mrs. Hogan's out-house, which was already occupied by her husband.

The neighbor kids joined us in our pursuit of the marauding pigs, who were by now rooting up flower beds and gardens. Anyone knows that it is almost impossible to make a pig mind, and they were as slippery and tricky as a football player.

It took the whole afternoon to corral the wandering animals who were as exhausted as we were. The whole neighborhood was in an uproar about damage that was inflicted on their property. Who was going to pay for the pig escape?

"Just wait till that man gets home," stormed Mama, trying to repair the broken fence. "I'm really going to tell him 'what for' this time."

Poor Dad, I worried, was only trying to help out with a little extra meat in the pot this fall. I hoped Mama would be cooled down by the time he came home. I hated to hear her blame my father.

As the sun was setting, I saw Dad as he walked up the hill with a pail of buttermilk in each hand. I ran to tell him what happened. "Oh, no," he moaned. "Well, that's the end of the pig business, for sure."

And it was. Dad reluctantly allowed Farmer Moir to haul his swine to the packing plant where they brought only a few dollars. When he handed the money to Mama he smiled faintly and said, "Just about enough to buy a slab of salt pork."

The hillside was back to normal in a few weeks and the neighbors didn't hold it against Dad for the escape of the pigs.

The folks realized that they couldn't squeeze blood out of a turnip, anyway, so they didn't ask for any damages.

"Just stick to raising chickens," Mama advised Dad. He had given up hopes of becoming a city farmer. "Chickens are a double-barreled investment. We get eggs and meat and it doesn't cost that much for feed."

"And they're fun to play with," brother Bobby agreed.

There was no need of an alarm clock in those days because the early rising roosters would begin to crow before daylight. The old hens would leave their roosts, looking for tidbits that were thrown over the fence. We kids were amused when the amorous roosters chased and conquered the hens in a never ending love-making ritual. Little did we realize that the lady chickens didn't mind the rough treatment.

My sister and I would often race to the coop when the sounds of excitable cackling pierced the air. Another egg had been laid. It was a joyful feeling to reach into the straw-filled nest and bring forth a freshly laid egg. Sometimes we were chased by a ruffled hen who wanted to squat forever on an empty nest. Although some of our baby chicks were hatched beneath the warm bodies of their mother, most of the chicks were purchased from the Boote Hatchery in Mitchell.

Early in the spring when the frost was still in the ground, Dad brought home baby chicks in cardboard boxes. They peeked out at us through the holes that provided them with air. Dad emptied the tiny balls of fluff onto the paper-lined stall in the basement. A few heat lamps and jugs of water were placed in the center to ward off the chill. The loud chirping soon became quiet little peeps as they snuggled together and closed their eyes in sleep.

"Now just leave them alone for a while," cautioned Dad to Bobby, who wanted to cuddle a black one. "Too much handling is bad for them. Wait about a week and then you can gently stroke their heads. For now you can just look, but don't touch."

Watching the chicks grow was our favorite pastime. In a few weeks they were pecking and scratching, and feasting on cornmeal mash. But alas, soon there were complications and the weak ones died, one by one, kicking and gasping. We so wanted them to survive, not realizing that by summer they would be put in a pot, anyway.

The adopted chicks were fun to take care of but they weren't as lovable as the chicks that were hatched by their natural mothers. Mama always allowed a few of the setting hens to raise families.

Often a maverick hen hid her nest of eggs until hatched and surprised all of us when she clucked into the yard, followed by her cheeping offspring, darting in and out.

"Isn't that the prettiest sight you ever saw?" Dad smiled warmly when the mother hen squatted down to provide a safe shelter for her chicks. "She will fight to the death if anyone tries to harm those chicks."

We kids learned to keep our distance and not to disturb them, for fear of getting our eyes pecked.

There were a few years when Dad lost money in the chicken business. There was no way to foresee the destructive forces that could wipe out a flock of birds. Predators, including rats and weasels, arrived in the middle of the night and left only the feathers lying on a blood-stained floor. Cats and dogs could also maim and kill chickens.

Another danger was the wind and the hail that struck without warning, drowning the unprotected chicks. Many times we kids were sent out to search for the strays that didn't make it to the coop in time.

I felt sorry for the ones that were found huddled beneath some weeds or a pile of boards. The wet shivering chicks were carried into the house where they were dried off behind the cookstove. Within a short time they would be back on their feet and giving a weak chirp of thanks for being rescued. The kitchen smelled "chickeny" for a few days.

My brothers, sisters and I tried to keep the mother hens and their chicks under strict surveillance. We watched as they picked, scratched and searched their way along the footpaths and weed patches that criss-crossed the hillside. Every evening we "counted noses" to see if all were safe and sound.

One evening our favorite speckled mother hen and her brood of nine children were missing. We tearfully reported our loss to Dad who was watching the sunset. It was his favorite time of the day.

"Don't worry," he soothed, sitting down beside us on the back porch. "She will find her way back home." He went on to explain that chickens had an instinct that helped them to return home, no matter how far they roamed. "They will show up pretty soon."

Just as the red glow of the sunset was fading into twilight

we heard a faint cheeping sound accompanied by a muffled "cluck, cluck." Coming through some high mustard weeds was our missing hen and her little family. They headed straight for the chicken coop, skipped through the open door and disappeared.

"Will we be like those chickens when we grow up and move far away from here? Will you still be here when we come back to roost?" These questions we kids asked of a sentimental father.

"I'll always be here waiting for you," he answered, trying to speak with conviction.

"Well, you kids better get into the house now and eat your supper. I'll go out and lock up the chicken coop for the night." It was time for us to go to bed again—with the chickens.

The Milwaukee Railroad

It can be said with humor that I "cut my teeth" on a steel railroad track. At an early age I became accustomed to the "choo-choo" trains that passed by only a few yards from our house.

It was fun to stand near the tracks with older brothers and sisters and watch the box cars, emblazoned with the emblems of every railroad line in the country, grind by us, rocking and rolling. The cars were a good lesson in spelling and geography.

"That's the Northern Pacific. There's the Chicago, Milwaukee, or Baltimore and Ohio, the Northwestern or the Rock Island Line." On and on the names were repeated until the orange colored caboose came into sight, and that was the end of another freight train, either arriving at or leaving Mitchell.

During the late twenties and thirties when I was a child, I didn't realize that Mitchell was an important part of the fast-growing passenger and freight service of two railroad lines, the Chicago, Minneapolis, St. Paul and Omaha (part of the Northwestern), on the north side of town, and the Chicago-Milwaukee that claimed more buildings, bigger yards and miles of track (that went from Mitchell over hill and dale and streams and rivers to Aberdeen, to Rapid City, to Sioux City, Ia.), located in midtown.

No wonder the city was named in honor of Alexander Mitchell, who was an early day president of the Milwaukee Railroad.

This prairie country was being turned into a network of railroad transportation. There was a great demand for a faster route to and from Dakota where people were coming to seek new horizons. The freight cars were needed to haul tons of building materials, fuel, livestock and grain. As early as 1880 there were freight trains pulling their loads through this area.

It wasn't until the early 1930's that we became acquainted with some of the personnel of the section gangs that worked by the sweat of their brow, laying or repairing tracks and road-beds.

We were living on the west edge of town where the tracks of the Milwaukee Railroad laced across our back yard. Our family had a front seat, watching the crews repair and replace the rails and ties, worn from the passage of the heavily laden freight and passenger cars.

Section crew of the Milwaukee railroad. Two men on the left were from Greece. Man with hands on hips was the section boss.

"Now you kids keep your distance. You don't want a piece of steel hitting you," bellowed an enormously large man dressed in blue denim work clothes. We looked up into a severe face with a bristling red beard and a mustache that curled up on the ends. We knew that he was the "boss man" because he was always shouting instructions to other workers who handled picks and shovels, perhaps digging up a rotted wooden tie.

Two of the men wore sombreros and their skin was tanned. I thought they looked like gypsies. When they spoke to each other, their words were in another language. Dad told us they were from Greece and came to Mitchell as immigrants to be "gandy dancers" (railroad workers).

They always welcomed us with pleasant smiles and greetings in broken English, and offered us a bite from their tin buckets during lunch break. We knew their work was hard. Their clothes were grimy and saturated with sweat.

"I have a little boy about your age back home in Greece," the one they called "Nick" told brother Bobby. "When I get enough money saved, he will come to America to live with me." "That's nice," Bobby said politely. "I hope he goes to my school when he comes." The dialect was sometimes hard to understand but they tried hard to communicate with us.

"O.K., men, back to work. This job has to be done before the evening passenger leaves tonight, so I want no gold bricking." The boss broke up our conversation. It was time anyway for us kids to head for home. "See you tomorrow," we yelled back at our friends who waved their sombreros.

For many years we children watched the section crews working through all kinds of weather, from the sweltering heat of the summer to the bitter cold of winter time. They rode to their daily labors on the small deck of a motor-driven "hand car," which also carried their picks and shovels.

I knew that they worked like the devil for their pay, and it was a dog's life to be a "steel driving man" for the railroad.

There were countless other jobs with the railroad for those who wanted a day's wages for a long day's work or work on the night shifts that were essential to keep the wheels moving. Each worker played a role in keeping the freights and passengers running on schedule, from the brakemen, switchmen, firemen, engineers and conductors to the crews who maintained the round house, coal chutes and water tanks.

Carpenters and masonary workers originally had constructed the round houses, chutes, water tanks, office freight buildings and the depots that offered temporary rest for weary travelers.

It was during the middle of the Thirties that we and other families living on the South Side became part and parcel of the great Milwaukee Railroad in a way, by living near the tracks and sprawling property which was owned by multimillionaires back east, we thought.

We kids began short cuts through the yards despite the signs that were posted everywhere, saying "Keep Off." When I recall that period, I'm amazed that we survived the dangerous trespassing.

"I wish you kids would walk over to Sanborn Street, then to school or town," Dad often pleaded. "You could lose an arm or leg or get killed by those trains." The thought of falling under those wheels frightened us for a while but those thoughts soon were forgotten when time was compared between the long walk of about ten blocks, with the "hop, skip and a jump" across the tracks.

The round house pond, a small body of waste water from the round house, sometimes proved to be a barrier when it over-flowed into Dry Run Creek. When this happened, a foot bridge could be used. It was put together with discarded planks from bridges, brought in by the crews and stacked along the tracks.

Once the swollen creek was forded, there was a steep hill to climb where a path was worn smooth by the foot traffic of the south siders. Sometimes a load of cinders was dumped over the banks and a new route had to be found. "I swear your kids are like mountain goats," neighbors told Mama as they watched us scale the obstacles to get to our destination.

After reaching the other side of the tracks and barriers, we realized there had been danger from the steam-spitting, bell-clanging, black iron monsters that puffed along, back and forth through the yards to switch the cars into the right formation. We soon learned how to dodge the boxcars that could easily have crushed us.

At first the railroad men tried everything to discourage our trespassing. The "Dick" (railroad policeman), Bill Carrick was just too soft hearted to refuse to let us cross his domain. One time I almost jumped into his arms when leaping off of a coupling between two boxcars. "If I had a pretty little daughter like you, I wouldn't want her crossing these tracks," he told me. "Don't your parents worry about you?"

"We're careful," I stammered, not really understanding the problems we were causing.

When I look back and think about all of the close calls we had then, I am truly amazed that none of our family was dismembered by a train. A few of our neighbors weren't so fortunate. A Mrs. Cooper and two of her children were killed while crossing a railroad bridge on the outskirts of town. A twelve-year-old Johnson girl was crushed to death between two boxcars which had been separated barely wide enough for her to squeeze through. She didn't know the switch engine was connected to the other end, and pushed the cars together where she was squeezing through. Others, including some of the employes, met accident or death in the yards when they miscalculated the speed of the moving cars, or how quickly the engineers could apply steam brakes.

Another problem that concerned both the railroad officials and the families whose children sneaked across the tracks was the influx of bums or hobos.

Men, women and even sometimes children rode the rods or empty freights in search of employment and often "jumped freight" in Mitchell to either beg, borrow or steal a mouthful of food. Since we lived on the fringe of the railroad right-of-way, many of the tramps came to our house in search of a hand-out. "If they come to us for help, I guess we're not so bad off after all," Mama would comment, watching the departing ragged band walking back to their only means of transportation and traveling home.

A few of our neighbors didn't take kindly to the sons of the open road and would order them to leave or threaten to call the sheriff who would run them out.

"You don't know who those people are. They could be escaped convicts, child molesters or murderers," a concerned Mr. Schirmer told my dad. "I wouldn't let one sleep in my barn if it was 40 below zero. Your kids are taking an awful chance passing by the 'bums' roost,' especially your little girls. You read every day about some child being murdered by a sex maniac. I work down there and I know what's going on. The white ones are just as dangerous as the blacks."

This warning prompted the folks to tell us to stay clear of the "hobo jungle" from that day on. We obeyed, but could still see the campsites along the Dry Run Creek where the transients used the creek water to shave and bathe and to brew a pot of coffee. The campfires were also visible at night as they flickered through the intervening cottonwood trees that helped protect the huddled nomads. Early in the morning most of them would be hopping a freight train in their endless search for a place where the grass was greener.

The depression years lingered on without much hope of us moving to a better neighborhood, on the other side of the tracks. By this time most of the railroad men knew us kids by our first names and we were learning all about railroad matters by asking hundreds of questions. We were allowed to inspect an engine when it was being checked out by the maintenance crew. "Mr. Quinn, how much coal can that tender hold?" "Oh, I'd say about 15 to 20 ton," the friendly man answered, wiping his grease-stained face with a red bandana which was commonly worn around the necks of railroad men.

"The engines can't function on just coal. They need about 3,600 gallons of water to make enough steam," he explained as we watched another engine being filled from a storage tank. The water was chemically treated with soda, ash and lime, we were told.

"How come engines need sand?" Brother Bobby wanted to know. We thought the huge piles of shifting sand were just there for us kids to play in and the sand house just a place for the hobos to sleep during the winter.

"That sand is very important," we were assured by Joe Holtzner, another employe. "It is scattered on the tracks to help keep the drive-wheels from slipping."

"When I grow up, I'm going to be an engineer," Bobby promised sister Neeney and me. "I'll go out of town and all over America." "I wouldn't want to work in the round house. It's too noisy, smoky and hot," I chimed in. "I don't know how those welders can stand wearing those big helmets and look at those flying sparks all day. It feels like a blast furnace just standing near the doorway." "That banging and clanging and the shishing and the roaring of that steam would be enough to drive me crazy," sister Neeney said. We watched the steam fitters, welders, machinists, fire builders, fire "knockers," oil boys and the "hostlers," whose endless job was to bring the engines in to the right stall until their next "run." The "call boys" were assigned to make sure the crews were available for the day or night shifts.

Most of the railroad men whom I remember as a child have passed away and have gone to that celestial train heaven, where trains are still puffing along, bound for glory land.

These men are but a few of the many I remember who were employed by the Milwaukee Railroad since its beginnings here in 1880: George Courey, John McGuire, Fred Hendrickson, James Quinn, the Paulin Brothers, Babe Parsons, James Hodson, Fred Whitkop, Joe Hoeltzner, Louis Knudson, Ed Kirsch, Fred Kemper, Frank Miller, Hubert Kearney, Harry Binderup, Joe Martell and Mr. Juenemann.

Switching Crews

I'm sure my favorite railroad employes were the switchman and the brakeman who spent most of their time in the great outdoors. They were as skilled as an athlete. They raced alongside the cars, grabbing a rung of the steel ladders, then waving a leather gloved hand to signal the engineer. It was dangerous work, especially during the winters when the cat walks were covered with ice.

All through the night these rugged caretakers transmitted their signals with bright lanterns that flashed in the dark freight yards. We kids were often awakened by the noise of the boxcars clanging together while switching. It sounded like thunder. I admired the men who labored in the cold, wet, dark, and sometimes foggy nights.

Yet there were many times when these dedicated men were cussed out by an impatient public for the train's delays on the Sanborn Street crossing. (There was no overpass at this time.)

During the late 1930's, when we kids were enrolled at Junior High on North Sanborn, the Railroad was blamed for our being late for school on many occasions.

"You better get a head start this morning. They may be

Milwaukee steam engine, with switchmen and brakemen

switching at the crossing," Dad reminded us while setting a plate of pancakes on the breakfast table.

"I sure wish we lived on the other side of town so we wouldn't have to be always blocked off by the railroad," brother Bobby complained.

"Well, they were here first," Dad smiled, "and I don't think they are going to move. Don't get mad at the switchmen. They're only doing their job. Maybe some day the city will build an overpass and that will solve the problem." "I'll be a hundred years old by that time," Bobby replied.

The noon hour rush continued to be the worst time of day to walk or drive on Sanborn Street. There was a mad dash of pedestrians and drivers of vehicles to cross the tracks before the switch engines blocked their path.

While the angry populace waited, cursing and fretting, the boxcars slowly rolled along, with the switchmen trying not to notice the impatience of the people at the crossings.

"Why, during the noon hour? Don't they know we only have an hour to get home and back? If this keeps up I'll lose my job."

"It's a disgrace for us taxpayers to put up with this nonsense. Why doesn't the mayor do something about it?"

"What if an ambulance or a fire truck comes along, then what? A person could die or his house could burn down."

The "Home away from home," Chicago, Milwaukee caboose

"If this keeps up, I'm moving away from the south side." All of this complaint and horn blowing fell upon deaf ears of the flagman who stood holding a "stop" sign until the cars had passed by.

For school kids, who were always behind schedule anyway, it meant a fast run for home, so as to be back on time at 1 p.m. when the school bell rang.

It wasn't until 1950 that the long-awaited bridge, or overpass, was constructed to solve traffic problems between the City of Mitchell and the Milwaukee Railroad.

After all these years, I am still living on the south side of town and have to drive across the Sanborn overpass just about every day. I never fail to gaze across the network of tracks and remember when the ubiquitous railroad men ruled this domain with a wave of a gloved hand. I can still see them in early dawn or in twilight when the yards are covered with shadows. Some of these yard men I remember were the Schirmer Brothers, Henry and Fred, Joe Mussingman, and our good buddy, Harry (Shorty) Halverson.

Borrowing Coal

We kids knew the need, at an early age, to help prepare ourselves and the family against the onslaught of the bitter cold winters that came each year, with snowing and blowing.

"I don't know why we have to live in South Dakota," one of us was always complaining when the temperatures dipped to around 20 degrees below zero. We envied the people who lived below the Mason and Dixon line or on the sun-kissed shores of California or Florida.

"We have to keep both stoves fired up. So bring in anything you kids find that will burn. Pile it behind the chicken coop," Mama instructed us. "Those old ties that the railroad throws away can be chopped up, and the boxes and crates that the grocery stores don't want will make good kindling." Nothing went to waste.

One day we noticed some of our neighbors picking up coal that fell from the coal cars. So my two brothers, sister and I joined the bucket brigade and grabbed up all the shiny chunks of black gold that we could find. Our small tin pails were stashed in a hiding place when we went to school, and then retrieved and filled with coal when we made the trip back home.

Part of Milwaukee railroad crew

In no time there were many coal pickers, so some began to borrow from the loaded cars sitting on the tracks.

"Don't you kids realize that you can get arrested for stealing that coal?" the railroad "Dick" asked, when he saw us hurrying away.

"We need it real bad," Bobby replied, knowing that kind-hearted Bill wouldn't take precious fuel back from us. "Well, you can have a few buckets now and then, but remember, this coal costs the Railroad a lot of money."

One cold afternoon when the sun dogs were visible in the sky we kids were again in the process of gathering coal. We were suddenly startled to hear a deep voice say, "Hello dere, children. Whacha doin' down dere?" (Maybe the devil has caught up with us, I thought.) I looked up to see a shadowy figure of a man dressed in workman's overalls and cap. His face was covered with coal dust. He stared at us over the edge of the car. We were petrified with fear until he smiled, revealing a toothy grin that matched the whites of his eyes. "Are you Mr. Williams who takes care of the coal cars?" asked Bobby, now no longer afraid. "Yes, I am," he replied, "and you children better get out of the way or you might fall into the elevator and that would be the end of you." (We didn't know at first that Williams was a black man.)

"I'll throw some big chunks down this time but you shouldn't come back no more to this place. It's too dangerous for little tykes like you."

On our way home we stopped now and then to rest our arms from the strain of carrying the coal buckets, and discussed the negro who gave us a helping hand and some good advice. "I think he's a nice 'nigger' man and we don't have to be afraid of him," sister Neeney decided for us. "They picked a good one for that job because he is already black, and folks can't tell if he's dirty or not."

"I don't think a white man wants that kind of work," I joined in, looking back at the clouds of coal dust swirling around the chutes and settling on the round house pond. The real nice, hard working black man, Mr. Williams, lost his life while on the job a few years later. Workmen found his mangled body lying on the tracks. One of the coal cars had run over him.

Borrowing coal from the Milwaukee and also the North-western railroad began to gain in momentum as the hard pressed poor people needed more than just a few buckets at a time. Cars and pick-up trucks were put to use carrying

Milwaukee Railroad yards in Mitchell. Depot in left center, roundhouse at right, towering coal chute in right center.

gunnysacks bulging with coal. Many people exchanged some of the black stuff with friends for food or other items that were needed. One of the local bakery truck drivers often exchanged day-old rolls and bread for a few bags of coal from my dad.

"I think coal hauling is getting out of hand," Uncle Pete remarked to the folks. "Last night I counted twelve cars or trucks parked on the side of the hill. It's getting to be big business."

The big business was nipped in the bud when the Milwaukee officials decided to get tough with coal thieves. Extra "Dicks" were placed on patrol around the chutes and arrests came thick and fast. Names began to appear in the newspaper.

But when the guilty parties were brought into court they were usually met by a sympathetic judge who understood the need for fuel. If the bread winner was placed behind bars it would mean more county relief for his family.

Judges Thompson and Danforth suspended most of the jail terms and fines and tried to persuade the county officials to supply more fuel to the needy who had no other alternative than stealing, to keep from freezing to death.

When I look back and remember those years, I often wonder if the Milwaukee Railroad officials ever knew how many tons of coal they supplied to the depression generation. Those who borrowed their fuel from the tracks owe the Railroad a debt of gratitude.

The Depot

We children thought the most important part of the Milwaukee Railroad was the travel agency in the depot. This grand old brick station almost became our home away from home. It was a bee hive of activity, what with passenger trains arriving and leaving (hopefully on schedule) at various hours of the day and night.

The building that faced north at the south end of Main Street was a cozy haven after we kids had crossed the wind-swept tracks during a snowstorm. It became a cool spot in the desert when temperatures rose to a "boiling point" along the railroad yards that seemed to be the hottest place on earth.

Once inside the depot the first place we girls visited was the ladies' room to enjoy the comfort of an indoor toilet. "It sure must be nice to have a bathroom in the house," I sighed to my little sister while tapping out some liquid soap from the dispenser to wash my hands. "There's always plenty of paper towels and toilet paper, too," she agreed, taking lots of time. "Well, hurry up, I gotta go too," I said. "The trains will be coming pretty soon. We don't want to miss anything."

The waiting room was at the east end of the depot where wooden oak benches awaited the weary travelers. Neeney and I made sure of our "reserved seat" by usurping the space long before the trains pulled into the station.

"I sure wish we could go away somewhere once," I whis-

Milwaukee Depot constructed in 1909 (well kept and still standing).

pered to Neeney, while enviously watching a well-dressed family surrounded by their luggage, waiting patiently for the conductor to call "All aboard." "You have to be rich to ride trains. Where do you want to go, anyway?"

"Someday I'm going to get on one of those passengers and go to Hollywood, and get in the movies," I predicted. "When I come back, rich and famous, this depot will be filled with home town folks, wanting to see me."

My dreams weren't taken too seriously by my sister who knew that wishing wouldn't make it so, but the friendly conductors often joined in our make-believe world, stopping to chat, with a glance now and then at their big pocket watches that ticked away the minutes. Their watches were attached to long chains.

"Well now, where in the world are you two girls traveling today?" they asked us, good naturedly, "New York? Chicago? San Francisco? How about a trip to Sioux City? That's not too far away."

Our laughter was interrupted by someone shouting, "Here comes the passenger from the east, and it's right on schedule." Neeney and I raced to the windows to get a good look at the travelers as they stepped down from the train, assisted by a porter in a dark blue uniform and blue visored cap.

Suitcases, boxes and bags were often carried by an energetic little man, Jimmy Moreland, who was the only "red cap." He proudly scurried back and forth from the train to the depot, assisting anyone who would pay for his services.

We watched in silence the joyful reunions that always took place in and around the depot. In a few minutes the people left in automobiles and on foot, and the depot was empty again (except for Clarence Wangsness, the ticket agent who we remembered as always too crabby to say "hello"). Sometimes he did peer at us with a look of disapproval because we hung around his window and watched him sell tickets. We probably made him nervous. "He's sure not friendly," Neeney said. "He acts like we don't belong here. I wish he was nice like Mr. Olenberg, the baggage man. He never gets mad when we watch them unload the baggage cars."

The times we loved the best by far were when we could be in the depot during the Christmas holidays when the spirit of the evergreen season was everywhere. There were shouts of "Merry Christmas" echoing throughout the complex, festive red and green paper swooping down from the high ceilings to form red ruffled bells in the center. They shimmered and sparkled in the sunlight and swayed in the breeze from the doors that were constantly opened or shut.

Sitting in a corner on the east end near the windows was a magnificent Christmas tree dripping with twinkling lights, colored balls and ornaments, strings of red cranberries and white popcorn, strands of tinsel in silver and gold, and last but not least, a glittering star that almost touched the ceiling.

What a warm feeling engulfed us as we sat on the oak bench next to the sparkling green tree, admiring the panorama of beauty that reflected in the frosted window panes.

"I wish we could have a Christmas tree at home," Neeney sighed, gazing at her image in one of the mirror-like balls. "Mama says we can't afford to buy a tree, let alone all those expensive lights and decorations, and the Good Fellows and Salvation Army just bring toys and food." "Maybe next year we will have more money," I consoled my little sister.

Our dreams of having our very own Christmas tree was interrupted by one of the railroad men dressed in a Santa Claus suit. The annual Christmas party for the children of the railroad employees was held each year at the depot.

I recognized "Santa Claus" as one of our old friends. "How would you little girls like a sack of candy?" he asked, trying to disguise his voice. We never turned down anything free and held out our hands. A white sack bulging with candy and nuts was placed in my hand by this kind-hearted train man, who gave treats to all the children. Mama always wished that Dad was a railroad man because they "make a good living."

I'm sure we kids were a nuisance to some of the railroad folks who probably thought we should be in our own back yard instead of mingling with them.

There were other times when we chose the west end of the depot to watch people. The lunchroom was located in this area and the hungry, weary tourist, small groups of railroad men, and some townspeople stopped by for a cup of coffee and a little talk. The waitresses soon learned to take the teasing and flirtations of the switchmen and engineers good naturedly. "I bet you tell that to all the girls," they would say.

The railroad men all looked alike to me and walked with a sway as if they were still on the moving trains.

The traditional uniforms of blue overalls with matching jackets, blue and gray striped caps and jaunty neck scarfs, were often purchased at the Louis Lipschultz Clothing Store, one block north of the Milwaukee depot. This store sold famous name brands in men's work clothes such as "Lees," "Oshkosh," "Big Mac," and other durable wear that was the trademark of a railroad man.

Saved From Attack

Despite warnings from some of the neighbors and our parents, we kids were too young to realize that there were people in this world who could be dangerous.

We were aware of the kidnappings, murders and assaults upon children from reading newspapers or hearing the frightening news over the radio. But it always happened to someone else.

"Now remember, you three," Mama repeated to her youngest offsprings, "if you have to cross the railroad yards, stay together for your own protection." "The railroad men are always around," Bobby answered, with not too much concern. "They will help us if a bum tries to kidnap us." Mama was more worried about us two girls, who might be accosted by some derelict passing through on a freight train. "Just keep your eyes and ears open," she would warn us, watching us get ready for school.

Mama's advice to beware was swept away in the "cobwebs" of my mind. One sunny afternoon I decided to go to the dime store to buy some ribbons for my hair. Neither sister Neeney nor brother Bobby knew that I was going to cross the tracks without their company.

My thoughts were on the purchase I was going to make as I strolled between two rows of boxcars, when suddenly a boy jumped down from an open doorway and grabbed me from behind. He turned me around and I looked into a pock marked face that made my stomach turn. "Don't you dare scream," he warned, "or you'll be sorry." He pointed to a knife in a leather sheath attached to his belt. I was so scared I thought my heart was going to jump out of my throat and I prayed that I wouldn't pass out from fright. I recognized him—a local youth with a reputation of not being "all there."

"What do you want?" I tearfully asked, as he jerked me towards him. "You'll find out," he sneered. "You're going to give me a little lovin.' I'm going to take you into this boxcar where no one will hear or see us. Don't you let out one peep."

All I could think of was Mama's warning about the transients but here was this strong-muscled local teenager threatening me. I had often passed him on the street corner where he sold papers, and sometimes I saw him hanging around the entrance of the local pool hall.

"He's going to kill me," I thought, and I struggled as he

pushed me into the car, cutting my arm on a piece of loose tin. I tried to kick, bite and scratch but he held me in a vise-like grip.

"Why doesn't someone come along to help me? Mama, why didn't I listen to you?" I moaned. Then I resigned myself. This was the end.

I couldn't believe my ears when I heard a voice angrily shout, "Hey there! what the hell are you doing with that girl? Leave her alone." The boy released his hold on me and leaped to the ground. I could hear running footsteps on the gravel as the boy left with someone after him.

I jumped from the boxcar, so shaken with fright I could hardly stand. Approaching me a few yards away was a young man in faded work clothes with a dusty cowboy hat held in one hand. He grinned and I knew that he was the person who had saved me.

"Did that kid hurt you?" he questioned me, putting his arm around my still-shaking shoulders. "I couldn't catch him. He crawled under a boxcar. Lucky for him. Do you live around here? What is your name? This is no place for a little girl like you. How old are you?"

I finally composed myself long enough to answer all of his questions, while trying to conceal my embarrassment.

My new hero escorted me through the railroad yards and explained that he was riding the rods to Montana, and just happened to come along at the right time to hear the commotion.

"You tell your parents what happened back there so they can get the sheriff on that kid's tail," he said, leaving me at the edge of the yards. "He should be locked up."

"I sure will," I replied, looking up into quite a handsome face, sprinkled with freckles that matched the color of his tousled hair. "And before you go, what is your name?" I asked. "Johnny Sturdivent," he grinned. "Can you remember it? Most people call me Rusty. My home is way down in Oklahoma."

"Well, bye now, I gotta be going. Have to catch the next freight." "Bye," I answered, and watched him till he disappeared. I thanked God as I walked down the cinder path towards home.

Dad and Mama were in the garden pulling weeds and right away they knew that something was wrong. Mama asked,

"What in heaven's name happened to you? You look so pale. How did you get your dress torn and dirty and your arms all scratched up?"

"I fell down the hill and into a pile of cinders," I lied. I just couldn't tell them about the degrading experience that left me scared and ashamed. If they knew the truth they would go after the simple-minded boy who assailed me.

"It don't hurt," I told Dad, as he examined my bruised arm, now turning black and blue and throbbing. "I'll change my clothes and come back and help you pull weeds."

I washed my hands and face and combed my hair that I had planned to make pretty with some satin ribbons that I never bought because of my ordeal. I gazed into the faded mirror above the sink and saw a demoralized little girl of eleven who stared back at me. "Do all boys act like that when they grow up?" I asked myself, "or are some of them good and kind, just like Johnny Sturdivent? He was a young man whom I knew I'd never see again."

It took a long time to get over the traumatic experience, and I had to keep it secret, even from my sister with whom I shared all of my hopes and dreams. The teenager who threatened me was still walking the streets with a bundle of newspapers tucked under his arm. I'm sure he would have been sent to the State Training School or Redfield if the authorities had known about his assault upon a minor. The scars on my arm faded away but not the uncertainty that remained in my thoughts about myself and my future. Because my family was poor and had to accept handouts from more prosperous people who lived in nice homes in better neighborhoods, would we always be taken advantage of by those who thought they were better than we were? When I was old enough to have my first date, would I be ashamed of being "that girl from the wrong side of the tracks"?

The Engineers

"He was going down the grade, making ninety miles an hour, when the whistle broke into a scream. He was found in the wreck with his hand on the throttle and was scalded to death by the steam." These are words from the classic "Casey Jones," a legendary song about a fearless engineer and his railroad engine.

To a small girl like me, the engineers were the nonchalant, happy wanderers of the vast network of railroading. They kept the puffing monsters under control, with the help of their sidekicks, the firemen. We kids surmised that the firemen really did all the hard work of coal shoveling and gauge watching, while the engineer, with his cap cocked to one side, and his red or blue bandana jauntily tied around his throat, just sat on his perch controlled the speed and blew the whistle.

I'm sure the life of an engineer and fireman was lonely at times because of their absence from their homes. Sometimes they were gone days before they returned from their runs to Murdo, Rapid City, Sioux City, Aberdeen or other points. Their pay was based on the miles shown on their time sheets.

The freight engineers manned the smaller switch engines, which were used for assembling of freight trains or positioning cars for unloading of fruits, vegetables or other supplies, and storage in warehouses adjacent to the tracks.

Many of the railroad employes and engineers lived in and around the railroad addition neighborhood. It was just a hop, skip, and a jump from railroad property. The Simpson Hotel, on South Duff Street, offered rooms for rent to the engineers and firemen from out of town, on "layover."

The Merchant's Hotel and Coffee Shop on South Main Street was another well-known rest haven with clean rooms and good meals at reasonable rates. If a man wasn't a teetotaler, the Hoffman Bar, across the street, provided a relaxing atmosphere of companionship and one could buy a glass or two of foaming beer, or a couple of "boilermakers."

This sometimes helped to ward off the loneliness of being away from home, wives, sweethearts, or girl friends. The whistles of the steam engines always served to carry a mournful, melancholy sound as the long freights pulled away from the yards. It was a good-bye to their families, who patiently waited for their return.

We kids didn't know the engineers too well, as they were here today and gone tomorrow. They did wave at us and sometimes "tooted" the whistle. They knew that all little boys and some little girls wanted to grow up to be engineers for the Chicago, Milwaukee, St. Paul and Pacific Railroad line.

Listed here are but a few of the many firemen and engineers of the great steam locomotives which crossed South Dakota and surrounding states. (I want to thank Orlo Livingston and George McDougal for their help in the story about the engineers and firemen.) If there was a hall of fame for trainmen, these names should be in it: Frank Livingston, Orlo Livingston, George McDougal, Harry Veit, George Gowling, O. M. Heather, Fred Harges, Donald Dale, Richard Kelley, Oscar Andres and Robert Montgomery.

Knights of the Road

"Hangin' 'round the water tank, just waitin' for a train" was a nostalgic song of the Thirties about bums, tramps, hobos and many others who were out of work. During 1932, when the depression was at its worst, there were 15,000,000 people unemployed.

Husbands, fathers and brothers pulled up stakes, leaving families behind to seek any kind of livelihood. Without a dime to reach their destination, it was either hitchhike or hop a freight train. "Brother, can you spare a dime?" was often asked.

These men were the migrants who were willing to pick fruit for five cents an hour, chop wood, or pull weeds. During the harvest season, thousands were hired to help in the fields from North Dakota to Kansas.

The freight trains unwillingly carried these "free loaders" across the vast countryside. It became so bad, the railroad companies hired special police detectives to rid their lines of those unwelcome riders. The police were called "Dicks" or "Bulls" and sometimes used drastic means to clear the freights and railroad yards. In the southern states, the migrants, if caught, were sometimes sentenced to a brutal work detail in prison.

During one year, 700,000 people were ejected from trains.

Harvest hands and hobos, riding the freight cars in search of work during hard times.

Among these rejects from society were women and girls and many under-age children. Many of these inexperienced travelers were killed by the steel railroad car wheels as they fell or were thrown off fast moving boxcars. Some with no identification were buried in an unmarked grave in a "potter's field."

Woodie Guthrie, a song writer of that period, depicted the plight of these depressed nomads in words and song. His works are now considered classics, as they were indeed a part of this nation's struggle for survival.

During the Dirty Thirties, we observed this migration across the land. Living within view of the Milwaukee Railroad yards, and a block or so from trains, it was only natural to watch and wonder where they came from and where they were going. Dad used to tell us about the caste system and distinction between a "bum," "hobo," or "tramp." The hobos, or "knights of the road," as they liked to be called, were truly the "happy wanderers." They followed the sun, like will o' the wisps from sea to shining sea. Work was not in their make-up. They were too lazy to work and maybe too honest to steal. A handout could be obtained from a sympathetic housewife or a farmer to tide them over to the next town.

I remember Mama giving a hearty lunch to many grimy, ragged hobos. While we kids peeked out from the kitchen window, they wolfed down trays of sandwiches, cake and coffee. The old story of hobos leaving messages to other knights of the road must have been true. Mama fed many of them during the great depression. She felt compassion for these homeless people.

Thousands of bums passed through Mitchell during this period. They usually jumped from the trains on the outskirts of town, along the railroad embankments. The "no bums allowed" signs in most towns led them to seek out the hobo jungles. The jungles could be found near the railroad in a secluded spot, hidden from the railroad police. There was a jungle in Mitchell behind the roundhouse, where a small creek trickled into the roundhouse pond. We kids walked by their encampments many times without any fear, although they never attempted to talk or ask questions. I'm sure they only wanted to rest, brew a pot of coffee or soup, and to be on their way. We kids called their debris littered sanctuary "The Bum's Roost."

The bitter cold of the winter months didn't stop the ever-moving hordes of men, although it did slow them down to a degree. I remember seeing men standing on the couplings between box cars, as the ice-coated trains rumbled past our house. Others were huddled together in the open doorways of box cars.

The old sand house, east of the roundhouse (where the sand was kept warm for the steam engines), was a warm place to sleep; that is, if a railroad "bull" was sympathetic and allowed bums to stay.

I'm sure another depression like the Dirty Thirties will never come along again, but if it should, I wonder, will the bums, tramps and hobos ride the rails again, as they did then? Could history repeat itself?

Farewell to the Railroad

In order to write this chapter about the Milwaukee Railroad, I revisited the familiar surroundings of the bottom lands, roundhouse pond, and footpaths that led to the tract of land where the roundhouse and the depot were located.

The bottom lands where the cat tails used to grow near the banks of the pond are now a hard-surfaced bicycle trail. Gone are the Russian olive trees that grew on the hillsides. A newly constructed footbridge crosses dry run creek, but there are no signs of the cinder paths that wandered along the steep incline. I found myself in a knee-high mass of tangled fire-weeds and underbrush where the water from the spring rains used to gurgle and sparkle in the sunlight.

Where once we kids took the short cut through the yards there is now a barricade with a "cyclone" fence. "No Trespassing" signs are posted everywhere. I've been told that there is now a severe penalty if anyone is caught on railroad property.

"How many years have the towering coal chutes been gone?" I wondered, as I listened for the sounds of yesteryear but only heard the rustle of the waving grass.

"I'd sure love to see again one of the big old steam engines puffing along the steel rails," I thought to myself, remembering how we used to wave at the engineers when they pulled the cord for the piercing whistle, or rang the big brass bell.

Has it really been more than forty years since I saw the wandering hordes of outcasts passing through this city on the freight trains that were taking them to some unknown place? I wondered how many of them struck pay dirt beyond the blue horizon and how many came to the end of the trail along a railroad track.

The next stop, and the one I saved for last, was the now aging Milwaukee Depot still standing as a reminder of times now forgotten.

I felt a tug at my heart-strings and a wave of nostalgia flooded over me as I stepped on the cracked and broken concrete surrounding the passenger depot. Withered grass and fireweeds were finding a hiding place along the crumbling steps and sagging foundation. A sudden gust of wind churned up dust, and scraps of paper blew against the grimy windows of the old depot.

"Would anyone care if I tried the door handle?" I wondered, but there wasn't a soul stirring or a train moving in the ghostly yards standing deserted and silent.

The heavy door that used to welcome us kids with a "squeak" and a "bang" was now security-locked. I felt rejected. But I could see into the waiting room where a lone oak bench was still standing against the wall. Could that be the same bench that offered my little sister and me the best seat in the house to watch the trains come in and leave?

High above the main entrance in the center of the depot was an empty space where the paint was faded and peeled away like a disfigured work of art. That was where the large clock used to be fastened, its face revealing to one and all the exact reminder that time and trains waited for no one. "I hope that wonderful old clock is reposing on the wall of a retired railroad man," I thought.

"Well, what do you know?" I laughed, the rest room is still here. I remembered it as a welcome comfort station that provided us with the relief after our long walks to town.

From the sign that read "Ladies Room," my gaze shifted to where I saw with surprise the white marble water fountain still intact, but stained with rust from the water that used to refresh thirsty travelers, railroad employes and kids like us who loved to drink the gurgling waters.

I turned my attention to the railroad tracks and the string of box cars that bore new names of national railroad lines on their wood or steel bodies. They weren't familiar to me any more. Was there still a Rock Island Line?

Across the yards I could see what was left of a once great business that provided a livelihood for hundreds of Mitchell employes. A shell was all that was left of the "home for the steam engines," the old time-worn roundhouse. Later it was maintained by a skeleton crew who take care of the oil-burning diesels. I sure wish I could turn back time and see once more the blues and the grays of the overalled railroad men, now replaced by a new breed dressed in blue jeans and sweatshirts. Now the Milwaukee may be gone forever.

Although the sun was sinking and it was nearing twilight time, I didn't want to leave. I felt as though I belonged in this place, where the ghosts of the past were still with me.

Was that my imagination or did I hear a haunting voice calling from the darkened train station? "Train leaving for

Townspeople waiting for returning soldiers at the Milwaukee Depot in Mitchell, circa 1917.

all points east—Bridgewater, Emery, Canton, Sanborn and Chicago. A-a-l-l- aboard!"

Who are those two little girls getting on that gold-colored "passenger" with happy smiles on their faces? Do I see their family, who have to stay behind, shedding tears?

Why is that black "passenger" arriving in a mist, awaited by people with heads bowed? Why is a flag-draped casket being unloaded from the baggage car? I remember the war and I see troop trains with faceless soldiers peering through the dimly lit windows at a town they may never see again.

Now I find myself sitting in the luxurious coach of a dream train, taking me away from both the good and bad times of a small midwestern town. I'm going to find my dream somewhere beyond the borders of this state.

The train is gaining speed and the lights of my home town are fading from view. Now all I can see is darkness when I look out the window. I have changed my mind. I want the train to stop so I can get off and walk back home. In my heart I never really wanted to leave my home, be it ever so humble.

Now I see white pigeons flying like doves of peace over the towers of the coal chutes. The war has ended and there are smiles on the faces of the railroad men. There are bells ringing everywhere.

But suddenly there is silence. I don't hear the rumble and the roar of the passengers and freight trains. The aging steam engines have gasped their last breath and stand silent on the weed covered tracks.

Where have all the old time railroad men gone? Are they sitting alone somewhere, dreaming of that glorious time in history when railroads were the heartbeat of the nation?

The depot is shrouded in silence, too. Will it now be destroyed, along with other buildings that have served so faithfully? Please let it stand as a reminder of our heritage and as a tribute to the dedicated railroad men who moved in and out of its portals.

My search for yesterday was over. It was time to leave the past behind. But, as I walked away I could hear the "shishing" of a steam engine, and wasn't that a mournful wail of a train whistle echoing across the bottom land, on a final run?

395

Corn Palace, Story I

"Isn't that something?" "Never saw anything quite like it." "It's really beautiful." "How do they get all that corn and grain up there to make those pictures and designs?" "How many years has there been a Corn Palace?"

These were comments and questions of relatives and friends when they came to visit our home town, Mitchell. They were referring to the sprawling brick building that covered almost an entire block on north Main Street. We home folks knew it as the World's Only Corn Palace—a tourist attraction that helped put Mitchell on the map.

We kids accompanied Mama and Dad and our country cousins to see this corn-decorated building which some city slickers called "a year-round free meal for the birds and mice."

"It was here when I came to this town in 1910," Dad said, while everyone stood gawking at it. The Corn Palace was constructed on this site in 1921. "They say the first one was located down on the corner of Fourth and Main in 1892. Later it was moved to the corner of Fifth and Main, right where Rozum's garage stands," Mama told her relatives. They were all ears to hear the story of our famous landmark.

"I wish I had a camera. I'd take a few pictures," Uncle Lee said, walking across the street to obtain a better look. "You can get some picture postcards over at Barnes Cafe. They have some good ones that were taken by two local photographers, Mr. Stair and Mr. Hersey."

The Barnes Cafe and grocery store was across the street, in the very shadow of the Corn Palace. It served also as a mini Chamber of Commerce building for tourists who wanted information and perhaps a few postcards. (During early years there weren't many mementoes and souvenirs.) Unlike today where the exploitation of the "Palace" has mushroomed into a million dollar industry.

When everyone had seen enough, we all piled back into our relatives' car and conversation continued about the famous Corn Palace.

"You should come back in September during the Corn Palace festival, if you really want to see the sights," I told my little cousins, who were sitting with their noses pressed to the car windows, not wanting to miss a thing. They light up the Corn Palace at night and it looks just like a gigantic Christmas tree." "And there are all kinds of rides and free

Mitchell Corn Palace in 1926

shows on Main Street," sister Neeney chimed in. By this time eyes were as big as saucers as we told them all about Corn Palace week and the magical carnival.

"Put your pennies away for Corn Palace week," we kids were told by our parents and friends when a stray nickel or penny was found in the bottom of a coin purse and given to us. "It costs a nickel to ride the merry-go-round and fifteen cents for a ride on the little train that is pulled by a real live steam engine."

"Oh yes, a candied apple costs five cents. That's an awful lot of money," I thought, checking again my few pennies that I kept safely banked in an old tobacco tin.

After fifty years, I can clearly recall the first time that we children were taken up town to see the spectacular carnival panorama on Main Street. It was the year 1928. Night had already fallen over the city and it was time to see the sights.

"Now don't you kids walk too far ahead of me. You might get lost in the crowds," Mama cautioned my sister and me. We were too excited to walk at a snail's pace beside our mother. She never could move very fast because of her chronic backache and aching feet. "When you get to Main Street, you wait for me, you hear?"

We were living on North Edmunds Street at the time. It

was only a four-block walk east on Seventh to reach the "main drag."

From out of a moonlit sky we suddenly saw the twinkling lights of the Corn Palace laced between the branches of trees that grew thick in that area. It was a thrill that can come only to a child whose imagination cannot be contained.

"Oh, isn't it beautiful?" I sighed to my little sister as we stood transfixed by the brilliant cascades of colored lights that were drawing us on.

"Hurry up, Mama," we coaxed, "everything has already started." From where we waited on Seventh Street and Main we gazed in awe at a harvest festival in full swing.

"Mama, can we have a box of popcorn?" we begged, when we saw the red and white popcorn wagon near us. She placed a few coins on the window sill and a pleasant lady handed each of us a paper box filled with fluffy white popcorn. A

Corn Palace Midway, circa 1943

generous supply of melted butter topped off its crunchy goodness.

"Now you kids will have to wait until I see the aerial acts before we go any farther, so stay close to me. There are going to be a lot of people coming this way in a few minutes. We can stand on the porch of Aunt Christine's cafe to see better." We grabbed her coat tails and followed her through the swarming mass of people around the Corn Palace.

"Where do all of these people come from?" we asked as we looked across the sea of humanity, standing shoulder to shoulder. "Oh, oh!" Mama exclaimed, "there goes the guy up the ladder who's going to dive off that platform, way up there."

I stood on tiptoe and followed Mama's finger pointing at a man "decked out" in what looked like underwear. He was climbing swiftly to a sky-high perch, the Mitchell band was playing a fast stepping march, then it suddenly stopped. The agile acrobat, now barely visible, was waving to the crowds below. My neck was getting stiff from rubber necking.

"I don't believe it," one of the nervous bystanders said to Mama. "Will he really dive into that tank of water, after they set it afire with gasoline?" "That crazy fool will be killed," said another, wondering if we would see an accident happen to the dare devil about to thrill the fun-seeking populace. "I can't look, I told my little sister, half hiding behind Mama's coat. "Tell me when it's over."

After what seemed to be an eternity, I heard the band playing the grand finale and the cheers and applause of the people who had seen the spectacular death-defying stunt. In a few minutes the crowds dissipated and moved back towards the center of the midway where the rides were going and barkers for the tent shows were ballyhooing their freak exhibits or games. They wanted the jingling coins that were burning holes in the pockets of local youth. We kids, along with Mama, were swept along with the tide of fun seekers, searching for a make-believe world that came to life only during Corn Palace week.

After walking through the maze of electric cables that supplied power to the rides and for side-shows, we found ourselves on the south end of Main.

There was a dance hall on one side of Main Street where people were kicking up their heels to the music of a three-piece band, playing on a platform. "This is the 'Bowery dance',"

Mama informed us as she pushed aside some of the on-lookers so we could have a better view. "Your Dad better not be out there with some whirling dervish. He's supposed to be tending bar at Navin's." "Let's get out there and do the toddle," I suggested to my little sister. "Nope," she answered, taking another bite of her sticky, candied apple. "I'd rather ride the tilt-a-whirl." (She was always game for anything daring.)

"Now you girls wait right here and I'll go into Navin's and bring Dad out so he can watch you ride those little cars over there," Mama said. It was one of the few times that Mama entered a beer joint. She always remarked that she wouldn't be found in one. It was no place for a lady, she thought. I could hear the sounds of boisterous merry-making and gales of laughter coming from the smoke-filled bar. There was a pugent smell of beer and fried onions.

I thought Dad looked real elegant in his white starched shirt and black bow tie around a white collar, when he came out. "You put the girls in the cars and I'll get the tickets," he told Mama.

"I can get in by myself," Neeney insisted, when Mama tried to lift us into the miniature cars. Even the horns beeped.

The "Carnie" man released an iron lever and we were off on a bumpy ride to nowhere. "Gee, this is sure fun," I thought to myself as I "steered" the little car and bashfully peeked at the mothers and fathers who smiled and looked pleased when their children passed by.

"Hi, Mama and Dad," I boldly called to my parents after I saw other small fry waving and throwing kisses. Dad returned my wave, and smiled, each time that I passed by, but Mama remained emotionless. (For some reason it was hard for her to show her feelings, especially in public.)

The joy ride ended all too soon. Mama waited to grab us by the hand and take us back up the street, and then home.

"Here's a couple quarters I got tonight for tips," Dad said, holding up the money. "I think we can afford to give the kids another ride on the merry-go-round. After all, Corn Palace only comes once a year."

Mama took the money and placed it in her shabby leather pocketbook. "I should really spend this for some hamburger, but I guess they should have a good time once in a while. Now don't forget to come right home after the bar closes," she told Dad with a severe look. Everyone knew that floozies flocked to Mitchell during Corn Palace week and frequented saloons.

"Hurry up, let's hop on the prettiest horses," Neeney yelled to me, leaping up on the circular platform that held the wild-eyed mustangs. They looked life-like with flaring nostrils and open mouths. The prancing mechanical horses in black, brown, white and dapple gray were mounted on brass rods that rose up and down to the "ump pa pa" music of a steam calliope playing inside the revolving ride.

I selected a snow white steed and clambered into the saddle, placing my feet in the wooden stirrups. I grabbed the leather reins with one hand and hung on to the brass pole for dear life, with the other. The carousel slowly began to move. I don't think anyone can describe the exhilarating feeling stirred in the soul of a child, taking her first ride on a merry-go-round. As for me, I was in seventh heaven.

I was transported into another world as I rode with the herd of magical ponies. The whirling lights and the faces of the bystanders were almost a blur. I dreamed I was a princess riding away with gypsies.

"Hey, it's time to get off, little girl," a "Carnie" man yelled, jolting me back to reality. "You will have to buy another ticket if you want another ride."

"Maybe I'll be back tomorrow," I told him hopefully as I jumped down to the ground. I felt giddy and a little weak-kneed as I walked to the edge of the crowd where Mama stood waiting. "That sure looked like fun," she smiled while brushing away a tear. "We better get home now. It's getting late. Maybe, just maybe, we will come up Saturday for the last day of Corn Palace."

"All the neighbors are heading for town," we kids reminded Mama, Saturday. "You promised a 'maybe' about tonight. Please, can't we go just for one more time? You don't have to give us any rides, we will just stand by and watch." "Well, all right," she finally gave in, "but you kids have to polish my shoes while I get dressed. It will take me a while to get into my corset."

Brother Bobby raced into the bedroom where he found Mama's scuffed shoes underneath the bed. In the meantime I found the bottle of black shoe polish on the kitchen window sill. "I get to polish them," I demanded, "because I'm neat and won't make a mess." I pulled and twisted but I couldn't get the cork out.

"Here, let me do that," Dad said. "You don't want to end up looking like a nigger baby," and he took the ebony bottle. Mama's black shoes looked almost like new with the spit and polish shine that Dad applied.

"Tell Mama to hurry up, we begged Dad when he took the shoes into the bedroom. "We don't want to miss a thing."

"Well, who is this beautiful dressed-up lady?" we heard Dad exclaim as Mama sashayed into the dining room. She did indeed look as glamorous as a movie queen. A wide-brimmed hat was pulled down over one eye, making her seem mysterious and vampish. Her navy blue dress was transformed into an elegant gown by adding a strand of shimmering rhinestones. When she wrapped herself into a black cloth coat with a rabbit fur collar, she looked almost well endowed but not really fat. "Everybody gets dressed up for the last night of Corn Palace week, so here I am, world," Mama gayly announced. And so we left our little house on Edmunds Street and walked through the darkened streets until we again stood in the sparkling lights from the Corn Palace.

For a few hours we could forget we were poor and pretend that we were rich.

"We were going to be packed into these streets like sardines," Mama said, trying to keep the jostling crowd from stepping on us. "And keep your mouths shut because they're beginning to throw confetti by the bagsful.

We weaved our way, in, out and under until we came to a standstill in front of Chris' Inn, an eating place famous for hamburger, draught beer and hot popcorn. "I can't go any farther," Mama groaned. "My feet are killing me."

She was lucky to find an empty booth that had just been vacated. "Do you kids want a hamburger or do you want to spend your nickels on the little train?"

Neeney, brother Bobby and I chose the train ride and left, with Mama's warning ringing in our ears. "Stick together and when you're done, come right back over here. Now scoot."

She misjudged the size of the crowds pushing three small children around, ages four, five and six. Within a few minutes I lost my grip on my brother's hand and found myself being pushed along in a melee of arms and legs attached to faceless people. "Mama, Mama," I cried, but no one heard or paid any attention to a little girl who was lost.

Somewhere along the way I found a space to get un-

Crowds watch street attraction at Corn Palace in 1927

tangled from the strangers, next to the tilt-a-whirl that I was always afraid of. Everyone was having the time of their lives but me. "Maybe if I stay in one spot, Mama will find me," I hoped.

"Hey, little girl, are you lost?" I heard a voice that I thought would guide me back to Mama. But when I looked up, there was a grizzled old man reeking of alcohol. "No, I'm not lost," I angrily shouted, and escaped back into the crowd so he wouldn't bother me anymore.

By this time I was so panic stricken I didn't know which way to turn but I knew I would have to make someone listen to me and not be too bashful to ask for help.

Finally I spied a man sitting in a high ticket booth in front of a tent that had pictures of dancing girls painted on a soiled canvas. He was selling tickets so I waited until he wasn't busy, then quickly asked, "Can you tell me which way is the Corn Palace?" I knew that I lived almost directly west of there. Then I could find my way.

He looked down at me, unconcerned, a cigaret dangling from his lower lip, but he smiled, "Listen, little girl, you're way down here on First Street, five blocks south of the Corn Palace. You just go over there by that store, then walk straight north, and stay close to the buildings. Good luck, kid."

I took the advice of the carnival man and inched my way along this unfamiliar part of the street, hoping to find my way home. I didn't even glance at the rides, the cotton-candy stands, or the Kewpie dolls and balloons that now seemed meaningless.

Always watching above the heads and shoulders of the moving throng, I finally saw the glowing lights of the Corn Palace (like a lighthouse in a storm) and I knew I was close to home and Mama.

The hour was growing late and the night air was becoming cold when I walked west on seventh street. I wrapped my sweater a little tighter around my shaking body to keep my teeth from chattering. The street was becoming darker, the bushes along the sidewalk reminding me of monsters that roamed during the witching hour. I was getting scared but tried not to cry. "Big girls don't cry," I told myself.

Suddenly from out of the shadows I saw two figures approaching and I could hear arguing. When they appeared under the streetlight, my heart rejoiced. It was Mama and Dad. I couldn't hold back the tears. I ran toward them as fast as my legs could carry me.

Dad lifted me up into his arms and hugged me. He told me how worried everyone was and how they all had searched the Midway for me. Mama wasn't as sympathetic at the moment. She tried to hide her concern. "Do you know that you ruined the whole evening for everyone? I should give you a good spanking."

"Now, Mother," Dad soothed. "It's all over and I'm glad that she's safe and sound. Kitty Cat is only five years old." "Well, that's the last time I'll ever take a bunch of kids up town during Corn Palace week," Mama promised, with a tired yawn. "Let's get home and get some sleep. I'm worn out."

I was the happiest little girl in the world when I crawled into the bed beside my sleeping sister. As I snuggled up to the warmth of her body, I soon felt drowsy and lapsed into a deep slumber. The "Sandman" took me away to the land of nod where the nightmare of being lost was erased. I knew that in the days ahead the story about me getting lost would be repeated by Mama to our relatives and friends, or whoever visited us.

Corn Palace, Story II

The annual Corn Palace festival, an annual harvest event, was soon forgotten but remembered again each fall.

After we moved from North Edmunds to West Fourth Street, the distance of about sixteen blocks was just too far to walk and there was no extra money for such foolishness. It wasn't until we lived on the south side of town that our interest was renewed in the Corn Palace. From our house on the hill we could see the ferris wheels turning in the sunlight above the canvas tops of the merry-go-rounds and the tent shows.

"You kids don't have to tag along behind me anymore," Mama said. "You're all old enough to go by yourselves. But remember, the nickels are going to be few and far between. I hope the boys can find jobs on the Midway, since school will be excused every afternoon." "We don't need a lot of money," I told her, optimistically. "The best things are free. I read in the paper that the Mitchell band will play for all of the street acts." During those years a wooden platform was constructed at three sites along Main Street to provide free entertainment. "Oh, I can hardly wait till Monday when the first show begins at 12:30 sharp," I exclaimed.

The walk home from school was made very quickly by all of us and the neighborhood kids. Excitement crackled in the air. "I'm not even stopping to eat dinner," brother Bobby shouted as he raced on ahead of us. "See you guys on the Midway!"

By the time Neeney and I reached the first block on South Main the streets were already jammed with people. There were the old timers dressed in their Sunday best, trying to hold their ground against the pushing and shoving youngsters. Young couples leaned together with arms entwined, whispering sweet nothings to each other. Silly cowboy hats with balls of fringe were perched on their heads. Every young miss felt that she had to have a date for the week's festivities.

"We won't be able to see," I told Neeney, as I tried to keep track of her. She was searching for an open space. "Why don't you kids look where you're going?" a plump lady angrily shouted when we squeezed her feathered Kewpie doll into her face.

"Here's a good spot," sister finally called, and I climbed around a lanky man holding a youngster on his shoulders.

"We should have come earlier," I complained, feeling the foot of the little boy resting on my head.

"Why can't they start on time?" the restless natives grumbled as the scheduled time slipped by with no entertainers in sight. The Mitchell band continued to play marches as the people patiently waited near the high wooden platform in the noon-day sun.

"Here they come now." The message spread through the crowd. An energetic band of acrobats bounded onto the stage, wearing spangled tights that revealed every curve or bulge of their athletic bodies. (Some of the onlookers responded with shrill whistles and a few hubba, hubbas, as they ogled the curvacious females.)

"Oohs and ahs" escaped the audience as the back bends, cartwheels, hand stands and other pretzel-like acrobatics were performed before the transfixed street audience.

The hand clapping and whistles of applause were deafening. The crowd appreciated the free show that had now ended. It was time to tour the Midway, to see what strange and unusual sights awaited us, urged on by the Carnies who viewed us all as pigeons.

"You kids can't go into that side-show," one of our older brothers told us, when we paused in front of a gaudy tent. "That's a hoochie coochie place where the women hardly wear any clothes. They do a dance called the shimmy."

"How do you know?" we girls asked, staring at the pictures of buxom women, garishly painted on the canvas that rose and fell in the wind. "I heard some of the boys talking about it in school," he answered. "We have to be eighteen before we are allowed to buy a ticket. And only men are allowed to see that kind of stuff."

"I'd sure like to be a mouse in a corner during one of those shows." I winked at my sister and we giggled.

During the Thirties the Corn Palace Midway had more of a variety to offer than today. Along with the professional acts, hired for the entire week, there was also local talent able to sing and dance, or present novelty numbers.

Among these Mitchellites was Les Montgomery, whom I remember singing "Should I?" Maxine Fixmer and Mary Lou Bergeson delighted their audiences with acrobatic routines.

The rare whistling abilities of Lila Ruth Drenkow and

Free street attraction near Corn Palace, taken in 1931

Mrs. Myrtle Stolt Kaponin's voice added a touch of culture with her lovely singing of arias from operas.

My favorite entertainers were the beautiful little Danforth Sisters, June and Carol, who tap danced and sang to the music of the Mitchell band.

The dark-haired, blue-eyed girls, daughters of a judge, were admired and envied by some of us young ladies whose dreams were to be stars on the main street stages.

I often wished that I was in their shoes when they danced in front of the footlights, bathed in the adulation showered upon them.

"Aren't they darling?" "Just too cute for words," "They're just living dolls." These were some of the compliments coming from the bystanders.

"They should be good. They've been taking singing and dancing lessons for years, and their folks can afford to buy all the costumes and expensive tap shoes," I said half aloud to my sister, hoping some of their admirers would hear.

My jealous remarks fell on deaf ears and silence prevailed when the two dimpled darlings cuddled up to the microphone and sang "Rendezvous With A Dream" in clear, sweet notes, like song birds.

I yearned to dress just once in one of their many costumes, like the Hawaiian grass skirts and leis or the satin and rhinestone trimmed tuxedoes with top hats. I would have given anything for a pair of tap shoes adorned with taffeta bows.

"Some day these people will come to see me when I am famous," I dreamed. "I'll be rich and beautiful and somebody—not just a poor little girl who lives in a small town."

"Let's get out of here and head up to the north end of Main Street," said my sister, elbowing me. "We don't want to miss the sway pole act."

Watching some daring young man or woman in a high, dangerous act always made me fearful for them.

These human flies found the Corn Palace Midway one of the best places in the country to display their unique, spine chilling feats. I don't know how many accidents have occurred during the years but I know of one death when a broken trapeze let a man plunge to his death on the pavement below.

In the flexible pole act which we watched, Johnny Swaypole pushed his luck to the limit. From his lofty perch he paralyzed the onlookers by hanging from his nose to his toes while the band played a waltz.

Corn Palace (picture taken in 1939)

All too soon the free show was over and the crowd relaxed and mingled around the Corn Palace, admiring the decorations on the building. About to begin inside was a star-studded stage show that boasted some of the big names in show business. Some came from the far corners of the world.

"There's Paul Whiteman," I told my little sister, pointing to a picture of the famed band leader, in a glass enclosure beneath the marquee.

"I bet Mama would love to hear him. She always listens to him on that 'Chesterfield' program over the radio."

"I wouldn't go in there if they paid me," Neeney answered, with hardly a glance at the attractions. "Those shows are for old people who can't do anything else."

"Let's go back down the street and find that freak show where there's a lady that is half alligator. I'm going to spend one of my dimes to see her."

"Hurree, hurree, hurree, step right up ladies and gentlemen, boys and girls, and see the freaks that we have gathered from all over the world." We listened gullibly as the carnival barker coaxed the crowd of hesitant people to "step in a little bit closer."

Pointing to a picture of a gigantic ape-like man, uprooting trees in a jungle on the front of the canvas tent, he proclaimed, "This is the wild man from Borneo, captured and brought back alive. He can tear a man apart with his bare hands. . . . But don't worry. He is chained to the inside of a steel cage. . . . He walks, he talks, he's almost human, and has hair on his belly. You won't believe what you see."

"And on my left," he pointed his cane at "Gilda," who was supposed to be half woman and half alligator. "You will shiver and shake when you see her devour raw fish and slither across the floor."

By this time our curiosity was really aroused and we were convinced that we were about to see something wonderful, despite the hecklers who told the barker that his show was just a fake.

Challenging them and saying he would return their money if they weren't satisfied, the barker insisted "Gilda" was real. "I wouldn't trust you as far as I could throw a bull by the tail," one man told him. By this time the barker was hoping the unbelievers would leave, and let the suckers stay.

"Do you still wanna go in?" Neeney asked me, as we studied the pictures of a three-headed boy, and the "man who was turning to stone." "O.K.," I finally agreed, untying the corner of my handkerchief where I kept my nickels and dimes. "This may be our only chance to see some real live freaks."

The minute we walked into the tent we realized that we had indeed been taken for suckers.

"Robert the Ponyboy" was nothing more than a "double-jointed cripple" who walked on his hands and knees. The "three-headed baby" looked exactly like a jar of pickled pigs feet. The alligator woman, "Gilda" was an ugly woman with some skin disease that made her appear dried out and scaly, like a snake.

"I bet that's the man who is turning to stone," another onlooker cried as he pointed to a young boy lying on a sheet-covered couch. He was a skeleton, skin and bones, and what was left of his hard-as-a-rock body was not the muscular adonis pictured out front.

"These people aren't freaks. They're only persons with severe handicaps. They are more to be pitied than anything else," a sympathetic woman told the rest of us. "There should be a law against the exploitation of these poor people. We are just as much to blame for coming in here to gawk at them."

By this time, I was feeling sorry for such misfits who should have been in a hospital instead of in a drafty, dirty tent.

"We haven't seen the wild man from Borneo yet," Neeney insisted, when I wanted to leave. "He's crouched over there in the corner of that cage. I'm not afraid of him," and she walked right up to the steel bars. "Boo!" she cried, then waited for his reaction. The animal-like creature made a leap towards my little sister. I was scared to death that she would be clawed to bits. Maybe this freak is the real thing, I thought.

"But nothing happened," Neeney stood her ground and out-stared the wild-eyed creature who tried to look ferocious beneath his long hair that hung in matted strings around his face. Still playing the role of a savage beast, he jumped to the ground and crawled into a corner where he grabbed a headless chicken and proceeded to chew on the blood-stained bird.

"See," sister Neeney boasted, "he is scared of me, but he gets paid to act wild."

I had had enough excitement for one day and suggested that we spend the rest of our money either for some cotton candy, hot dog or a candy apple.

Dad had promised that he would give us a few extra nickels from the tips that he earned "parking cars" on the side streets.

There wasn't a day that we missed on the Midway, rain, shine, or snow.

Many times a drizzling October rain sent the fun seekers running for shelter beneath the tents and canopies along the Main Street. I remember at rare times snowflakes falling, transforming the Midway into a winter wonderland. It didn't stop the children from riding the real live ponies through mounds of slush and dirty straw. We made it to the Corn Palace festival, year after year.

Although it was a glorious event in the daylight, it became more magical at night, when the lights from the Midway glowed in a giant kaleidoscope.

Above the noise of the rides, music and ballyhoo of the carnival barkers, the loudspeakers advertising the picture show at the Roxy Theatre echoed in vibrating tones. Who could resist seeing an adults only movie, starring Hedy Lamar in "Ecstasy." Some of the nude scenes were the talk of the town and were considered obscene then. Today that same movie would probably be rated family entertainment.

So were the hoochie coochie shows that started when the sun went down. They were considered vulgar and hence not fit for viewing. These tantalizing girlie shows were often asked to leave town before the festival was over. "Indecent and immoral" was the label attached to this form of entertainment by some of the local church groups.

Still the shows drew a good share of the town's populace, as might be expected. Peep shows that were staged out front on a high wooden platform were popular. Like moths drawn to a flame, we kids hurried to the south end of the Midway when we heard the sounds of drums and the twang of Hawaiian guitars coming from one of the tents.

The music sounded beautiful to me. I recognized the song, "Sweet Leilani" from a movie. I noticed that most of the people pretended to keep a discreet distance from a "hula" show but the barker egged them on, especially the men, encouraging them to move in a little closer to the dark-skinned beauties.

411

"Come on, boys," he would exhort. "These little ladies don't bite. They just want to entertain you for only a tenth part of a dollar. Just get your hands out of your pockets and step inside and I guarantee, you will gaze upon your own little 'missus' in a different light." All the men looked sheepish but they peeked at the brazen hussies.

"Tell you what I'm going to do. I'm going to have Jackie, Billie, and Bobbie Jo do a little number right here on this very stage, and if they can't convince you to see the rest of the show, well then, you're a cold bunch."

"How come they have boys' names," Neeney asked our brother, who was all eyes. "All famous stars change their names," he replied, not glancing away from the swaying bodies of the natives from the islands. "If you look, you will go blind," someone joked in the crowd. "I'll chance one eye," a fat man laughed, covering an eye with a beefy hand.

As for me, I thought the imported girls were pretty, despite the heavy mascara that made them look artificial. Their costumes were only a bra and fringed skirt made out of something like cellophane that hugged their well-rounded hips. Paper leis of pink, blue and green dangled from their necks and over their ample bosoms. Clinging to their clouds of dark, wavy hair were large paper orchids in exotic colors.

Long fingernails that were painted red matched the lipstick that glistened on sultry lips. "How could anything so pretty be called naughty?" I thought, looking around at the thinning crowd who were leaving, afraid that they would be seen by some of the prudish citizens.

It was time for us kids to wander on down the street to see what else was free. We found it on the next block when we were hemmed in by a crowd of men and boys with a few sprinkles of the fairer sex. They were arguing with the barker of the wrestling and boxing tent show. "This is what I want to see," Neeney said, pushing herself up front—"a good fight." I reluctantly followed her, although I didn't have the stomach to watch any bloodshed.

"Aren't those brutes ugly?" I heard a lady exclaim. "Look at those flattened noses and twisted ears." "Those are called cauliflower ears," a bystander told her. "Why do they want to ruin their looks for a few bucks?" the lady asked. I also wondered as I peered up into the wretched looking faces of the carnies who boxed or wrestled all comers.

"You hay shakers are all yellow," the muscle-bound pugi-

Throngs on Mitchell Main Street (picture taken in 1920's)

list declared in a raspy voice. Isn't there a man out there who will try to last a round with one of my boys?" This remark inflamed some of the farm boys, who lashed back with verbal abuse at the wrestlers who were flexing their bulging bisceps and dancing on the platform. "I wouldn't want to jump into that ring with one of those hairy apes," someone said. "I wonder who is going to be crazy enough to do it." They turned and looked at each other.

Finally, from out of the crowd, a young man accepted the challenge and was pushed up onto the platform by the strong arms of his friends. I compared him to David going into combat with Goliath. "Don't worry," Neeney said. "He won't get hurt. It's a 'put on'." I still wasn't convinced that there wasn't likely to be any broken bones or gouged eyes.

Fake or not, I did manage to see one wrestling match during my lifetime and I didn't enjoy it.

There were many young men from these parts who were willing to lock horns with the carnival people and were admired by their many fans who spurred them on. A few of them were Marion Haines, Dick Hayes and Frank Bohr of Mitchell, and the well-known Joe Shelley of Parkston.

For those who liked to gamble, there were numerous stands. Many folks, including most of the lawmen, called them "gyp joints" and warned the local people not to be persuaded to play. Some stands were shut down before the week's end. Carnival people weren't considered trustworthy and their tarnished image hasn't improved over the years. "Never give a sucker an even break," was a well known phrase attributed to the carnies.

Yet we kids (too dumb to know better), continued to lay our money down on some of the games and hoped to win, despite the odds.

"I bet I can knock every one of those milk bottles down with three balls," Neeney boasted to the bystanders, who already knew about her skill at softball. She was a "dead eye Dick." Still the elusive prize of a stuffed teddy bear was not within her reach. She often became angry at the proprietors and told them that they were crooks.

My luck was usually as bad as my sister's, and no matter how hard I tried throwing darts, pulling strings, dipping into tanks of water or trying to maneuver the crank on the steam shovel, I couldn't win a prize. The best I could do was take a small prize such as a celluloid button that read "Confucius Says." I would have given anything to own one of the dimpled faced Kewpie dolls that stood on the top shelf, with its pink feathers.

Our brothers and other macho males could usually be found playing the machines in the Penny Arcade. This was also an early day pornography shop, where nudies of women could be purchased from coin operated boxes. The pictures were sometimes discarded on the paper-littered streets, only to be picked up by the younger children who gazed in curiosity at the forbidden art.

"I wonder if that Gypsy woman can really tell about the future. I'd sure like to know what I'm going to be when I grow up," I told a girl friend when we stopped at a safe distance from the Gypsy's tent. Squatting on a low stool in front of a moon and star-painted stand, the fortune teller babbled to the passing crowd in a foreign sounding voice, "Let the Gypsy tell your fortune, only twenty-five cents."

The black-eyed, dark-skinned lady was in a flowing purple robe, decorated with bangles and beads that sparkled. Dangling from her wrists were bracelets of silver and gold that matched the hooped earrings in her pierced ears. Shining black hair cascaded around shoulders wrapped in a pink flowered shawl. I thought she was pretty and unlike any of the women I had seen.

She turned and gazed at us with her smoldering, hypnotic eyes and then smiled to reveal her perfect white teeth. "Come here, little girls. I'll tell your fortune for free. Don't be afraid. I won't hurt you."

As if in a trance, we accepted her invitation and walked into another world behind the fortune teller. There were only a few chairs and a small table where a deck of cards was spread into a semi-circle. I was expecting to see a glowing crystal ball and a Persian carpet, but there was nothing like that there.

The Gypsy motioned for us to sit down and then took the hand of my friend and began to trace the lines on her outstretched palm.

"Oh my!" she said softly, "you have a great life line. You're going to live a very long time." Following along another shorter line, she gasped, "Oh no! I see many heartbreaks in your love life." My little friend giggled. "But I see you're going to serve humanity. Perhaps you will be a teacher, a nurse or even a doctor."

Then she clasped my hand firmly in her own and began

to trace softly across the criss-crossed lines of my palm. It tickled.

"My little one," she exclaimed, "I see for you a great future. Do you know that you're going to move away from this town and become very rich and famous some day? Your palm reveals that you are very creative. Perhaps you will be a musician."

"Gee, that's nice," I thought, wanting very much to believe the gypsy who could predict my future. Yet I knew there wasn't much likelihood of me ever being able to attain success. I lacked confidence.

"That's all I can tell you now, but I hope all your dreams come true," the exotic lady said. "Tell your family and friends to stop by and I'll tell their fortune." I reached into my pocket and handed a dime to the soothsayer who made me feel happy, if only for a day.

"Do you believe what she told us?" my friend asked, when we walked away from the Midway and headed for home.

"No, I guess not. She's just something to amuse us," I laughed. Yet I secretly wished that some day the fortune teller's predictions would come true. I wanted to believe her.

I couldn't begin to list the many shows and events along the seven blocks of Main Street that I remember. For me it all began about 50 years ago and there are enough stories to fill books.

For many folks living here, Corn Palace week was an important part of their lives and for some it meant much needed added income.

I have seen many changes over the years from the time I was a wide-eyed little girl chewing on a candy apple until today when I only attend the main Corn Palace show, and don't find the Midway interesting any more. For me, the magic and make-believe of the Midway has faded into the mists of yesterday.

When I look back at those fun-filled days of the harvest festival, I also remember the melancholy that I experienced when the festivities came to a close. It was the saddest time of the year.

"Don't forget to set the alarm clock so we can get up at six o'clock," my brother reminded Dad, when they arrived home around midnight, the last Saturday night of Corn Palace week. "Don't worry," Dad shouted out from behind his bedroom door, "we will be there before the rooster crows." It was a race between the town kids to be the first ones on the deserted Midway to search for lost or discarded items.

"We're going, too," Neeney whispered to me in the darkness of our room. "We might as well have some of the money or whatever stuff the boys bring home. When you hear the pots and pans rattle in the morning you better get out of bed, fast." "Do you think girls do that sort of thing?" I sleepily asked her. "Well, I'm going to, whether you go along or not." "O.K., I'll go," I promised, and rolled over against the wall.

Our brothers weren't too enthusiastic about two little sisters following them down the hill the next morning but we kept a safe distance from them. Clutched in our hands were brown paper bags.

By the time we reached the south end of Main Street a pink and gold sunrise was coming. The town was sleeping and in need of a rest after six days of celebrating. A few ragged awnings on the store fronts were "flapping" in the morning breeze. Two stray dogs barked at us from an alley where they too were rummaging in the over-flowing garbage cans.

"I think we won't be noticed," Neeney laughed. "The town looks pretty dead. I don't see any other kids yet. I'm heading for the rolo plane first. People lose money from their pockets when they ride that thing." We raced past our brothers who had stopped to investigate some empty boxes near a half dismantled bingo stand.

"Hey, you kids, why don't cha look where you're going," one of the town drunks said in slurred speech when we bumped into him sitting on the curb near the gutter. "You jus' about spilled my (hic) wine." "Don't you ever get filled up?" my sister asked him impertinently. Corn Palace week was an excuse for the local winos to imbibe.

Most of the swings, benches and rides were already stripped. Only the steel skeletons stood silhouetted against the sky.

"Look what I found—a quarter," my sister gleefully shouted, kneeling beneath the stripped-down rollo plane. I'll bet there's a lot more. Did you find anything yet?" she asked.

By this time the town began to stir and people came to probe and pick their way through the debris laden streets. Strewn from gutter to gutter were empty popcorn boxes, crumpled and dirty paper leis, felt banners, cotton candy, half eaten candy apples, tiny bits of confetti, and paper programs from the Corn Palace show, marked with dirty footprints. I stood and watched the accumulated rubbish being swept and shoveled into trash piles by the hard-working employes of the street department.

"Hey, wait a minute," I asked one of the men, as I stepped in front of his straw broom. "Can I have that Kewpie doll lying there?"

"There isn't much left of it," he remarked. "It's really been battered and most of the feathers are gone." He held it up for me to see and no doubt wondered why I wanted it.

"I grabbed the celluloid doll, that was attached to a broken cane, and was thrilled to have her even though her once pretty face had been pushed in and one arm dangled. Carefully I placed the half nude doll into my grocery sack and walked away from the curious street sweepers. I had saved another orphan doll from the dump ground.

The late autumn sun was directly above us when we decided to call it a day and hurry home with our assortment of second-hand souvenirs from the Corn Palace. Taking one last look at Main Street where the "Carnies" were dismantling the last of the rides and tents, I felt a twinge of sorrow and wished that the sounds of music and laughter could linger forever.

"You kids sure made a haul," grinned Mama, picking up a damaged statue of an elephant. "I'll put him on top of the organ beside the black panther lamp."

The trinkets, plaster of Paris statues, emblems, balloons and stuffed toys were scattered across the dining room table like a pirate's booty. The coins and a few dollar bills were neatly stacked.

By nightfall the walls of the bedrooms were cluttered with Corn Palace memorabilia, placed there by the loving hands of children who didn't mind taking the cast offs from the people on the other side of the tracks.

My beloved Kewpie doll was put on my pillow where I also laid my sleepy head and dreamed of a rhinestoned carousel in a pink cotton candy sky.

Home, Sweet Home

"Be it ever so humble, there is no place like home," is a song we used to sing. I believe it represents the feelings of most people when they remember their childhood, even during the depression years.

Most of my childhood was spent living in substandard housing, where the roofs leaked and the "bathroom" facilities were outdoors. Sometimes a few months free rent was given to us by landlords, providing that Mama and Dad reinforced the sagging foundations, patched up porches and cracked walls. Dad was a house painter, so the leftover paint and muresco from his paint jobs were mixed together to create a new color for both the interior and exteriors of our abode.

I loved to watch Dad spread on a coat of muresco, which is a water paint, on plaster walls and then take a sponge, dip it in a different color, and create a feathered design. I thought it looked beautiful and it also concealed the zig-zagging cracks. On occasion, a generous landlord would get us a roll of tar paper and a few shingles to patch a hole in the roof. This only lasted until a severe storm hit, when the pots and pans had to be hurriedly placed below the leaking ceiling. The ugly water spots left a rusty stain that couldn't be removed.

Although we moved more times than I can remember, it was around on the edges of town, usually where the sidewalks stopped far from our door. I yearned for a concrete walk, where I could pull my wagon easily, push a doll buggy or play "hop scotch." Only a well-worn path circled our premises, which were always muddy after a summer shower.

Mitchell had its share of shanty neighborhoods, where the poor folks lived, many near the railroad property or on the outer fringes of town. Yet, there were many lovely homes and apartment buildings, where the more prosperous people lived. These stately homes of brick, masonry, and wood have weathered the years and many are just as beautiful today. We kids knew where the "rich people" lived, as we walked past their places on our way to school and up town. Picking out our favorite house was something we often made a game of, wishing some day it would become ours.

The Spangler mansion, across the street, north from the court house, was my dream home. It reminded me of a colonial manor on a southern plantation. The magnificent white columns and arched portals, the patios and verandas gave it an air of aristocracy.

Walking through the darkened streets at night, we also looked longingly at the better homes along the tree-lined avenues. As the soft glow from the lamps and chandeliers flowed through the arched doors and picture windows, a feeling of envy filled my soul and I would compare this with our standard of living. I continued to dream of a mansion on a hill surrounded by weeping willow trees and lilac bushes swaying in the soft breezes of a spring morning.

Yet we loved our own house and were happy when it came into view after walking many blocks through the cold, dark night. As we entered the front door, the wave of warmth from the pot-bellied stove greeted us. The flame always shining through the isinglass door, threw shimmering shadows on the walls and linoleum floor. It was good to be home again, no matter how humble home was.

My favorite "southern style" mansion is still standing, across the street from the court house. It hasn't lost any of its grandeur. Draisey Real Estate Company now owns it.

Many of the other older homes have been moved or razed and are being replaced by parking lots or shopping centers. Others have been remodeled with new siding and paneling to make them look new again. I am glad to see that so many are being reclaimed again by householders who liked the style and way of life that were held in high esteem.

The house where I was born was on North Edmunds, adjacent to a cement plant, has been demolished. A vacant lot next to a railroad track leaves no visible signs of our second home on West Fourth Street.

My beloved "house on the hill" still stands at 522 South Main, and it keeps calling me back. The neighborhood has changed, perhaps for the better, but the Milwaukee Railroad is still only a block away. The roundhouse pond, which served as our recreation area during both summer and winter months, is now covered by an asphalt bicycle trail. The once muddy and dusty streets are being rebuilt with pavement and curbing. New trees and shrubbery have replaced the Russian olive trees that used to fill the hillside and creek bottoms.

I paid a visit to my childhood home this past summer and it was like walking back into the pages of time. Although the exterior is almost the same, with the exception of some new windows and doors, I was anxious to view the interior. The young married tenants, new owners, were kind enough to allow me this privilege. They proved to be interested in the history of this old home. I don't know who built the house, only the name of the owners during the depression years. We rented it from a Jones family.

A flood of nostalgia engulfed me as I stepped from the remodled back porch into the kitchen. It looked about the same with its hardwood floors and woodwork that I remember scrubbing clean when I was a young girl. I mentally placed our old Monarch range, kitchen table and chairs in their places. The sounds and smells of soup bubbling in the kettle on the wood-burning stove gave me a happy remembrance.

I crossed over into a spacious, paneled family room, which served as a bedroom and living room for our large family. Those floors, now covered with plush carpeting, once saw the fun and laughter of couples dancing to a fiddle and banjo music, perhaps in a square dance.

The bedroom which served as my parents' hide-away from the cares of the day, is now a beautifully paneled den. Many problems of the depression were discussed within those walls, sometimes in laughter, and other times in anger or despair. Thoughts of cold winter winds buffeting the storm windows again took me back to my childhood. As I searched the room, I felt there was something missing. Why did I expect things to be the same after forty years? It was the wide bay window that I finally realized was gone—replaced with a new wall and paneling. That old window served as our lookout to watch the neighbors, people passing by, or an approaching dust storm, or to admire a rainbow after a summer's shower.

After inspecting the downstairs, I asked to see the second floor, where my old bedroom was located. As we stepped into the darkened hallway, I placed my hand on the railing of my familiar staircase, where my sister and I played games and slid down the mahogany banister. A light turned on revealed the polished lustre of its now antique veneer. How many times did we kids climb those stairs sleepily in the evening and noisily clatter back down in the morning? I could almost hear Mama scolding us for making so much noise.

After ascending the stairs and spending a few minutes in the bedrooms, which are intact with the same doors and woodwork, I felt homesick pangs and wished I could turn back the hands of time and share once more this household with my brothers, sisters, Mama and Dad.

With a lump in my throat and a few threatening tears,

I slowly walked out of the house and back into the sunlight. The woman living there questioned me about the years I had spent on the premises. I pointed to the spot where the old cement cistern was located near the back porch. I described the Russian olive trees that grew around the house and into the alley, and told them of the neighbor kids who shared in our fun and games in the spacious yard; the dust and snowstorms that practically shook the foundations of the aging brown house. I mentioned the time-weahered front porch, with its carved corner posts and latticed and spindled railing. I sat here for hours in the noonday sun, reading a book.

My house guards the precious memories of a past generation, in beauty and dignity. I hope this house continues to offer the comfort and pleasure to other families that it did for us. Liwe an old friend, I plan to stop by now and then to relive the joys and sorrows of our yesterdays.

Working For Armour's

There isn't much to tell about my Junior and Senior High school days, because when I think about that time and place I still feel the rejection that I experienced as a teenage girl.

Although I was bright and received good grades, I felt a sense of not belonging to the school society which was often snobbish. Popularity seemed to have priority. I realize now that my own insecurity and low opinion of my background played an important role in my decision to quit school and become a dropout.

"If it makes you that miserable, why don't you quit?" Mama told me when she sensed my unhappiness. "Look at me, I only went through the sixth grade and I'm no dummy. There are a lot of jobs around town that you can get without a high school education."

"I don't want to take care of any more kids or clean up other people's houses," I replied. "I want a nice clean job and decent pay."

"I hear that Armour's are hiring. Why don't you try over there," suggested Dad, who was always concerned about my problems.

Armour's was an industrial plant located on East Ash street arjacent to the Milwaukee Railroad.

Scores of Mitchellites were employed in egg breaking, butter wrapping, chicken plucking and cream buying. Many of our neighbors worked at the monotonous jobs.

I often saw them coming home after a day's toil. They always looked tired, had soiled uniforms from work with eggs and chickens. Some looked as though they were "dragged through a knot hole."

Yet the pay was above average compared with jobs around this small city where hand skills were more important than brains.

I looked out the kitchen window across the railroad tracks and focused my eyes on the sprawling Armour's plant. "I'm going to give it a try," I told my parents. "I'll go over there the first thing in the morning."

But a feeling of fear and anxiety came to me when I awoke and remembered my promise to find a job. I wanted to crawl back under the covers and stay there, but I realized that it was now or never. "Just think of all the pretty clothes I could buy from the catalogue," I reassured myself. I quickly got dressed and went downstairs for a piece of toast and a cup of coffee. Dad and Mama waved encouragement as I went down the footpath that crossed the roundhouse pond near the railroad tracks. With a hop, skip and a jump, I cleared the rails and found myself standing in the midst of trucks, employes and cackling hens.

"Go right over there near the creamery. That's the office," a brawny employe directed me, when I shyly asked the whereabouts of the employment office. I entered a large white-walled place where typists and bookkeepers were moving about, keeping records, time sheets and payrolls of the Chicago based company. I felt uncomfortable when they looked at me but tried to appear unconcerned. Maybe they think I'm too young; just a kid, I worried. I suppose they wonder why I'm not in school.

Finally a nice, well-groomed office girl came to my rescue, handing me the necessary papers for my application. I scanned the long lists of questions and felt embarrassed when I had to admit to minimal education.

While I sat nervously on a hard-backed chair, my application was scrutinized by an assistant manager who looked serious behind a pair of horn-rimmed glasses. I bet he has a good education, I thought.

"Everything looks fine to me," he finally said, with a pleasant smile. "Take this form to the superintendent of the creamery section, Al Davis. I'm sure he has a place for you in the print room. They come and go all the time."

I was hired immediately by a man dressed in white clothing from his cap to the well creased, spotless trousers.

"Get yourself a couple of white uniforms, some hair nets and a good pair of white rubber boots," he said. "It gets pretty damp in the print room where you're going to work. Be here at 8:00 in the morning. Your card will be on the rack next to the time clock." I heaved a sigh of relief. I was happy to be an employe of Amour's.

It wasn't easy to become adjusted to the rigid routine that awaited me during the first few weeks of employment. All newcomers were given the cold shoulder treatment by the other workers who acted as if they "ownd a piece of the rock." Many were afraid of losing their seniority to young people who flocked into Mitchell seeking the good pay (35 cents an hour) that was offered by Armour's.

Annual Christmas party. Employes of Armour Creamery. (Many Mitchell residents worked at various times for Armour.)

There was also a kind of caste system among the numerous departments where the office personnel were at the top of the totem pole. Following the supervisors and straw bosses were the print room employes such as test room girls, butter wrappers, churn boys and cream dumpers.

The egg breakers deserved a higher berth than the chicken pickers, who in my estimation, worked hardest for their pay.

There was an influx of humanity every morning as employes arrived like an army of ants, in cars, pickups, bicycles and on foot, dedicating their day's labor to "the company store." At that time there were no unions or a guaranteed minimum wage, no laws against health hazards. For most of them there was no choice. They were the low income people and needed this kind of work.

As for me, I was slowly emerging from my timidity and I learned to get along with my fellow employes. Most of us had something in common—we were all poor and under-educated. The better jobs went to the floor women who had a little high school education.

Sometimes authority gave some the "big head," or superior attitude, toward others. The women retaliated by calling them names when their backs were turned.

"That old bitch," was a common expression, expressed by

425

disgruntled women and girls, jealous of their superiors.

I tried my best to take orders and do my share, but I, too, sometimes rebelled at an imperious command, barked in a demeaning way, especially by the male "straw bosses."

"I wasn't hired to pick chickens," I protested one day when we were told to help out in that department during the rush season at Thanksgiving and Christmas. I don't feel like going over there among those smelly feathers, blood and entrails. I soon learned that being transferred to different departments was expected of an Armour employe.

"If you flirt a little with Dick or Elmer (the foremen) they will give you a soft job. . . . I notice the way all the guys give you the eye when you walk through the plant," Evelyn pointed out. She was a veteran who knew all about bosses, and who was stepping out, and what girl had a bad reputation.

"I'd give my eye teeth if I could get next to the new manager. He can put his shoes under my bed any time," one girl would say.

Romance never blossomed for me while I worked among the men and boys whom I thought were never going to make it anyhow and I didn't want to get stuck in what I felt was a "one horse town," and marry a local boy.

I had plans for the future. I was saving my money to buy pretty clothes and to own a good car. Some day my prince would come and carry me away from the other side of the tracks. I was only biding my time. Boy friends couldn't hold my interest for very long. Many of them rightfully called me fickle.

I'm sure I could write a book about Armour's and the area folks who were employed by them. They were the backbone of the working class.

This establishment which had its beginning many years ago closed its doors on June 2, 1968. Competition from the larger commercial plants wiped out a two million dollar annual payroll.

Somehow I deeply feel that this company should be commended for giving employment to so many, from truck drivers, churn boys, egg breakers, cream dumpers, butter wrappers, engineers and maintenance men, to test room employes and office personnel, including managers, assistants and office help. They played an important role in preserving the economy of Mitchell.

Chicken Pickers

The hardest workers of all Armour employes were those who labored in the chicken picking section. I didn't know how difficult it was until I did the work myself.

Some of the butter wrappers were recruited to help out in the chicken department during the rush seasons, like Thanksgiving and Christmas. It was also a good way to earn a larger pay check. But we younger girls got a taste of a dirty stomach-turning job. It took a lot of work and no special skill.

The chicken picking building was located between the creamery section and the egg buying station, where farmers sold their products. The cackling of the excited chickens could be heard for blocks and many tried to escape across the railroad tracks, only to be recaptured by a local chicken raiser and added to his own flock of barnyard fowl.

We were told not to wear anything fancy and to cover our hair with a bandana or scarf. Rubber boots and aprons were needed to keep us from getting saturated with water and blood.

I'll never forget the first time I walked into this slaughter house. The steamy, unpleasant odor of feathers and chicken droppings assailed my nostrils. "This is certainly no place to wear perfume," I joked to a co-worker, while a foreman led us to our spot below a revolving chain which had steel shackles. It reminded me of a medieval torture chamber.

The squawking chickens were handed through an open window by one man, while another worker hung them, struggling on a shackle. The next step was the killing. A worker holding a razor-sharp knife stabbed the chickens' throats while blood splattered. Each chicken was still only half dead.

While still kicking and flapping its wings, the fowl was then plunged into a tank of scalding hot water to loosen the feathers. As they emerged, each employe grabbed one to pluck. Small washers were on each shackle for a tally, to determine the number cleaned. We were told that a worker must pick her share. So fingers flew fast, stripping the birds of all feathers, including the wing and pin feathers, which often cut hands and fingers. A plucker also had to be careful not to bruise or tear the skin of the poultry, which was to be labled "top grade."

427

At first the shifts of sometimes ten-hour days passed fairly quickly. Later it became sheer misery to work and walk with the revolving chain around the feather-littered floor. As I looked into the faces of some of the older women, who were approaching middle age, I felt sympathy for them. Their features bore the marks of the tiresome work, with no future. There wouldn't even be any retirement benefits when they were too old to work. While having these mind-provoking thoughts, I wondered what I was doing there and thought that I should return to school. Would I be spending the rest of my life working on an assembly line?

Still, there was humor and jokes to tell when that long awaited rest period came, and all were given a coffee break of ten or fifteen minutes. The candy bars, sandwiches, fruit (and I suspect, a few shots of whiskey) were appreciated by the weary employes.

The younger, prettier girls rushed to the rest rooms to study themselves in a faded mirror and refresh their make-up so as to look more presentable. They liked to flirt with the foreman or supervisors. This could earn them an easier job.

The head men who bossed the crews had worked their way up to their envied position; but many were resented. The old timers, who started their laboring days at Armour's during the twenties, sometimes didn't like the new help or the new foreman. Sometimes everyone wanted to be the boss.

To pacify the sometimes exhausted and frustrated workers, records were played, purchased by a committee to pick out the latest hits. The music was sometimes inaudible because of revolving, creaking chains, the barking of the foremen, or the endless cries of the poultry victims. But everyone did learn the music and lyrics to "Elmer's Tune," "South," and "Three Little Fishies," because they were played hundreds of times.

The backbone of the staff, who had themselves and families to support, took the hard monotonous work in stride; but they really didn't have much choice. The teenagers still wanted to have a good time after a long day of "pickin' chickens." There were many wedding, barn, house and road house dances to attend. It was the jitterbug age and the depression generation wanted a good time. After a night on the town, many didn't show up for the early morning shift; a few were miserable with hangovers. Most of the chronic absentees were eventually fired by the foremen. I'm sure just about half of the blue collared population of Mitchell who worked a stint at Armour's can relate to this account of activities there.

Not everyone could stand the grueling hours of hard work. Some lasted from a few hours to a day, at the most. It seemed like slave labor, but for the majority of the Armour employes, it was the only means of making a livelihood.

Armour's Truck Drivers

The canary yellow trucks with "Armour's" painted on the side panels, drove literally millions of miles to villages, towns, hamlets, farms and buying stations to purchase the products for the processing plant at Mitchell.

These trail blazers didn't drive on good roads. Many roads were muddy. The drivers were bitten by unfriendly farm dogs, changed flat tires, had blow-outs, and engine breakdowns. During rain storms and howling blizzards, the familiar trucks could be seen from dawn to dusk, and many times pulled into the plant late at night to unload their perishable cargo.

Some of the truck drivers were promoted to field men who checked on the outlying buying stations to make sure that only the top grades of poultry, eggs, and cream were being purchased. These men were very important to the Railroad Street plant.

Managers, assistant managers, and foremen were transferred from state to state. From their experience and seniority earned in the small plants, they received promotions to the larger plants in the more populated cities.

The office workers also had important positions—doing paper work for millions of hours stamped on the time cards and a payroll of two million paid yearly to the employes; keeping record of other expenditures, such as taxes and purchase of supplies. Armour Creameries played an important role in preserving the economy of Mitchell and the surrounding communities.

The hard-earned checks with the familiar Armour Creameries stamped across the top were cashed and quickly spent. Employes had no voice in deciding what their work was worth. There was no limit to the number of hours in a working day, and no time-and-a-half for extra hours.

Finally, in 1945, the employes won their battle to join a union, receive more pay and have better working conditions. There were also provisions for paid vacations of from two to four weeks, yet there were no retirement benefits for the workers at that time.

Hundreds of Mitchell residents embarked on their working careers at this plant. Many were fortunate enough to operate their own businesses in later years. Romances and marriages bloomed among the many young employes who decided that "two could live as cheaply as one." There were no rules to limit the number of employes from one household. (There were five from our family during World War II.)

I'm sure there are many former employes of Armour's who would just as soon forget that they worked at this kind of job during those depression times. Today, some are in the chips, so to speak. Others look back with pride and want to remember those days when they rose with the sun and worked till sunset. They are the ones who remained to earn those last pay checks to add to their nest eggs and increase their social security. One of my old friends, "Lillian," racked up thirty-two years there. She was a faithful employe until 1968, when the doors finally closed.

There were no gold watches or service pins, no plaques or recognition, no thanks from the multi-million dollar corporation, whose headquarters were in a Chicago skyscraper.

The plant, originally the Turner Creamery, closed all operations, June 2, 1968. Competition from the larger commercial plants was the main reason given for discontinuing production. The old building still stands at East Ash and Railroad Street and has been converted into a cheese factory.

While writing my reminiscences, I wanted to revisit the place where I was employed as a teenager. Armour Creameries is still visible on signs painted across the deteriorating building. The once busy office, where typewriters clacked and business machines buzzed, is deserted. High weeds, crumbling concrete, and boarded up windows are mute testimony to what was once a booming industry.

As I peered through a modern glass door of a remodeled structure being erected where the "print room" once stood, a workman invited me in to inspect the old creamery section where the revolving wooden churns once stood. I could almost see again the huge mounds of golden butter being transferred into the coolers to await processing.

Downstairs, I took note of the debris laden steps, broken machinery, pipes rusting, and deteriorating walls. This was where the millions of eggs were candled, broken, and shipped out as egg products; where countless pounds of condensed and dried milk were manufactured. The "No Smoking" sign was still intact on a wooden partition, where some long ago employes scribbled their names. I placed my hand on the circular stairway, with its paint chipped railing, and walked again in the footsteps of my past.

While I observed the now stilled work area, I thought I heard the sharp click of the time clock, which stood beneath the staircase. I could recall some of the names of the workers who checked in and out. Most of them are still living; others have passed on, to be remembered only by close friends and relatives.

End of the Depression

The Dirty Thirties will long be remembered as the decade when the Great Depression spread its economic devastation throughout the entire world, when many states suffered dust storms and crop failures; when many caught the helping hand of the government.

History books will record the benefit of Works Progress Administration (WPA) which gave jobs to millions of unemployed, the drought and the dust storms which stripped the soil and vegetation from the land, the construction of roads and highways, buildings, schools, dams, lakes and parks through WPA or PWA. The greatest still standing memorial to that time is the majestic groves of trees that stand across the midwest. They grew from the sun-parched soil as tiny seedlings, planted by WPA employes and farmers.

Our family was slowly emerging from the distressed economy, along with everyone else, during the early 1940's.

We could almost see the light at the end of the tunnel. Happy days were coming again.

There was also an uneasy feeling of suspicion and hatred for a dictator in Germany who was in the headlines of our newspaper. Everyone was discussing Adolph Hitler and wondered why he wanted more territory and why he wanted to kill and destroy innocent people, especially Jews, who only desired to live in peace.

"I can honestly say I'm ashamed of being a German," confessed Mama, when we discussed the war in Europe that finally spread to all the world.

"Why doesn't the United States do something about it?" we children questioned. "Hitler's going to kill everybody if he isn't stopped." No one seemed to have the answer.

Although I was concerned about this mad man whose followers saluted him with "heil, Hitler," my world was still wrapped around such ideas as buying the latest fashions in clothing, my boy friends and my secret desire to be a movie star. My friends made the prediction that I would become famous some day.

I was reluctant about going to work at Armour's on the swing shift one night, but knew if I didn't show up that I would be fired. I hated the turkey pools where the over-sized birds had to be prepared for the Christmas holidays. Armour's were proud of their top graded turkeys that were shipped to all parts of the United States. I tried to forget the smells and the discomfort of the damp building where the turkeys were picked as I worked that night.

The next afternoon, Sunday, December 7, 1941, the news came over the radio that Pearl Harbor had been bombed by the Japanese. The United States was at war.

Depression Slanguage

Full of applesauce
Full of beans
In a pig's eye
Blacker than the ace of spades
Doesn't amount to a hill of beans
Not worth his salt
Jumping from the frying pan into the fire
It's Greek to me
Raked over the coals
Scarcer than hen's teeth
Harder than finding a needle in a haystack
Cool as a cucumber
Smooth as a pickerel
Green as grass
Dibs (wanting a share)
Knock your block off
A fool and his money are soon parted
Blinder than a bat
Liar, liar, pants on fire
Rubber neck
Chewing the fat
Red as a beet
White as a sheet

Depression Talk

Salt it down
Till the cows come home
Painting the town red
Homely as a mud fence
Happy as a lark
Stuck up
Going high hat
Mean as the devil
Crepe hanger
Hunky dory
Slower than molasses in January
Tight as a drum
Loose as a goose
Wild as a gypsy
Hotter than a pistol
Flat as a pancake
Couldn't hit the broad side of a barn
Too lazy to work, too honest to steal
Hot ginger and dynamite
Full of pee and vinegar
Licked-off butter bread
Don't have a pot or a window to throw it out of
Wish in one hand and spit in other
Red as a spanked baby's butt
More fun than a barrel of monkeys
Kicked the can
Woudn't be found dead
Laugh before breakfast, cry before supper
Ornery as they come
Fishy eyed
Bad apple in every barrel
Strong as an ox
Dumb as an ox
Hungry as a bear
I could eat a horse
Sly as a fox
Yellow belly
Hot under the collar
Get under the skin
Tan your hide
Tattle tale, tattle tale, hanging on a bull's tail
Stab in the back
Hairy as an ape
Today the chicken, tomorrow the feathers

You made your bed, sleep in it
Misery loves company
Loaded for bear
Quiet as a mouse
Shiny as a bald man's head
Bald as an eagle
Whistling girls and cacklin hens always come to bad end
Chickens always come home to roost
Happier than a black boy eating watermelon
Clean as a whistle
Tired as a dog
Poor as a church mouse
Bright as a dollar
Hard as a rock
Rough as a cob
Older than the hills
Slippery as an eel
Losers weepers, finders keepers
Don't count your chickens before they are hatched
Running like a jackass with its ears cut off
No room to talk
Big as a blimp
Easy as pie
Take your medicine
Crabby as an old maid
Can't squeeze blood out of a turnip
Smart as a whip
Cute as a bug's ear
Putting on the dog
Clear as a bell
Birds of a feather flock together
Love me, love my dog
Mad as a wet hen
Closer than six in bed
Don't let the bedbugs bite
If wishes were horses, beggars would ride
Four sheets in the wind
Throw a bull by the tail
See slivers in others eyes and not logs in one's own
Six axe handles across
Nervous as a hen on ice
Boss in the chicken coop when the rooster isn't there
Never let your right hand know what your left hand is
    doing
It's no skin off my nose
Hit the hay
In a pig's eye

As helpless as a boar with teats
Crazy as a pet coon
Drunk as a skunk
High as a kite
Broad as a barn
Tall as a pine
Running like a chicken with its head cut off
If that don't take the cake
Look what the cat drug in
For crying out loud
Fit to be tied
Chewing the rag
Getting down to brass tacks
Knee high to a grasshopper
Lower than a snake's belly
Like it or lump it
Making dough